THE U.S. MERCHANT MARINE AT WAR, 1775–1945

THE ★★★★ U.S.
Merchant
Marine

AT WAR, 1775–1945

EDITED BY BRUCE L. FELKNOR

NAVAL INSTITUTE PRESS   ANNAPOLIS, MARYLAND

LIBRARY OF CONGRESS CATALOGING IN PUBLICATION DATA

The U.S. Merchant Marine at war, 1775–1945 / edited by Bruce L. Felknor.
p.   cm.
Includes bibliographical references (p.   –   ) and index.
ISBN 1-55750-273-0 (alk. paper)
1. Merchant marine—United States—History. 2. United States—History, Naval. I. Felknor, Bruce L.
VK23.U18   1998
387.5'0973—dc21   97-49860

Printed in the United States of America on acid-free paper ∞
05 04 03 02 01 00 99 98   9 8 7 6 5 4 3 2
First printing

FRONTISPIECE: An Allied merchantman in World War I, her bow already under water, begins her slide to the bottom as the last two living men aboard (one obscured in shadow) abandon ship by lifelines. (National Archives, War and Conflict Collection, 694)

For many brave souls . . .
asleep in the deep.

Contents

Preface

This book germinated in a trunk, where in 1994 I came across a few fifty-year-old issues of the *North Atlantic Occasional News, Tanker Edition.* That grandly titled news sheet (daily when at sea) had a circulation of five or six carbon copies on flimsy paper and was posted on bulletin boards in crew and officers' messes and elsewhere about the SS *Sappa Creek*—a T-2 running aviation gasoline in fast-tanker convoys from Delaware Bay refineries to English ports.

I was "Sparks" in that ship, and like many counterparts across the world, I used this ship's paper to share with my shipmates, merchant and navy, the news of the day, which was condensed and rewritten from short-wave broadcasts in International (Morse) Code. An article about this aspect of merchant marine life during wartime intrigued the *American Legion* magazine, but not enough to publish it.

The fiftieth-anniversary commemoration of D-Day and the Normandy landings stirred further memories, and I suggested to my agent, Jane Jordan Browne, a book of U.S. merchant marine stories from World War II. She pointed out that, given the timetables of book production, I was already a couple of years too late—which I, as an old editor, should have recognized on my own.

Then she came up with the prescription for this book: "Broaden it," she said, "make it all the wars." That worked, and I thank her.

The research involved in this inquiry consumed much time between 1994 and 1997; it was nearly always fascinating and absorbing, though occasionally profoundly frustrating.

The memories evoked by this study are familiar to anyone who went to sea in World War II—great tension at moments of high alert or when thrown about by a vicious storm, a wild mix of boredom and exaltation at the wondrous beauty of the sea (glorious or terrible beauty), and the underlying unvoiced dread when the dull clang of the hull echoed depth charges exploding close by.

Finishing the book at last brought a sense of relief almost like that of a wartime seafarer watching those blessed tugs opening the net at the entrance to a safe harbor. Finally, do not misconstrue these reflections as implying any claim to personal bravery. I was there, but one of the lucky ones, unscathed by anything worse than sunburn. I sent only one SOS, from the Liberty ship *Jonathan Edwards* when another freighter knifed into her engine room one foggy dawn—but that was in Long Island Sound, safely inside the nets, a scant month before V-E Day.

No medals. Only memories. And abiding respect for those who risked all and were maimed, or who died.

Acknowledgments

First I must thank my wife, Edith, for the generous forbearance with which she tolerated the mayhem this book worked on what might otherwise have been an orderly three years. She also supplied a critical eye and much other sound editorial assistance.

This work being an anthology—in which my own voice supplies only connective tissue and which is augmented here and there with bits and pieces of my own writing—I have tried scrupulously to acknowledge all my sources, and wherever permissions were necessary, to secure and state them.

The first half of the book, covering the eighteenth and nineteenth centuries, quotes many authors whose writings long have been in the public domain. I am grateful for their labors and for freedom of access to the fruits of those labors.

More recent works—generally speaking, those copyrighted after 1919—are identified here. Long excerpts from writings still under copyright are identified, with permission to use them, in footnotes at the beginning of the chapter where the writings appear.

Numerous shorter references and quotations from recent books appear here, and while I have tried to acknowledge the source of each such use, in most cases I am quoting from these works under the "fair use" provisions of copyright law because the total bulk is small both in the present work and in the work quoted. In a few cases quotations from these works appear here only for critical appraisal and refutation, a central element of fair use.

There are a few sad omissions from my list of permissions. A long excerpt from a 1942 book by Robert Carse appears with attribution but no permission. That book slipped into the public domain apparently because both he and his wife, also a writer, died just at the time in 1970 when the copyright should have been renewed.

I really had hoped to use many long sections from the work of Felix Riesenberg, now dead for a quarter century, but after months of detective work had to abandon the idea because I could not locate a living heir nor could his agent. I have used a small number of quotations that I believe fall within the scope of fair use. In the Riesenberg case as well as that of Carse, staff members at the Authors Guild helped me greatly in becoming oriented to the peculiarities of copyright law.

Readers may note in the World War II sections of this book a great many quotations—all with permission—from two books in particular. This is to explain why I have leaned on them so heavily. One is *Liberty Ships* by John Bunker. Mr. Bunker, a merchant seaman in that war, is with Riesenberg surely the most pungent and authoritative chronicler of the proud role he and his fellow mariners played in winning that war, and he is perhaps the most prolific as well. I am most grateful for permission to quote him *in extenso.*

The other book extensively quoted is the long and detailed work (538 pages in quarto), *Ships of the Esso Fleet in World War II*, published in 1946 by the Standard Oil Company (New Jersey). I have used it so frequently for several reasons, the first of which is its content. It assembles the wartime history of every one of the 135 Esso tankers in copious detail, including log excerpts and long, careful interviews soon after the fact with the men involved.

The second reason is related to the first: as America entered that war, Esso owned and operated by far the largest U.S. tanker fleet. It ran seventy-three tankers under the U.S. flag and another sixty-two under its Panamanian subsidiary, vis-à-vis the forty and twenty-seven tankers, respectively, of its two largest competitors, Standard Oil Company (New York; or Socony) and Texaco.

As the attentive reader will observe in other books of World War II stories of the merchant marine, most of the Esso ships treated here were the small stage on which some of the war's classic tales of tragedy and gallantry played out.

Esso's successor, Exxon Corporation, and its shipping subsidiary, SeaRiver Maritime, Inc., have recently republished *Ships of the Esso Fleet* for their employees, and it is a pity that it is not more widely available; the book is a major resource for any author investigating the role of the merchant marine in World War II. I acquired a copy of the first edition in 1946 from a fellow tankerman (I was one, though never for Esso).

As in every book I have ever undertaken, I am deeply indebted to many libraries and reference librarians, especialy the Deerfield (Illinois) Public Library and its resourceful and generous reference head, Judy Hortin. Through the interlibrary loan (which God preserve) and other sources, she and her staff spirited out arcana that even their original sources thought gone forever.

Dorothy T. King, librarian of the Long Island Collection at the East Hampton Library in New York (to whom I was sent by Helen S. Rattray, editor of the East Hampton *Star,* and Beth Gray, director of the East Hampton Public Library) dug out the information I needed both on Robert Carse's background and the fact that his work used here was indeed in the public domain.

Victoria Callahan of the Sunset Publishing Corporation not only immediately answered my queries but just as quickly provided photocopies of the remarkable saga of Capt. John Cameron, the World War I captive of the German raider *Wolf.*

I thank Stephen Arbogast of Exxon for putting me in touch with Arthur J. Stephen, manager of external affairs at SeaRiver Maritime, for permissions, and also to Mr. Stephen for finding and lending the original negative of that remarkable photograph of oil-drenched survivors in their lifeboat at the moment of rescue. Copies of it have been reproduced in several books but never (that I have seen) with identification of its source.

On several counts I am grateful to my old friend Woody Price, recently retired as head of federal affairs for CSX Corp., whose subsidiary SeaLand is the container ship pioneer. Jim Henry and Larry Evans of the Transportation Institute supplied badly needed information and contacts at critical moments. Through them I reached Anita Potyen at the Library of the Seafarers' Harry Lundeberg School of Seamanship, who immediately found and faxed to me an early work for the Seafarer's International Union, North America (SIUNA) by John Bunker, a document that drew only blank stares from some dozen librarians. Kathleen Hunt of the National Maritime Union's (NMU) District 4, and her predecessor, Kenneth Palinka, also supplied information and documentation that many others thought unobtainable.

In my research into armed guard voyage reports, German U-boat logs, and photographic and cartographic records from World War II, I extend hearty thanks to the staffs of those research rooms at the National Archives at College Park, Maryland (Archives II), and most especially to those in Textual and Still Pictures research, and also to Angie Van Dereedt at Archives I, downtown.

I made extensive and profitable use of these libraries both in "real time" and in the cyberworld: the Donnelley at Lake Forest College; Northwestern University; Loyola University (Chicago); the Regenstein at the University of Chicago; the Chicago Public Library; and the excellent local libraries at Highland Park, Lake Forest, Libertyville, and Waukegan, Illinois. (But my heart belongs to Deerfield.)

Thanks also to Frank Braynard at the American Merchant Marine Museum and to the librarians at the Schuyler Otis Bland Memorial Library, both at the Merchant Marine Academy in Kings Point, New York.

Many people in the rights-and-permissions end of the publishing world gave me generous assistance in tracking down authors or their heirs or help in determining that certain authors were not traceable. The most generous of these were Fred Courtright of Norton, Peter London of Morrow, and Norma Johnson of Greenwood, by coincidence all former publishers of mine. Thanks also to Gladys Vargas of John Hawkins & Associates, agents to the late seamen-authors Carse and Riesenberg.

Several people to whom I turned for permissions also gave me substantive help or useful clues in tracking sources. These include Prof. Jerome R. Garitee; my friend and fellow "Dutch Treater" Lowell Thomas Jr.; Charles Dana Gibson; Julia Morton of the Kent State University Press; and last but far from least, Patricia A. Sappington of the Naval Institute Press.

In seeking out illustrations, Joanna C. Britto, manager of the office of rights and reproductions at the National Portrait Gallery, and Lyn Gardner and John Pemberton at the Mariners' Museum Library at Newport News, Virginia, were of great help.

I gratefully acknowledge permission to use the following works.
Bloody Winter, John M. Waters. Copyright © 1984 by John M. Waters. By permission of Naval Institute Press.

Count Luckner, the Sea Devil, Lowell Thomas. Copyright © 1932 (renewed 1960) by Lowell Thomas. By permission of Lowell Thomas Jr.

CSS Alabama: Builder, Captain, and Plans, Charles Grayson Summersell. Copyright © 1985 by Charles Grayson Summersell. By permission of University of Alabama Press.

Escape from Archangel: An American Merchant Seaman at War, Thomas E. Simmons. Copyright © 1990 by Thomas E. Simmons. By permission of University Press of Mississippi.

History of U.S. Naval Operations in World War II, Samuel Eliot Morison. Vol. 1, *The Battle of the Atlantic.* Copyright © 1947 by Samuel Eliot Morison; copyright renewed. Vol. 10, *The Atlantic Battle Won.* Copyright © 1959 by Samuel Eliot Morison; copyright renewed. By permission of Little, Brown & Company.

How America Went to War: An Account from Official Sources of the Nation's War Activities, 1917–1920; vols. 2–3, *The Road to France,* Benedict Crowell and Robert Forrest Wilson. Copyright © 1921 (renewed 1949) by Benedict Crowell and Robert Forrest Wilson. By permission of Yale University Press.

Liberty Ships: The Ugly Ducklings of World War II, John Bunker. Copyright © 1972 by John Bunker. By permission of Naval Institute Press.

Merchantman? Or Ship of War: A Synopsis of Laws, U.S. State Department Positions and Practices Which Alter the Peaceful Character of U.S. Merchant Vessels in Time of War, Charles Dana Gibson. Copyright © 1986 by Charles Dana Gibson and used by his permission.

Operation Drumbeat: Germany's First U-Boat Attacks Along the American Coast in World War II, Michael Gannon. Copyright © 1990 by Michael Gannon. By permission of Harper & Row.

Raiders of the Deep, Lowell Thomas. Copyright © 1928 (renewed 1956) by Lowell Thomas. By permission of Lowell Thomas Jr.

Sea Lanes in Wartime: The American Experience, 1775–1945, Robert Greenhalgh Albion and Jennie Barnes Pope. Copyright © 1942 (renewed 1960) by Robert Greenhalgh Albion and Jennie Barnes Pope. By permission of W. W. Norton.

Ships of the Esso Fleet in World War II. Copyright © 1946 by Standard Oil Company (New Jersey). By permission of SeaRiver Maritime, Inc.

The Fighting Liberty Ships: A Memoir, A. A. Hoehling. Copyright © 1996 by A. A. Hoehling. By permission of Naval Institute Press.

The Republic's Private Navy: The American Privateering Business as Practiced by Baltimore during the War of 1812, Jerome R. Garitee. Copyright © 1977 by Jerome R. Garitee and used by his permission.

U-Boats Offshore: When Hitler Struck America, Edwin P. Hoyt. Copyright © 1978 by Edwin P. Hoyt. By permission of University Press of America.

With the permission of NMU District 50, as noted elsewhere, I made substantial (and grateful) use of articles from the NMU's newspaper, the *Pilot,* and at shorter length its history, *On a True Course* (1967). I am similarly grateful to the SIUNA and the library at the Lundeberg School noted above for access to and permission to use John Bunker's *The Seafarers in World War II* (1951).

Virtually all the illustrations are in the public domain. Two required permissions. "The Fight Between Alabama and the Kearsarge" by G. W. Seitz is from the National Portrait Gallery, Smithsonian Institution, and appears here courtesy of the Smithsonian's Office of Rights and Reproductions. "Destruction of the Federal Merchantman Harvey Birch by the Confederate War-Sloop Nashville" appears courtesy of the Mariners' Museum, Newport News, Virginia.

My principal source for logistical information and projections on the Military Sealift Command in the epilogue to part 5 is 1991 congressional hearings on sealift performance and requirements.

Introduction

This is a book of sea stories, true tales of heroes, victims, and survivors against long odds—volunteers who served their country in war on the high seas. They were the civilian seamen of the U.S. merchant marine in America's wars of the eighteenth, nineteenth, and twentieth centuries.

Collections of sea stories abound, among them wartime tales of merchant mariners from the Revolution to World War II. Most of these books are now obscure, but many of them contain a fascinating and long-forgotten story or two. The old books, like their modern successors, focus on a particular war, or at least on an era. My research has discovered no other work that assembles dramatic stories of merchant seamen in all of America's wars in a single volume, as this one undertakes to do.

"All wars" here treats only overseas wars in which control of the sea was a vital and seriously contested issue and in which great numbers of U.S. merchantmen came under enemy fire. Omitted are the Mexican-American War, the ten-week Spanish-American War and the Korean, Vietnam, and Persian Gulf Wars against nonsea powers.

The reader will find the privateers of the American Revolution and the War of 1812, the steam-and-sail raiders of the Civil War, and both world wars at sea—on, above, and beneath the sea. Tales of sinkings, escapes, and the occasional triumph; of heroism and death, sadism and gallantry, ice-choked waters, and seas on fire—all are little-known tales that make the heart beat faster.

Most of these accounts are collected from works of both scholarly and popular maritime historians of the nineteenth and twentieth centuries, the early stories long in the public domain. Some of these are retold in my words, but in every case my original sources are cited. Stars (one at beginning and one at end) denote excerpted material. Arcane and archaic terms of gunnery and the sea are defined in the glossary.

In several selections from older works, I have divided extremely long paragraphs into shorter ones, to make reading easier for the modern eye. For consistency of style, in treating units of measurement, such as gun bores, speed rates, and tonnage, I have switched numerals to words or vice versa, but done no other violence to the original.

Especially in the World War II chapters, many selections are drawn directly from logs or reports of survivors in U.S. Navy Armed Guard or shipping company records and a few from my own experience and observation as a seafarer in the war years.

Permissions to reprint substantial extracts from copyrighted works appear at the beginning of each chapter. Sources of shorter quotations are cited where they appear.

THE U.S. MERCHANT MARINE AT WAR, 1775–1945

The American Revolution

IN THE AMERICAN COLONIES, SCATTERED along the Atlantic Coast, sailing was second nature, whether for fishing, transportation of people and their property, or trading. In the coastal towns, seamanship was learned soon after walking. So, everywhere, was marksmanship and the handling of guns, for hunting—which supplied an important part of the colonial diet—and protection from marauders whether quadruped or biped.

There was a large, vigorous, and growing merchant marine in the American colonies. As the historian Winthrop Marvin put it, "The merchant ships and sailors of America steadily increased, until at the breaking out of the Revolution there were more people in Northern New England—Maine and New Hampshire—engaged in shipbuilding and in navigation, than there were in agriculture, and Massachusetts was said to own one seagoing vessel for every hundred of its inhabitants" (Marvin, *American Merchant Marine*, 11).

British encroachments on the livelihood and freedom of shipowners and sailors in the 1760s contributed to the growing readiness of the colonies to revolt. From 1764 British Navy ships were stationed along the coast from Maine to Delaware to serve as revenue cutters, searching sloops and schooners, and even open boats hauling farm produce across the bay, delaying many cargoes and seizing all that were or seemed to be contraband under the hated tax laws, the Stamp Act, and later the Townshend Acts.

Colonial seamen were seized, accused as deserters from the King's Navy, and pressed into service aboard British warships. In one egregious incident the man-of-war *Maidstone* sailed into Narragansett Bay to Newport and

> began impressing seamen from the merchant ships in the bay, and finally took the entire crew from a ship just home from the year-long voyage to the coast of Africa. It seems impossible now [1919] that a naval officer should be guilty of such needless cruelty as taking men under such circumstances, but the truth is that the naval officers of that period found pleasure in cruelty. It was because of inhumanity—the harshness with which men were treated in the navy—that impressment was necessary. The friends and relatives of the impressed seamen were unable to obtain redress, but they expressed their feelings by burning one of the *Maidstone*'s small boats.
>
> (Spears, *Story of American Merchant Marine,* 81)

Impressment was frequent and by no means practiced only by the British but at least as much by other maritime powers. After the American Revolution was won, England resumed and even accelerated the practice, which became a major precipitant of the War of 1812. But during the Revolution, the British had an ugly refinement with regard to the impressment of black sailors, of whom there were surprisingly many. Throughout the war, they "faced special jeopardy. Any Negro on an American ship captured by the British was automatically assumed to be a slave and could be sold as 'enemy property' along with the captured ship and cargo. If the black managed to produce papers proving he was not a slave, they were impounded as 'court documents'; he was then left without papers and was subject to enslavement by anyone in Jamaica who cared to haul him in front of a magistrate" (Cohn and Platzer, *Black Men of the Sea,* 72–73).

Even while the British incitements and provocations of the 1760s and early 1770s went on, however, the American colonies constituted

> a latent sea power of the first importance. The merchant ships of the colonies, hastily fitted out as privateers, were an active factor in the struggle for independence. It must be remembered that the

merchant vessel of that day, large or small, usually went to sea armed for its own protection, and that far larger crews than would really be required for the ordinary ship's work were carried to man the guns and swivels against pirates or national enemies. Thus, old records note the clearing from Boston for Carolina of a sixty-ton vessel with ten men, or twice as many as such a craft would now carry; the clearing for Jamaica of a larger ship with one hundred and forty men and fourteen guns; the sailing for Barbadoes of a one-hundred-and-fifty-ton vessel with eighteen men, as many as would now be found aboard a thousand-ton ship, and the sailing of a two-hundred-ton vessel with twenty men for Nevis. The merchant seaman of the eighteenth century was compelled not only to know how to "hand, reef, and steer," but to be expert in the use of great guns, and of musket, pike, and cutlass. Of course such men were ready when the war came. There was no more commerce. British cruisers put an end to that. The slow vessels of the colonies were laid up in port; the swift ones were sent a-privateering.

(Marvin, *American Merchant Marine*, 11–12)

The Continental Congress authorized letters of marque and reprisal four months before the Declaration of Independence, which one colony (Rhode Island) had already done, quickly followed by Massachusetts and several others.

The privateer, as understood at the outbreak of the war for American independence, was a ship armed and fitted out at private expense for the purpose of preying on the enemy's commerce to the profit of her owners, and bearing a commission, or letter of marque, authorizing her to do so, from the Government. Usually the Government claimed a portion of the money realized from the sales of prizes and their cargoes. The owners, of course, had a lion's share, though a considerable portion was divided among the officers and crew as an additional incentive to securing prizes. In fact, it was this division of the spoils, rather than the wages, that induced many of our best seamen to enter this peculiarly dangerous service. It frequently happened that even the common sailors received as their share, in one cruise, over and above their wages, one thousand dollars—a small fortune in those days for a mariner.

(Maclay, "Privateers," 309)

1 Maine Men and Boys
⋆⋆ Take a British Schooner

The "Shot Heard 'Round the World" was fired by "an embattled farmer" near Concord, Massachusetts, on 19 April 1775. But its echoes did not reach Machias, Maine—that northeasternmost outpost of the Massachusetts Colony—until early May.

When word of the battles of Lexington and Concord did get to Machias, it precipitated a young man named Jeremiah O'Brien into momentous events, which would include his victory in the first naval action of the American Revolution, command of the commonwealth navy of Massachusetts, success as a privateersman, and a difficult time in British prisons afloat and abroad.

Jeremiah, along with his five brothers, had been educated by his father, taught "to read and spell, to handle the plough, the pitchfork and the rifle, to raft timber and sail a boat." These men of Maine and their "brave men's mothers and brave men's wives" were more than ready for the declaration of hostilities the provincial congress was at the point of adopting.

At Machias a town meeting had already fired off to the General Court of the province a florid protest against the crown's "iron chains of tyranny" that threatened them with "servitude equal to Egyptian bondage." This pioneer settlement lay just upriver from the marshy coast, where hundreds of acres of grass awaited the scythe, where unbroken forest ascended to the north and west as far as the imagination could fly.

There also the Machias River awaited dams and sawmills, and the lacework of coves and bays along the coast awaited commerce; only

---

This story is retold from accounts in two works published in 1902, John Randolph Spears's *The History of Our Navy* and Rev. Andrew M. Sherman's *Life of Captain Jeremiah O'Brien, Machias, Maine*. They are the sources of direct quotations that appear here.

recently they had been lair and haven for a century of pirates, among them the notorious Samuel Bellamy. Machias lay so far to the east that its pioneers thought they were in Nova Scotia. Only when they petitioned that province to grant land for a township did they discover that they were in the province of Massachusetts—from which Maine was not separated until 1820.

"Jere" O'Brien was a natural leader, an active participant in operating his family's two sawmills, tough, strong, and well liked. And although he did not brood about it, the casual contempt of local tories for his Irish ancestry, if anything, further fired his ardent patriotism.

When a town meeting decreed the erection of a Liberty Pole, Jeremiah and two of his brothers were in the vanguard, seeking out the tallest tree, felling and stripping it but for a defiant plume of green at its peak, and emplacing it in the heart of the village where no resident tory or visiting Briton could miss it.

Shortly after this juncture, a pair of merchant sloops arrived from Boston under the escort of a British Navy schooner, the *Margaretta*. The sloop *Polly* bore the personal effects of several Boston families seeking refuge in remote Machias from the austerity of Boston under British occupation and from the prospect of mayhem stirred by its rebellious populace.

Also aboard was a Boston commercial agent and broker who had been instrumental in the settling of Machias and in effect was its banker, "Captain" Ichabod Jones. Jones owned the sloops, and his son's family was among the refugees.

The cargo of the other sloop, the *Unity*, was provisions for Machias, which Captain Jones had regularly supplied for years in exchange for lumber from the village's sawmills. But this time sparks were struck when the *Margaretta*'s young commander, a British Navy midshipman named James Moore, took umbrage at the Liberty Pole towering over Machias and demanded its removal.

Along with its cargoes and the guns of the *Margaretta*, this little flotilla had brought details of the bloodshed at Lexington and Concord, and patriotic tempers and suspicions were running high. The rumor spread that the *Unity*'s return cargo of lumber was to be used for barracks for British troops at Boston. Into this stew, Captain Jones introduced a petition to the village that additional Boston families be received on future voyages and stipulating that the sloop *Polly* as well as the *Unity* return laden with Machias lumber.

By a divided vote, those at the village meeting narrowly agreed, but soon hotter heads prevailed. A plot was hatched to arrest the officers of the *Margaretta* at church, seize their schooner, and use its guns to defend their settlement against future British encroachment. At the afternoon church service on 11 June, the plotters were armed and ready, but before they could act Captain Moore sensed danger and escaped through a window, fleeing with his officers and Ichabod Jones to a waiting dinghy, which was quickly rowed out to their schooner where they clambered aboard.

The *Margaretta* quickly weighed anchor and dropped downstream, with the frustrated patriots giving chase, peppering the schooner with musket fire from canoes and small boats. The *Margaretta* fired several rounds at them from her swivel guns, and the incident petered out. Captain Moore sent word to the village that if either Captain Jones or his sloops were harmed, he would return in force and burn the village.

At this, the enraged and defiant men of Machias rushed toward the schooner's new anchorage downriver and rained musket fire on her from the high south bank. The *Margaretta* could not elevate her guns high enough to fire on the top of the bank. She weighed anchor again and broached sharply to ride farther downstream to a better position. But in the sudden turn the boom of her mainsail snapped, seriously crippling her. The vessel managed to get out of range as night fell, and the attackers dispersed. In her retreat the *Margaretta* encountered a small sloop and impressed her master to serve as pilot in the local waters. This was not difficult, for the pilot was a well-known Machias tory, one Captain Tobey.

The following morning, Monday, 12 June, a spontaneous waterfront gathering of local youths reviewed Sunday afternoon's events. A temporary resident from New York, Joseph Wheaton, suggested to Dennis O'Brien, a younger brother of Jeremiah, that they seize the British schooner. These two picked up a couple of accomplices, and rowed out to Ichabod Jones's sloop *Unity*, already partly loaded with lumber and riding at anchor in the river. Despite the profuse objections of her master, the boys took her over and maneuvered her in to Scott's wharf, tied her up, and sent up a rousing cheer. This immediately drew a crowd, including Jeremiah O'Brien and two other brothers, Gideon and John.

When Jeremiah heard the scheme, he shouted, "My boys, we can do it!" Quickly the group assembled such armament as came to hand: twenty fowling pieces, with enough powder and ball for three rounds, thirteen haying forks, and several axes. They took aboard a small bag of bread, a few chunks of pork, and a barrel of water. And somewhere in the village they found an old wallpiece—a long-barreled, large-bore rifle too heavy for a man to shoot offhand. For it they improvised a swivel mount from an old windlass.

By now a real crowd had gathered on the wharf, and from it by common consent the nucleus of the group picked about thirty-five husky young volunteers for a crew, including four O'Brien brothers. Only with difficulty could the two youngest brothers, Dennis and Joseph (the latter only sixteen), and their father, sixty, be excluded. The boys, however, disappeared into a hiding place in the sloop.

The British Captain Moore, meanwhile, climbed into his rigging to watch this bustle of activity through a spyglass. By the time the wallpiece went aboard the *Unity*, he had weighed anchor and was on his crippled way seaward. En route he encountered an American merchant schooner, the *Westport*, arriving from Norwich, Connecticut. He made fast to the *Westport* and confiscated her main boom and gaff to replace his own wrecked rigging. He seized her provisions for the *Margaretta's* larder and effectively placed her master, Robert Avery, under arrest aboard the British vessel.

Robert Foster, a young man from East Machias and a lieutenant in the Massachusetts militia, after consulting with Jeremiah O'Brien, located a schooner, the *Falmouth Packet*, in the East Branch of the Machias River near his home, that could take part in the action. He recruited a volunteer crew and procured arms, and set out downstream to meet the *Unity* at "The Rim," where the East Branch joined the main stream.

However, Foster had the bad luck to run hard aground, and he sent word to the *Unity* that he would not be able to float the schooner until high tide at midday. But adrenalin flowed too freely aboard the *Unity* to brook delay, and with three loud cheers they sent Foster's messenger back to report that they could "take the Englishman without the *Falmouth Packet*," and they would proceed alone.

About the time the *Unity* sighted the *Margaretta*, it began to dawn on the ardent young crew that the spontaneity and enthusiasm that had brought them thus far was no substitute for a single line of command.

What they confronted was, after all, a British Navy vessel twice the size of their sloop with a trained crew of forty men. At its broadside gun ports were four six-pounders on each side, and on its rails were twenty swivel guns firing 1-pound balls. There were two wallpieces, like their own sole major weapon. And there were forty muskets, forty cutlasses, forty pikes, forty boarding axes. Beyond this were two boxes of hand grenades, ten pairs of pistols, and an ample supply of powder and ball.

Joseph Wheaton, the young New Yorker who had first suggested this venture, quickly spoke up to nominate Jeremiah O'Brien as captain, and he was unanimously confirmed. Edmund Stevens was elected lieutenant. Jere O'Brien's first act as captain was to solidify that unanimity, and he offered a boat to anyone wishing to return to shore. Three men, who had been among the most aggressive on the wharf, took the opportunity and departed. After they had left, the stowaways, the littlest O'Briens, were discovered, and both subsequently acquitted themselves gallantly.

As the *Unity* pursued the retreating *Margaretta,* her crew improvised breastworks out of her partial cargo of lumber. It has never been explained why the larger vessel sought to avoid a fight it surely could have won in the normal course of events. Speculation has included the fact that Captain Moore's fiancée and another lady were aboard the *Margaretta.* He might have had orders from his own commander, Admiral Graves at Boston, to avoid a quarrel. Humane considerations may have deterred him from depopulating the sloop and sinking it with his vastly superior armament.

But in the event, the fleet little sloop soon overtook the schooner, and at last Captain Moore from his quarterdeck hailed the audacious young skipper of the *Unity:* "Sloop ahoy! Keep off or I'll fire!"

But Captain O'Brien rejoined, "In America's name, I demand your surrender."

The *Margaretta* repeated her warning, and from the *Unity* Lieutenant Stevens shouted back, "Fire away and be damned!" At once the schooner fired one of her stern swivels, killing a lad named McNeil at the *Unity's* wallpiece and mortally wounding James Coolbroth, who stood beside him. Jonathan Knight stepped up to the wallpiece, reloaded, took careful aim, and put a ball through the head of the *Margaretta's* helmsman. The historian John Randolph Spears speculates soundly that Knight "was probably from the backwoods and a moose-hunter, for he was bright enough and skillful enough to pick off the man at the schooner's helm.

And that shot drove everybody off the schooner's quarterdeck, so that she was left, as a sailor might say, 'to take charge of herself.' "

At the same instant the *Unity*'s crew loosed a heavy volley of musketry at the crew of the *Margaretta* on her main deck. With no one at the helm the larger vessel broached to under the sloop's bowsprit, which tore into the schooner's mainsail. John O'Brien, posted at the bow, leaped aboard the *Margaretta* just as the vessels parted. Seven of the British crew fired their muskets at him and all seven missed; then they charged him with bayonets. John jumped overboard and, while British muskets rained balls on the water all around him, he swam for the sloop, now some thirty yards off, and was hauled aboard safely.

Captain O'Brien then ordered the sweeps manned and these long oars, together with adroit helmsmanship, brought the sloop alongside the schooner, while others of the Yankee crew prepared to lash the two together for boarding. The sloop's dauntless crew had no bayonets but twenty of them were prepared to board with their pitchforks.

The British captain reappeared on the rail of his quarterdeck, bearing his sword and cheering on his men against the Yankee woodsmen and haymakers. As the Americans gained ground in their audacious attack, Captain Moore himself began lighting and throwing hand grenades amid the crew on the deck of the *Unity*. He spotted Jeremiah O'Brien and hurled grenade after grenade at him, but the American seemed to bear a charmed life. Eighteen-year-old Samuel Watts raised his rifle, aimed carefully, and sent a ball into the British captain's chest. A second shot followed, and the gallant Moore fell backward, sword still in hand, mortally wounded.

At this juncture, with the *Unity*'s meager ammunition virtually exhausted, Captain O'Brien turned to his boarding party, who had been ordered to lie behind any available cover against the *Margaretta*'s musket fire. "To your feet, lads!" he shouted. "The schooner is ours! Follow me! Board!"

The boarders leaped to their feet, hurtling over the *Margaretta*'s railing on O'Brien's heels. In the face of this charge of the pitchforks, the schooner's second officer, now in command, turned and fled below to his quarters. Of the leaderless remainder of the British crew, those still standing threw down their cutlasses and pikes and surrendered.

After a moment to catch his breath, Jere O'Brien hauled down the British ensign, and young Wheaton (the visiting New Yorker whose suggestion had set the whole event in motion) scurried up the ratlines and cut away the pennant halyards. It was noon.

The *Unity's* crew saw to the repair of the *Margaretta's* rigging and put her deck in order, and they sailed her docilely back to port where her dead—including the unfortunate Robert Avery, who had been killed in the battle—could be put ashore and her wounded given medical care. The *Margaretta,* as well as the sloops *Unity* and *Polly* seized from Ichabod Jones, were adjudicated prizes of Capt. Jeremiah O'Brien and his crew, and the proceeds distributed among them—victors in America's first naval battle.

Before the end of the month the Massachusetts General Court adopted a resolution thanking Jeremiah O'Brien and his sturdy companions for their courageous doings. The Machias Committee of Safety, meanwhile, authorized O'Brien to take over the seized sloop *Unity,* mount on her the guns of the conquered *Margaretta,* and rechristen her *Machias Liberty.*

In July, the British Navy schooner *Diligent* showed up off Machias with her tender, the *Tapnaquish.* At once O'Brien in the *Machias Liberty* accosted the *Diligent,* and both the schooner and her tender surrendered on the spot. The *Diligent* and the *Machias Liberty* thereupon became the Navy of the Colony of Massachusetts, and its Flying Squadron, Jeremiah O'Brien commanding.

O'Brien served later as a privateersman, adding new British conquests to the prizes he had already taken, until in 1780 he lost a fight at sea and was captured with his ship (at that time the *Hannibal,* which he and his brothers had built at Newburyport). After a year in a prison ship and then being sent to jail in England, he managed to escape and find passage home. He returned to sea, successfully commanding yet two more American ships before the war was won at last, and he settled again in Machias.

There was in the America of those days no system for training seamen and officers; sailors learned by observing and doing, and they polished their gunnery by hunting and rose to command by demonstrating ability to engender loyalty and obedience.

Students of O'Brien's career have remarked his modest place in the history books, but he rose out of obscurity only when the need was present and returned there willingly when the need was past. He was greatly respected in Machias, where he settled after the war, and over the years his name has been honored in ways that would have pleased him: in Machias on the local Fort O'Brien Memorial and on several navy vessels bearing his name, including an early torpedo boat and a World War II escort vessel.

Finally, a World War II Liberty ship, Hull No. 806, was christened *Jeremiah O'Brien* and participated in the Normandy Invasion. She was one of several refurbished fifty years later to take part in memorial ceremonies off Normandy. The *O'Brien,* moreover, manned by remnants of her original crew, was the only one of the lot to make it there under her own power. Jeremiah O'Brien would have been pleased by that combination of chance and courage and patriotism and volunteerism. That was the fiber of his life.

2   Naval Battles, Private Ships
★★

Three days after Jeremiah O'Brien struck the British ensign of the *Margaretta,* the Continental Congress named George Washington commander of the American army that was precipitated into existence by the events of Lexington and Concord.

There was no U.S. Navy. Preliminary steps toward colonial naval enterprises like that of Massachusetts were the American colonies' seaward line of defense. Olive branches still were proffered tentatively both in Parliament and the Continental Congress in the summer of 1775, and along much of the American coast local resentment focused more on harsh acts by individual British warships and their captains than on the crown.

Then, at the end of October, news of two events changed the world. The king, persuaded that the colonies were in open rebellion, hired 20,000 crack Hessian troops to help subdue the unruly Americans. And a British Navy martinet, Capt. Henry Mowatt, was assaulted by local hotheads at Falmouth (later Portland, Maine), who then took shots at his man-of-war anchored there. Mowatt retaliated by having cannonballs heated red-hot and bombarding the town with them, burning it to the ground and sending its men, women, and children fleeing homeless into the chill winds of the coming Maine winter.

Immediately—on 1 November 1775—the Massachusetts General Court authorized "the Fixing out of Armed Vessells, to defend the Sea Coast of America, and . . . Erecting a Court to Try and Condemn all Vessels that shall be found infesting the same." John Adams saw the act,

---

Principal sources for this chapter are Gardner W. Allen's *A Naval History of the American Revolution* (1913), William H. Clark's *Ships and Sailors* (1938), Edgar Stanton Maclay's *A History of American Privateers* (1895), and John R. Spears's *The History of Our Navy* (1902) and *The Story of the American Merchant Marine* (1919).

written by Elbridge Gerry, as one of the most important documents in American history (Allen, *Naval History,* 1:43; Spears, *Navy,* 197).

Massachusetts, Connecticut, Rhode Island, Pennsylvania, and other colonies sped the development of what would soon become their state navies. The Continental Congress, which had authorized a Continental Navy on 13 October, was galvanized to implement it, and by the end of 1776 thirty ships were in service. However, but for a few glorious victories that still live in legend, they were not a major factor in the war. Only nine of them

★

were afloat in 1781 and, by the end of the war, only one was still active— the *Alliance.* . . . All the others were either destroyed, captured, or put out of commission by superior British squadrons.

However, if the navy did not . . . match the success of the Continental militia, there was one class of American ships which did do so—our merchant marine. Yankee merchantmen [constituted] the real navy of the Revolution.

No one knows just how many American merchant ships turned from their peaceful pursuits to go forth and fight, not in line of battle, of course [with some notable exceptions, as will be seen]—they were too small for the heavyweight slugging matches of the day—but as privateers, armed vessels commissioned by the Continental Congress and the legislatures of the several newly formed states to go out and capture English merchantmen.

[Wholly unlike the wars of the twentieth century, the Revolution found the American merchant marine quite at home with the idea of mounting guns.] All during the eighteenth century, merchantmen sailed as a matter of course armed to the teeth. They had to be prepared to fight their way through not only pirates but hostile ships, warships, and privateers of nations at war, either openly or tacitly, with Britain.

[A 60-ton vessel would require five men to sail it and five more to man its four cannons.] Merchant sailors in those days were trained not only to "hand, reef, and steer" but also to fight the ships's big guns, to use muskets and pistols and, when the order "Board her!" came, to swarm overside armed with pikes and cutlasses, ready and able to mow down French sailors similarly armed.

Thus when the Revolution came and British squadrons cruising along the coast ended all commerce, the Yankee ships had but one field open to them—privateering. The older and slower ships naturally were laid up, but the smaller and swifter ships went out to reap the harvest the war offered. They doubled their guns, they tripled their crews, and they depended upon their superior skills to outrun and outwit the British frigates assigned to convoy the British merchantmen.

★   (Clark, *Ships and Sailors*, 62–63)

But if the armed ship and fighting sailor were nothing new, the Revolutionary War placed a new emphasis on the offensive role of the merchant mariner, and the structure of compensation for the privateersman brought the ordinary seafarer the prospect of financial security and even wealth. It must be said that this—plus the relatively relaxed discipline in privateers—was an impediment to recruiting for the (tiny) Continental Navy when it was established, though it too adopted a compensation scheme for prizes of war. (The division of proceeds from the prizes taken by a privateer is discussed at considerable length in chapter 5.)

What with an infant Continental Navy, state navies of various sizes and capabilities, and privateers commissioned by the states, the congress, and sometimes both, there was little precise identification of what vessel or captain was which. Moreover, there was considerable shifting of ships and men from one category to another. Occasionally a joint operation would include all categories, and a state or the congress might borrow a vessel from the other for a particular emergency. Chains of authority in young America were often vague or unformed. Improvisation, not precedent, usually carried the day.

Relieving the gunpowder crisis of 1775 was a case in point. The patriots rallied by Paul Revere who stood up to the British at Lexington and Concord did not have enough guns and those with guns had too little powder and ball. Two months later "the Battle of Bunker Hill, the most glorious defeat recorded in the annals of American warfare, [was] fought and lost because the supplies of gunpowder, brought by the colonists in old-fashioned cowhorns . . . failed them. . . . The want of gunpowder became chronic" (Spears, *Navy*, 1:26).

Early in July when Washington took command of the Continental Army poised to drive the British from their occupation of Boston, he was appalled to discover that his troops had no powder for their cannons and only enough for each rifleman to fire a few rounds.

When it examined the state of trade in the colonies, Spears tells us, the congress determined that the gunpowder trade demanded its most urgent attention. There was only one plausible source of supply: the British supply ships, enjoying untrammeled access to Boston and other American harbors, providing an almost inexhaustible supply of powder for the great warships of the British fleet—and shortly for their invading troops.

Because the colonies had no navy, the Crown's munitions ships faced no threat; laden with guns and powder and all the stuff of war, they entered colonial ports unarmed and unconvoyed. This was about to change. Yankee seafarers along the coast pointed out this source of supply to colonial legislators and others.

☆

Massachusetts, Rhode Island, and Connecticut provided small cruisers on their own account and sent them out seeking the enemy's supply ships. . . . Washington . . . took hold of this matter and brought it to the attention of the Congress. . . .

[Early in October Congress learned that two unarmed brigs had left England on 11 August] loaded with arms, powder, and other stores for Quebec without convoy, which [would be] of importance to intercept.

☆   (Spears, *Navy,* 26–28)

☆

[Immediately Congress shared this information with Washington, who, having no navy of his own, hurriedly and informally] borrowed two vessels from Massachusetts and sent them to the Gulf of St. Lawrence to intercept [the two British ships].

These were the schooners *Lynch* and *Franklin,* the first carrying six guns, ten swivels, and seventy men, under the command of Capt. Nicholas Broughton, and the second carrying four guns, ten swivels, and sixty men, commanded by Capt. John Selman. [His first and second officers were also named John, and the schooner was promptly and] jokingly dubbed *The Three Johns.*

☆   (Maclay, *Privateers,* 64–65)

Fortunately for the two rich prizes they sought, *Lynch* and *Three Johns* made a startling navigational blunder and, heading northeast from Boston, failed to cut eastward around Nova Scotia and wound up not in the Gulf of St. Lawrence but the Bay of Fundy.

This misfortune was handsomely redressed within a month. Washington had written in his own hand the commission for another Massachusetts schooner, the *Lee,* and on 29 November 1775, under Capt. John Manley she took one of the richest prizes of the war, the ordnance ship *Nancy,*

☆

laden with two thousand muskets and bayonets, eight thousand fuses, thirty-one tons of musket shots, three thousand rounds of shot for twelve-pounders, a 13-inch mortar, two six-pounders, several barrels of powder, and fifty "carcasses," or great frames for combustibles [for] setting buildings on fire.

☆   (Maclay, *Privateers,* 66)

A similar capture was made by the *Franklin,* under the command of James Mugford of Marblehead, the following spring after the British had been driven out of Boston. It was the ship *Hope,* with a large cargo of military stores including 1,500 barrels of powder. Under the noses of the British fleet, still at anchor in the harbor after the troop evacuation, Mugford took her into Boston through a narrow channel, Pulling Point Gut, too shallow for the men-of-war to follow, and her munitions were unloaded in plain view.

Two days later, accompanied by a smaller privateer, the sloop *Lady Washington,* with a crew of six and armed only with a few swivels, muskets, and blunderbusses, Mugford headed back through the same channel but ran hard aground. Capt. Joseph Cunningham in the *Lady Washington* anchored beside him as night drew near.

Knowing the British would be on him in strength to avenge their insulting and damaging loss, Mugford prepared his complement of twenty-one officers and men for a boarding party after dark. He loaded his cannon with musket ball and saw that his company was ready with spears and muskets as well as their cutlasses and pistols.

Between nine and ten o'clock muffled oars were heard approaching and Mugford hailed the unseen boats. A voice from the dark replied that they were from Boston.

"Keep off or I will fire," he shouted.

The voice called back not to fire for God's sake, for they were coming aboard.

Instantly Mugford's cannons belched their lethal charge of musket balls and his men loosed their volley of musket and pistol fire. Before the guns could be reloaded boarders from the first two or three of twelve or thirteen boats were clambering over his rail. The spears of the *Franklin* impaled many and thrust them off; one crewman was certain he had killed nine. Mugford stood by the rail with his cutlass and as a hand grabbed the rail from overside he chopped it off; thus he dispatched five boarders.

British attackers screamed in the blackness as spears found them or their boats sank under them. Four or five of the boats—with some twenty men in each—took on the little sloop, but the *Lady Washington's* half-dozen fought them off.

Finally the boarders gave up and made for their remaining boats, but not before one British lance found the gallant Mugford and pierced him through. He was the *Franklin's* only casualty, while the boarders lost sixty or seventy of their approximately two hundred.

John Manley, captor of the munitions ship *Hope,* quickly became a favorite of General Washington. On New Year's Day of 1776 Washington

☆

appointed Manley commodore of his fleet, and he hoisted his pennant on board the schooner *Hancock,* which had just been added to the force. The terms of enlistment of the soldiers who had manned the vessels having just expired, new crews were recruited from the seafaring population [i.e., merchant mariners] along shore. . . .

In January, Manley took two prizes off Nantasket [on Massachusetts Bay] and was convoying them to Plymouth when he fell in with a British 8-gun schooner and had a brisk engagement in sight of the enemy's fleet in Nantasket Roads. The [British] schooner sheered off and ran into Boston Harbor.

Washington wrote to Manley on 28 January: "I received your agreeable . . . account of your having taken and carried into Plymouth two of the enemy's transports. Your conduct in engaging the 8-gun schooner with so few hands as you went out with, your attention in securing your prizes, and your general good behavior since you first engaged in the service, merit my and your country's thanks." He [added], "I wish you could inspire the captains of the other armed schooners under your command with some of your activity and industry."

A few days later Manley had another encounter with the enemy. [Coming out of Plymouth on 30 January, an armed British brig sent from Boston to take Manley ran him aground near Scituate.] The brig came to anchor and fired not less than four hundred times upon the privateer; but, very remarkable, no man was even wounded. [One ball entered the *Hancock's* stern; the next day 130 balls were found on the shore.]

☆   (Allen, *Naval History*, 1:70–72)

As a commentary on British marksmanship, this report is not as surprising as it may seem. The British Navy in this era relied not on aimed shots but sustained rapid fire. The Americans, however, true to their tradition of marksmanship, took careful aim and made each shot count, an important element in the success of Yankee privateers.

Manley was given command of a new 32-gun frigate, also named *Hancock*, in 1777, and that June he took the British 28-gun frigate *Fox*. But the next month he lost both the prize and his own ship and was confined in a British prison ship in New York. After being exchanged the next year, he turned to privateering in the *Cumberland*—which he soon lost.

☆

He then was given command of the privateer *Jason*—in which he was nearly captured again by a British frigate. He was spared by a sudden squall, which dismasted him but drove off the frigate. At this, his crew drew the natural conclusion that their captain's luck had fled. Convinced that he was now a poor risk as skipper, they mutinied.

But Manley was still confident of his fortune and, wresting a cutlass away from one of the sailors . . . threatening to kill him, he killed the sailor and several others, and then, single-handed, drove his crew to refitting the *Jason*. In two days, the dismasted vessel was able to hoist sail enough to beat south, and off Sandy Hook Manley attacked and captured two British merchantmen, [whose] value with their cargoes was more than enough to repay the loss of the *Cumberland* and the cost of the *Jason* as well.

☆   (Clark, *Ships and Sailors*, 73–74)

After Cornwallis surrendered at Yorktown in October 1781, the last two years of the Revolution were fought almost entirely at sea, and from the American side mainly by privateers and the state navies—which were all but indistinguishable from one another.

Capt. Joshua Barney had run the gamut: the Continental Navy, privateers, capture and confinement in—and escape from—the notorious British prison ship *Jersey*. Six months after Yorktown he found himself commanding the Pennsylvania navy's *Hyder Ali*, convoying

☆

a fleet of merchantmen from Philadelphia out to sea. The *Hyder Ali* carried sixteen six-pounders and 110 men. [Off the Delaware capes the fleet encountered three British vessels, a frigate, a 16-gun brig, and another brig, the *General Monk* with sixteen 12-pound carronades and two long six-pounders]. The frigate could not get around the shoals, [one] brig went hunting the convoy, and the *General Monk* came after the *Hyder Ali*.

As the Englishman approached, Capt. Barney saw his immense superiority in men and metal, but determined to make a fight, [using wile as well as weapons]. Calling his officers and men around him, he said, "If I direct you to prepare for boarding you are to understand me as meaning that you are to remain at your guns, and be ready to fire the moment the word is given. If on the contrary I order you to give him a broadside, you are to consider me as calling for boarders, and to hold yourselves ready to board as soon as we gain a proper position."

[Shortly] the *General Monk* ranged up within a dozen yards or less, and in a loud voice [the British captain] demanded that the *Hyder Ali* strike her colors.

"Hard aport your helm—do you want him to run aboard us?" bawled Capt. Barney to the man at the wheel.

The [quick-witted Yankee] seaman understood his cue and clapped his helm hard astarboard. The enemy's jib boom caught in the fore rigging of the *Hyder Ali* and [remained entangled there] during the short but glorious action that ensued. The *Hyder Ali* thus gained a raking position of which she availed herself to [the utmost]. More than twenty broadsides were fired in twenty-six minutes and scarcely a shot missed its effect, entering at the starboard bow and [exiting] through the port quarter. In less than half an hour [the British vessel] struck her colors, one more royal victim of an American privateer.

☆   (Spears, *Navy*, 211–15)

3 Bravado and Battles
⋆⋆ and Traitorous Swabs

Browsers in old books about the Revolution are often rewarded with heroic tales of seafarers that leap off the page at full speed and in vivid color. But war at sea, then as ever, was experienced as long stretches of boredom punctuated by intervals of surging adrenalin, and many of the privateers' logs are as laconic as the old salts who skippered them:

⋆

Filled away in pursuit of a second sail in the N.W. At 4.30 she hoisted English colors and commenced firing her stern guns. At 5.20 she took in the steering sails, at the same time she fired a broadside. We opened fire from our larboard battery and at 5.30 she struck her colors. Got out the boats and boarded her. She proved to be the British brig *Acorn* from Liverpool to Rio Janeiro [*sic*], mounting fourteen cannon.

[The logs reflected frustration, as well. Witness this plaintive 1778 entry in the master's log of the privateer *Scorpion*.]

This Book I made to keep the Accounts of my voyage but God knows beste what that will be, for I am at this time very Impashent but I hope soon there will be a Change to ease my Trubled Mind. On this day I was Chaced by Two Ships of War which I tuck to be Enemies, but coming on thick Weather I have lost site of them and so conclude myself escaped which is a small good Fortune in the midste of my Discouragements.

[Salem was the foremost privateering port of the Revolution, and from its pleasant harbor there put to sea] 158 vessels of all sizes to scan the horizon for British topsails. They accounted for four hundred prizes, or half the whole number to the credit of American arms afloat. This preeminence was due partly . . . to a seafaring population which was born and bred to its trade and knew no other. . . .

Adapted and excerpted from chapter 3, "Out Cutlasses and Board," in Ralph D. Paine's *The Old Merchant Marine,* (1921, 31–42).

[One of the Salem shipmasters stood out in almost any dimension. He was a swashbuckling privateersman, a master of drama and derring-do; he was Capt. Jonathan Haraden,] who captured one thousand British cannon afloat and is worthy to be ranked as one of the ablest sea-fighters of his generation. He was a merchant mariner, a master at the outbreak of the Revolution, who had followed the sea since boyhood. But it was more to his taste to command the Salem ship *General Pickering* of 180 tons which was fitted out under a letter of marque in the spring of 1780.* She carried fourteen six-pounders and forty-five men and boys, nothing very formidable, when Captain Haraden sailed for Bilbao with a cargo of sugar. During the voyage, before his crew had been hammered into shape, he beat off a British privateer of twenty guns and safely tacked into the Bay of Biscay.

There he sighted another hostile privateer, the *Golden Eagle,* larger than his own ship. Instead of shifting his course to avoid her, Haraden clapped on sail and steered alongside after nightfall, roaring through his trumpet: "What ship is this? An American frigate, sir. Strike, or I'll sink you with a broadside."

Dazed by this unexpected summons in the gloom, the master of the *Golden Eagle* promptly surrendered, and a prize crew was thrown aboard with orders to follow the *Pickering* into Bilbao.

[But just as the *Pickering* approached that Spanish harbor, a strange sail appeared, heading for the port. It was evident that the stranger would overtake the *Pickering* and her prize before they could enter the harbor. Again Haraden cleared for action. The vessel turned out to be the *Achilles,* one of the most powerful privateers out of London, with forty guns and 150 men, or almost thrice the fighting strength of the little] *Pickering.* She was, in fact, more like a sloop of war. Before Captain Haraden could haul within gunshot to protect his prize, it had been recaptured by the *Achilles,* which then maneuvered to engage the *Pickering.*

Darkness intervened, but Jonathan Haraden had no idea of escaping under cover of it. He was waiting for the morning breeze and a chance to fight it out to a finish. He was a handsome man with an air of serene composure and a touch of the theatrical such as Nelson displayed in his

---

*She was named after the quartermaster general of the Continental Army, Timothy Pickering, for whom many others have been named.

great moments. Having prepared his ship for battle, he slept soundly until dawn and then dressed with fastidious care to stroll on deck, where he beheld the *Achilles* bearing down on him with her crew at quarters.

His own men were clustered behind their open ports, matches lighted, tackles and breechings cast off, crowbars, handspikes, and sponge-staves in place, gunners stripped to the waist, powder-boys ready for the word like sprinters on the mark. Forty-five of them against 150, and Captain Haraden, debonair, unruffled, walking to and fro with a leisurely demeanor, remarking that although the *Achilles* appeared to be superior in force, "he had no doubt they would beat her if they were firm and steady and did not throw away their fire."

It was, indeed, a memorable sea-picture, the sturdy *Pickering* riding deep with her burden of sugar and seeming smaller than she really was, the *Achilles* towering like a frigate, and all Bilbao turned out to watch the duel, shore and headlands crowded with spectators, the blue harbor-mouth gay with an immense flotilla of fishing boats and pleasure craft. The stake for which Haraden fought was to retake the *Golden Eagle* prize and to gain his port. His seamanship was flawless. Vastly outnumbered if it should come to boarding, he handled his vessel so as to avoid the *Achilles* while he poured the broadsides into her. After two hours the London privateer emerged from the smoke which had obscured the combat and put out to sea in flight, hulled through and through, while a farewell flight of crowbars, with which the guns of the *Pickering* had been crammed to the muzzle, ripped through her sails and rigging.

Haraden hoisted canvas and drove in chase, but the *Achilles* had the heels of him "with a mainsail as large as a ship of the line," and reluctantly he wore ship and, with the *Golden Eagle* again in his possession, he sailed to an anchorage in Bilbao harbor. The Spanish populace welcomed him with tremendous enthusiasm. He was carried through the streets in a holiday procession and was the hero of banquets and public receptions.

Such a man was bound to be the idol of his sailors and one of them quite plausibly related that "so great was the confidence he inspired that if he but looked at a sail through his glass and told the helmsman to steer for her, the observation went round, 'If she is an enemy, she is ours.'"

It was in this same *General Pickering*, no longer sugar laden but in cruising trim, that Jonathan Haraden accomplished a feat which Paul Jones might have been proud to claim. There lifted above the skyline three armed merchantmen sailing in company from Halifax to New York, a brig of fourteen guns, a ship of sixteen guns, a sloop of twelve guns. When they flew signals and formed in line, the ship alone appeared to outmatch the *Pickering,* but Haraden, in that lordly manner of his, assured his men that "he had no doubt whatever that if they would do their duty he would quickly capture the three vessels."

[And so they did; Haraden captured those vessels] "with great ease," one witness said later, simply "by going alongside of each of them, one after the other."

[Here is another] story of this master sea rover of the Revolution, sailor, and gentleman, who served his country so much more brilliantly than many a landsman lauded in the written histories of the war. While in the *Pickering* Haraden attacked a heavily armed royal mail packet bound to England from the West Indies, one of the largest merchant vessels of her day and equipped to defend herself against privateers. [The packet was a] tough antagonist and a hard nut to crack. They battered each other like two pugilists for four hours, and even then the decision was still in the balance. [Haraden then] sheered off to mend his damaged gear and splintered hull before closing in again.

He discovered that all his powder had been shot away excepting one last charge. Instead of calling it a drawn battle, he rammed home this last shot in the locker and ran down to windward of the packet, so close that he could shout across to the other quarterdeck: "I will give you five minutes to haul down your colors. If they are not down at the end of that time, I will fire into you and sink you, so help me God."

It was a bluff magnificent—courage [that was] coldblooded and calculating. The adversary was still unbeaten. Haraden stood with watch in hand and sonorously counted off the minutes. It was the stronger will and not the heavier metal that won the day. To be shattered by fresh broadsides at pistol range was too much for the nerves of the gallant English skipper whose decks were already like a slaughterhouse. One by one, Haraden shouted the minutes, and his gunners blew their matches. At "four" the red ensign came fluttering down, and the mail packet was a prize of war.

Another merchant seaman of this muster roll of patriots was Silas Talbot, who took to salt water as a cabin boy at the age of twelve and was a prosperous shipmaster at twenty-one with savings invested in a house of his own in Providence. Enlisting under Washington, he was made a captain of infantry and was soon promoted, but he was restless ashore and glad to obtain an odd assignment. As Colonel Talbot he selected sixty infantry volunteers, most of them seamen by trade, and led them aboard the small sloop *Argo* in May 1779, to punish the New York Tories who were equipping privateers against their own countrymen and working great mischief in Long Island Sound. So serious was the situation that [Gen. Horatio] Gates found it almost impossible to obtain food supplies for [his command,] the northern department of the Continental Army.

Silas Talbot and his nautical infantrymen promptly fell in with the New York privateer *Lively,* a fair match for him, and as promptly sent her into port. He then ran offshore and picked up and carried into Boston two English privateers headed for New York with large cargoes of merchandise from the West Indies. But he was particularly anxious to square accounts with a renegade Captain Hazard who made Newport his base and had captured many American vessels with the stout brig *King George,* using her for "the base purpose of plundering his old neighbors and friends."

On his second cruise in the *Argo,* young Silas Talbot encountered the perfidious *King George* to the southward of Long Island and riddled her with one broadside after another, first hailing Captain Hazard by name and cursing him in double-shotted phrases for the traitorous swab that he was. Then the seagoing infantry scrambled over the bulwarks and tumbled the Tories down their own hatches without losing a man. A prize crew with the humiliated *King George* made for New London, where there was much cheering in the port, and "even the women, both young and old, expressed the greatest joy."

With no very heavy fighting, Talbot had captured five vessels and was keen to show what his crew could do against mettlesome foemen. He found them at last well out to sea in a large ship which seemed eager to engage him. Only a few hundred feet apart through a long afternoon, they briskly and cheerily belabored each other with grape and solid shot. Talbot's speaking trumpet was shot out of his hand, the tails of his coat were shorn off, and all the officers and men stationed with him on the quarterdeck were killed or wounded.

His crew reported that the *Argo* was in a sinking condition, with the water flooding the gun deck, but he told them to lower a man or two in the bight of a line; they then pluckily plugged the holes from overside. There was a lusty huzza when the Englishman's mainmast crashed to the deck, and this finished the affair. Silas Talbot found that he had trounced the privateer *Dragon,* of twice his own tonnage and with the advantage in both guns and men.

While his crew was patching the *Argo* and pumping the water from her hold, the lookout yelled that another sail was making for them. Without hesitation Talbot somehow got this absurdly impudent one-masted craft of his under way and told those of his sixty men who survived to prepare for a second tussle. Fortunately another Yankee privateer joined the chase, and together they subdued the armed brig *Hannah.* When the *Argo* safely convoyed the two prizes into New Bedford, "all who beheld her were astonished that a vessel of her diminutive size could suffer so much and yet get safely to port."

Men fought and slew each other in those rude and distant days with a certain courtesy, with a fine, punctilious regard for the etiquette of the bloody game. There was the Scotch skipper of the *Betsy,* a privateer, whom Silas Talbot hailed as follows, before they opened fire: "You must now haul down those British colors, my friend."

"Notwithstanding I find you an enemy, as I suspected," was the dignified reply, "yet, sir, I shall let them hang a little bit longer,—with your permission,—so fire away, Flanagan."

During another of her cruises the *Argo* pursued an artfully disguised ship of the line which could have blown her to kingdom come with a broadside of thirty guns. The little *Argo* was actually becalmed within short range, but her company got out the sweeps and rowed her some distance before darkness, and a favoring slant of wind carried them clear. In the summer of 1780, Capt. Silas Talbot, again a mariner by title, was given the private cruiser *General Washington* with 120 men, but he was less fortunate with her than when afloat in the tiny *Argo* with his 60 Continentals. Off Sandy Hook he ran into the British fleet under Admiral Arbuthnot and, being outsailed in a gale of wind, he was forced to lower his flag to the great seventy-four *Culloden.* After a year in English prisons Talbot was released and made his way home, serving no more in the war but having the honor to command the immortal frigate *Constitution* in 1799 as a captain in the American Navy.

★

Epilogue

☆

The American people owe a vast debt of honor to the private armed ships of the Revolution. The Continental Navy was, in the main, a poor experiment. At no time was it a formidable factor in the war. Its ships were for the most part small and weak; its crews ill disciplined; its commanders distinguished more for personal intrepidity than for the professional skill and wisdom which could come only from long naval experience. John Paul Jones won his most famous victory in a French-built ship, and our only American-built frigate which came out of the war with a brilliant reputation was the swift and beautiful *Alliance*, launched at Salisbury Point on the Merrimac and so shamefully mishandled in the battle of the *Bon Homme Richard* and the *Serapis* by the traitor and madman, Landais. Indeed, the *Alliance* was almost our only frigate which came out of the Revolution in any way whatever. Nearly all of our other regular ships were destroyed or captured in the course of the war by the overwhelming British squadrons. The thirty Continental cruisers of 1776 had shrunk in 1781 to nine, carrying 164 guns. But in the same year the American privateers, converted out of merchantmen, and managed by individual shipowners, numbered 449, mounting in all 6,735 guns. The American privateers of 1775–83 captured or destroyed three times as many of the enemy's ships as did our frigates and sloops-of-war.

The audacity of the Yankee privateersmen was astounding. Paul Jones met some of them right on the British coast, whither they had gone before him. They hung like hawks in the Irish Channel and the North Sea, and the wrath and fear which they aroused were far greater than the

Reprinted from *The American Merchant Marine*, Winthrop L. Marvin (Yale University Press, 1919, 12–16).

results of any of our land victories. Silas Deane, one of Franklin's fellow commissioners to Paris, wrote home to the Marine Committee of Congress in 1777 that the exploits of our many privateers and few cruisers "effectually alarmed England, prevented the great fair at Chester, occasioned insurance to rise, and even deterred the English merchants from shipping goods in English vessels at any rate of insurance; so that in a few weeks forty French ships were loaded in London on freight—an instance never before known." So frightened were the merchants that they demanded naval protection for the linen ships crossing from Ireland to England. "In no former war," mournfully declared an English newspaper of the period, "not even in any of the wars with France and Spain, were the linen vessels from Ireland to England escorted by warships." In 1777—the year of Bennington and Saratoga—the men at sea in our merchant vessels transformed into privateers almost equalled the strength of the Continental army under the immediate command of Washington. They scoured the Atlantic from the Orkneys to Yucatan. A letter written home from Grenada in 1777 gives a graphic idea, from the British standpoint, of the havoc of these privateers: "Everything continues exceedingly dear, and we are happy if we can get anything for money, by reason of the quantity of vessels taken by the Americans. A fleet of vessels came from Ireland a few days ago. From sixty vessels that departed from Ireland not above twenty-five arrived in this and neighboring islands, the others, it is thought, being all taken by American privateers. God knows if this American war continues much longer, we shall all die of hunger. There was a ship from Africa with 450 negroes, some 1,000 weight of gold dust and a great many elephant teeth—the whole cargo being computed to be worth 20,000 pounds—also taken by an American privateer, a brig mounting fourteen cannon."

. . . From July 1775 to December 1777, American shipowners had received commissions for 174 of their idle ships as privateers. These vessels mounted 1,836 cannon and their crews comprised from 9,000 to 10,000 sailors. New Hampshire, with only twenty miles of seacoast and one port (Portsmouth) had sent out eight privateers before the end of 1777; rich and patriotic Massachusetts, fifty-three; Rhode Island, six; Connecticut, twenty-two; New York, though her great port was held by the British, seven; Pennsylvania, thirteen; Maryland, twenty-one; South Carolina, six, and North Carolina, three. For this hazardous but profitable work the best ships in the American merchant fleet were chosen. Already, almost a hundred years before the development of the astonishing Yankee clippers, our shipwrights had begun to produce a class of vessels of superior speed, and our seamen were famous for their hardihood. Later in the war vessels were designed and built especially for privateering, but the smart mechantmen which put to sea with their ugly rows of teeth from 1775 to 1777 were, most of them, able to run away from the king's cruisers.

Some of these early privateers were extraordinarily successful. Several of them took as many as twenty British prizes in a single voyage, and one is said to have taken twenty-eight prizes. Of course this was exceptional luck. It was due to getting into the track of a West India convoy, or hovering off Halifax or the Gulf of St. Lawrence in the path of supply ships and transports. While the war enriched some American shipowners, it impoverished others. Not all privateers came home with wealth and glory. A large number never came at all. Many of these vessels, built for the uses of peace, were overloaded with guns and overpressed with lofty canvas, and they sailed and were never after heard from. Twenty-two vessels with more than a thousand men are said to have vanished in this way from the Massachusetts town of Newburyport, on the Merrimac, during the Revolution.

No mere greed of gain animated the owners of our private armed ships in the War for Independence. Indeed, merchant vessels though these were, they held a semipublic, national character. They were as a rule swifter than our few regular warships, and often better fitted and found. They were, of course, very much more numerous, and they were often called on to perform difficult tasks for the Continental government. They carried our envoys to and fro between our coasts and Europe. They conveyed despatches and kept France and our other friends on the Continent informed of the temper of our people and the actual progress of the war. They transported specie and brought to us time and time again the arms, ammunition, and supplies so indispensable to the patriot army. If we had depended on our navy alone for all this service afloat in the Revolution, we should have leaned upon a breaking reed.

★

The War of 1812

THE WAR OF 1812 COINCIDED WITH AND WAS complicated by the last phase of Britain's bitter conflict with France in the Napoleonic Wars. Both empires had meddled in the affairs of the young United States most arrogantly, contemptuously, and piratically. France had manipulated the Prussian seizure of hundreds of U.S. ships. Great Britain had resumed and magnified her nefarious practice of boarding U.S. merchant ships to kidnap seamen for involuntary service in British Navy crews.

The Embargo Act of 1807, enacted at Pres. Thomas Jefferson's behest, protected U.S. merchant ships by keeping them at home—but idling them threatened to ruin their owners. The embargo was finally recognized as counterproductive, and in November 1811 Jefferson's successor, James Madison, called on Congress to consider war with Britain, which it finally declared in June 1812.

Meanwhile, the Continental Navy, created in 1775, was disbanded in 1784, a few months after the army was mustered out. In 1798, after incessant French piracy and naval harassment of U.S. shipping and the continuing depredations of the Barbary pirates, a Navy Department was established and the United States Navy came into existence. Undeclared naval war with France began immediately and lasted several years. The navy was too small and too preoccupied with French warships to protect U.S. merchant ships on the high seas, and what defense merchantmen found came from their own guns.

4 Provocations and Privateers

★★

Thomas Jefferson was president from 1801 to 1809, and because "Jefferson and his party disliked line-of-battleships," the young U.S. Navy in 1812 had "not one two-decked man-of-war afloat, and only half a dozen serviceable frigates" and eleven sloops.

★

[It had] seventeen national vessels, not one of them first class in power or size, mounting 442 guns, and carrying 5,000 men, to match against the 1,000 ships, the 27,000 guns and the 150,000 seamen of our great and confident antagonist. The United States and England in 1812 were the David and Goliath of the ocean. Our little navy did its work valiantly. It won ten out of twelve single-ship actions, [including such glorious triumphs as the defeat of the British *Guerrière* by the USS *Constitution* ("Old Ironsides")].

But the naval student and the historian know what the people do not always remember—that because we had no battleships nearly all our frigates and sloops were finally blockaded by overwhelming squadrons, and that the last frigate which ran the gauntlet, the *President,* met with defeat and capture before she could clear the land.

[The War of 1812 was fought on the sea] not by national ships, which were few, but by privateers, which were many. [They] were usually improvised from merchant vessels; they were always manned by merchant crews.

There were, at least, 40,000 native-born American merchant seamen at the breaking out of the War of 1812, or enough to man the U.S. Navy eight times over. There was no opportunity for them in the national

Adapted and excerpted from "Impressment and Embargo, 1801–15," in Winthrop L. Marvin's *The American Merchant Marine* (1919, 124–30).

service, and the independent temperament of most of these Yankee tars would turn naturally, anyway, to the freer and more gainful, though more perilous, life of privateering. The thoroughgoing Yankee sailor was then, as he is today, the *beau idéal* of the ocean rover. He was a consummate master of his calling, a keen lookout, a clever helmsman, bold and active aloft, of ironlike physique, famed the world around for his vigor and endurance. He had his full share of the Yankee characteristic of thriftiness. He could appreciate the profit-sharing plan which made every man and boy of a privateer crew an interested partner in the enterprise. He had a native aptitude for firearms, large and small, and a wicked predilection for those ugly tools—the boarding pike and cutlass.

Above all, the Yankee seaman of 1812 was self-reliant. He learned his trade and lived his life in a world of merciless enemies. The first thing he realized when, as a boy, he went to sea, was that if he was to keep out of the clutches of press-gangs and buccaneers, he must depend upon himself; his government could not and perhaps would not save him. The British tar had a man-of-war ever ready to protect him; the Yankee tar probably never had seen one of the few and rare frigates or sloops that flew the gridiron ensign. His own stout heart and steel nerves and muscles were his only shield and buckler in his rough knocking about the world.

The net result was a splendid fighting man, often a little too forceful and aggressive for matter-of-fact naval discipline but a perfect privateersman. Yet real discipline was not lacking in these private armed ships of 1812. There were instances in which they actually outfought and took regular British cruisers; man for man and gun for gun, they were as superior to British privateers as was the *Constitution* or the *Wasp* to the stately vessels that flew the pennant of the king.

These matchless seamen had matchless ships ready to their hands. The "right of search" and the practice of impressment, as enforced by France and England, had set a tremendous premium upon long legs and lofty canvas. The result was that the average U.S. merchant ship, brig, or schooner was fine-lined and tall-sparred beyond all European precedent. Our ports were full of these swift vessels when war was declared. It was an easy matter to throw a few more broadside guns aboard, to mount a "long Tom" eighteen-pounder on a pivot amidships, and to clear the 'tween decks for hammocks for fifty or a hundred men. These privateers of 1812 got to sea with amazing rapidity. Within sixty days after the declaration, 150 of them were harrying British commerce in the North

Atlantic. Meanwhile, only eight warships of the United States had managed to escape from port.

The British blockade of the coast was rigid and unceasing. It extended from Long Island Sound to the Mississippi. New England was at first exempted because of her supposed sympathy with the British cause, but the victories of the *Constitution* and the exploits of the swarm of northern privateers soon drew a cordon of watchful cruisers across the bay from Halifax to Cape Cod. The U.S. coasting trade straightway became so hazardous that it was virtually abandoned. Flour, which sold for $4.50 per barrel in Richmond and $6.00 in Baltimore, brought $12.00 in Boston. Rice, worth $3.00 a hundred weight in Charleston and Savannah, was worth $12.00 in Philadelphia. Coffee doubled in price. For Hyson tea by the chest $4.00 a pound was offered. Salt brought $5.00 per bushel. Sugar, which was quoted at $9.00 a hundred weight in New Orleans in August of 1813 and $21.00 or $22.00 in New York, had advanced to $40.00 in December. New York's exports fell from $12,250,000 in 1811 to $209,000 in 1814. The blockade was helped by a last embargo, laid as a distinct war measure on 17 December 1813, and intended especially to prevent disloyal New England shipowners from trading with the country's enemies.

Between the war and the embargo, U.S. ocean carrying now became almost nonexistent. But our great antagonist was far more vulnerable, and she suffered even worse. In June 1813, the British people were paying the famine prices of $58.00 a barrel for flour, $38.00 for beef, and $36.00 for pork, while lumber cost $72.00 a thousand. It was this economic distress more than our brilliant victories in a dozen naval duels which brought Great Britain at the last to terms, and this distress was the work less of our national warships than of our privateers. The regular navy of the United States in the War of 1812 comprised on the ocean only twenty-three vessels of all classes, mounting 556 guns. These twenty-three men-of-war captured 254 naval and merchant ships of the enemy. But the Yankee privateers of 1812–15 numbered 517, mounting 2,893 guns. These private-armed ships, nearly all of them merchant ships with merchant crews, took no fewer than 1,300 prizes. The money value of British ships and cargoes captured by our government cruisers in the second War for Independence is estimated at $6,600,000; the money value of ships and cargoes captured by our privateers at $39,000,000. In this terrible attack upon England's "pocket nerve" our great merchant marine proved six times as potent as our little navy.

The better class of our privateers were very much more successful in their work of commerce destroying than our small regular cruisers of the same tonnage. Nearly all our navy brigs and schooners that got to sea were pursued and caught by British frigates. Their loss is attributed to an official mania for overloading these smart little craft with heavy batteries. Private enterprise was wiser. The privateers as a rule "ran light." They were thus able to outsail their ponderous foes, and yet, when there was need of fighting, these armed merchant ships rarely failed to whip a Briton of equal power.

The audacity of the Yankee privateersmen was as astonishing as their numbers. The master of a British merchantman, who had been three times captured and as many times recaptured, declared when he reached the shelter of his home port that he had sighted no fewer than ten U.S. privateers in a single voyage. These intrepid adventurers haunted the West Indies. They hung upon the flanks of rich convoys, and cut out the choicest vessels in night and fog with exasperating defiance of the guardian line of battleships and frigates. But the most dramatic and effective work of the Yankee privateers of 1812–15 was done . . . right on the British coast and in the chops of the English Channel. This produced in Britain a comical blending of fury and despondency, which found voice in the memorials of the merchants of Liverpool and other seaport towns. A typical remonstrance is that of the merchants of Glasgow, adopted at a meeting called by public advertisement in September 1814 under the auspices of the Lord Provost. Scotland's trade had been severely harried, and no less a personage than Sir Walter Scott narrowly escaped being carried off by these indomitable Yankee rovers. The Glasgow meeting unanimously adopted resolutions [complaining]

> That the number of privateers with which our channels have been infested, the audacity with which they have approached our coasts, and the success with which their enterprise has been attended have proved injurious to our commerce, humbling to our pride, and discreditable to the directors of the naval power of the British nation, whose flag, till of late, waved over every sea and triumphed over every rival.
>
> That there is reason to believe that in the short space of less than twenty-four months, above eight hundred vessels have been captured

by that power whose maritime strength we have hitherto impolitically held in contempt.

That at a time when we are at peace with all the world, when the maintenance of our marine costs so large a sum to the country, when the mercantile and shipping interests pay a tax for protection under the form of convoy duty, and when, in the plenitude of our power, we have declared the whole American coast under blockade, it is equally distressing and mortifying that our ships cannot with safety traverse our own channels, that insurance cannot be effected but at an excessive premium, and that a horde of American cruisers should be allowed, unresisted and unmolested, to take, burn, or sink our own vessels in our own inlets, and almost in sight of our own harbors.

What manner of men and of ships these were, that did this bold and telling work, can be gathered from . . . [Edgar Stanton] Maclay's . . . recent . . . history. . . . The privateer was no mere harpy of the deep; it was ready and eager for battle. The famous brig *Chasseur* captured the king's cruiser *St. Lawrence.* There were other instances where the royal colors went down before our merchant flag, and there were combats of privateer against privateer almost without number.

These facts are worth remembering, as tokens of the brave and self-reliant spirit that animated the U.S. merchant marine after England and France, by orders and decrees and impressment, had spent long years in an endeavor to crush the enterprise of our merchants and the manhood of their crews. The oppressive policies of the giant powers of Europe and our own embargo may have encouraged sharp practices here and there and made some U.S. sailors smugglers and some U.S. shipowners hypocrites. But the merchant marine, as a whole, came out of the long ordeal of 1801–12 sound and honest and brave to prove its worth in the supreme test of war.

Great Britain did not formally renounce impressment in the peace treaty of 1814–15. But the vital truth is that this injustice was shot to pieces by the broadsides of our few frigates and our many privateers. Never afterward could the "right" to steal sailors from the decks of U.S. ships and compel them to serve an alien flag, or fight their own flag, be reasserted.

★

5 Privateers and Privateersmen

☆☆

Soon after the creation of the U.S. Navy it became apparent that the prospect of rich rewards from privateering made naval recruitment difficult. In 1800 Congress authorized navy crews to share in the proceeds of prize vessels taken by warships.

☆

When the prize is of equal or superior force to the vessel making the capture, it shall be the sole property of the captors. If of inferior force, it shall be divided equally between the United States and the officers and men making the capture. . . . All public ships in sight at the time of making prize shall share equally. Twenty dollars to be paid by the United States for each person on board an enemy's ship at the commencement of an engagement which shall be burned, sunk, or destroyed by any U.S. vessel of equal or inferior force. All prize money accruing to the United States is solemnly pledged as a fund for payment of pensions and half pay should the same be hereafter granted. If this fund is insufficient, the faith of the United States is pledged for the indeficiency; if more than sufficient, the surplus is to go to the comfort of disabled mariners, or such as may deserve the gratitude of their country.

☆ (Maclay, "Privateers," 310)

Even when the "prize" was so badly shot up she could not make port, prize money was put up on special occasions. When "Old Ironsides" (USS *Constitution*) destroyed HMS *Guerrière* in the summer of 1812 a grateful Congress appropriated a $50,000 bonus to be shared by her crew, and repeated the gesture later when she sank the king's 38-gun frigate *Java*. A similar bonus was put up when the *Constitution* later

Adapted and retold from the chapter of this name in Edgar Stanton Maclay's *History of American Privateers* (1895, as reprinted in *Deep Water Days*, Oliver G. Swan, ed., 1929). It is augmented with excerpts from Jerome R. Garitee's *The Republic's Private Navy* (1977), which appears with the author's kind permission.

bested the British *Macedonian,* but that 38-gun frigate did reach New London under a prize crew.

In the case of merchant vessels captured as regular prizes by navy ships, the eventual proceeds (after adjudication by a prize court) were divided into twenty equal parts, of which three went to the captain. Two shares were divided among the sea lieutenants and sailing master. Another two were split up among the marine officers, surgeon, purser, boatswain, gunner, carpenter, master's mates, and chaplain. Three parts were shared by the midshipmen, surgeon's mates, captain's clerk, schoolmaster, boatswain's mates, steward, sailmaker, master-at-arms, armorer, and coxwain.

Each succeeding category grew more numerous: Three parts went to the gunners' yeomen, boatswain's yeomen, quartermasters, quarter gunners, coopers, sailmaker's mates, sergeants and corporals of the marines, drummer, fifer, and extra petty officers. Finally, seven parts were shared among some two hundred men and boys: seamen, ordinary seamen, marines, and boys.

If a prize brought $50,000, this would mean the captain's share was $7,500—a snug fortune for a naval officer who regularly earned from $600 to $1,200 a year. The seamen, marines, and boys in the last group cited above would receive about $87 apiece—almost a year's regular wages.

Some navy ships brought in prizes valued at more than a million dollars. "One of the boys in the *Ranger,* fourteen years old who less than a month before had left a farm to ship in this cruiser, received his share [in the form of] one ton of sugar, thirty to forty gallons of fourth proof Jamaica rum, some twenty pounds of cotton, and about the same quantity of ginger, logwood, and allspice, besides $700 in money" (Maclay, "Privateers," 313).

The government also allowed a bounty for prisoners brought to port—originally $20 a head and later raised to $25; this applied to privateersmen as well as navy crews.

★

[But the privateersman, in most cases,] preferred to rid himself of prisoners at the earliest possible moment. There were several reasons for this. Even had the bounty been as high as $100 it would not have paid the successful privateersman to accumulate prisoners, especially when on a long voyage—and there could be no telling how long a cruise would last—for the cost of feeding amounted to a large sum. Then the danger of having too many prisoners was shown dozens of times when the captured rose on their captors and not only recovered their own vessel, but made prisoners of the privateersman.

☆   (Maclay, "Privateers," 314)

The apportionment of shares on a privateer was quite different, as demonstrated in an itemized list in *The Republic's Private Navy*.

☆

Arrangements among privateer crewmen for the distribution of prize proceeds were more complicated than those of commissioned traders. The *Highflyer's* Articles of Agreement were typical of privateer staffing and prize distribution schemes. The following plan was utilized:

1 Captain	14 shares
1 1st Lieutenant	9 shares
1 2nd Lieutenant	7 shares
1 Sailing Master	8 shares
1 Surgeon	8 shares
4 Prize Masters	6 shares each
1 Carpenter	4 shares
1 Gunner	4 shares
1 Boatswain	4 shares
1 Clerk	2½ shares
1 Drummer	1½ shares
1 Gunner's Mate	2½ shares
1 Ship's Steward	2½ shares
1 Boatswain mate	2 shares
1 Carpenter's mate	2 shares
1 Captain's Steward	2½ shares
1 Cook	2 shares
1 Captain of the Forecastle	2 shares
2 Quartermasters	2 shares each
1 Armourer	2 shares
41 First Class seamen	2 shares each
11 Ordinary seamen	1½ shares each
13 Ordinary seamen	1 share each
1 Ordinary seaman	¾ share
1 Boy	1 share

The assignment of 2.5 shares to the drummer suggests that boys did not occupy that position. [The position] required exposure during combat and some drummers, including the one of the privateer *Globe,* were killed in action. Ordinary seamen (eleven of them on *Highflyer*) were normally required to know the common duties of seamen in regard to ropes, sails, and some steering but were not required to be experts. First-class or able-bodied seamen were expected to handle all facets of the watch, steering, anchoring, and everything to do with the sails. The *Highflyer* carried forty-one of the all-important first-class seamen at two shares each.

The *Highflyer's* articles listed a total of 220 shares for the officers and crew. Eight and one-quarter "reserved" or "deserving" shares were unassigned in the articles. Two first-class seamen names were followed by the notation "runaway at Baltimore," and one ordinary seaman was marked "returned sick" and then "discharged." Advances to the crew ranged from ten to thirty dollars except in the case of the surgeon who received seventy-five dollars. Other privateers followed similar but not identical crew positions and distribution patterns.

☆   (Garitee, *The Republic's Private Navy,* 134–35)

It is revealing to compare the compensation schemes of navy vessels and privateers. The latter was much more egalitarian. As stated previously, a navy captain with a prize worth $50,000 would net $7,500 (plus his regular pay, which would have run between $600 and $1,200 annually). By comparison the master of a privateer with a prize of similar value would net about $3,200, with no base pay.

But where the navy boatswain would receive some $200, his privateering counterpart would receive about $900. And the navy's ordinary seaman would net about $87 vis-à-vis his privateer counterpart's share of about $280. Small wonder that recruiting was much less of a problem for the owner of a privateer than for the navy.

☆

[Still, it was a problem at various times and places (e.g., Baltimore).] With the unusual demand for men in peak periods of activity, Baltimore vessels sought men elsewhere. The privateer *Rolla's* log for November 1812, only twenty days out of Baltimore, recorded stops at Bristol, Providence, Falmouth, and Boston for men. Her cruise terminated in December 1812 "for want of officers and men." The privateer *Bona* entered at Norfolk for men, enrolling one black man after he gave proof that "he was not a slave." Commodore Joshua Barney's *Rossie* "touched in at Newport, Rhode Island, for officers and men and proceeded to the West Indies." A Baltimore merchant firm reported that vessels were scarce in December of 1812 and that no men were available when vessels were on hand.

Some shortages resulted from combat losses at sea and from the manning of prizes. The *Syren* cleared with eighty men but in her effort to enter the blockaded Delaware River after a successful cruise, she was handled by only twenty men. The 55-ton *Wasp*, clearing with forty men, found it necessary to ship a boatswain, a seaman, and three Frenchmen at Charleston. Joshua Barney reported the recruitment of six prisoners from prizes to the *Rossie* but carefully noted that they were not British subjects. British subjects were not permitted to serve on U.S. private armed vessels. Apparently, some captains still enrolled them when they were desperate for men. The privateer *Globe*'s journal contained a notation that seven prisoners had "entered" as seamen. Captain Thomas Boyle of the *Chasseur* admitted that he "did accept the Services of some men he took prisoners." Boyle made them [state in writing] that they had signed on voluntarily, that they would obey regulations, and that they were to receive one share each. A captain at sea took anyone he could find after his own crew began to shrink. New men might prolong a cruise and increase profits.

☆   (Garitee, *Republic's Private Navy*, 135)

As time at sea grew longer, crews shrank but appetites did not. Concern for the larder would gradually become constant, and it required improvisation, confiscation, and barter or purchase of food from neutral vessels when encountered.

☆

[Garitee cites a Baltimore schooner *Wasp* that stopped a small] vessel of twenty-one tons and "took out some Yams and coffee and let go." The same privateer bought a barrel of sugar for $22.00 from another vessel and when short, served out a pound of pork, a pound of bread, and "plenty of peace" for each man per day. Near the end of the voyage, with provisions dwindling, the men survived on one-half pound of bread per man daily and "as much Turtle Soup as they can devour." The *Kemp*'s log noted that two essentials, rum and cordage, were taken out of a prize vessel when needed by the privateer. Captains were permitted to remove items for the use of their vessel, and they usually had a need for food toward the end of a long cruise or voyage.

Clothing was the responsibility of the individual crew members, and the owners accepted no responsibility for providing such items. They did sell clothing on board and owners William and James Bosley provided, at their own cost, winter clothing for the *Tartar's* crew. To outfit himself, a crew member was able to sell part or all of his prize ticket or to spend his small advance from the owners. One court dispute illustrated the cost when a store owner outfitted and loaned money in exchange for a prize ticket. Hezekiah Joel signed onto the *Rolla* in Massachusetts and was sold shirts from $2.00 to $4.00 each, a jacket, a "Superfine Coat" ($35.00), hose, and braces. His shoes cost $2.00, and his two pairs of "Duck Trowsers" were $1.50 apiece. He also purchased, among other items, a mattress, two blankets for $6.00 each, a sea chest for $5.00, and, perhaps for shore use, an umbrella. Joel was outfitted with thirty items for a total of $181.00 according to the store owners. He obviously got what he could for his shares in the *Rolla* while others were content to use their fifteen dollars advance to outfit themselves in a less splendid fashion. Where Joel, perhaps a "greenhand," expected to use a mattress on the crowded *Rolla* is uncertain. Even hammocks were a luxury below decks where space was scarce.

There were other ways to fill the need for clothing. Cotton duck trousers were commonly sewn together from old sails by the seamen. Prize vessels provided clothing also but not always as spoils of war. The *Kemp* sold its own crew $632.75 worth of clothes taken from the prize *Lady Mary Pelham,* but that sum then became part of the *Kemp's* prize account. Seaman John Barnes's account with the agent of the *Kemp* listed $26.00 owed by Barnes for trousers or "slops" purchased on board the vessel.

Charts, compasses, sextants, and other nautical items were available in Baltimore, particularly at Fells Point. James Ramsay, part owner of the privateers *Sarah Ann, Caroline,* and *Fairy* operated the best-known chandlery and grocery in Fells Point. He advertised charts, compasses, quadrants, sextants, day and night telescopes, lamps, rules, scales, dividers, and other items for sale in October 1812. Another advertisement placed by John Allen of Thames Street in Fells Point boasted that his was the new and only manufactury in Baltimore of ships' compasses, quadrants, and other instruments and that he also gave navigation lessons.

Navigational instruments were another item taken from prizes at sea. Capt. Thomas Boyle of the famous *Comet,* in response to a charge that he had kept prize items for himself and the owners, admitted that nautical instruments were taken from prizes. From the prize ship *John,* Boyle said he also took out among other items signals, canvas, twine, grap shot, and other arms while also distributing liquor and a "few pigs" among the crew. From the *Henry* he took shot, powder, and sailcloth, while the *Hopewell* provided ammunition as well as coffee and sugar, which were "divided among the crew" and a "few Teripins" when the *Comet's* stores were depleted.

☆ (Garitee, *Republic's Private Navy,* 124–25)

In June of 1812 Congress authorized the commissioning of privateers to seize British merchantmen, and the owners of a vessel seeking such authorization had only to apply to the collector of the port. *The Republic's Private Navy* quotes an actual commission for the schooner *Patapsco* of Baltimore.

☆

JAMES MADISON, President of the United States of America.

TO ALL WHO SHALL THESE PRESENTS, GREETING:

BE IT KNOWN, That in pursuance of an Act of Congress passed on the *eighteenth* day of *June* one thousand eight hundred and twelve, I have commissioned, and by these presents do commission, the private armed *Schooner* called the *Patapsco* of the burthen of *159* tons, or thereabouts, owned by Andrew Clopper, Levi Hollingsworth, Amos A. Williams and Henry Fulford of the City of Baltimore mounting *6* carriage guns, and navigated by *40* men, hereby authorizing *James M. Mortimer* Captain, and *William Ross* Lieutenant of the said *schooner Patapsco* and the other officers and crew thereof to subdue, seize and take any armed or unarmed British vessel, public or private, which shall be found within the jurisdictional limits of the United States or elsewhere on the high seas, or within the waters of the British dominions, and such captured vessel, with her apparel, guns and appurtenances, and the goods and effects which shall be found on board the same, together with the British persons and others who shall be acting on board, to bring within some port of the

United States; and also to retake any vessel, goods and effects of the people of the United States, which may have been captured by any British armed vessel, in order that proceedings may be had concerning such capture or recapture in due form of law, and as to right and justice shall appertain. The said *James M. Mortimer* is further authorized to detain, seize and take all vessels and effects, to whomsoever belonging, which shall be liable thereto according to the Law of Nations and the rights of the United States as a power at war, and to bring the same within some port of the United States in order that due proceedings may be had thereon. This commission to continue in force during the pleasure of the President of the United States for the time being.

> Given under my hand and seal of the United States of America, at the city of Washington, the *17* day of *September* in the year of our Lord, one thousand eight hundred and *12* and of the Independence of the said states the *Thirty seven.*
>
> By the President JAMES MADISON
> JAMES MONROE Secretary of State

★   (Garitee, *Republic's Private Navy,* 96–97)

★

The first and greatest element of success with a privateersman was audacity. Without that, above all other things, he was doomed to ignominious failure. The navy man who came home from a voyage without meeting an enemy or taking a prize suffered little loss of esteem. In fact, both in the Revolution and the War of 1812, the naval commanding officer who put to sea and returned to port with a whole skin was regarded, at least by naval administrators, as a singularly fortunate and capable officer. Not so with a privateersman. To return to port empty-handed was to commit the greatest sin of the profession. Hence we find that the privateersman was preeminently a bold and daring man, and when such qualities were combined with skillful seamanship we have the ideal privateersman.

A good illustration of the "audacious impudence" of privateersmen is had in the case of the *Paul Jones* of New York. This vessel put to sea at the outbreak of the War of 1812 with a complement of 120 men but with only three guns. Almost her first prize was the heavily armed British merchantman *Hassan,* carrying fourteen guns and a crew of twenty men, while her cargo was worth some $200,000. The *Paul Jones,* though carrying only three guns, was pierced for seventeen. It is said that the commander of the *Paul Jones* sawed off some spare masts to the length of guns, painted them black, and, being mounted on buckets, rolled them out of his empty ports as effective imitations of heavy ordnance. Then filling his rigging with his superfluous force of men, so far overawed the enemy that they surrendered as soon as the privateer, with her dummy guns, got fairly alongside. The Americans then helped themselves to such of the *Hassan's* guns and ammunitions as they needed and went on their way rejoicing.

☆   (Maclay, "Privateers," 314–15)

☆

[With rare exceptions, the rights of neutrals were scrupulously observed. This was an explicit requirement.] Accompanying the commission, copies of it, and the law authorizing the commissions, the sponsors of the private armed vessel were given "suitable instructions for the better governing and directing the conduct of the vessels, so commissioned, their officers and crews." Such instructions were ordered by the law authorizing commissions. Designed along with bonds and other requirements to prevent abuses of the system, they evolved out of the long European struggle to control private armed vessels at sea or to punish them in the courts upon their return. War of 1812 instructions read as follows:

> To Captain ————— Commander of the private armed —————
> called the —————
>
> INSTRUCTIONS
> *For the Private Armed Vessels of the United States*
> 1. The tenor of your commission under the act of Congress entitled
> "An act concerning letters of marque, prizes, and prize goods," a
> copy of which is hereto annexed, will be kept constantly in your view.
> The high seas, referred to in your commission, you will understand,
> generally, to extend to low water mark; but with the exception of the
> space within one league, or three miles, from the shores of countries
> at peace both with Great Britain and with the United States. You may
> nevertheless execute your commission within that distance of the
> shore of a nation at war with Great Britain, and even on the waters
> within the jurisdiction of such nation, if permitted to do so.

2. You are to pay the strictest regard to the rights of neutral powers, and the usages of civilized nations, and in all your proceedings toward neutral vessels, you are to give them as little molestation or interruption as will consist with the right of ascertaining their neutral character, and of detaining and bringing them in for regular adjudication, in the proper case. You are particularly to avoid even the appearance of using force or reduction with a view to deprive such vessels of their crews, or of their passengers other than persons in the military service of the enemy.

3. Towards the enemy vessels and their crews, you are to proceed, in exercising the rights of war with all the justice and humanity which characterizes the nation of which you are members.

4. The master and one or more of the principal persons belonging to captured vessels, are to be sent, as soon after the capture as may be, to the judge or judges of the proper court in the United States, to be examined upon oath, touching the interests or property of the captured vessel and her lading: and at the same time are to be delivered to the judge or judges, all passes, charter parties, bills of lading, invoices, letters and other documents and writings found on board; the said papers to be proved by the affidavit of the commander of the capturing vessel, or some other person present at the capture, to be produced as they were received, without fraud, addition, subduction or embezzlement.

By command of the President of the United States of America.

JAMES MONROE
Secretary of State

The clause in the "Instructions" referring to "the justice and humanity which characterizes the nation of which you are members" may appear quaint to readers in a century characterized by total wars, but in 1812 it reflected the values and self-image of the new republic. Its insertion in a warlike document reflects its general acceptance at the time, while the record of the Baltimoreans at sea suggests that it was taken seriously. Five British masters attested to the good treatment they received on board the Baltimore privateer *Harpy*. The privateer *Kemp* released a British brig "out of humanity to an Italian lady and family" traveling on that brig. The *Sparrow* was praised by a British captain for not touching private items and for purchasing poultry. The *Federal Gazette* received a report on the good treatment of British prisoners on U.S. privateers and commented that this was "as it should be." A New York newspaper applauded the "correct and liberal" conduct of the U.S. privateersmen. Whether the U.S. captains acted as liberally and humanely toward their own crews is another question, but in their dealings with the enemy there is little evidence that they failed to uphold the new republic's standards.

☆   (Garitee, *Republic's Private Navy*, 97–98)

☆

When the schooner *Industry,* Captain Renneaux, a prize to the privateer *Benjamin Franklin,* Captain Ingersol, of New York, reached that port on 24 August 1812, it was learned that the craft belonged to a widow whose only dependence was on the earnings of that vessel. Although the *Industry* had two thousand dollars' worth of goods aboard, the American restored her and her cargo to the widow.

☆   (Maclay, "Privateers," 315)

Another instance of a gentle act by a warlike skipper came to light in a letter published in a London newspaper at the end of 1914. It related the capture of a British merchantman laden with wheat by a U.S. privateer. When the captain entered the captain's cabin of his prize, his eye fell on a small wooden box with a slot in its top, labeled "Missionary Box."

☆

On seeing this the U.S. captain seemed not a little astounded and addressed the Welsh captain as follows:

"Captain, what is this?" pointing to the box with his stick.

"Oh," replied the honest Cambrian, heaving a sigh, "'tis all over now."

"What?" said the U.S. captain.

"Why, the truth is," said the Welshman, "that I and my poor fellows have been accustomed every Monday morning to drop a penny each into that box for the purpose of sending out missionaries to preach the Gospel to the heathen; but it is all over now."

"Indeed," answered the U.S. captain, "that is very good."

After pausing a few minutes he said: "Captain, I'll not hurt a hair on your head, nor touch your vessel," and he immediately departed, leaving the owner to pursue his course to his destined port.

☆   (Maclay, "Privateers," 316)

6 ★★ An 1812 Privateer Captures a British Letter of Marque

★

The watch had been roused from their lazy retreat after a hard sleep of two hours and the customary duties of the morning watch were being commenced as the lookout went aloft. After he had reached his post in the crosstrees, he quietly seated himself, supporting his back against the head of the mast; then his strengthened eye swept around a clear, unbroken horizon, until it stopped in the direction of one point abaft the beam, and after a long and attentive gaze he sung out at the top of his hoarse voice, "Sail ho!" For a few minutes all was excitement, but as it was now a dead calm and very little appearance of wind, the chance was small to get within speaking distance shortly.

The duties of the morning watch and breakfast being finished, the cruiser was got into complete readiness for action. The great probability was that the strange sail was a man-of-war, as it was not a position for merchant vessels to be in without convoy. It was a matter of little import to the officers or men, whether the stranger was a man-of-war or merchant vessel, for having so little to do in the last fifteen days, they were eager to wet their palates, and cared not whether it was a chase, or an action.

Hour after hour passed away, and no ripple or cat's paw was seen on the surface of the ocean, neither was the bearing or distance of the two vessels altered. Two bells was struck, and not a change—the same interminable calm prevailed; but the young seaman who had the lookout aloft, reported that the stranger was a ship, having a breeze from the eastward and bearing down upon the cruiser, her top gallant sails being lifted. The cat's paw and overfalls came dancing over the deep, and before a half hour passed the breeze was settled and steady.

By Capt. George Little. Reprinted from *Deep Water Days*, Oliver G. Swan, ed. (Philadelphia: Macrae Smith, 1929).

"I hope the stranger will keep in the same mind as she is now," observed the commander, "and we shall be better acquainted before dark."

Every yard was now trimmed to the breeze on the larboard tack, and a few minutes brought the stranger in sight from the deck, but as soon as her hull was lifted, she suddenly hauled close to the wind, on the same tack with the cruiser.

"I am of the same opinion," replied the first lieutenant, "but that movement tells me that he is some fat merchantman, or letter of marque, perhaps, and calculated when he first saw us that he would make a prize."

Innumerable were the conjectures in relation to the character of our neighbor. Again and again were the glasses put in requisition to see if anything could be discovered to decide conflicting opinions. The stranger had taken in studding sails and was close by the wind, bearing directly abeam of the cruiser. All doubts that had been entertained of her character were now dispelled; she was certainly not a man-of-war, and even if she were an armed vessel, it was now apparent that she did not admire the looks of the cruiser.

"That craft to windward," said the skipper, "does not appear like a sleepy merchantman; she carries a stout sail, square yards, and shows us as bold a side as a frigate, for she is as upright as a dish, and were it not for this move, and I believe it is only a maneuver, I should decide that she was a man-of-war. However, we will swagger up to her, and if my conjecture is right, we shall have use of all our muslin shortly."

All the light sails were therefore got in readiness, and Long Tom was prepared to enter into conversation with the stranger, if required. The northeastern breeze freshened and blew briskly. It was now a fair trial of speed between the two vessels, but the cruiser had the advantage, for she not only lay a point nearer to the wind, but actually head-reached quite as fast, so that by sunset the relative distance between the two was very much lessened, not being more than a half mile apart; it became evident that the stranger was an Englishman, and would not risk an action if it could possibly be avoided. After night had set in, the cruiser shortened sail to drop in the wake of the ship, so as to keep her close aboard, during the night. This maneuver was effected, and by eight o'clock the cruiser was about musket shot distant from the ship.

The night was clear, and the moon had risen and was calmly sailing on, far up in the blue ether, silvering the deep with her gentle radiance and showering a flood of sparkles on every billowy crest that rolled up and shivered in her light. Everywhere objects were discernible with as much distinctness as under the noonday sun. The breeze sang through the rigging with a joyous sound, singularly pleasing after the silence and monotony of the fore part of the day; and the waves that parted beneath the cutwater rolled glittering astern along the sides, while ever and anon some billow larger than its fellows broke over the bow, sending its foam crackling back to the foremast. Around the deck the men were gathered each one beside his allotted gun, silently awaiting the moment of attack. The cutlasses had been served out, the boarding pikes and muskets were convenient for use, the balls had already been on deck, and the cruiser only waited for some demonstration on the part of the foe to open the magazine and commence the combat in earnest; but no manifestation was made, for she kept on her way under a cloud of sail in profound silence, evidently wishing to avoid the combat altogether or defer it until morning.

With the break of dawn the first demonstration of attack on the part of the foe was given. The ports were thrown up and displayed eight pieces of cannon, and the English bunting removed all doubts respecting her character, which could not be misunderstood for her broadside was poured into the cruiser without further ceremony. The enemy's shot produced very little effect upon the cruiser, only cutting away some ropes and a few airholes through the sails.

"You had better elevate the muzzle of your gun," said the old gunner, "and then mayhap you will cut away our trucks. Long Tom will pepper you after a different fashion when it comes to his turn to speak."

As soon as the enemy had delivered her broadside, she bore away, and the contest became a running fight; the ship delivered her stern chasers in fine style with some effect, but the cruiser had not as yet fired a shot. Nevertheless, as she was superior in point of sailing, she closed in rapidly with the enemy and took her position on the starboard quarter of the ship.

"It is a pity to wing the craft," said the gunner, as he stood by the Long Tom, impatiently waiting the command to fire, "so I'll send a decent messenger to that quarterdeck."

The fire from the enemy did considerable execution, and the crew, impatient of restraint and exasperated at the sight of blood, were eager to lay alongside, and they did not hesitate to speak their minds to that effect.

"Very well," said the commander, evidently pleased at the impetuosity of the men, "in twenty minutes we shall be alongside of that ship, and I expect every man will do his duty. Prepare, then, for boarding."

Just then a shot from the enemy cut away the cruiser's main topmast.

"Is Long Tom ready?" shouted the skipper.

"Fire!"

A loud cracking was heard immediately after the discharge of Long Tom, and when the smoke cleared away the enemy's quarter boardrail and taffrail were cut away. The compliment was immediately repeated by Long Tom with great effect, and the two 18-pound carronades, filled with grape and langrage shot, were delivered in a manner that drove the Englishmen from their quarters, after which the cruiser shot alongside and grappled the mizzenchain of the ship.

"Boarders way!" shouted the skipper.

The assailants, with the young seaman (who had been stationed in the crosstrees) and boatswain at their head, boarded on the starboard quarter, rushing with an impetuosity that drove the Englishmen as far as the mainmast. Here they once more rallied, and the conflict on the part of the foe, exasperated as they were at the prospects of losing their ship, was so furious that for a moment the assailants retreated; but the brave young seaman and the boatswain, perceiving the check of their shipmates, threw themselves into the hottest of the fight and with voices that reverberated far away on the ocean, shouted, "Follow us, shipmates, she is ours!"

The dexterous arm of the young seaman and the science of the boatswain dealt out destruction to all who had the temerity to oppose them, while the undaunted first lieutenant drove the Englishmen on the starboard side. For a short time the wild uproar of the fight, the groans of the wounded and dying, baffled all description. The conflict, however, was soon decided, for the crew of the ship, consisting of mongrel Frenchmen and Englishmen together, were driven by the furious Yankees as far as the foremast and then sung out for quarter. At the same moment the English bunting was hauled down, and the contest was at an end. This beautiful prize ship was a Gurnsey letter of marque, mounting sixteen guns with a complement of fifty men. This ship, with two heavy British brigs of the same character, had captured a U.S. merchantman, the captain, a first officer, and three men of which were now prisoners on board.

The English ship was ordered to the United States under escort of a prize crew; the U.S. prisoners aboard were released and the cruiser set sail for fresh conquests.

☆

7 ★★ The Incredible Captain Thomas Boyle

Few privateersmen of the War of 1812 cut a more dashing figure than Thomas Boyle, the gallant and flamboyant master of two fleet Baltimore schooners. Both were built by the master of Fells Point, Thomas Kemp. In his first command, of the *Comet* during the first three months of the war, Boyle took rich prizes one after another, consistently besting better-armed vessels. One such was a Portuguese warship big enough to carry his *Comet* on deck. Boyle defeated the warship and captured three well-armed British merchantmen the ship was escorting, though one of them was "all cut to pieces and rendered unmanageable."

Boyle's second vessel was a much larger and faster ship, the Kemp-built, 356-ton topsail schooner *Chasseur.* Her armament featured sixteen long-range twelve-pounders, and she had a crew of 150 (including prize masters and extra seamen to sail prizes home with their cargoes). She was known as the "Pride of Baltimore," and could show her heels to any British warship afloat. On his first cruise in the *Chasseur,* out of New York and while en route to his hunting grounds along the European coast, Boyle took numerous prizes, sending the rich ones home with prize crews and burning the worthless ones.

★

[His *Chasseur* was never outsailed in fair winds or foul. Out of sheer] "wantonness," said an admirer, "she sometimes affected to chase the enemy's men-of-war of far superior force." Once when surrounded by two frigates and two naval brigs, she slipped through and was gone like a phantom. During his first cruise in the *Chasseur,* Captain Boyle captured eighteen valuable merchantmen. It was such defiant rovers as he that provoked the *Morning Chronicle* of London to splutter "that the whole coast of Ireland from Wexford round by Cape Clear to Carrickfergus, should have been for above a month under the unresisted domination of a few petty fly-by-nights from the blockaded ports of the United States is a grievance equally intolerable and disgraceful."

This was when the schooner *Syren* had captured His Majesty's cutter *Landrail* while crossing the Irish Sea with dispatches; when the *Governor Tompkins* burned fourteen English vessels in the English Channel in quick succession; when the *Harpy* of Baltimore cruised for three months off the Irish and English coasts and in the Bay of Biscay and returned to Boston filled with spoils, including a half million dollars; when the *Prince de Neuchâtel* hovered at her leisure in the Irish Channel and made coasting trade impossible; and when the *Young Wasp* of Philadelphia cruised for six months in those same waters.

[The *Prince de Neuchâtel* had the honor of beating] off the attack of a 40-gun British frigate—an exploit second only to that of the *General Armstrong* in the harbor of Fayal. This privateer with a foreign name hailed from New York and was so fortunate as to capture for her owners three million dollars' worth of British merchandise. With Capt. J. Ordronaux on the quarterdeck, she was near Nantucket Shoals at noon on 11 October 1814, when a strange sail was discovered. As this vessel promptly gave chase, Captain Ordronaux guessed—and events proved correctly—that she must be a British frigate. She turned out to be the *Endymion*. The privateer had in tow a prize which she was anxious to get into port, but she was forced to cast off the hawser late in the afternoon and make every effort to escape.

The breeze died with the sun, and the vessels were close inshore. Becalmed, the privateer and the frigate anchored a quarter of a mile apart. Captain Ordronaux might have put his crew on the beach in boats and abandoned his ship. This was the reasonable course, for, as he had sent in several prize crews, he was shorthanded and could muster no more than thirty-seven men and boys. The *Endymion,* on the other hand, had a complement of 350 sailors and marines, and in size and fighting power she was in the class of the U.S. frigates *President* and *Constitution.* Quite unreasonably, however, the master of the privateer decided to await events.

The unexpected occurred shortly after dusk when several boats loaded to the gunwales with a boarding party crept away from the frigate. Five of them, with 120 men, made a concerted attack at different points, alongside and under the bow and stern. Captain Ordronaux had told his crew that he would blow up the ship with all hands before striking his colors, and they believed him implicitly. This was the hero who was described as "a Jew by persuasion, a Frenchman by birth, an American for convenience, and so diminutive in stature as to make him appear ridiculous, in the eyes of others, even for him to enforce authority among a hardy, weather-beaten crew should they do aught against his will." He was big enough, nevertheless, for this night's bloody work, and there was no doubt about his authority. While the British tried to climb over the bulwarks, his thirty-seven men and boys fought like raging devils with knives, pistols, cutlases, with their bare fists and their teeth. A few of the enemy gained the deck, but the privateersmen turned and killed them. Others leaped aboard and were gradually driving the Americans back, when the skipper ran to the hatch above the powder magazine waving a lighted match and swearing to drop it in if his crew retreated one step further. Either way the issue seemed desperate. But again they took their skipper's word for it and rallied for a bloody struggle, which soon swept the decks.

No more than twenty minutes had passed and the battle was won. The enemy was begging for quarter. One boat had been sunk, three had drifted away filled with dead and wounded, and the fifth was captured with thirty-six men in it of whom only eight were unhurt. The American loss was seven killed and twenty-four wounded, or thirty-one of her crew of thirty-seven. Yet they had not given up the ship. The frigate *Endymion* concluded that once was enough, and next morning the *Prince de Neuchâtel* bore away for Boston with a freshening breeze.

★   (Paine, *Old Merchant Marine*, 120–24)

Ordronaux and dozens of other privateers were as tough and resourceful as Boyle, but not one was more flamboyant. It is not known just how Captain Boyle managed to deliver it, but his most impudent message to London was a proclamation actually posted on the door of the great marine insurance exchange, Lloyd's of London, that August. Copies appeared at home in Baltimore's *American and Commercial Daily Advertiser* (2 November 1814). Referring mockingly to the British blockade of the United States, Boyle heaped insult upon outrage by declaring his own blockade of the United Kingdom.

✩

PROCLAMATION

Whereas it has become customary with the Admirals of Great
Britain, commanding the small forces on the coast of the United
States, particularly with Sir John Borlase Warren, and Sir Alexander
Cochrane, to declare all the coast of the United States in a state of
strict and rigorous blockade, without possessing the power to justify
such a declaration, or stationing an adequate force to maintain and
blockade—

I do, therefore, by virtue of the power and authority in me vested
(possessing sufficient force) declare all the ports, harbours, bays,
creeks, rivers, inlets, outlets, islands and sea coast of the United
Kingdom of Great Britain and Ireland in a state of strict and rigorous
blockade. And I do further declare, that I consider the force under
my command adequate to maintain strictly, rigorously and effectually
the said blockade. And I do hereby require the respective officers,
whether captains, commanders or commanding officers under my
command, employed or to be employed on the coast of England,
Ireland and Scotland to pay strict attention to the execution of this
my Proclamation. And I do hereby caution and forbid the ships
and vessels of all and every nation in amity and peace with the
United States from entering or attempting to enter, or from coming
or attempting to come out of any of the said ports, harbours, bays,
creeks, rivers, inlets, outlets, islands or sea coast, under any pretence
whatsoever. And that no person may plead ignorant of this my
Proclamation, I have ordered the same to be made public in
England.

Given under my hand on board the *Chasseur,* day and date as
above.

THOMAS BOYLE
By command of the commanding officer,
J. J. Stansbury, Sec.

Undoubtedly, the *Chasseur*'s sailing ability and her sixteen long twelve-
pounders assured Boyle that he would never have to explain his concept
of blockade to a British court.

The operation of Baltimore schooners, such as the *Chasseur,* and other
U.S. privateers infuriated the British public and the admiralty. Vigor-

ous efforts were made to catch the U.S. seawolves. In one chase, the *Chasseur* put two broadsides into "a frigate of the second class" but received some punishment in exchange. One 24-pound shot struck Boyle's foremast about twelve feet from the deck and "cut it nearly a third off." Another "struck the gunwale of port No. 5, tore away all the sill and plank shear," dismounted the gun, went through the deck, and wounded three men. Henry Watson was "compelled to have his thigh amputated, and is maimed for life" according to the schooner's journal. After escaping from four men-of-war at once, Boyle perceived a trap set for him by two man-of-war brigs. He "edged down upon one of them, which was of the largest class," but after she fired at him, Boyle "fired a shot to him, displayed the Yanky flag, hauled upon a wind, and outsailed them both with ease." On the very next day, 6 September 1814, Boyle "got among three men-of-war, and narrowly escaped capture" in a calm. On the seventh, Boyle was "chased by 4 men-of-war but outsailed them with ease." Three days later, he outsailed one of five man-of-war brigs sent out especially to nab the *Chasseur.*

Even with the intensified pressure from the British Navy, Boyle made more prizes in English waters. Dogging a convoy of thirty-three vessels, Boyle waited until "a perfect gale" separated the ship *Carlbury* of London, bound from Curaçao via Jamaica, before making his move. Leaving such bulky items as cotton, cocoa, tobacco, and hides on the *Carlbury,* Boyle removed the smaller and more valuable goods to the safety of his own hold before ordering the *Carlbury* into a U.S. port. Dogging another convoy in late September, west of Ireland, Boyle jumped the brig *Amicus,* of and for Liverpool from Lisbon. Removing a small quantity of valuable woolens, Boyle sent the brig with her remaining cargo of wool and fruit into port. Down to only sixty men, Boyle brought the *Chasseur* with her hold jammed with prize goods and forty-eight prisoners into New York on 29 October 1814. In three months' cruising in English waters off Halifax and Bermuda, Boyle had taken eighteen prizes, sending in nine while parolling 150 prisoners. Focusing on the *Chasseur's* cruise and the productive U.S. sloop-of-war *Peacock,* a Baltimore editor offered the two cruises as "fresh proof" and "clear indications" that commerce raiding was the best way to defeat Britain. U.S. seamen, the editor boasted, were now "the admiration of Europe and the terror of England."

While Thomas Boyle returned to Baltimore to consult with the owners, *Chasseur*'s foremast and some of her yards were altered to allow her to convert to brig or brigantine rigging at will. Probably because he was planning to cruise in crowded West Indian waters where he would have less elbow room. Boyle replaced ten of his long twelve-pounders with the popular hard-hitting and quickly loaded carronades. Moving from the North River to an anchorage at Staten Island, the brig *Chasseur* broke for the open sea on 23 December 1814. Heavy seas knocked down her "Fore Top Gallant Mast" and cost her one man who was carried "overboard by the Wash of a Sea" and never seen again. After reaching Barbados on 5 January, Boyle exchanged shots with a large sloop-of-war, burned a schooner within sight of a British admiral's ship, and escaped a pursuing frigate or 74-gun ship-of-the-line "with ease." On 15 January the sometimes reckless Boyle showed his more prudent side when he refused to take a British ship only a half mile away but "within Neutral limits."

Thomas Boyle was just as resourceful as a situation demanded. With squalls pushing a heavier frigate close upon the fleeing *Chausseur,* the commander threw over ten guns and his spare yards and started releasing his water to lighten the brig. Finally, as the frigate kept coming, he moved two long twelve-pounders aft. Once he had the *Chausser*'s rails sawn away to give the guns more play, they drove off his tormentor. On 3 February Boyle beat all hands to quarters, cleared for action, and loaded his remaining guns with round and grape shot. In fifteen minutes the 335-ton *Coruna* struck [her colors] but was unable to follow Boyle's sailing instructions because the crew "was all run below from fear." Boyle replaced his lost guns with those of the *Coruna* and ordered her and her cargo of coal, coarse clothing, cheese, crockery, and hardware into the United States. While dogging a huge convoy of 110 vessels, Boyle's wait for the inevitable laggard paid off when the ship *Adventure*, out of London for Havana, fell behind. Boyle snapped her up, divested some cargo, and sent her into a U.S. port.

Some prizes came easily, but others did not want to come at all. Boyle lost six well-armed ships and two brigs near Puerto Rico after unsuccessfully attempting to separate them. Off Santo Domingo he turned a ketch taken with a volley of musketry while a Jamaica-bound ship struck as soon as the black *Chasseur* pulled alongside and hoisted her flag. It took Boyle two days to divest that vessel's rich cargo. On 15 February 1815 Boyle pursued an innocent-looking schooner showing only three gunports on one side. The *Chasseur's* commander "hastily made but small preparation for action, expecting no fighting." Much to his chagrin the schooner uncovered a tier of ten gunports and unloosed a broadside when the unsuspecting American was within pistol range. Responding with all his great and small guns, Boyle's closeness, forcing him to try a boarding operation, permitted him to see not only extra men concealed under his opponent's bulwark but "the blood run Freely from her Scuppers" from the *Chasseur's* desperate return fire. Boyle's order to board, "quick and cheerfully obeyed," induced the battered adversary, His British Majesty's schooner *St. Lawrence,* formerly the famous private-armed schooner *Atlas* of Philadelphia, to surrender. Carrying fourteen 12-pound carronades, a long nine-pounder, and seventy-five men plus some marines, the *St. Lawrence* lost at least six men killed and seventeen wounded. She was "a perfect wreck in her hull and had scarcely a Sail or Rope Standing" but the *Chasseur* was hurt in her sails and rigging also. Thomas Boyle, who had lost no men on his first cruise on the *Comet,* had to record five men killed and seven wounded, including four very serious cases. He converted the wrecked *St. Lawrence* into a "flag of Truce" for Havana, carrying the wounded from "motives of humanity" much appreciated by her former captain.

★ (Garitee, *Republic's Private Navy,* 159–61)

★

Lieutenant Gordon of the *St. Lawrence* gave his captor a letter that read, in part: "In the event of Captain Boyle's becoming a prisoner of war to any British cruiser I consider it a tribute justly due to his humane and generous treatment of myself, the surviving officers, and crew of His Majesty's late schooner *St. Lawrence,* to state that his obliging attention and watchful solicitude to preserve our effects and render us comfortable during the short time we were in his possession were such as justly entitle him to the indulgence and respect of every British subject."

★ (Paine, *Old Merchant Marine,* 121)

The Civil War

DURING THE DECADE BEFORE THE CIVIL War, the controversy over slavery and the growing sectional rivalry began to sap the former shared sense of national patriotism to which southern leadership had contributed so much. One fruit of the old consensus had been unanimity in legislative support for the U.S. merchant marine, including substantial subsidies for U.S. mail steamships. In 1858, southern congressional leadership scuttled these subsidies. The result—on the eve of the Civil War—was a slowdown in shipbuilding, the closing of shipyards, and, in Winthrop Marvin's phrase, "to drive the stars and stripes from the great highways of commerce several years before the stars and bars had been hoisted above the first Anglo-Confederate cruiser" (Marvin, *American Merchant Marine*, 320).

This blow had little immediate effect on the building of wooden ships, but it was virtually a preemptive strike against "the few marine engine and boiler works [and the young, ambitious shipyards] now experimenting with iron hulls" (Marvin, *American Merchant Marine*, 320).

When the South opened fire on Fort Sumter on 12 April 1861, the United States had approximately 2.5 million tons of shipping registered for foreign trade, most of which was scattered across the seven seas and nearly all of which was owned in the North. This immense and far-flung fleet, therefore was "the lawful prey of Confederate cruisers and privateers. Nearly all of them were sailing ships. All were unarmed and defenseless, for merchantmen no longer carried the six-pounders, nines, or twelves that had frowned from the ports of important trading craft in the first years of the nineteenth century" (Marvin, *American Merchant Marine*, 121).

The few ships owned by the South were immobilized within a week of Fort Sumter when the North declared a complete blockade of all southern seaports—long before there were enough Union warships to enforce it. Navy vessels on distant stations were hastily recalled, and Yankee industrial might was invoked to initiate a crash shipbuilding program.

There was no possibility that the Confederacy could match the North in shipbuilding or evade a Yankee blockade once it was in place. Southern strategy turned first to privateering, then to raiders, to cripple the northern war effort. For the North, the problem was to shut off southern imports at once.

The Role of the Merchant Marine

It is striking that the role of American merchant mariners in manning the ships and waging the sea war of both sides in the Civil War has been so little noted in the contemporary (*fin-de-siècle*, twentieth-century) surge of books, films, and television programming about the Civil War. For as Professor Marvin noted, writing nearly a century earlier,

> without its great merchant marine of 1861, the United States could never have drawn the relentless cordon of the blockade about the Southern coasts, which in the end smothered and starved the Confederacy. More than half of the ships, four-fifths of the officers, and five-sixths of the men who performed this vital work came directly from the merchant service. When the Civil War began, the United States Navy contained only thirty steam ships of war, with about twice as many obsolete sailing vessels. There were 1,450 officers and 7,600 seamen. Before the war ended, this force had been expanded to 600 steamers, 9,000 officers, and 51,000 seamen.
>
> The 7,500 volunteer officers who joined the navy between 1861 and 1865 were a superb body of men, intelligent, zealous, skillful, and brave. Most of them were captains, mates, or engineers of the

merchant marine. They were thorough masters of their calling, and with a few months of instruction in gunnery, signalling, and the navy routine in general, they became so efficient that on many of our vessels in 1863–64 they were performing all the duties of watch and division officers, and in not a few cases had risen to actual command. They were followed into the navy by forty thousand merchant sailors.

[The government could not idly await the slow process of construction; the blockade had to be effected immediately.] The arduous work of cruise and blockade required something more powerful than 90-day gunboats. So the Navy Department purchased scores of iron-and-wooden merchant steamers of the coastwise and West India service and converted them into excellent "merchant cruisers."

Until the end of the war it was these merchant ships that made up the bulk of our blockading squadrons. Some of them, notably the *Vanderbilt* . . . the *Santiago de Cuba,* the *Rhode Island,* and the *Connecticut,* proved to be among the most valuable ships of our entire fleet because of their excellent speed and "coal endurance." Until a fast special class of light steamers was built in 1863–64, the large converted merchantmen were almost the only vessels [in our navy] that could overtake the flying British blockade runners. Without their help an adequate blockade could never have been maintained by the regular navy sloops and frigates—fine ships of their type, but heavy, slow, and encumbered with worse-than-useless top-hamper.

The War Department as well as the Navy Department drew deeply upon the great resources of the merchant marine. The transports which conveyed General Burnside's expedition to the North Carolina [coast] and General Butler's to New Orleans were bought or chartered merchant vessels. This mobility by sea which enabled us to send great bodies of troops to any point along the beleaguered coast of the Confederacy, or to shift the base of army operations suddenly from Washington to Hampton Roads, would have been impossible had not the North possessed a large fleet of commercial ships and a hardy seafaring population.

(Marvin, *American Merchant Marine,* 338–40)

Charles Dana Gibson, the scholar and commentator on maritime law and warfare, amplifies the point in two ways. As to vessels, "the penetration of the South by the Union's Armies of the West depended almost entirely on the Mississippi River and its tributaries, [using watercraft nearly all of which were] chartered, hired, or temporarily commandeered. [Similarly] on east coast inland waters such as the Chesapeake Bay and Virginia river systems . . . Union Army fleets [were used] for specific campaigns (Gibson, *Merchantman? Or Ship of War,* 14–15)."

Most of these rivercraft were chartered. As to who manned them, "armed and armored steamers utilized on the Mississippi as army gunboats carried mixed civilian and military crews as a fairly regular thing. Crew composition seemed more a matter of availability. This appears to have been the first time in our history [when] civilians and military were intermingled in the manning of vessels of the army or navy" (Gibson, *Merchantman? Or Ship of War,* 15).

8 Effective Blockades,
★★ Devastating Raids

★

If the blockade was to be effective before new warships could be rushed to completion, armed steamers were needed to take up immediate patrol stations off the southern ports. South they went—everything from ocean liners to East River ferryboats, and they did their job well. Hundreds of other steamers, some almost too rotten to float, were used as transports and supply ships.

New York was not only able to furnish most of these, but its highly developed shipyards and marine-engine works on the East River made possible the wholesale construction of new warships that constantly reinforced the navy, until at the close [of the war] it numbered some seven hundred vessels. . . .

The effects of the Confederate raiders, however, proved more significant, as far as U.S. commerce was concerned, than the blockade and the transport service. They were few in number, but they dealt Yankee shipping such a deadly blow that it failed to recover until World War I, a half a century later. Just as in 1814, when the shipowners of Britain had howled to high heaven at the depredations of Yankee privateers upon their vessels, so now the New York Chamber of Commerce was issuing frantic complaints against the southern raiders that were dotting the seas with the flaming wrecks of local sailing vessels. To the eastward, lamentations rose in similar vein from one shipping port after another.

History was certainly repeating itself fifty years later; on both occasions the navies of those frantic shipping circles, the Royal Navy in 1814, and the northern navy in the 1860s, were strangling by rigid blockade all

---

Reprinted with the permission of W. W. Norton & Co. from the chapter "Reversed Roles" in *Sea Lanes in Wartime: The American Experience, 1775–1945,* Robert Greenhalgh Albion and Jennie Barnes Pope (1942, 150–73, passim).

the commerce of the enemy. Yet their own shipowners and merchants scarcely noticed that successful blockading in their horrified concentration upon the lesser activities of the enemy raiders. Those Confederate raiders fell into three groups—the privateers, the lesser cruisers, and, most devastating to Union commerce, the British-built *Alabama* and her consorts.

The first to appear—and to disappear—were "the last of the privateers." Privateering had been abolished [through an] international agreement by the European powers in 1856 at Paris, but the United States had not participated. Panic spread through northern shipping centers at Pres. Jefferson Davis's announcement in April 1861 that the Confederacy would grant "letters of marque and reprisal." Lincoln threatened five days later that any such vessels would be regarded as engaged in piracy. The crew of the captured privateer *Savannah* were actually put on trial for piracy at New York but were saved from the gallows by the Confederate ultimatum that a corresponding number of captured Union officers were being held as hostages and would suffer a similar fate.

A small and mongrel assortment of vessels operated out of southern harbors, chiefly New Orleans, Charleston, and the North Carolina inlets. They were augmented by some vesels from the North Carolina state navy. A few privateers made a tidy profit. They caught some forty Yankee victims, more than half of which were condemned by regular prize courts in southern ports. By the summer of 1861, the practice died of malnutrition because of the increasing difficulty of getting the prizes through the tightened blockade into ports—and the consequent dearth of prize money. Only a lone privateer, the *Retribution,* once a tug on the Great Lakes but now refitted as a schooner, was left by early 1863. In January she seized the schooner *Hanover* and in February the brig *Emily Fosdick* in the Bahamas—a final act in the history of privateering.

The rest of the southern raiders, although often denounced as privateers or even as pirates, were all formally commissioned warships of the navy of the Confederate states, and in many cases their commanders were officers of the "old navy." The *Sumter,* a former passenger steamship of the New Orleans–Havana run and the *Nashville* of the New York–Charleston line, were passenger steamers seized in southern ports. The *Georgia,* built to order in a British yard, was such a shoddy piece of work that she lasted for only three months of active service in 1863. In the latter part of 1864, two other British-built vessels were the blockade-runners *Tallahassee,* alias *Olustee,* and the *Chickamauga.*

The bulk of the effective raiding was the work of the "big three"—the *Alabama, Florida,* and *Shenandoah.* All were large, fast vessels, equipped with both steam and sail and built in England. Despite the protests of the vigilant northern minister at London, the British government did not stop them from slipping out to sea, where they received their armaments from other vessels from England.

The *Alabama,* justly the most celebrated, left the Mersey in July 1862 to be commissioned off the Azores four weeks later and was steadily "on the go" under Capt. Raphael Semmes until sunk by the *Kearsarge* off Cherbourg in June 1864. The *Florida* had an even longer nominal career—between March 1862 when she sailed from England, and October 1864 when she was rammed and captured by the *Wachusett* in the neutral harbor of Bahia. She spent, however, a good part of her time lying idle at Nassau, Mobile, and Brest; and her chief activity came between February and August 1863 when she was aided by a series of tenders as subraiders. The *Shenandoah* left England in September 1864 ostensibly on a merchant voyage. Early the next year she visited Australia and then went north to accomplish her chief damage in the Bering Sea.

Most of these raiders' victims were burned at sea. A few were allowed to proceed after giving a bond payable to the Confederacy six months after the war. The usual reason for such surprising clemency was the presence of more passengers than the raider cared to take aboard or of a neutral cargo. It was also a means by which the raider could rid herself of an accumulation of prisoners from destroyed ships. By the time the raiders were at sea, the blockade had become too tight to reach the ports with prizes, as the privateers had done earlier. . . . The bulk of the captured vessels was put to the torch—much in the same way as were the British victims of U.S. privateers in 1814. The procedure was pretty much a regular ritual. The doomed vessel was stripped of whatever the raider wanted in rigging and stores, and the officers and crew were taken off as prisoners. Combustibles were then set ablaze in cabin and forecastle or other enclosed places.

Altogether some two hundred northern vessels would be burned, scuttled, or sent in for condemnation between May 1861, when a privateer caught the lime-laden *Ocean Rover* from Rockland below New

Orleans, and July 1865, ten weeks after Appomattox, when the *Shenandoah* burned her last victims. The intervening years saw few weeks when at least one raider was not at work, but after the privateering interval, four were the most ever to be cruising at any one time. The peak of this destruction at sea coincided with the "high tide of the Confederacy" in the six months before Gettysburg.

The story of that raiding has been told many times by eyewitnesses and by recent authors, but always from the viewpoint of the raiders themselves. Their point of view often reminds one of the little boy who stood

The incendiary crew of the Confederate raider *Nashville* rows back after firing the Yankee clipper *Harvey Birch* in the English Channel, homebound from Le Havre. The *Birch* was the first Atlantic victim of the raiders. (Courtesy of the Mariners' Museum, Newport News, Va., PNC35)

with tears in his eyes before a picture of lions devouring Christian martyrs: "One poor little lion," he sobbed, "didn't get any martyr." Our concern here is for the hunted Yankee square-riggers.

The old U.S. merchant marine was at its peak, as far as size was concerned, at the outbreak of the war. The combined stimuli of the California gold rush, the flood of Irish and German immigration, the increased European demand for wheat and cotton, along with various other factors, had more than doubled it between 1846, when it stood at 2,562,000 tons, and 1861, when it reached 5,539,000. . . .

The raiding hit with particular force the pride of the merchant marine, the clipper ships, and other large seagoing sailing vessels. The bulk of the tonnage lost was in sixty-four full-rigged ships and sixty barks, which were like ships except for their labor-saving fore-and-aft rig on the third mast. Only one steamship was destroyed; these were less numerous and from their nature could escape more easily. The rest of the losses concerned much smaller vessels—thirty-odd brigs and forty-five or so schooners. . . .

The blows fell upon some sea lanes much more heavily than upon others, although none of the major fields of commerce escaped scot free. Altogether, the transatlantic run yielded some twenty-six victims totaling about 16,200 tons; the Far East and Africa, twenty-seven of 22,500 tons; the Cape Horn route to San Francisco, six of 5,000 tons; the Caribbean, thirty of 8,300 tons; the rest of Latin America, twenty-seven of 14,700 tons; the coastal trade, fifty of 15,500 tons; and the whalers, forty-three of 12,800 tons. The largest ships and most valuable cargoes were caught on the Far Eastern and West Coast runs, which, with the whalers, suffered the heaviest relative damage. . . .

The first distinguished victim on the Atlantic shuttle was the 1,462-ton clipper *Harvey Birch* of New York, the second largest of all the vessels destroyed. She was burned by the *Nashville* in November 1861 as she was returning in ballast after delivering grain to Havre.

[Eleven months later, in the fall of 1862, the North Atlantic became the theater for Raphael Semmes's depredations in CSS *Alabama*, which are discussed in some detail in chapter 9. But the Far East trade offered inviting targets to the raiders. The Pacific and South Atlantic sea lanes, the latter the route "around the Horn" to the Pacific for ships from the east coast, were less crowded and less dangerous than the North Atlantic. The South Atlantic, where it narrows somewhat between the bulges of Africa and Brazil, became a favorite hunting ground.]

Raiders Lurk "Between the Bulges"

[There, between the bulges, raiders] could lie in wait both for the clippers rounding the Horn to California and for the shipping bound to the farther ports of South America. This region, too, was sufficiently remote to avoid effective Union pursuit. The first half of 1863 found the "big three" all there at once, while the *Sumter* and the *Shenandoah* likewise haunted these waters in their turn.

Early in her career the *Florida* there burned three rich Far Eastern victims, averaging almost half a million dollars apiece in value. In February 1863 she caught Abiel Low's 1,362-ton clipper ship *Jacob Bell* homeward bound with teas. The next month, it was the 941-ton *Star of Peace* on her way from Calcutta to Boston with a general cargo, including saltpeter for the Du Pont powder works. The third capture in April was the 420-ton *Oneida,* a little old ship bound from Shanghai to New York but with a cargo of great value.

At the same time the *Florida* was busily making hauls in the trade between New York and San Francisco. This trade was not quite what it had been at the height of the gold rush a dozen years before, but until the transcontinental rail connection was opened in 1869, most of the general cargo for the West Coast was still going by square-riggers around the Horn. Foreign vessels were barred from this "coastal" trade, and with ships and cargoes just about as valuable as those from the Far East, the *Florida* found plenty of loot. Unlike the China trade, where vessel and cargo had the same owner, these were common carriers representing the new trend toward divorce between shipowning and cargo. The *Commonwealth,* for example (one of these victims and a common carrier), had a mixed cargo for San Francisco valued at $470,000 and belonging to 217 merchants—quite a difference from the Lows' sole ownership of the clipper *Contest* and her cargo. The *Crown Point,* also destroyed by the *Florida* on this run, and the *Tycoon,* caught by the *Alabama* in that same 1863 season, had similar ladings almost as valuable.

Vessels trading with South America found it dangerous going "down between the bulges" in that spring of 1863. Four vessels, carrying guano (bird dung) from the Pacific, made the least fragrant of the Confederate bonfires. But the raiders had compensation, as far as smell was concerned, when they set fire to some of the cargoes of Rio coffee. Even in the early months when the *Sumter* was abroad consuls in Brazilian ports found cargoes were scarce for vulnerable U.S. ships there. Wool shipments from Buenos Aires went up in smoke, too; one of the last of the South Atlantic losses, burned by the *Shenandoah* at the beginning of her career late in 1864, was bound from England to the Argentine.

Attacks along the Atlantic Coast

[The first attacks along the Atlantic coast came from Carolina privateers but the chief onslaught occurred in 1863 when] a succession of sailing vessels under some of the *Florida's* men on detached service swept up the coast from Hatteras to Portland.

They left a trail of burning hulks. Lt. Charles W. Reed, with twenty men and one gun in the brig *Clarence,* captured off Brazil, set out to raid the Union base at Hampton Roads. He caught some vessels off Hatteras, including the bark *Mary Alvina* bound from Boston to New Orleans with "3200 bbl. pork, beans &c" for the Union army, but he found Union vigilance too keen for his original project. Transferring his flag to the bark *Tacony,* he proceeded up the coast, destroying shipping along the way. None of his prizes was particularly valuable, but the impact on northern nerves was tremendous.

Panic spread when the newspapers told of what was happening to the incoming transatlantic ships . . . [through the] encounters of the "Pirates off Nantuckett." Headlines . . . told of "The Oceans Lit Up by the Rebel Sea Devils" . . . . Meanwhile the *Florida* herself had been heading northward, capturing several valuable vessels on the way. Within fifty miles of New York, she had a successful brush with an improvised northern cruiser but finding too many more in the vicinity, hurried south to Bermuda. By the time the good news of Gettysburg and Vicksburg had come, the North found that the worst of its maritime menace had also subsided.

There were some further coastal scares, with the *Florida* back again for some of them; but the closest to the *Tacony's* exploits were the hit-and-run raids out of Wilmington by the fast British-built blockade runners, the *Tallahassee,* alias *Olustee,* and the *Chickamauga.* In the summer of 1864, the *New York Herald* headlined "Operations at the Entrance to our Harbor," along with news of Farragut at Mobile Bay and of Sherman at Atlanta. The *Tallahassee* scuttled a coasting schooner off the Jersey coast rather than spread the alarm to the shore by the flames from her burning hulk. Then she suddenly appeared off Fire Island, near the very entrance of the unsuspecting port of New York. The plan was to dash into the East River through Hell Gate and to set fire to the shipping at the crowded wharves. An unobservant pilot, on the lookout for business, came aboard before spying the Confederate flag and "a more astonished man never stood on deck of vessel. He turned deadly pale and drops of perspiration broke from every pore." Seizing the pilot boat *James Funk* as a decoy, the raiders caught "no less than six vessels in as many hours," including another Sandy Hook pilot boat. Ironically, the harbor raid had to be abandoned because a Hell Gate pilot was not to be found. Turning eastward, the *Tallahassee* continued her destructive course from Nantucket up the Maine coast to the Bay of Fundy. She caught some transatlantic shipping and also burned many coasters laden with lumber or Cape Breton coal. Despite the naval vessels swarming on her trail, she found her way from Halifax safely back through the blockade to Wilmington.

Two months later, rechristened the *Olustee,* she was through the blockade again. Off the Delaware Capes she destroyed six vessels, including an army transport brig, luckily not full of troops, bound from Fortress Monroe to New York. The transport's captain and crew, because of her military status, were deposited in a southern prison. Hotly pursued by a northern cruiser and with coal nearly gone, the *Olustee* had to rush back to port but again made good her escape. Meanwhile the *Chickamauga* was also out of Wilmington, raiding within fifty miles of Sandy Hook and off Block Island. She destroyed several coasters and vessels in the Cuban trade; but by late autumn all was finally quiet along the seaboard.

The coastal raiders had had to hit and run in fear of the warning spread along shore by the telegraph to Union bases; but the other cruisers did a thorough and devastating job against the whalers without interference.

Of all U.S. shipping, the whalers—scattered through remote seas—caught it hardest, losing almost a tenth of their fleet. For generations, New Bedford and Nantucket had done a thriving business with whale oil—in heavy demand for illumination in America and Europe—brought in by little secondhand vessels from their adventurous prowlings. The Civil War years brought ruin to this flourishing trade. . . . The real nemesis of the whalers was the *Shenandoah,* which took over the *Florida's* orders to cruise primarily against whalers in the Pacific when the latter was seized at Bahia.

Leaving Melbourne, Australia, early in 1865, the *Shenandoah* swooped down on four whalers in port at Ascension Island, now Ponape, in the Carolines. Leaving there in April just as Lee was surrendering at Appomattox, Capt. James Dredell Waddell, her skipper, cruised over toward Japan and picked a solitary victim. Late in July, he came upon a big concentration of whalers in the Bering Sea. After burning one, he accosted a trading schooner fresh from San Francisco and saw a newspaper dated 15 April with a telegraphic report of Appomattox but with plenty of implications that the Confederates might not be through fighting. Giving himself the benefit of any doubts about the war's being over, he proceeded to his work of wholesale destruction. Eleven vessels were burned in less than a week, with two spared to carry the crews home. Two days later, eight more were put to the torch by a vessel that had never been within two thousand miles of the country whose flag she flew. An officer of the *Shenandoah* wrote of that last grim and distant act of Confederate raiding:

> The red glare from the eight burning vessels shone far and wide over the drifting ice of those savage seas; the crackling of the fire as it made its devouring way through each doomed ship fell on the still air like upbraiding voices. The sea was filled with boats driving hither and thither with no hand to guide them, and with yards, sails and cordage, remnants of the stupendous ruin there progressing.

[The panic spread by the raiders in northern shipping circles raised insurance rates much higher than actual losses warranted; they ran as high as 2 percent of the value of the cargo in the Far Eastern trade but overall averaged less than 0.5 percent. But in the summer of 1863 the rates rose as high as fifteen times their prewar levels.]

Such were the circumstances that produced the "flight from the flag." Increasingly common after mid-1863 were such notices as the following in the marine news columns:

Ship *Saratoga* of New Bedford, 542 tons, has been sold on British account, to hail from St. John, N.B.

Bark *Hudson,* late of New Bedford, has had her name changed to *Hae Hawaii,* and now hails from Honolulu, for which port she will sail in about 10 days.

Schooner *Chief of Barnstable* has been sold to Spanish parties for $6,500.

Ship *Henry Clark,* A1½, 512 tons, built at Kennebunk in 1857, has been sold at about $20,000 to go under the British flag.

Ship *Martin Luther,* A1½, 984 tons, built at Searsport in 1855, has been sold at Genoa on private terms to go under the Italian flag.

Even some of the newly built shipping was sold directly to go under foreign flags, as for instance this item from Portland:

Bark *Artemesia* (new) recently built by B. W. Pickett of Cape Elizabeth, 447 tons, sold the past week to Claudio Lanicrold of Valparaiso for $43,000.

For every vessel the raiders destroyed, the Yankee merchant marine lost eight others as an indirect result. A moderate amount of tonnage was being transferred to foreign registry before the war. In the first war year, it had amounted to 117,000 tons. By the second year, ending in June 1863, it had grown to 220,000 tons. Then it suddenly jumped—in the panic of the "great terror" and its attendant high war-risk rates—to 300,000 tons for the third year but dropped back to 133,000 tons for the fourth year. This meant the loss to the U.S. merchant fleet of 1,613 vessels, about 774,000 tons.

The blow fell hardest on the big sailing vessels, the full-rigged ships and barks that had been the pride of the old merchant marine and the mainstay of the foreign trade. During the course of the four war years, 990 ships and barks were "sold foreign"; 213 were "lost at sea," about half of them being destroyed by the raiders; and 55 condemned as unseaworthy. Meanwhile, only 378 new ones were built, leaving a net loss of 880 of the big square-riggers.

A picture of the sinking *Alabama,* which sold well in the North, carried the inscription, "Built of English oak, in an English yard, armed with English guns, manned by an English crew, and sunk in the English Channel." That hinted at the bitterness that the northerners felt at England's shamelessly unneutral attitude in connection with the raiders. . . .

Finally in 1871, England agreed in the Treaty of Washington to submit the question of damages for unneutral conduct to an international arbitration commission. This group met at Geneva in 1872 to analyze the *Alabama* claims.

Probably the total direct damage to northern shipping and cargoes amounted to somewhere between twenty and twenty-five million dollars, about one-fifth of which represented the vessels themselves. The victims totaled nearly 100,000 tons; of that, the *Alabama* alone got about one-third; the *Florida,* with her tenders, and the *Shenandoah* accounted for another third; while the remaining third was shared about equally between the lesser cruisers and the privateers. The Americans claimed plenty. Not only did they want damages for losses actually caused by those raiders but also the amounts paid in war-risk insurance in general, and even the U.S. Navy's expenses of $3,375,000 for fitting out vessels to chase the raiders.

The commissioners whittled this down to the damages inflicted by the *Alabama,* the *Florida* and her tenders, and the *Shenandoah* after leaving Australia. The final award came to $15,500,000, including interest. It was a good bargain for England at that—to have reduced so effectively the competition of the U.S. merchant marine, not only during the war but for a half century thereafter.

★

9 Building the Ships

★★

The first raider the Confederates acquired was a small packet steamer, *Habana*. She was hurriedly converted and armed and renamed *Sumter*. The burning wrecks she left in the North Atlantic under the command of Raphael Semmes, of whom much more is to come, gave two clear messages, an ominous one for northern shippers and an encouraging one indeed for the Confederacy.

But the *Sumter* was a mere improvisation and a hasty one at that. Lacking shipyards that could craft the perfect raider, the South found a ready, covert, and duplicitous ally in England and a brilliant agent to serve as the Confederacy's naval commissioner in London—Capt. James D. Bulloch.

Captain Bulloch—uncle of a three-year-old Yankee named Theodore Roosevelt—was effectively the head procurement officer of the Confederate Navy.

★

[He was, as Winthrop Marvin observes, entrusted with large] funds and extraordinary power to expend them for the best interests of the Confederate cause. He recognized very early that sail craft and converted merchant steamers were not fit instruments to chase and seize the peerless Yankee clipper ships. He secretly procured the building in British yards of two vessels modeled after the latest type of British steam sloops-of-war. Indeed, both the *Florida*, when she ran the blockade of Mobile, and the *Alabama*, in her fight with the *Hatteras*, passed themselves off as cruisers of Her Majesty's navy. They were, of course, inferior in all points save speed to our larger men-of-war, but they were very formidable vessels for the peculiar service for which they were designed. They were the first steam commerce-destroyers. The *Alabama* and *Florida* were graceful, fine-lined corvettes, bark-rigged with a full spread of canvas. They were capable of cruising under sail alone and could, therefore, keep the sea for long periods without recoaling. Their steam machinery was supposed to be sufficient to enable them to overtake the fastest of [the U.S.] clipper merchantmen and to escape from our heavy warships.

It was an obvious breach of neutrality to build these ships in Britain for use against a friendly power, and Captain Bulloch cleverly managed to encourage the fiction that they were intended for the service of some continental power at peace with all the world. In all this the Confederate agent was met more than halfway by the British government. The first of the Anglo-Confederate cruisers was the *Florida,* built at Liverpool on British man-of-war designs. It was pretended that she was the property of Italy, but though the Italian Consul at Liverpool officially denied this, and the U.S. Minister, Charles Francis Adams, protested that she was really a Confederate vessel and gave formal evidence to support his charge, the *Florida* was not interfered with. She was allowed to sail from Liverpool in March 1862 for the British colony of Bahama, where she received her battery of British naval guns and filled her magazines with British ammunition.

Under cover of the British flag, the *Florida* ran into Mobile outwitting the Union cruisers, which took her for a British corvette inspecting the blockade. At Mobile the *Florida* completed her outfit and shipped a crew, and then, escaping to sea on a dark and stormy night, she began in January 1863 her destructive work on the North Atlantic. At Nassau in the Bahamas the British authorities, in defiance of the obligations of neutrality, allowed the *Florida* to take aboard a three months' supply of coal. Thus provided, the *Florida* hovered like a hawk on the trade routes between Boston, New York, and Brazil, seizing fourteen prizes [and wreaking the havoc noted in chapter 8].

✫ (Marvin, *American Merchant Marine,* 322–23)

The exploits of the *Florida* were dwarfed by those of her sister ship, *Alabama,* which came off the ways at Birkenhead in July of 1862. As she slid into the Mersey she bore not a name but a number, hull 290. The motto on the wheel at her quarterdeck was apt: *Aide-toi et Dieu t'aidera* (Help yourself and God will help you). Command of this perfect commerce-raider was given to Raphael Semmes, a dashing former Union

Navy officer and Confederate patriot, who had terrorized Yankee shippers in the Confederate Navy's first raider, the *Sumter.*

On the morning of 29 July, Captain Bulloch put on board the not-quite-completed 290 a "gay party of ladies and gentlemen" who sailed down the Mersey on a trial trip. Customs "officials went along also to see that no international wrong was done. It was a complimentary jaunt enjoyed by all with a seasonable luncheon in the cabin about noon, but later a tug came alongside and the surprised party were all requested to pass over the side into her. The feast was cleared away, the bunting taken down, and there was lively bustling to get the '290' in shape for her maiden voyage on the high seas, as she was ordained never to see Liverpool again. In the darkness of the early morning of the last day of July, she turned her prow out of the bay on the coast of Wales where she had been at anchor and plowed northward through the Irish Sea, then around the north of Ireland and vanished in the broad ocean" (Meriwether, *Raphael Semmes,* 168).

Under a temporary crew the 290 made her way to the Azores, where Raphael Semmes had been sent separately to join her. Another ship loaded with munitions and supplies also met her there. When he first glimpsed the cruiser, Semmes's reaction was enthusiastic. She was indeed a beautiful thing to look upon.

☆

A Perfect Steamer

She was about 900 tons burden, 230 feet in length, 32 feet in breadth, 20 feet in depth, and drew, when provisioned and coaled for a cruise, 15 feet of water. Her model was of the most perfect symmetry, and she sat upon the water with the lightness and grace of a swan. She was bar-kentine rigged, with long lower masts, which enabled her to carry large fore-and-aft sails, as jibs and try sails, which are of so much importance to a steamer in so many emergencies. Her sticks were of the best yellow pine that would bend in a gale like a willow wand without breaking, and her rigging was of the best Swedish iron wire. The scantling of the vessel was light, compared with vessels of her class in the federal navy, but this was scarcely a disadvantage as she was designed as a scourge of the enemy's commerce rather than for battle. She was to defend herself simply, if defense should become necessary. Her engine was of 300 horse power and she had attached an apparatus for condensing from the vapor of sea water all the fresh water that her crew might require. She was a perfect steamer and a perfect sailing object.

☆   (Porter, *Naval History,* 628)

The crew of the 290 was recruited on the island of Terceira from crews of other vessels then in port, who had been gathered to hear Semmes offer them a berth. They were a wild mix of nationalities and backgrounds.

☆

[There] was an anxious moment after Semmes had made his address inviting seamen from the crews to enlist. He had enticingly stated the case to them, briefly describing the cause of the South as a struggle for liberty, painting the delights of strange skies and foreign ports with "liberty on shore" and mentioning the prospects for combat with the foe. Especially careful had he been to emphasize the financial side—the unusually good rate of pay he offered them and the chances for big prize money if all turned out successfully. He must have been eloquent if results were the test, as he got nearly all the available fellows, or eighty out of the total of ninety. It was a happy ending for the first and only "stump speech" ever made to the crew of the *Alabama.* Semmes, Bulloch, and the British captain were all kept busy till late that night arranging matters for the newly enlisted men so they could make remittances home. Semmes was gratified that so many were married, as he felt that for this reason he could rely on them all the more.

☆   (Meriwether, *Raphael Semmes,* 176–77)

With a few important exceptions, all the officers were new to Semmes. His seasoned and trusted aide, John McIntosh Kell, held the critical post of executive officer, and the surgeon and chief engineer had served with Semmes in the *Sumter.* The assistant surgeon was an Englishman, and Captain Bulloch's brother was another officer. The first paymaster was a renegade Yankee sympathizer who tried to raise a mutiny but was discovered and discharged.

Late in August, all was ready, and the 290 sailed off into the Atlantic. There, at sea in the broad ocean, she was commissioned at last.

☆

[Semmes acknowledged that he] was impressed with the spectacle.

While the reading was going on, two small balls might have been seen ascending slowly, one to the peak, and the other to the main-royal mast-head. These balls were so arranged that, by a sudden jerk of the halliards by which they had been sent aloft, the flag and pennant would unfold themselves to the breeze. A curious observer would also have seen a quartermaster standing by the English colors, which we were still bear-ing, ready to strike them, a band of music on the quarterdeck, and a gunner (lockstring in hand) standing by the weather-bow gun. All these men had their eyes upon the reader; and when he had concluded, at a wave of his hand, the gun was fired, the change of flags took place, and the air was rent by a deafening cheer from officers and men: the band at the same time playing "Dixie," that soul-stirring national anthem of the new-born government. Thus amid this peaceful scene of beauty, with all nature smiling upon the ceremony, was the *Alabama* christened; the name 290 disappearing with the English flag.

In this way on Sunday, 24 August 1862, was born the *Alabama;* on another Sunday a little over a score of months later she died.

☆   (Meriwether, *Raphael Semmes,* 175)

10　Semmes and the *Alabama*
★★

For a few days after the commissioning, Semmes concentrated on drilling his crew. They were all merchant seamen, though to the captain's pleasure several of them had seen service on men-of-war. He welded them into a tough and loyal ship's company, and they were ready for action when, on 5 September and hardly a hundred miles from the position of her commissioning, the *Alabama* ventured into the whaling grounds off the Azores and happened on her first prize.

The ship was the whaler *Ocmulgee,* and she had a huge whale alongside that the entire crew was busy stripping of blubber and trying it out into whale oil. Semmes sailed up to the whaler, struck his British flag, and ran up his Confederate colors to the astonished dismay of the whaler's skipper. Until nine o'clock that evening the *Alabama*'s crew removed beef, pork, and such other supplies as desired from the *Ocmulgee* but put off burning the ship until daylight to avoid alarming other Yankee whalers in the vicinity.

The next morning the whaler's crew was taken aboard the raider, with their own small boats and whatever they wanted from their own stores, and the Confederate crew prepared the *Ocmulgee,* oil soaked from years of whaling, for the torch. Bunks were chopped up for kindling and heaped together with mattress straw and lard from the galley, one pile in the forecastle and one in the cabin. Then men of the wrecking crew climbed into their boats alongside; firesetters ignited the bonfire on command and raced to the boats and then returned to the raider.

In the *Ocmulgee*'s case, $50,000 worth of ship and refined whale oil were subtracted from the Yankee economy, converted to oily smoke

---

The excerpts that follow are reprinted with the permission of the University of Alabama Press from Charles Grayson Summersell, *CSS Alabama: Builder, Captain, and Plans* (1985, 37–44).

and wreckage. With the burning party back aboard the raider, Captain Semmes sailed in close to the island of Flores, where the *Ocmulgee's* crew put off in their own boats with enough provisions (from their own ship) to see them safely to shore.

☆

Not until after the first prize was taken and *Alabama* was again on her course was the first muster held aboard the cruiser. This procedure speedily became the usual Sunday routine. Muster included general inspection and cleanup of men and ship, close-order drill, and practice of emergency bills. It was an occasion for reading the Articles of War and for changing the civilians in the crew into disciplined man-of-war's men. Both crew and officers knew that punishment for misconduct could be swift and sure. For a sailor's offense, a confinement in irons was immediate, and if more grave, a court martial was convened on his case before the day was over. Miscellaneous seamen soon began to shape up under coercive discipline. Perhaps even more important in the shaping-up process was the inducement of money. Rate by rate, *Alabama's* crew were paid twice as much as their counterparts in the Royal Navy. More than this, each man looked forward to his pro rata share of the value of all prizes burned. This money, they had been promised, would be appropriated at the end of the Civil War by the Congress of the Confederate States. The prize money was never actually awarded, but the crew of *Alabama* carefully noted with bright hope the value of each ship and cargo destroyed. Prize money was the chief topic in wardroom and in forecastle.

Only two days after the whaler was burned, the schooner *Starlight* was overtaken, boarded, and made prize. She was crowded with passengers, including women and children, and was bound to Boston via Flores. The well-armed Confederate boarding party sent Capt. Samuel H. Doane and his men to the raider. Second Lieutenant Armstrong was made prize master in charge of *Starlight*, with orders to reassure the women passengers. Semmes had just heard of the shameful treatment of *Sumter's* former paymaster, Henry Myers, who upon being captured by Union officials in Tangier had his head shaved and was put in irons. In retaliation Semmes put Doane and his crew of seven in irons. When Doane complained, Semmes agreed that it was an indignity but explained the treatment of Myers. He could have added that unmanacled prisoners were dangerous for the raider, particularly those who, like Captain Doane, were able to navigate. Confinement in irons continued for the following seven or eight captures. For this action Semmes was understandably criticized by the northern press. Next morning the prisoners were paroled and, with the passengers, were landed at nearby Santacruz. *Alabama* then put to sea. . . .

On 8 September *Alabama* captured another whaler, *Ocean Rover,* the third prize in three days. She was a bark well soaked with sperm oil collected during three years out, having on board 1,100 barrels. The prisoners were moved to the raider and *Ocean Rover* was put under a prize crew until morning. The whaling master, Capt. James M. Clark, asked to take his boats and crew to the nearby land, about five miles distant. Although it was a long haul, Semmes agreed. The six whaleboats were packed full of provisions and gear and departed on a smooth sea—a rich haul for the ship's company.

While the Confederate was lying off the island with the two prize vessels nearby, a large ship approached. *Alabama* quietly followed and began a chase that lasted four hours. When the range was closed sufficiently, a 32-pounder showered water on the deck of the whaler, and she hove to. She was the bark *Alert,* the fourth prize and third whaler taken in four days. She was just a short while out of New London and well provided with stores, winter clothing, and some tobacco, which the Confederate crew particularly enjoyed. This vessel was the one in which Richard Henry Dana Jr., who wrote *Two Years before the Mast,* had served as a seaman during a voyage from San Diego to Boston in 1836. The officers and crew of *Alert* were paroled and allowed to go in their own boats to the nearby land. The three captured whaling ships were then fired. With the excitement of so many captures in rapid succession, *Alabama*'s crew had very little sleep. *Alert* was valued at $20,000. No sooner had the prize crews returned to the raider and the boats run up than a vessel was sighted coming in toward land. She was chased, boarded, and discovered to be the whaling schooner *Weathergauge,* valued by the Confederates at only $10,000. Next day the crew of *Weathergauge* were landed in their own boats, and the vessel was burned.

The raider was still running in the track of the whaling vessels. During the next twelve days *Alabama* made prize of and burned the following whalers: brig *Altamaha* ($3,000); ship *Benjamin Tucker* ($18,000);

schooner *Courser* ($7,000); bark *Virginia* ($25,000); and bark *Elisha Dunbar* ($25,000). In less than two weeks *Alabama* had captured ten ships and burned every one. The crews of the first three whalers, *Altamaha*, *Benjamin Tucker*, and *Courser*, numbering seventy, were allowed to take their whaleboats filled with provisions and personal gear. There were eight boats in all, and *Alabama* towed them to the island. Because the weather turned foul, the crews of the later captures, *Virginia* and *Elisha Dunbar*, were kept on board the raider.

Prisoners' Complaints

Captain Tilton, master of *Virginia*, later complained bitterly of his treatment while a prisoner in CSS *Alabama*, saying that he and his crew were put in irons in the lee waist of the cruiser with an old sail over them for protection and a few planks to lie upon. Because the guns were kept run out, the sea came in the side ports and by morning the prisoners were wet with sea water. Tilton said that only one iron was loosened at a time and the food was beef, pork, beans, rice, bread, tea, and coffee. Semmes said this was more or less correct. Captain Gifford, of *Elisha Dunbar*, told of his experiences also but did not mention the food or water.

Semmes resolved to leave the whaling grounds and try his luck along the coast of the United States, where the grain fleet, carrying the harvest from rich grain fields of the American West, might make him a successful reaper. The crew needed relaxation and a rest from the sleepless nights and hard days chasing and firing prizes, enduring wet jackets in bad weather, and facing appalling dangers in boarding during a squall.

The boarding party was strictly forbidden to appropriate articles of merchandise from the prizes that were not specifically called for by the paymaster. Time was required to establish discipline in such matters. Nevertheless, sometimes a sailor would manage to steal liquor and dress up in some of the outlandish garb found on the vessels—beaver hats, long-tailed coats, or women's finery. Returning on board in such a ludicrous state would evoke great merriment from the ship's company, even when the drunk was hustled straight to the brig. Semmes was much interested in keeping his crew healthy during the changes from cold climate to hot, fair weather to foul. He had two doctors on board, Galt and Llewellyn, and strict orders were enforced about cleanliness in daytime wear and blue flannels at night. Semmes felt satisfaction in pointing out that of the men of his own crew and the approximately two thousand prisoners taken by *Sumter* and *Alabama* not a man was lost by disease.

All was not work, and much camaraderie and merriment were afforded when the crew gathered on the forecastle after duty hours and the evening meal. Sinclair described the meal as beginning with the strong issue–grog that cheered the sailor after his working day. With legs doubled up under him, Jack would sit on the deck, a piece of canvas for a cloth and tin dishes. He cut the salt pork or beef with a sheathknife, washing down the meat, hardtack, and beans with coffee. All this was hurriedly wolfed down because he eagerly looked forward to his main object, a pipe of tobacco.

Finally all were ready for the evening's entertainment. The fiddle, tambourine, and other musical instruments were kept on board to be used for song and dance. Some of the men tied handkerchiefs about the waist to represent women, imitating the sighs and giggles and flirting eyes of the fair sex. This never failed to bring roars of laughter. There was singing of tunes loved by all, and yarns and stories [told] that captured the attention of the most hardened. At the end, "Dixie" was sung with a will, even by the denizens of the streets of Liverpool.

In fact, one of the ways so many seamen were recruited from among the prisoners on board was this evening entertainment, plus the high pay and the twice-daily ration of grog. Semmes himself would enjoy the evening's song and dance. He would sit on the bridge, located just forward of the funnel, where he could hear the entertainment on the deck below. The men knew this and were keenly delighted by his real though remote presence.

By the beginning of October the cruiser had reached the Banks of Newfoundland and was sailing in the stormy area of the Gulf Stream, where shipping abounded because of the swift current that aids ships in their passage to Europe. On 3 October two large vessels that looked [to be] American came into view. *Alabama* waited until they were close enough for a gun to bring them to, when the quarter boats were sent out to make the prizes. The first was the 1,119-ton ship *Emily Farnum* from New York to Liverpool, under Capt. N. P. Simes. She proved to be the first cartel, the first released under ransom bond, and the first that had flour and grain cargo documented as neutral. *Emily Farnum* was released with the obligation of taking with her all of *Alabama*'s fifty or sixty prisoners in addition to those from the next prize.

The other prize was the 839-ton ship *Brilliant* with grain from New York to England. Ship and cargo together were valued at $164,000, the most valuable prize so far. Her captain, George Hagar, later gave the first published account of the capture of a ship by *Alabama* and of the Semmes technique in taking the prize. Hagar complained that his own crew were pressed into service in moving from *Brilliant* the supplies wanted by the Confederates. He wrote a protest to the *New York Journal of Commerce* giving the names of the officers and a description of the "Confederate Steamer Propeller Alabama." Captain Hagar's denunciation of the deed and his description of the raider were widely circulated in the hope it would lead to her capture. New York insurance companies joined in the clamor against the Rebel raider. Mariners of 1862 in a clearly identifiable foreign bottom could pass CSS *Alabama*, and that Confederate cruiser, with no smokestack and no sign of steam propulsion, might look like a peaceful and well-laden sailing vessel, probably of British registry. The next time the same mariners saw *Alabama*, she might have the appearance of a different rig, even two smokestacks achieved by a black wind sail.

If the neutral were boarded by *Alabama*, he might think that the boarding party were all British, because perhaps they were. No wonder the Yankee press gave contradictory accounts of that Confederate sea warrior and very unreasonably frequently called the cruiser a privateer, or even a British pirate. *Brilliant* was the first of *Alabama*'s prizes to be protested to the British government. The raider's attacks on the grain fleet off New York marked the beginning of the decline of the U.S. merchant marine, as shipping retreated from U.S. bottoms to foreign. Regardless of the sentiment in New England, three Englishmen from the Yankee's crew enlisted for service in *Alabama*. As day was ending, *Brilliant* was set afire, and she burned through the night. Two Russian ships, attracted by the flames, came up to learn whether rescue was needed. . . .

The second grain ship to meet the torch at the hands of the Confederate boarding party was the 409-ton bark *Wave Crest*, valued at $44,000. Before she was burned *Wave Crest* furnished supplies and was used for target practice by Confederate guns.

While the grain ships moved in the Gulf Stream clockwise across the Atlantic, *Alabama* moved counterclockwise toward the west and south.

In October and November the weather turned foul, making the work of the boarding parties more dangerous. Identification of prizes became difficult as the number of sails increased. In the rough weather the boarding party had to fight through wind, wave, and fog to reach and identify suspected targets. The ability of some mariners, particularly Master's Mate James Evans, to make correct guesses as to the nationality of vessels often prevented unnecessary boarding. There was no doubting the lines of the next vessel, however, and *Alabama* stretched off in pursuit of her. Semmes wrote a detailed account of the chase of this graceful hermaphrodite brig. The pursuit lasted well into the night. She proved to be the 293-ton *Dunkirk*, loaded with grain and valued by the Confederates at $25,000. Her crew was moved to the raider, and the prize was burned. One of the prisoners from *Dunkirk* was a deserter from CSS *Sumter*, George Forrest.

On 11 October "Sail ho!" introduced *Tonawanda*, a large 1,300-ton packet ship from Philadelphia carrying grain and passengers, including women and children. Because of the value of the ship ($80,000), Semmes was reluctant to release her, but there was no alternative because of the passengers. The decision was made to put a prize crew aboard her and let her stand by for a couple of days. Soon another, more valuable, prize was taken. She was the 1,062-ton grain ship *Manchester* from New York bound for Liverpool under command of Capt. John Landerskin. Ship and cargo, valued at $164,000, were burned. The crews of *Manchester*, *Wave Crest*, and *Dunkirk* were all placed aboard *Tonawanda*, which, under ransom bond, was pledged to carry them to safety. A young slave named David White was traveling with his master on *Tonawanda*, and Semmes took him aboard *Alabama* as a mess steward. He was in effect emancipated by the raider because he was enemy property. David became attached to Dr. Galt and never tried to escape. An ordinary seaman from *Tonawanda* enlisted for duty on the raider. . . .

"What Happened to the Morning Paper?"

Manchester was an example of a ship that brought a fresh supply of newspapers. Semmes was an avid reader of the northern press, amassing valuable military intelligence from the frank and outspoken journalists, especially the location of Union vessels pursuing the raider. Semmes wrote, "Perhaps this was the only war in which the newspapers ever explained, beforehand, all the movements of armies, and fleets, to the enemy." It was a standing joke in *Alabama*'s wardroom for officers to ask, "What happened to the morning paper?" Another source of current intelligence was mail from captured ships, which the Confederates carefully read. Newspapers from the grain ship informed the Confederates that the New York press was increasingly aware that CSS *Alabama* was destroying Union vessels. Ship owners of the North demanded protection against the Rebel pirates.

While the October weather worsened, with the wind blowing half a gale, *Alabama* found her next prize, the bark *Lamplighter*. It was unnecessary for the raider to chase this prize because *Lamplighter* came barreling down upon the unrecognized Confederate. It was just as well that she arrived early in the day because the storm became so intense that it would have been impossible to board her at a later hour. The 365-ton ship was burned, but not before the boarding party helped themselves generously to the welcome tobacco in her cargo.

Yankee Flag Collection

After the fierce storm subsided, all hands turned to and made repairs. It was generally claimed that *Alabama* had on board two of everything, and this enabled her to refit after the storm. The signal-quartermaster took out the collection of Yankee flags from his locker to air them. The number of captured flags had grown to seventeen in only six weeks.

The last days of October 1862 were stormy off the coast. Nine ships were boarded, but all proved to be neutral. The cruiser war was reducing the number of Yankee merchantmen, even though *Alabama* and *Florida* were the only Rebel raiders working at this time. On 21 October, however, a large ship that looked like a Yankee came in from the northwest and was soon under the guns of the Confederates. She was the 945-ton ship *Lafayette*, the first of two prizes of that name, and she was valued at $100,337. Her grain cargo had certificates claiming neutrality. Because the depredations of *Alabama* were now well known to the New York merchants, claims of neutrality were beginning to appear. Semmes pored over his law books, and the admiralty court on board *Alabama* condemned the cargo. After removal of the prisoners and some supplies, the Confederates burned the vessel late at night. Three days later, having boarded a number of neutrals, *Alabama* captured the 279-ton schooner *Crenshaw*, yet another grain vessel, though smaller than some. The prisoners having been removed, ship and cargo, valued at only $33,800, were burned.

While the irate Federals stormed and declared that gunboats would be sent to the Newfoundland Banks, *Alabama* turned toward New York. Off the New England coast in rough weather she captured the 284-ton bark *Lauretta*, the third grain vessel seized in five days. The Confederates valued her at $32,880. Her captain, Marshall M. Wells, and his crew were moved to *Alabama*, and the prize was burned. The New York press published a long account of the seizure of *Lauretta*, claiming that Semmes had burned or confiscated property of neutrals and that all of this information would be sent to the British government since some of the property was declared British. . . .

On 2 November, as *Alabama* moved southward, her lookouts discovered a sail, and the chase began. Sunday Muster was in progress, and even during the pursuit the reading of the Articles of War continued. Finally the Confederates fired a blank shell, and the vessel hove to. She was the 376-ton ship *Levi Starbuck*, under Capt. Thomas Mellen. The ship and her cargo, valued at $25,000, were burned. Because *Levi Starbuck* was a whaler, she was supplied for a long voyage of thirty months. She yielded miscellaneous stores very welcome aboard the raider, particularly cabbages, turnips, and such antiscorbutic vegetables. For over seventy days *Alabama's* crew had been living on a diet of dried beans, salt pork, and dried beef. The seamen called this meat "salt horse." The story of the burning of *Levi Starbuck* appeared in *Harper's Weekly*, with the report that USS *San Jacinto* was going in search of the raider. This periodical elaborated the charge that *Alabama* was a British pirate, an accusation that was repeated more and more often. The article read in part as follows:

> Here is a vessel built in a British dock-yard, by a member of the British Parliament—Mr. Laird; armed with British guns, manned with British sailors; fitted out under the auspices of British officials, in defiance alike of the remonstrances of our Minister and of the Foreign Enlistment Act; going to sea under British protection, and commencing at once her career by the destruction of ten helpless

and defenseless whalers. If this craft be not a British pirate, what would constitute one?

As bountiful October yielded to November, *Alabama* continued her southward course, running counter to the Gulf Stream, headed for the West Indies. She discovered a sail and was in pursuit when a larger vessel came on that looked more inviting. The Confederate quickly captured and boarded the larger. She was the 599-ton ship *Thomas B. Wales,* often called *T. B. Wales*—an East Indiaman returning to Boston with women and children on board, including a former U.S. consul, George H. Fairchild, his family, and the wife of the master. Passengers and crew were transferred to the raider. Semmes enjoyed the presence of the women, and the voices of children replaced for a time the gloom of war in his thoughts. The prize, valued at $245,625, was soon burned. Some spars and a nearly precise replacement for the mainyard lost in the storm were obtained from this ship, and *Alabama* recruited eleven seamen from *Wales*. This brought her complement to 110, while her full complement would have been 120. It was a typical situation—*Alabama* undermanned but not by many hands. Union admiral David D. Porter, who knew Semmes well, admired him, disliked him, and vainly pursued him, wrote,

> Was there ever such a lucky man as the Captain of the "Alabama"? If he wanted a cargo of provisions it fell into his hands. If he required to visit a dock-yard to fit out his ship, a vessel came along filled with cordage, canvas and anchors. If he wanted lumber, a lumber vessel from Maine came right into his path; and if he needed to reinforce his crew, renegades from captured vessels would put their names to the shipping articles, after listening to the thrilling tales of the Norsemen, of burning ships and abundant prize-money.

According to plan, *Alabama* went to Fort de France, Martinique— her first port since Terceira—to meet her collier, *Agrippina*. There the Confederates discharged prisoners, sent the coal ship to a different rendezvous for security reasons, and all hands enjoyed a visit from the flamboyant bumboat women peddling fruits and tropical wares. What the officers tried so hard to avoid, happened.

Near Mutiny, Narrow Escape

Enough liquor was smuggled aboard to set the stage for a near mutiny, the closest call the raider ever had to the real thing. A drunken sailor threw a belaying pin at Lieutenant Kell, and a temporary defiance of authority erupted. Semmes ordered the ship to general quarters, as in battle, and had the ringleaders doused continuously with water until they gasped for breath. Within two hours the "mutiny" had ended. Control of liquor taxed *Alabama*'s discipline. Rum was regularly issued to the crew, as in the U.S. Navy at that time and in the Royal Navy as well. Yet *Alabama*'s officers were not allowed liquor. Strenuous efforts were made to keep uncontrolled spirits from flowing aboard.

Alabama's adventures at Martinique had not ended, however. Capt. Alexander McQueen of *Agrippina* had indiscreetly boasted of his connection with the now famous raider, and as a result USS *San Jacinto*, star and villain of the *Trent* affair, arrived and blockaded the harbor, with the assistance of signals from shore. Although the well-known U.S. warship had every advantage of size and armament, *Alabama* had the advantage of speed. By night, the Confederate escaped. This incident almost duplicated the escape by Semmes in CSS *Sumter* from USS *Iroquois*—a year earlier and also at Martinique. Among the ships pursuing *Alabama* only three actually found her: USS *Hatteras*, sunk by *Alabama;* USS *Kearsarge*, which sank *Alabama;* and USS *San Jacinto*, from whose guns *Alabama* escaped in the darkness. Near misses were scored by USS *Tuscarora* and USS *Wyoming*. Finding the Confederate raider was, at one time or another, a mission of nearly all ships of the U.S. Navy capable of outgunning her. The solution of smaller ships hunting in pairs was never exploited.

Departing Martinique, *Alabama* proceeded to the second appointment with the collier at Blanquilla, Venezuela. There the raider took on coal and put ashore George Forrest, the one-time deserter from *Sumter*, who probably had been the main mover in the near mutiny. Semmes set the next coaling rendezvous at Arcas Cays. Within the marine league of Venezuela, *Alabama* encountered a Yankee whaling schooner, *Clara L. Sparks*. Semmes made the decision to release her because of Venezuela's neutrality, much to the relief of her captain.

Leaving Blanquilla, *Alabama* cruised in the Caribbean with the primary mission of capturing one of the California treasure steamers. Meanwhile prizes were sought along the way. It was not until 30 November, however, that the Confederates seized the 136-ton bark *Parker Cook* of Boston, under command of Thomas M. Fulton and bound for Santo Domingo with a general cargo. Ship and cargo were valued at $10,000. She yielded badly needed provisions: cheese, Boston bread, crackers, beef, pork, and especially fruit. Then she was burned. From *Parker Cook* the Confederates obtained Boston and New York newspapers that confirmed what Semmes had already guessed, that he was winning the cruiser war. Fear of Confederate raiders had become so great as to cause real or alleged transfers of ownership of American ships and cargoes to foreign registry. These transfers were eloquent testimony by the enemy that insurance rates had risen to such heights as to attest the success of the cruiser war.

★

11   The Death of the *Alabama*
★★

In June 1864 off Cherbourg, Semmes dueled the Union sloop-of-war *Kearsarge*, knowing she carried heavier guns but not that she was clad in hidden chain armor. The fight ended in the sinking of *Alabama,* with little damage to the Union sloop. So ended the Confederate threat to Union merchant shipping.

★

Soon after our arrival at Cherbourg an officer was sent on shore to ask permission of the port admiral to land our prisoners of the two captured ships. This being obtained without trouble or delay, Captain Semmes went on shore to see to the docking of the ship for repairs. Cherbourg being a naval station and the dock belonging to the government, permission had to be obtained of the emperor before we could do anything. The port admiral told us "we had better have gone into Havre, as the government might not give permission for repairs to a belligerent ship." The emperor was absent from Paris at some watering place on the coast and would not return for some days. Here was an impediment to our plans which gave us time for thought, and the result of such thought was the unfortunate combat between the *Alabama* and the *Kearsarge.*

The latter ship was lying at Flushing when we entered Cherbourg. Two or three days after our arrival she steamed into the harbor, sent a boat on shore to communicate, steamed outside, and stationed off the breakwater. While Captain Semmes had not singled her out as an antagonist and would never have done so had he known her to be chain-clad (an armored ship), he had about this time made up his mind that he would

---

Reprinted from "The Sinking of the Confederate Steamer *Alabama*" in John McIntosh Kell's *Recollections of a Naval Life* (1900, 244–251). Mr. Kell was Raphael Semmes's executive officer.

cease fleeing before the foe and meet an equal in battle when the opportunity presented itself. Our cause was weakening daily, and our ship so disabled it really seemed to us our work was almost done! We might end her career gloriously by being victorious in battle and defeat against an equal foe we would never have allowed ourselves to anticipate.

As soon as the *Kearsarge* came into the harbor Captain Semmes sent for me to come to his cabin and abruptly said to me: "Kell, I am going out to fight the *Kearsarge*. What do you think of it?" We then quietly talked it all over. We discussed the batteries, especially the *Kearsarge's* advantage in 11-inch guns. I reminded him of our defective powder, how our long cruise had deteriorated everything, as proven in our target-practice off the coast of Brazil on the ship *Rockingham,* when certainly every third shot was a failure even to explode. I saw his mind was fully made up, so I simply stated these facts for myself. I had always felt ready for a fight, and I also knew that the brave young officers of the ship would not object— the men would be not only willing, but anxious, to meet the enemy! To all outward seeming the disparity was not great between the two ships, barring the unknown (because concealed) chain armor. The *Kearsarge* communicated with the authorities to request that our prisoners be turned over to them. Captain Semmes made an objection to her increasing her crew. He addressed our agent, Mr. Bonfils, a communication requesting him to inform Captain Winslow, through the U.S. Consul, that "if he would wait till the *Alabama* could coal ship he would give him battle." We began to coal and at the same time to make preparation for battle. We overhauled the magazine and shell rooms, gun equipments, etc.

The *Kearsarge* was really in the fullest sense of the word a man-of-war, staunch and well built; the *Alabama* was made for flight and speed and was much more lightly constructed than her chosen antagonist. The *Alabama* had one more gun, but the *Kearsarge* carried more metal at a broadside. The seven guns of the *Kearsarge* were two 11-inch Dahlgrens, four 32-pounders, and one rifled 28-pounder. The *Alabama's* eight guns were six 32-pounders, one 8-inch, and one rifled 100-pounder. The crew of the *Alabama* all told was 149 men, while that of the *Kearsarge* was 162 men. By Saturday night, 18 June, our preparations were completed. Captain Semmes notified the admiral of the port that he would be ready to go out and meet the *Kearsarge* the following morning. Early Sunday

Crewmen of the notorious Confederate raider *Alabama* abandon ship as the armored Union sloop-of-war *Kearsarge* keeps firing. Behind the two vessels is the steam yacht *Deerhound,* an accidental English witness, which rescued survivors. Inset at bottom are busts of Raphael Semmes (right) and the Union victor, Captain Winslow. (Lithograph by G. W. Seitz, reproduced by permission of the National Portrait Gallery, Smithsonian Institution, NPG.84.369)

morning the admiral sent an officer to say to us that "the ironclad Frigate *Couronne* would accompany us to protect the neutrality of French waters."

Many offered to join us. William C. Whittle Jr., Grimball, and others; also George Sinclair and Adolphe Marmelstein, officers of the *Tuscaloosa,* and others who were in Paris came down to join us; but the French authorities objected, and they were not allowed to do so. Between nine and ten o'clock, 19 June, everything being in readiness, we got under way and proceeded to sea. We took the western entrance of the harbor. The *Couronne* accompanied us, also some French pilot boats and an English steam yacht, the *Deerhound,* owned by a rich Englishman (as we afterward learned), who, with his wife and children, was enjoying life and leisure in his pleasure yacht. The walls and fortifications of the harbor,

the heights above the town, the buildings, everything that looked seaward, was crowded with people. About seven miles from the land the
Kearsarge was quietly awaiting our arrival.

"You Have Destroyed the Enemy's Commerce"

Officers in uniforms, men at their best, Captain Semmes ordered them
sent aft, and mounting a gun-carriage made them a brief address:

> Officers and seamen of the *Alabama:* You have at length another
> opportunity to meet the enemy, the first that has presented to you
> since you sank the *Hatteras.* In the meantime you have been all over
> the world, and it is not too much to say that you have destroyed and
> driven for protection under neutral flags one-half of the enemy's
> commerce, which at the beginning of the war covered every sea. This
> is an achievement of which you may well be proud, and a grateful
> country will not be unmindful of it. The name of your ship has
> become a household word wherever civilization extends. Shall that
> name be tarnished by defeat? [An outburst of Never! Never!] The
> thing is impossible. Remember that you are in the English Channel,
> the theatre of so much of the naval glory of our race. The eyes of all
> Europe are at this moment upon you! The flag that floats over you is
> that of a young Republic that bids defiance to her enemies, whenever
> and wherever found! Show the world that you know how to uphold it.
> Go to your quarters!

We now prepared our guns to engage the enemy on our starboard side.
When within a mile and a quarter he wheeled, presenting his starboard
battery to us. We opened on him with solid shot, to which he soon
replied, and the action became active. To keep our respective broadsides
bearing we were obliged to fight in a circle around a common center,
preserving a distance of three-quarters of a mile. When within distance
of shell range we opened on him with shell. The spanker gaff was shot
away, and our ensign came down. We replaced it immediately at the miz-
zen masthead. The firing now became very hot and heavy. Captain
Semmes, who was watching the battle from the horse block, called out to
me, "Mr. Kell, our shell strike the enemy's side, doing little damage, and
fall off in the water; try solid shot." From this time we alternated shot

and shell. The battle lasted an hour and ten minutes. Captain Semmes said to me at this time (seeing the great apertures made in the side of the ship from their 11-inch shell, and the water rushing in rapidly), "Mr. Kell, as soon as our head points to the French coast in our circuit of action, shift your guns to port and make all sail for the coast." This evolution was beautifully performed; righting the helm, hauling aft the fore trysail sheet, and pivoting to port, the action continuing all the time without cessation—but it was useless, nothing could avail us.

Before doing this and pivoting the gun, it became necessary to clear the deck of parts of the dead bodies that had been torn to pieces by the 11-inch shells of the enemy. The captain of our 8-inch gun and most of the gun's crew were killed. It became necessary to take the crew from young Anderson's gun to make up the vacancies, which I did, and placed him in command. Though a mere youth, he managed it like an old veteran. Going to the hatchway, I called out to Brooks (one of our efficient engineers) to give the ship more steam, or we would be whipped. He replied she "had every inch of steam that was safe to carry without being blown up!" Young Matt O'Brien, assistant engineer, called out, "Let her have the steam; we had better blow her to hell than to let the Yankees whip us!" The chief engineer now came on deck and reported "the furnace fires put out," whereupon Captain Semmes ordered me to go below and "see how long the ship could float." I did so, and returning said, "Perhaps ten minutes." "Then, sir," said Captain Semmes, "cease firing, shorten sail, and haul down the colors. It will never do in this nineteenth century for us to go down and the decks covered with our gallant wounded." This order was promptly executed, after which the *Kearsarge* deliberately fired into us five shots! In Captain Winslow's report to the Secretary of the Navy he admits this, saying, "Uncertain whether Captain Semmes was not making some ruse, the *Kearsarge* was stopped."

Was this a time—when disaster, defeat and death looked us in the face—for a ship to use a ruse, a Yankee trick? I ordered the men to "stand to their quarters," and they did it heroically; not even flinching, they stood every man to his post. As soon as we got the first of these shot I told the quartermaster to show the white flag from the stern. It was done. Captain Semmes said to me, "Dispatch an officer to the *Kearsarge* and ask that they send boats to save our wounded—ours are disabled." Our little dingey was not injured, so I sent Master's Mate Fulham with the request. No boats coming, I had one of our quarter boats (the least damaged one) lowered and had the wounded put in her. Dr. Galt came on deck at this time and was put in charge of her, with orders to take the wounded to the *Kearsarge*. They shoved off in time to save the wounded.

When I went below to inspect the sight was appalling! Assistant Surgeon Llewellyn was at his post, but the table and the patient on it had been swept away from him by an 11-inch shell, which made an aperture that was fast filling with water. This was the last time I saw Dr. Llewellyn in life. As I passed the deck to go down below a stalwart seaman with death's signet on his brow called to me. For an instant I stood beside him. He caught my hand and kissed it with such reverence and loyalty—the look, the act, it lingers in my memory still! I reached the deck and gave the order for "every man to save himself, to jump overboard with a spar, an oar, or a grating, and get out of the vortex of the sinking ship."

As soon as all were overboard but Captain Semmes and I, his steward, Bartelli, and two of the men—the sailmaker, Alcott, and Michael Mars— we began to strip off all superfluous clothing for our battle with the waves for our lives. Poor, faithful-hearted Bartelli, we did not know he could not swim, or he might have been sent to shore—he was drowned. The men disrobed us, I to my shirt and drawers, but Captain Semmes kept on his heavy pants and vest. We together gave our swords to the briny deep and the ship we loved so well! The sad farewell look at the ship would have wrung the stoutest heart! The dead were lying on her decks, the surging, roaring waters rising through the death wound in her side. The ship agonizing like a living thing and going down in her brave beauty, settling lower and lower, she sank fathoms deep—lost to all save love and fame and memory!

After undressing with the assistance of our men we plunged into the sea. It was a mass of living heads, striving, struggling, battling for life. On the wild waste of waters there came no boats, at first, from the *Kearsarge* to our rescue. Had victory struck them dumb or helpless—or had it frozen the milk of human kindness in their veins? The water was like ice, and after the excitement of battle it seemed doubly cold. I saw a float of empty shell boxes near me and called out to one of the men (an expert swimmer) to examine the float. He said: "It is the doctor, sir, and he is dead." Poor Llewellyn! Almost within sight of home, the air blowing across the channel from it into the dead face that had given up the struggle for life and liberty. I felt my strength giving out, but strange to say I never thought of giving up, though the white caps were breaking wildly over my head and the sea foam from the billows blinding my eyes. Midshipman Maffitt swam to my side and said, "Mr. Kell, you are so exhausted, take this life preserver" (endeavoring to disengage it). I refused, seeing in his own pallid young face that heroism had risen superior to self or bodily suffering! But "what can a man do more than give his life for his friend?"

The next thing that I remember, a voice called out, "Here's our first lieutenant," and I was pulled into a boat, in the stern sheets of which lay Captain Semmes as if dead. He had received a slight wound in the hand, which with the struggle in the water had exhausted his strength, long worn by sleeplessness, anxiety, and fatigue. There were several of our crew in the boat. In a few moments we were alongside a steam yacht, which received us on her deck, and we learned it was the *Deerhound*, owned by an English gentleman, Mr. John Lancaster, who used it for the pleasure of himself and family, who were with him at this time, his sons having preferred going out with him to witness the fight [than] to going to church with their mother, as he afterward told us.

In looking about us I saw two French pilot boats rescuing the crew and finally two boats from the *Kearsarge*. I was much surprised to find Mr. Fulham on the *Deerhound*, as I had dispatched him in the little dingey to ask the *Kearsarge* for boats to save our wounded. Mr. Fulham told me that "our shot had torn the casing from the chain armor of the *Kearsarge*, indenting the chain in many places." This now explained Captain Semmes' observation to me during the battle—"our shell strike the enemy's side and fall into the water." Had we been in possession of this knowledge the unequal battle between the *Alabama* and the *Kearsarge* would never have been fought and the gallant little *Alabama* have been lost by an error. She fought valiantly as long as there was a plank to stand upon.

History has failed to explain, unless there were secret orders forbidding it, why the *Kearsarge* did not steam into the midst of the fallen foe and generously save life! The *Kearsarge* fought the battle beautifully, but she tarnished her glory when she fired on a fallen foe and made no immediate effort to save brave living men from watery graves! Both heroic commanders are now gone—before the great tribunal where "the deeds done in the body" are to be accounted for, but history is history and truth is truth!

Mr. Lancaster came to Captain Semmes and said: "I think every man is saved, where shall I land you?" He replied, "I am under English colors; the sooner you land me on English soil the better." The little yacht, under a press of steam, moved away for Southampton. Our loss was nine killed, twenty-one wounded, and ten drowned. That afternoon, 19 June, we were landed in Southampton and received with every demonstration of kindness and sympathy.

☆

Epilogue

The Death of the U.S. Merchant Marine

Confederate raiders alone destroyed some 110,000 tons of northern-owned shipping during the war, and the economic impact of this destruction was amplified by horrified reports in the Union press. Early in the war, northern shipowners, devastated by their losses, began selling their tonnage to foreign buyers, and by war's end the tonnage lost by these sales far outstripped the raiders' destruction. More than 750,000 tons of shipping was sold abroad and at bargain prices. The U.S. fleet of deep-water merchant ships had been nearly 2.5 million tons in 1861, and by war's end it had shrunk by a million and more.

To be sure, other major causes unrelated to the war contributed to this decline, and a significant decline would have occurred in any event. But it took place, and it was immense—and for fifty years, until the eve of World War I, the U.S. deep-sea merchant marine was as dead as the *Alabama*.

The other loser, of course, was the Confederate cause. The raiders could not overcome the strangling effect of the impenetrable Union blockade of southern ports. Brilliant successes by the raiders alone could not win the war—and did not.

World War I

IN THE SUMMER OF 1914 WHEN GERMANY launched World War I, the United States had a small coastal fleet and a number of ships in service to South America. But it had almost no deep-water merchant marine. Ninety percent of U.S. exports and imports traveled in foreign ships. At the first signs of German bombast, they disappeared. "Overnight," writes Wallace West, "those 'foreign bottoms' which had carried our goods for so many years, vanished from the seas. We found our ports jammed with goods which we had planned to sell abroad but which now promised to rot on our hands" (West, *Down to the Sea*, 42–43).

12 The "European War" and American Trade
★★

Americans watched the development of the "European War" with grow-ing consternation. As the historian Allan Nevins put it, "The two chief maritime nations of the globe were straining every effort to defeat one another: the United Kingdom with more than nineteen million gross tons of shipping, and Germany with something less than six million" (Nevins, *Sail On*, 61). But while the United States had large lake and coastal fleets (nearly seven million tons), hardly more than a million tons was engaged in foreign trade.

★

Great Britain stood far and away in the lead not only in her ownership of ships but in her shipbuilding facilities. In the fifteen years preceding the war, she had built fully three-fifths of all the merchant shipping produced in the world.

The storm burst with Germany's invasion of Belgium. Within a single year the oceans presented an unexampled scene of havoc and confusion. The merchant navies of Germany and Austria were driven from the sea. Those ships not captured or destroyed had to tie up at home or intern themselves in neutral ports. Countless Allied ships were withdrawn for use as transports, auxiliary cruisers, hospital ships, and tenders. By the end of 1915 it was estimated that twelve million tons of shipping was thus in use. Meanwhile, German submarines and commerce raiders sank not merely hundreds of British, French, and Russian vessels but much neutral tonnage, especially Dutch and Scandinavian, as well. Accord-ing to Lloyd's, Great Britain during the first seventeen months of the war lost 338 merchant steamers and 264 lesser vessels, of 1,200,000 gross tonnage. Among the famous liners which went down during this period were the British *Lusitania* and the German *Cap Trafalgar* and *Kaiser Wilhelm der Grosse*.

In view of all these losses, and of the serious disorganization of commerce by blockades, embargoes, and war-zone proclamations, the merchant navy of the United States suddenly had to bear a staggering burden. In addition to taking over much of the transportation work ordinarily done by European shipping, it had to carry to the Allies a steadily increasing volume of munitions and other war material. Freight piled up in U.S. ports for lack of bottoms, until late in 1915 the congestion in New York, Philadelphia, and other centers made it necessary to establish railroad embargoes reaching far into the interior. Freight rates shot upward and insurance soared. In the fall of 1910 it had cost 20¢ a hundredweight to carry cotton from New York to Liverpool; in the fall of 1915 it cost $1.30. The charges for carrying wheat from the United States to Great Britain quadrupled. Farmers, manufacturers, and import merchants were all feeling the transportation pinch severely.

There was grave danger that U.S. economic life would be heavily disorganized if the merchant marine were not quickly and effectively expanded. Even those who were willing to pay trebled freights to bring in goods from Asia and South America, and quintupled or sextupled charges to take goods to Europe, had great difficulty in getting facilities. So much of the available cargo space was taken by the British, French, and Russian governments that private shippers could not obtain a half share. When Italy and Greece entered the war and began requisitioning ships for naval use, the hardships increased. Cotton growers who had obtained 12 1/2¢ a pound for their produce in 1913 found the price tumbling to 7¢ a pound; wheat growers suffered proportionately. A clamor naturally arose for government intervention.

First Steps in the Crisis

Before the war was three weeks old Congress had passed an act permitting the transfer of foreign ships to U.S. registry without respect to age. This was a revolutionary step: up to 1913 no transfers at all had been allowed save by special enactment, and under the Panama Canal Act of 1913 transfers only of vessels under five years old. As during the Civil War about three-quarters of a million tons of shipping had been sold abroad to escape Confederate capture or get the benefit of lower operating costs, so now in the fiscal year 1914–15 more than a half million tons of British, German, Belgian, and other foreign shipping was transferred to U.S. registry. In most instances this involved no change in the actual ownership. Title to many of these vessels had been held by such U.S. corporations as the United Fruit Company, Standard Oil, and United States Steel Products Company, and they had been operated under foreign flags for reasons of convenience or economy. But some changes in beneficiary ownership did occur.

☆

(Nevins, *Sail On*, 61–63)

In the meantime, the United States also had ready to hand a large volume of cargo space that could be filled with goods and powered to its destinations by that ancient resource—wind.

In the second half of the nineteenth century, steam power began to nudge the clipper ships, long the queens of the sea, out of favor for hauling freight. The square-rigged clippers, with their large sails set athwartships, were labor intensive. Many seamen had to swarm into the rigging to set or reef or furl the many rectangular sails promptly in a big blow or a change of course.

Then came new competition from the schooner, with its sails rigged fore and aft. Its huge sails had required many hands to raise or lower them—until the steam engine was adapted to power a winch, which could supply enough "muscle" so twelve or fifteen officers and men could sail a very large ship; a square-rigger of the same capacity would require a crew of 125. Three-masters gave way to four-masters, and schooners with even five, six, or seven masts.

In the emergency shortage of seaworthy vessels that began with Germany's declaration of war in 1914, schooners were no longer confined to the odd coastal load of coal but came into demand to carry on trade with both coasts of South America and even the West Indies. Indeed they hauled transatlantic cargoes until the U.S. government discovered "the ease with which the U-boats could blow the old schooners apart as they wallowed along, [and barred] them from all but coastwise and South Atlantic voyages" (Clark, *Ships and Sailors*, 284).

The occasional bark or brig—easier to handle than a full-size, square-rigged ship—also ventured out into deep water, but also was affected by the ban.

Germany was not hesitant to use force, threats, or bluster. A German submarine sank a British merchant freighter in October 1914 but first allowed its crew to abandon ship. In January U-boats sank two passenger vessels without warning, then Germany announced that waters around Britain were a war zone where any ship would be sunk. Submarines began to stop U.S. freighters and search them for "contraband cargo," which if found would justify sinking.

In June 1916, Germany flaunted her prowess in submarines with the first of two trips to the United States by the enormous submarine freighter *Deutschland*, which unloaded 750 tons of chemicals at Baltimore. No previous submarine had demonstrated the cruising range that would allow crossing the Atlantic and returning home safely.

A few months later a sister ship, the *U-53*, surfaced outside Newport, Rhode Island, awaited escort into the harbor, and anchored beside a U.S. cruiser at the fleet anchorage. There her captain, the German submarine ace Hans Rose, paid courtesy calls on the commandants of the U.S. Second Naval District and the Destroyer Force of the Atlantic Fleet. When the former, Rear Adm. Austin M. Knight, courteously asked if there was any courtesy he might pay the young German, Captain Rose blandly handed the admiral an envelope for delivery to German Ambassador von Bernstorff at Washington.

At the end of this visit, the *U-53* turned seaward, cruised a few miles to the southeast, then lay to overnight just off Nantucket Light. The next day she halted six steamships there and sank five of them (three British and two neutral, and released the sole American, inbound with a cargo of soda).

Rose only used a costly torpedo on one victim, which refused to sink. The others he put under water with shellfire or by opening their seacocks and scuttling them with explosives. Punctiliously, he allowed every crew time to abandon ship, and he dismissed a seventh vessel, a homebound American with unobjectionable cargo.

One of the ships, the British *Stephano*, had eighty-five passengers as well as freight; when passengers and crew were in their lifeboats, the submarine towed them over alongside the lightship and only then sank their ship.

U.S. Navy destroyers, alerted by radio distress messages from the targeted ships, raced out to the lightship and watched the end of the spectacle with astonishment. Eventually there were fifteen of them, and when one destroyer drifted between the U-boat and its target, Rose signaled the warship to stand clear because he intended to sink the merchantman.

The last victim was a Norwegian tanker, from which the submarine topped off its own fuel tanks before sending her to the bottom. The light-ship by now was riding low in the water with all her refugees. When the U-53 left the scene, the destroyers divided up the survivors from the lightship and took them to shore, leaving the lightship higher in the water and everyone present pondering the U-53's unspoken message. The *Deutschland* had demonstrated enormous cruising range with her cargoes of freight; U-53 showed off range and torpedoes.

The visit of the U-53 in October 1916 was the last evidence of German submarines along the Atlantic coast of the United States until May 1918. When they returned, a third sister of *Deutschland* and U-53 revealed yet another nasty capability of these giant *Unterseebooten:* laying mines.

U-151: Laying Mines and Keeping "Guests"

After sailing from Kiel in mid-April, the U-151 arrived on America's east coast a month later and prowled those waters for six weeks before return-ing safely home with a long list of triumphs. Her stores included more than a hundred large floating mines, which she sowed about equally on her first two side trips. Retracing the *Deutschland's* famous route to Baltimore, she booby-trapped Chesapeake Bay. Then she mined the entrance to Delaware Bay, the only seaward approach to Philadelphia.

However bland the recital may sound, these incursions were not with-out incident. After mining Chesapeake Bay the U-boat halted and sank three schooners: the *Hattie Dunn,* a three-master bound for Charleston; a brand-new four-master in ballast, the *Hauppauge;* and another three-masted schooner, *Edna.*

The submarine now had twenty-three "guests" from the trio of schooners, and because releasing them to reach the nearby shore in boats would have revealed the U-boat's still-undetected mission, they had to be kept aboard for the present. To the delight of U-151's crew, they also had plenty of fresh vegetables from the larders of the sailing ships.

Now the submarine proved the setting for an affecting reunion. After the war, the lecturer, broadcaster, and author Lowell Thomas looked high and low for the U-151's commander, Kapitänleutnant von Nostitz

The giant submarine *U-151* spent the spring of 1918 on the American coast laying mines and sinking ships. (National Archives, RG 19N, CR 13656)

und Janckendorf, to interview for his 1928 book, *Raiders of the Deep.* Unable to find him, he did locate Dr. Frederick Körner, who had been von Nostitz's boarding officer and who had kept extensive diaries.

Körner, Thomas wrote, spoke good English and was described by one of his former U.S. prisoners as "so polite that it almost got on our nerves." Thomas, in *Raiders of the Deep,* translated extensive extracts from Körner's diary. (This and following excerpts are used by the friendly permission of Lowell Thomas Jr.)

★

The captain of the *Edna* had just been sent below. He seated himself in the messroom and gloomily contemplated his fate in being a prisoner aboard a marauding submarine. The master of the *Hattie Dunn* came in through the narrow doorway. I happened to be near by. The two men shouted when they caught sight of each other, and shook hands with the utmost enthusiasm. They hadn't seen each other for thirty years. They were old friends and had been brought up together in the town of Saint George, Maine. They still lived in that community and were neighbors. Their wives were girlhood friends and saw each other every day. The two men had gone to sea. They had returned home only at long intervals, and their stays with their families were short. For thirty years their homecomings had never coincided. And now they were having their first reunion—in the bowels of a German submarine!

The captains of our three prizes were genuine old sea lions. They assured us that there hadn't even been a rumor afloat of our presence in U.S. waters. So remote had the possibility of a submarine attacking them seemed that they had each of them taken the first sound of our shots for naval gunnery practice off the coast. They were thoroughly familiar with the shore along which we were running and gave us excellent advice about our navigation. You see, their own fate depended on the success of our navigation.

We had no trouble at all with our prisoners. I don't suppose they particularly enjoyed the submarine cruise in which they found themselves compelled to take part. Quarters were close and uncomfortable and danger always at hand. It would, truly enough, have been trying for the nerves of anyone save a hardened submarine veteran. But they took things as cheerfully as possible. At first they were thoroughly uneasy. When, to begin with, we failed to shell their lifeboats (which, they erroneously had gathered from their propaganda-filled newspapers, was the usual custom of the U-boats), they formed a vague apprehension that we had something worse in store for them, possibly a cannibal stew. But when they found that we were doing as much to make them comfortable as our limited resources would allow—our officers sharing their bunks with their officers, our sailors with their sailors—they were thankful and they grew friendly. Some of them took their trip with us as an exciting adventure, and it certainly was all of that! After all, it was a pleasure for us to have them aboard. You see, we of the *U-151* had grown somewhat tired of looking at each other in such cramped quarters. So any new face was a welcome relief. We hoped, for our prisoners' sakes as well as our own, that we would encounter no accident while they were aboard.

★   (Thomas, *Raiders,* 298–300)

Approaching the entrance to Delaware Bay, the U-boat submerged to periscope depth to avoid the heavy surface traffic. But she blundered onto the bottom, and the shock disabled both steering gear and diving apparatus; the sub leaped and gyrated wildly as the channel's "freakish and powerful cross currents and eddies . . . caught us and were hauling us about . . . spinning us like a top" (Thomas, *Raiders,* 300).

☆

Up and up we went, and when we reached the surface we were still help-less and revolving like a crazy thing in waters where a ship might run us down at any moment.

Lights ahead and a looming form in the darkness. A large steamer came toward us. It passed us a few hundred feet away. Two other steam-ers passed close by.

"They would be as badly frightened as we," Von Nostitz said to me, "if they only knew how near they are to a U-boat." That was the only conso-lation he could think of.

The currents pulled us so near the lightship that we could hear its bell. It sounded like the tolling of a death knell. Down below the men worked feverishly, fighting to get the steering and diving mechanism back in order. Above we took occasion to throw overboard the mines stowed on deck. Luckily, we were in the very channel where they were to be placed.

"Close the hatches!" *Donnerwetter*! It was good to hear again that command to dive. The boat was in control.

We scurried down and lay on the bottom. The depths seemed a snug, comfortable place now, after our anxious time of drifting helplessly in the traffic lane on the surface. We utilized the interval to get the remainder of our mines ready for launching.

Up we came at 3 A.M. A heavy fog lay on the sea. We had no idea of our position. The currents had carried us heaven knows where during the time we were disabled. We went along, groping blindly through the fog. Then we came in earshot of that same lugubrious lightship bell that tolled in dismal monotony. It was as welcome as salvation now. We ran sub-merged to keep out of the way of traffic. With the earpieces of our under-water microphone on my head, I listened to the bell and we maneuvered the boat until the tolling sound was of the same loudness in each ear. That meant that we were steering straight toward it, or in other words, through the narrow mouth of the channel. A good place to lay the rest of our mines. We had no mind to do any more launching from deck in those waters, so we laid our mines from under water. This is one of the most difficult tasks of submarine maneuver. Everything went smoothly, though, and soon we were rid of the most burdensome part of our cargo. No doubt the fishes in the channel of Delaware Bay that night heard the sound of a cheer from the inside of an iron hulk thirty feet below the surface of the sea. It was the cheer that went up when we released our last mine.

With that great load off our shoulders, we came to the surface to take a look around. The fog was so thick that you could hardly have seen a light a dozen or so feet away. Our conning tower had scarcely emerged when we heard the hoarse toot of a fog horn right on top of us. It was the siren of a big steamer sounding its raucous cry at regular intervals. Our men gasped. Again the prisoners thought their last hour had come. We ducked as fast as we could and were lucky enough to escape with nothing more than a good stiff fright.

We were afraid to continue our course under water because we had no idea of the lay of the land around us. At last we decided that the fog on the surface would be a shelter.

☆   (Thomas, *Raiders*, 300–302)

The submarine plied the surface seaward through the fogbound cacophony of horns and whistles and sirens, impudently sounding her own shrill siren whenever a larger vessel's bellow sounded too close for comfort. By 10 P.M. the foghorns grew fewer, indicating their approach to the open sea. There *U-151* steered northeastward along the shoreline for perhaps her most audacious exploit.

Working on the surface off New York the sub extended a long line weighted with special fishing gear of a "newly devised implement for cutting cables" and dragged it to and fro along the bottom of the harbor probing for the Atlantic telegraph cables. When the equipment sensed a sudden drag indicating that a cable had been snagged, the *U-151* would stop while a special cutting mechanism would sever the cable.

Actually, two cables were successfully cut, one to Europe and another to South America. With that, at the end of May, the *U-151* resumed her role as a hunter of the deep, prowling America's Atlantic coast, sinking several more ships and releasing her captives in the powered lifeboats of one of them. She returned safely to Kiel at the end of June with a net bag of six schooners and fourteen steamers, in addition to two mined harbors and two cut cables.

13 The "European War"
☆☆ **and American Victims**

For all the toll of Allied ships taken by U-boats, and of neutral ships with war cargoes destined for England or France, no U.S. vessel was attacked by submarine until May of 1915. In January of that year, a wheat-laden, four-masted schooner, the *William P. Frye,* was sunk in the South Atlantic by a German surface raider, the *Prinz Eitel Friedrich.* The raider halted the schooner, boarded her, and ascertained her cargo and that it was destined for Queenstown, Australia. When dumping her cargo into the sea proved too labor intensive and time consuming, the U.S. crew was ordered into its boats and the *Eitel Friedrich* sank the *Frye.* That four-master became the first U.S. merchantman deliberately sunk in World War I.

Two U.S. freighters, SS *Evelyn* from New York and SS *Carib* out of Savannah, were sunk by mines in February, both in the North Sea, both carrying cotton, and both destined for Bremen, Germany. Ironically, both apparently were sunk by mines sown by Germany. After the *Carib* went down, with a loss of three lives, the German government issued a warning to all ships bound for North Sea ports to approach via waters north of Scotland, which had previously been declared safe.

On Saturday, 1 May 1915, a new U.S. tanker, SS *Gulflight,* was approaching the English Channel when she was torpedoed off the Isles of Scilly. The tanker, 360 feet long, was on her maiden voyage with 50,000 barrels of gasoline in her tanks and barrels of oil on deck, heading for Rouen via the channel and the River Seine.

About eleven o'clock that morning, she was steaming eastward in hazy weather, off Land's End at England's southwest corner. There she encountered two British patrol boats, the *Iago* and the *Filey,* which asked her destination. On hearing it was Rouen, they ordered the tanker to follow them to Bishop's Light, about twenty-five miles to the east.

The *Filey* then positioned herself a half mile off the *Gulflight*'s port bow and the *Iago* diagonally opposite and a little closer, on the starboard quarter. About an hour later, the tanker's second mate, who was on watch on the bridge, spotted an unmarked submarine on the surface—on the port bow some two and a half miles ahead—sailing directly across the course of the trio. He pointed the sub out to the captain and chief officer, who were also on the bridge.

The chief mate, Ralph E. Smith, went aft to notify the crew. He and the captain had noticed the sub too, but apparently the escorts, whose bridges were much closer to the water than the tanker's, had not, for they showed no response. This led the tanker's master to assume that the submarine was British.

As it turned out, the submarine was the German *U-30*, which had apparently been either stalking or evading the two patrol boats. Four or five minutes after being spotted from the *Gulflight*'s bridge, the sub, then dead ahead of the tanker, submerged.

Twenty-five minutes later, at 12:50 ship's time, a torpedo struck the tanker's starboard bow, sending an enormous curtain of water "high in the air, coming down on the bridge and shutting everything off from our view," the chief mate said. "After the water cleared away, our ship had sunk by the head so that the sea was washing over the foredeck and the ship appeared to be sinking."

Immediately, he rushed aft to see to the *Gulflight*'s two lifeboats. As he ran along the catwalk he noticed one man overboard on the starboard side, in water already black with oil. Meanwhile, in the engine room, the second assistant engineer, who was on watch, said the blow was so terrible that the ship "seemed to be tumbling to pieces. She appeared to be lifted high in the air and then to descend rapidly. I told the boys to beat it as quickly as possible and shut the engines down," he said.

At the instant of the blast, second mate Paul Bower recalled, the patrol boat *Iago*, then close in on the starboard quarter, "was so badly shaken by the explosion that her crew imagined that she also had been torpedoed."

All hands got safely into the boats except for two who had dived overboard at the moment of impact. They were a Spanish seaman and—of all people—the radio operator, whose prime reason for being there was to transmit a distress signal in exactly such an emergency.

The ship's cook was severely burned, and the *Gulflight*'s master, Capt. Alfred Gunter, suffered an apparent heart attack and died that night on one of the patrol boats. The weather had deteriorated from hazy to thick fog during the attack and its aftermath, and the patrol boats drifted about all night, finally able to land at Scilly at 10:30 A.M., Sunday, 2 May.

The *Gulflight,* badly damaged but still afloat, was beached and later towed to a safe anchorage.

May Day of 1915 saw other significant events. Germany had earlier declared British waters a war zone where any ships with cargoes for the Allies would be fair game. When the U.S. State Department rejected the German ambassador's suggestion that U.S. shipping be warned to avoid those waters, the ambassador chose 1 May to publish the warning in large ads in fifty major newspapers.

And the Cunard liner *Lusitania* left New York for London with 1,257 passengers, 149 of them Americans. She also had in her cargo hold a small shipment of 173 tons of ammunition.

As she sailed, U.S. government officials were contemplating the German newspaper ads and speculating about future German actions. President Wilson was out of Washington, and Secretary of State William Jennings Bryan and his counselor, Robert Lansing, would not comment; but on Monday, 3 May, the *New York Times* published a front page "dope story" (datelined Washington the previous day), "Gulflight Attack Arouses Washington."

The article (unsigned in conformity with managing editor Carr Van Anda's obsession against bylines) presented an acute analysis of German actions to date and a prediction of further actions to come—which within the week would prove devastatingly accurate.

Then, under a subhead reading, "Expect Attacks on Liners," it went on:

☆

Among administration officers the belief prevails that the German submarine warfare is about to be renewed in a more vigorous manner, and probably in a way that will endanger some of the great British passenger liners which are carrying large numbers of Americans to and from Europe.

This theory is based on the recent attitude of the German government with reference to the shipment of arms, ammunition, and other supplies from the United States to Great Britain and France. The latest German complaints of this character have been extremely emphatic, and it is apparent that the German government intends to take advantage of every opportunity to show resentment over the course of this government in permitting such supplies to go to the Allies. In some quarters here it is believed that the advertisement of the German embassy, which appeared in American newspapers yesterday, and which is to be repeated once a week for three weeks, was intended not merely as a warning to U.S. travelers to remain at home, but as notice to this government that the big passenger liners which carry large cargoes of American war munitions to Great Britain and France are to be made the victims of German submarines whenever possible.

★   (*New York Times*, 3 May 1915)

On Friday, 7 May, before the headlines had died down on the *Gulflight* sinking, the *Lusitania* was encountered off Ireland by Germany's *U-20*. The liner, despite warnings of German subs in the area, had come to a dead stop to take bearings. The U-boat was on the way home, low on oil and with only two torpedoes left, which her captain feared might be defective.

They were not. The proud liner, without having conducted so much as a lifeboat drill, sank in eighteen minutes of confused panic, taking to the bottom with her 1,195 of her 1,959 passengers and crew; only 25 of the 149 Americans on board survived.

Although the fate of the *Lusitania* brilliantly illustrated the accuracy of that *New York Times* analysis and prediction, chance played a larger role than planning in the timing and circumstances of the actual event. The size of the death toll helped make the affair a worldwide cause célèbre and galvanized the United States. The torpedoing of the U.S. freighter *Nebraskan* later that month (she did not sink) and the sinking of another, SS *Leelanaw*, by a submarine later in the year passed almost without public notice compared to the *Lusitania* affair.

★

For a year and a half after the *Lusitania*, the "main line" was not seriously molested. For a while, the Germans refrained from torpedoing passenger liners, even though some of them were openly carrying considerable quantities of munitions. In the summer of 1915, when the sinkings of that year were at their heaviest, the White Star liner *Arabic* was sunk with the loss of two Americans among the forty-four victims, and in the spring of 1916 German-American diplomatic relations were complicated by the deaths of more Americans in the torpedoing of the French Channel steamer *Sussex*. Ordinary little freighters by the dozen, some of them laden with American munitions or grain, went down during that summer of 1915, but by fall the sinkings tapered off and were not serious again until October 1916, when the average monthly toll rose to 175,000 tons for the next four months. Altogether during much of 1915 and 1916, most of the shrapnel, high explosives, and wheat from American ports reached England safely.

The submarines were not idle during that lull on the North Atlantic; they had shifted their activities elsewhere. The quiet waters and narrow bottlenecks of the Mediterranean made it an ideal field for operations. The Germans even sent down a considerable amount of submarine parts by rail to the Adriatic coast, where they were assembled. By the fall of 1916, war-risk rates to the Mediterranean were three times as high as to England; Britain began to send much of its shipping by the longer but safer alternate route around the Cape of Good Hope. Of the three American vessels sunk by U-boats to the end of 1916, two were lost in the Mediterranean trade.

☆   (Albion and Pope, *Sea Lanes,* 240)

As the war continued, and as cargoes destined for the Allies piled up on U.S. wharves, and as more and more of the European tonnage that could transport them went to the bottom, it grew ever more evident that the U.S. government would have to step in. President Wilson urgently advocated such action, saying, "Without a merchant marine, our independence is provincial and it is independence only on land and within our borders." After much debate, in September 1916 Congress created the United States Shipping Board (West, *Down to the Sea,* 44).

☆

The function assigned the board was to promote the development of the merchant marine, and to regulate foreign and domestic shipping. This was partly a "preparedness" measure: the board was to see that we had plenty of auxiliary ships if we were drawn into the war. It was partly a measure for the defense of our economic interests: the board was to furnish a fuller supply of ships for general trade, foster the merchant fleet, and free American shippers from the dictation of foreign owners who, on orders from belligerent governments, were directing what goods a ship could and could not carry. Very little attention was paid to the question of permanent policy. The act was an emergency step to meet a crisis. Incidentally, the board was authorized to enter the shipping business, with a revolving fund of fifty million to build, buy, lease, and operate its own fleet of merchant vessels.

During the last months of our neutrality, American shipbuilding continued to grow like a young giant fed on H. G. Wells's Food of the Gods. By midsummer of 1916 50,000 men were toiling like beavers in the various yards, and by the spring of 1917 the number had grown to 75,000. During the fiscal year 1916–17, our yards turned out for private owners almost 1,300 merchant ships of 655,000 gross tons. But this was not enough to meet the urgent demands of the time. Germany was rapidly increasing her submarine fleet, and at the end of January 1917, she announced that she would resume unrestricted submarine warfare. The sinkings of both Allied and neutral vessels became desperately serious. They threatened the isolation of Europe from the United States, the starvation of Britain, and the defeat of the democratic cause. As soon as the United States entered the war in April 1917 steps had to be taken to construct ships on a colossal scale.

Ships, Ships, and More Ships

To meet one of the most terrible hours of peril in the nation's life, the shipping board and its subsidiary agency, the Emergency Fleet Corporation, moved with frenzied energy. They possessed an ample grant of authority to do anything they pleased in the shipping field, and they were given practically limitless sums of money by Congress. Under Edward N. Hurley, who in the summer of 1917 took control of the board, prodigious feats were accomplished. To help build the needed "bridge to France," ninety German and Austrian ships of almost 600,000 gross tons were seized, and nearly as many Dutch ships in American ports, another 350,000 tons, were commandeered. The board also chartered or took over by some other form of agreement 161 neutral-owned ships of 687,000 gross tons. But its principal effort lay in a mighty feat of emergency shipbuilding; "the world's greatest shipbuilding spree," as one marine expert has called it.

No expense was spared. Before the war ended, the board had made commitments totaling $3,446,690,000. The prices paid for everything that had to do with ships, said William G. McAdoo, who as Secretary of the Treasury knew, were "appalling." Engines and other equipment, he wrote, "were purchased at such a staggering cost that I fancied more than once that the machinery we were buying must be made of silver instead of iron or steel." Wages for the army of workers enlisted—360,000 by the fall of 1918—went to unprecedented levels. To establish new shipyards the board spent about $150,000,000. In constructing the ships, the cost-plus system was generally adopted, the board assuring the shipbuilder the cost of his work, together with a profit that ranged up to 7.5 percent or even more. Money was squandered—but it produced results.

The grand achievement was the completion of 2,382 merchant ships of approximately nine million gross tons; the provision of facilities to carry half of the two million men sent to France (Britain carrying the other half), and keep them fed and equipped; and the complete crushing of the submarine menace. Many of the vessels were jerry-built affairs. They were made of steel, of wood, of composite materials, and even of concrete. After the war ended, shipping men regarded the product with amused disgust. "Anybody," wrote one observer, "built anything that somebody would brand a ship—of green wood and brittle concrete and baling wire and stove bolts—a hasty fleet of monstrosities." But they held together long enough to help win the war, and that was the vital consideration. To be sure, the greater part of the program was not finished until after the armistice; but this meant simply that if the war had run into 1919, as the government had expected it would, the prodigious fleet would have played an even greater part than it did.

☆   (Nevins, *Sail On*, 65–67)

14 A Vigorous Response
★★

★

In its new campaign of unrestricted submarine warfare, Germany announced that every vessel of any sort found in the waters around England and France or in the Mediterranean would be sunk. The one exception was permission for the United States to dispatch one ship each week to Falmouth, England, provided several minutely specified regulations were followed. Three days later, the United States severed diplomatic relations with Germany.

The U-boats went to work with deadly effectiveness. They laid mines close inshore to drive the shipping out to sea away from the protection of the patrol boats; and there sank them by the score. From Fastnet, that "rugged lonely rock with its tall lighthouse," off the tip of Ireland, on past Kinsale and off the end of Cornwall, they cruised in tireless relays. Although they centered their efforts as usual here, where Britain's sea lanes converged, the northern route and the approaches to France were not much safer. The losses hit 540,000 tons in February and did not drop below that again until September. Not only were the Germans successfully sinking a considerable part of the British merchant marine with its cargoes of precious foodstuffs beneath the waves, but this time they were frightening off many neutral cargo carriers. The dauntless Norwegians stuck to the dangerous work, but most others dared not risk their ships.

★   (Albion and Pope, *Sea Lanes,* 241)

Watching this toll mount, President Wilson concluded that U.S. merchantmen must be able to defend themselves and on 26 February, three weeks after severing relations with Germany, asked Congress to authorize arming them. The House of Representatives agreed with alacrity. The Senate dithered, immobilized by a filibuster organized by Wisconsin's senator Robert La Follette.

A week later (4 March, the anniversary of his second inauguration), the president deftly found the range of La Follette's "gang of five" and immortalized them as "a little group of willful men, representing no opinion but their own." And a week after that the State Department completed a study indicating that the ships could be armed by executive authority.

☆

[Secretary Lansing] announced that the United States had decided to place naval armed guards on all U.S. merchant ships sailing through areas which Germany had barred from commerce—a blockadelike prohibition that the United States refused to recognize. Lansing stated that the naval armed guards were for the protection of the lives of the persons on board and for the safety of the vessel. Confidential instructions provided to the master and the armed guard commander were emphatic that the armament was, "for the sole purpose of defense against the unlawful acts of the submarines of Germany." Up to that time, Germany had already sunk eight American merchantmen, which, at the time of attack, were within Germany's prohibited zone.

☆   (Gibson, *Merchantman? Or Ship of War,* 64)

The navy cooperated aggressively, fitting merchant ships with guns as heavy as the ship's structure would stand, frequently substantial naval cannon with bores of four to six inches. The mere fact of arming, however, did not ensure survival.

The front pages of the morning papers of 3 April 1917 were dominated by news of President Wilson's war message to an extraordinary session of Congress he had called to declare war on Germany. Beside it, in the *New York Times,* among other papers with various wording, was the headline, "Armed American Steamship Sunk; 11 Men Missing."

The ship was SS *Aztec,* the third armed freighter to sail for Europe from the U.S. East Coast, and the first sunk. She was torpedoed without warning at the mouth of the English Channel off Brest, about 9:15 P.M. ship's time.

The 23-year-old ship, 350 feet long, had a cargo of foodstuffs and other supplies. The torpedo caught her squarely amidships, and the initial explosion knocked out the wireless. The navy armed guard crew of a lieutenant and eleven enlisted men, all of whom survived, had no chance to use their substantial armament, 5-inch guns fore and aft. Heavy seas were running, and the *Aztec*'s first boat launched was smashed and its occupants presumed drowned. The other three boats were launched safely, and their passengers were picked up.

The Federal Shipping Board established a recruiting and training program for merchant marine officers and seamen. Officer candidates were required to have seafaring experience or, in the case of engineering officer candidates, equivalent experience with large engines. Shore schools were set up for future deck officers to learn navigation and engineer candidates to study marine engineering. Forty-three of these schools were established, at locations dotting the full length of the Atlantic coast, plus one at New Orleans, three on the Pacific coast, and three at Great Lakes ports.

Training programs for both deck and engine room crews schooled neophytes for a month and men with some experience for two weeks at shore installations, then sent them off for shipboard training and actual experience at sea.

Meanwhile the navy developed crash programs for training gun crew members for armed guard assignments. The first ships armed were passenger liners, which received more guns and larger crews, usually under the command of a lieutenant or lieutenant commander. But the navy's Ordnance Bureau was able very quickly to supply in quantity guns with bores in the 3- to 6-inch range for freighters and tankers. These were manned by smaller crews, usually a chief petty officer and about twenty seamen.

Obviously, the fleet could not be stripped of experienced spotters, trainers, and pointers to supply the burgeoning merchant marine, and there were nothing like enough trained gunnery officers available to command the number of crews needed. Seasoned chief petty officers—chief gunner's mates, chief boatswain's mates, and chief masters at arms, were drawn from the fleet, along with a decent nucleus of experienced seamen.

These were augmented with inexperienced crewmen from naval training stations ashore. They served and in the main excelled. The green men, most of whom were making their first voyage, gave good account of themselves and quickly became seasoned gunners.

The unfortunate *Aztec* was taken by surprise by the torpedo that sank her. This was by no means the standard armed guard experience.

☆

The Navajo's *Fourth of July*

[The steamer *Navajo* on 4 July 1917, was working slowly through a morning] mist in the English Channel when two shots, not in celebration of our national anniversary, broke the quiet. A submarine had seen the *Navajo's* superstructure, and as the mist broke away at the moment she was herself sighted about a mile distant. Then ensued a running chase in which the submarine fired forty rounds and the steamer twenty-seven. Only one of the submarine's shots took effect, striking under the port counter and causing a leak. The twenty-seventh shot from the *Navajo* hit and burst just forward of the enemy's conning tower, near the ammunition hoist, and caused a second explosion plainly heard on the ship. "The men who were on deck at the guns and had not jumped overboard," so reads the report, "ran aft, the submarine canted forward at an angle of almost 40 degrees, and the propeller could be plainly seen lashing the air." Then she plunged under. On the results of this action skeptical shore authorities would probably pass a doubtful verdict. "There was a submarine in the vicinity," they would say, "and she may have been injured." At all events, from then on the *Navajo* had a peaceful Fourth of July.

☆   (Westcott, "Sinkings," 107)

Ironically, the *Navajo* was destroyed by mishap after the gun damage to her stern plates was repaired. She made her way to a French port for repairs. After they were completed, she was bound for home when a fuel pipe exploded and set the ship on fire, which eventually caused her to be abandoned.

Official skepticism greeted virtually all reports of U-boat sinkings by merchant vessels. In this case it was not shared by officers of a destroyer that came to the *Navajo's* aid after the battle. When the *Navajo's* survivors reached home, her captain, J. F. MacDougall, and third officer, Edward Schafer, recounted the story of the battle at the request of a *New York Times* reporter.

☆

[Just after the submarine's shot that damaged the *Navajo's* stern, Schafer said,] "The Germans fired thirty more shots and then one of our gunners got home a shell, which struck the enemy well below the conning tower, and knocked the craft all to pieces. She went down stern first, just as the smoke of a British destroyer appeared on the horizon in answer to our call for assistance."

The officers of the destroyer examined the oily surface where the German craft had disappeared, and were satisfied, they told Captain MacDougall, that the U-boat had been sunk by the shell from the stern gun of the *Navajo.*

☆   *(New York Times,* 25 August 1917)

The *Luckenbach* 's Long Battle

A few months after the *Navajo's* memorable battle, and not far from its site, the U.S. freighter *J. L. Luckenbach* found herself in another extended battle with a U-boat. About daybreak, south of England's Isles of Scilly and steaming eastward for Le Havre, the *Luckenbach* passed a distant vessel on her port beam.

While the crews of both forward and after guns took their posts, Chief Master-at-Arms J. B. Trautner, commanding the armed guard, climbed into the freighter's rigging to get a better look. He saw what seemed to be a sail on the other craft; then he got a clearer look and realized it was a submarine. At that moment, the submarine opened fire on the *Luckenbach.*

The merchantman immediately replied with both guns. The sub's first shots fell about a half mile short; so did the *Luckenbach's.* The submarine closed a bit on the freighter, and Trautner asked the master of the *Luckenbach,* Arthur W. Street, to show the U-boat his stern. He turned away from the attacker at full speed, and ordered the radio man to send an SOS.

The submarine gained on the freighter and closed to about 2,000 yards. A shell from the submarine found the *Luckenbach's* forward deck on the port side and exploded down into the armed guard crew's quarters, started a fire there, and disabled the main line of the freighter's firefighting system.

A response to the SOS came from a U.S. destroyer sixty miles away. The USS *Nicholson* was helping screen an incoming convoy but could detach herself at once. She had more and bigger guns and was racing to the scene. The *Luckenbach* was sustaining more damage. Her main steam line was cut. A shell burst in the engine room, seriously wounding the first and third assistant engineers. The after gun was put out of commission, and her pointers dashed forward to alternate with their mates at the bow gun—which in all fired 167 rounds. The chief boatswain's mate, who had been spotting aft, now climbed atop the pilot house and spotted from there.

The *Luckenbach* was burning, listing, taking more water, but not yet sinking. Wireless signals crackled between the increasingly desperate freighter and the racing destroyer.

"How far are you away?"

"Two hours."

"Too late. Look for [life]boats."

"Don't surrender!"

"Never!"

A plume of smoke on the horizon grew into the speeding *Nicholson*, and she started firing as soon as she could see the submarine. A shell from either the destroyer or the freighter exploded in a solid hit on the sub's foredeck, and the *U-62* submerged and disappeared, having fired 225 shots at the hardy *Luckenbach*. The *Luckenbach* fired 202. She had been in the heat of battle four hours without a moment's surcease.

Remarkably, none of her crew, despite numerous injuries, was killed. The *Nicholson* escorted the *Luckenbach* to the safety of a nearby convoy bound for Le Havre. The armed guard crew was commended and Chief Master-at-Arms Trautner promoted to warrant officer. He had the grace to commend the merchant crew, albeit informally, for standing to their posts and passing ammunition to the constantly busy gunners.

So many men were injured, navy gunners and merchant seamen alike, that the assistant surgeon from the *Nicholson* stayed aboard the *Luckenbach,* along with medical corpsmen, to tend their wounds all the way into Le Havre.

When relations between the United States and Germany deteriorated to the point where they were finally severed, two vigorous actions were under study by U.S. statesmen. One was the arming of merchant ships. It was, as we have seen, dramatic and immediate.

The other took a bit longer but was of great value. That was the seizure of the numerous merchant vessels belonging to the Central Powers that were visiting U.S. ports when war was declared. Of particular importance were the great passenger liners, and the legal steps in taking them over for conversion to troop transports had to be accomplished hurriedly to prevent their crews from doing extensive sabotage to keep them out of U.S. service.

As it was, cylinders of reciprocating engines were smashed on many of the ships and some were significantly damaged. Repairs were effected on most of them within a few months, and this haul of big, fast ocean liners solved the military sea transport problem for the United States. (Some cargo vessels also were seized, but the really dramatic gain was in the seizure of the large passenger liners.)

Crowell and Wilson's monumental *How America Went to War* (1921) lists the major liner conversions (see table 1). Note that the list is headed by the *Vaterland*, the great pride of the German fleet, a 54,000-ton monster 904 feet long and capable of cruising at more than 27 knots (30 miles

TABLE 1. German Liners Converted to U.S. Troopships

Former names	Rechristened names	Date of first departure with troops
Vaterland	*Leviathan*	15 December 1917
President Lincoln	*President Lincoln*	19 October 1917
Cincinnati	*Covington*	19 October 1917
Koenig Wilhelm II	*Madawaska*	12 November 1917
Kronprinzessin Cecile	*Mt. Vernon*	19 October 1917
Grosser Kurfurst	*Æolus*	26 November 1917
Princess Irene	*Pocahontas*	8 September 1917
Neckar	*Antigone*	14 December 1917
Amerika	*America*	19 October 1917
President Grant	*President Grant*	26 December 1917
Hamburg	*Powhatan*	12 November 1917
George Washington	*George Washington*	4 December 1917
Kaiser Wilhelm II	*Agamemnon*	19 October 1917
Friedrich der Grosse	*Huron*	8 September 1917
Barbarossa	*Mercury*	4 January 1918
Rhein	*Susquehanna*	14 December 1917
Prinz Eitel Friedrich	*De Kalb*	14 June 1917
Martha Washington	*Martha Washington*	10 February 1918
Princess Alice	*Princess Matoika*	10 May 1918
Kronprinz Wilhelm	*Von Steuben*	19 October 1917

Source: Crowell and Wilson, *How America Went to War*, 342.

per hour in land-speed terms). Rechristened *Leviathan,* for years after the war she was the unquestioned queen of the seas.

☆

[Curiously enough, as Crowell and Wilson observe,] the Germans purposely damaged the machinery of their most magnificent vessel, the *Vaterland,* only a little. The Americans who surveyed the vessel surmised that this unexpected forbearance was due to ignorance and unfamiliarity with the machinery rather than to anything else. The *Vaterland* gave the German mariners their first experience with turbine engines, and when they tried to manage the big ship they found themselves in a pot of troubles. The vessel had floundered across the Atlantic on her last commercial trip and had limped into New York on three-eighths of her power.

☆ (Crowell and Wilson, *How America Went to War,* 342)

15 Coping with War at Sea

★★

Some crews were luckier than the *Luckenbach*'s, though to some degree lucky ships made their own luck. Consider the U.S. tanker *Silver Shell* steaming through that deadly hunting ground of the U-boats—the Mediterranean Sea—on 30 May 1917, when she was attacked by gunfire from a German submarine. The sub, in a long stern chase, had not yet drawn abeam of the tanker for a torpedo shot.

The senior wireless operator on the *Silver Shell* (a 5,605-ton tanker), who saw the battle from his wireless cabin "at the bullseye of the ship," published the following account in the *New York Times Magazine* for 8 July 1917.

★

U.S. Tanker Sinks U-Boat!

BY HAROLD T. MAPES

We had, altogether, a rather eventful trip on the *Silver Shell* from New York to Marseilles via Gibraltar and Oran, Algeria, 2,800 miles of which was through the extreme danger zone. We steered a course south of the Azores and from there on traversed a distance twice that of the regular steamer course in our maneuvers to keep out of the way of reported submarines. There were sixteen reported to me by wireless before we finally reached Marseilles. . . .

Out in the Atlantic (we were tossed about by a storm for three days), and a few days later we passed within a hundred feet of a submarine that was lying on the surface charging her storage batteries with her oil engines. For the next day's run she was plainly seen by the three watchers, and we could hear her engines running after we had lost her in the dark astern.

. . . A day later we also passed a wooden ship, bottom up, with a large hole in her side—grim evidence of what a torpedo could do. A few life preservers and a lifeboat were floating near, and nothing else.

We lay two days at Gibraltar, and while there an open boat was brought in with nine sailors, only two of whom were alive, and crazy as loons, having completely lost their memories.

The Mediterranean is a hotbed of submarines, twelve out of the sixteen reported to me being in those waters.

We lacked only a day and a half to complete our voyage when we encountered our next submarine. We sighted her about 6,000 yards off our starboard beam early in the afternoon of 30 May.

The alarm blast was sounded, and then the fun started. The course was changed to west, and the lifeboats were cast free and lowered to the main deck; the life belts were buckled on, and our small bundles of valuables thrown into the boats. Just then a shell from the submarine fell about a hundred yards short. The next one just missed the wireless cabin, falling into the ocean a hundred yards further on. Our 4-inch after gun had already opened up on them, our first seven shots falling nearly a thousand yards short of the submarine, even with the gun set at extreme elevation. [Warrant Officer] W. J. Clark, who commanded the armed guard on the *Silver Shell*, then knocked out the extreme elevation pin and gave her about 40 degrees. We then did better, dropping our shots close around the submarine.

They had 5-inch guns against our 4-inch ones, and to start with were outshooting us. The submarine was of the largest type, probably over three hundred feet long.

In the meantime they were making it very unpleasant for us. The shells would come screaming over our heads through the rigging and were bursting all around us. One of them had fallen short and not exploded, ricocheted right over the wireless cabin with only a couple of feet to spare.

I was sending out the SOS broadcast, giving our position, course, and speed, while Mr. Douglas, the junior operator, was strapping a life preserver on me.

I was listening under difficulties for an answer to our SOS call, as every time our after gun was fired, which was only twenty-five feet away from the wireless cabin, the concussion would knock my instruments out of adjustment, and the noise was deafening, along with the discharging of our gun and the exploding of the submarine shells.

The first answer was finally repeated from Algiers, and it had to be repeated a number of times because, apart from the noise, a Spanish ship was blocking our signals by repeatedly asking in Spanish: "What ship is that asking help?" She did not sign off, and it sounded like deliberate blocking, but finally I got it: "Help thirty-five miles northwest gunboat FQ." I then got into communication with gunboat FQ. She answered: "Coming as fast as possible."

From . . . the wireless cabin I could see the submarine [3,000 yards astern], plunging into a head sea, her gun crew hanging on every time she plunged. As her deck would be washed and they would be waist deep in the brine, they would load and fire between plunges. We could see the flash of their gun ten seconds before the shell would reach us, wondering in the meantime whether it would hit us or not—pleasant feeling I assure you, when one has about ten seconds to ponder over it at each shot.

On an oil tanker—boilers, engines, and wireless cabin—the vital parts of the ship are all right in the stern with the wireless cabin as the "bull's-eye." * To top it off, we had a cargo of more than a million gallons of gasoline. Nice position to be in, with a grand-stand seat in the "bull's-eye," straining your ears between explosions and gunfire for that weak answering signal that your SOS has been heard and that help is coming!

The firemen were below, making steam as they had never made it before, [and all three assistant engineers] trying to get the engine to turn up a few more revolutions. You sure have to hand it to them, as at any minute a shell might penetrate a boiler or the steam pipes, and they would all instantly be killed by the live steam or an explosion. They were getting 14 knots out of a ship that had never done better than 11 before.

William J. Clark, who had been a warrant officer on the U.S. battleship *Arkansas,* handled his guns and gunners like a veteran, and neither he nor his gunners showed any more nervousness or confusion than when they were shooting at barrels thrown overside out in the Atlantic on the way over for target practice, although [now] shrapnel was bursting close by on all sides, and they were in an exposed position, along with the engineers, firemen, and S. C. Harrison, the second mate, who was everywhere at once, lending a hand wherever needed: a quick, accurate thinker and a silent doer. They were the real heroes of the day.

The bos'n, also, who had got inside three suits of clothes, his Sunday ones on top, was seen a number of times brushing them off, and

---

* In later tankers, the wireless cabin adjoins the pilot house and bridge, amidships.

whenever a shell would come dangerously close he would let out a string of oaths and stop his work long enough to take a pinch of snuff.

Capt. J. Charlton, although crippled with rheumatism at the time, was on the bridge maneuvering his ship with precision and forethought. The mates and crew did good work, and there were only a few slackers to be found among them.

The submarine toward the last of the engagement was using shrapnel to clear our decks, and the shots were bursting all around and over the ship. She had closed in to about 2,300 yards, when we scored a hit aft of her conning tower. Her bow rose high in the air, and she sunk stern first, with her crew on deck. This was lucky for us, as she would have cleared our decks with her shrapnel in another fifteen minutes, and she would have probably shelled our lifeboats if we had been able to get away in them after the fight we had put up. She was unable to get in a position to torpedo us, thanks to the engineers and firemen.

The engagement lasted over an hour and a half; we fired thirty-five shots and they about forty, and it was the first authentic case of an American ship sinking a submarine by shellfire. We did not try to rescue any of her crew, as there were other submarines in the immediate vicinity that were advised as to our position by our SOS call, so it was up to us to get away as soon as possible. Luckily no one aboard was seriously hurt.

Shortly after the engagement I got a message that came in very weak, saying: "If possible steer southeast. Will meet you in an hour." This was a decoy message sent out by another submarine to lure us in her way, as I afterward could not get it confirmed. We had already been instructed not to heed messages sent out by ships that were not authorized or confirmed by a government land station.

At 7:05 P.M. gunboat FQ asked me our new position, which I gave her, and also details about the fight and sinking of the submarine. She wirelessed back, "Good work."

At 11:00 P.M. met gunboat FQ and exchanged messages by "Morse Lamp." We were instructed to proceed. Instead of thirty-five miles distant when SOS was sent out she probably was over a hundred miles away.

Next afternoon we arrived safely at Marseilles, France, the first American ship to make that port since war had been declared with Germany, and our blue-jackets wore the first American uniforms seen there; they attracted a great deal of attention. We will all probably receive prize money from the French government for sinking a submarine.

☆   (Mapes, "Wireless Man Tells," 7)

The U.S. press was eager to cover such stories when they came to light. Often only skimpy details were released. One victorious battle for a merchant ship first saw light of day through an unusual action by U.S. Secretary of the Navy Josephus Daniels—who also was a journalist and publisher of the Raleigh *News & Observer.* This account appeared on the front page of the *New York Times* of Sunday, 3 March 1917.

☆

Beat Off U-Boat in 2½-Hour Fight

WASHINGTON March 2—The story of an engagement lasting two and a half hours between a U.S. steamer and a German submarine, in which the U-boat was worsted, became known today through the action of the Secretary of the Navy in commending the chief petty officer of the U.S. Navy who was in command of the armed guard on the steamer: Chief Gunner's Mate Benjamin H. Groves is the man commended for zeal and efficiency in the performance of duty.

The engagement occurred on 13 January, when the steamer *Nyanza* encountered the submarine. It was 9:30 A.M. when the *Nyanza* saw a periscope about a thousand yards away and at the same time sighted a torpedo headed for the ship. The *Nyanza's* stern was swung clear in time to avoid the torpedo, and the *Nyanza* opened fire with the after gun. The submarine fell rapidly astern, then came to the surface, started her oil engines, and gave chase. At about 7,000 yards the U-boat opened fire with two guns, using shrapnel, and zigzagging in order to use both guns at the same time. This maneuver caused her to drop astern, but she came after the merchantman again, approaching to within 5,000 yards.

After a number of shots had fallen short the U-boat got the range, and the *Nyanza* was hit five times. One shot passed through the after-gun platform, through the wood shelter house and the iron deck, breaking a deck beam and passing out through the side of the ship. One shot exploded in the armed guard's messroom, wrecking it. Two shells exploded in a steam locomotive on deck, doing some damage. A shot hit the stern of the ship but did not go through.

"At about 11:15 the submarine had our range again," Groves says. "At the same time I had his range, and fired four shells quickly, causing him to come broadside and keel over, then suddenly disappear just as he had our range good. This leads me to think he did not quit from choice but from necessity."

"The engagement lasted two hours and thirty minutes. The *Nyanza* fired 92 rounds and the submarine approximately 200. The gun's crew throughout the engagement behaved coolly, doing their duty, and gaining experience, which I think will be manifested in the next attack. Three men of the gun's crew had their clothes torn more or less by the shrapnel. One engineer cadet was wounded and taken to the hospital on arrival in port."

The Navy Department's announcement of commendation says: "The promptness with which the periscope was picked up and the accuracy of fire denotes an efficiency on the part of the armed guard for which Groves, as commanding officer, was responsible."

★
                                    (*New York Times*, "Beat Off U-Boat," 1)

Victorious gunfights by such ships as the *Silver Shell* and the *Nyanza* were front page news because of their rarity. But official skepticism abounded. Sometimes the scoffers were the U.S. Navy; this time they were British. As Crowell and Wilson point out,

★

the master of the *Silver Shell*, John T. Charlton, gave further details in his report: "The speed of the *Silver Shell* had been raised to fourteen knots, but the submarine continued to gain. At about 7:00 P.M. one of the shots of the steamer struck the submarine flush, hitting the ammunition on the deck. There was a flash of flame, and within a minute she had disappeared."

An American naval officer at Toulon who investigated the engagement reported: "At the prefecture there is no report of any submarine being sighted in that vicinity since the engagement of the *Silver Shell*. There is no doubt in my mind but that the submarine was sunk."

Men have been hanged on evidence flimsier than this, but it was not proof with the admiralty. This was one of the first U.S. encounters with a submarine, and, if we accept the evidence as conclusive, the first U-boat sunk by Americans.

★   (Crowell and Wilson, *How America Went to War*, 519)

Another freighter–U-boat battle was even more remarkable for the way the merchantman reversed roles from target to attacker.

★

[On 4 June 1917, the armed guard of the U.S. freight] steamer *Norlina*, owned by the Garland Steamship Company, Baltimore, succeeded in all probability in sinking an enemy submarine as the result of an exploit, which, for audacity, ranks high. It was just before the days of cargo convoying. The *Norlina*, having discharged her cargo in a British port, was proceeding westward around the northern coast of Ireland in company with three British cargo vessels, all armed and steaming together for mutual protection. About five o'clock in the afternoon the group encountered U-boats. One of the British ships on the flank of the impromptu convoy staged a half-hour gun duel with an enemy submarine, without particular damage to either side. It ended when the U-boat submerged. Twenty minutes later another ship of the group, the British cargo vessel *Manchester Port*, broadcasted an SOS proclaiming that she was being attacked by a submarine directly off her stern. The armed guard of the *Norlina* were at supper; but, realizing that danger was imminent, they left their places at the mess table and set a close watch at the guns. About 6:30 the *Manchester Port* wirelessed that she had beaten off the U-boat and was not damaged.

The trouble now seemed to be over; but the armed guard still scrutinized the surface of the water, and the *Norlina* kept going at top speed. Suddenly a periscope appeared off to port, and almost immediately one of the gunners sighted a torpedo and shouted to the bridge, "Here she comes! Torpedo port side!" The chief officer ordered the helm put down hard to starboard, but it was too late. The torpedo was near the surface, its propeller kicking up a wake of whitecaps and its outline so plain that every petrified watcher on deck could see its red head and its tapering ten feet of length.

The *Norlina* was not only unloaded, but she was carrying so little ballast that she rolled heavily in the sea. Her empty, echoing steel tank of a hull formed, in effect, a gigantic bass drum; and as the half-ton torpedo came into her at forty or fifty miles per hour, it was as if the drum had been struck by the hammer of Thor. The boom was so loud that every person aboard the *Norlina* assumed without question that there had been an explosion, and at once the master gave the command to abandon ship. Some of the crew of foreigners fell into a panic, which was quieted only at the point of a gun held by one of the mates. Presently all boats were safely launched, and the entire ship's company left the supposedly sinking vessel, except her three navigating officers and Chief Boatswain's Mate O. J. Gullickson, commander of the armed guard, and his assistant. The U-boat commander observed the lifeboats leaving the *Norlina*, assumed that the ship was sinking, and started away at full speed on the surface to try to bag the other three ships, which had now turned and were racing away for dear life.

But the *Norlina* was not sinking. She was not even leaking, as those who remained on board soon discovered when they began sounding the bilges and inspecting the holds and engine rooms. The thing that could happen only once in ten thousand times had actually occurred. The torpedo had not exploded when it struck: it had bounded back off the hull and sunk.

Gullickson blew his whistle, summoning back the gunners. They came swarming up the Jacob's ladders and raced to their two guns. The submarine was now about a mile away and speeding toward the other ships. The engine-room force went back to their stations, the ship rapidly gained headway, the captain steering directly at the retreating periscope, and the *Norlina* opened fire. Meanwhile the U-boat commander had observed what was going on, and at the first shot the submarine turned and came tearing back again toward the U.S. vessel, evidently determined this time to make a good job of the sinking. The fighters on the *Norlina* gave credit to the courage of the U-boat commander for heading directly into the barrage of shell from the guns of the tanker. The marksmanship of the gun crews was excellent, and all the shots were falling close to the periscope. The U-boat came on intrepidly, reducing the distance finally to six hundred yards. Meanwhile the captain of the *Norlina* had stopped the engines and steered the ship so that it lay broadside to the submarine, a dangerous position, but one which allowed both guns full play. The war diary of Chief Boatswain's Mate Gullickson describes the denouement: "Suddenly shot from forward gun hit just in front of periscope, making it submerge and a light blue smoke come up from astern of the submarine. Periscope appeared again, range now six hundred yards, when a shot from the after gun hits it square on the water line, making small bits of steel fly, which may have been bursting of shell, and causing a great commotion of bubbles, etc., in the water."

Another observer on the *Norlina*, the wireless operator, reported to the owners as follows: "When about six hundred yards off our starboard quarter, a shell from our forward gun hit her and she submerged. Again she appeared, and our after gun hit her and blew away her periscope. Another shot from our forward gun fell right on top of her. There was a shower of black specks rising high in the air, followed by a great commotion of bubbles of water and a light blue smoke arising from the stern of the submarine. Our crew, which were lined up against the starboard rail watching the battle, gave a hearty American cheer when the submarine disappeared.

"The *Norlina* fired nineteen shots in all. One of the gunners afterward said we ought to have given them two more and make it twenty-one shots, the presidential salute."

This was another instance of a probable U-boat sinking not listed in the official record.

☆   (Crowell and Wilson, *How America Went to War,* 519–22)

The depredations of German U-boats were all too normal and all too frequent. Convoying freighters and tankers was a logical response to each month's new reports of staggering tonnage losses.

Although convoying freighters with the protection of heavily armed warships was a device as ancient as navies, effective convoys required training, discipline, and practice. These qualities do not leap to mind when the topic is the characteristic attributes of merchant skippers.

☆

A vociferous objection to the convoy plan came from the British merchant sea captains. It was all very well, they maintained, for naval officers, accustomed as they were to squadron maneuvers at sea, to talk about convoying; but as for merchant ships, they would never be able to sail in groups as was planned, without an accompaniment of collisions whose aggregate of destruction would be greater than the depredations of the U-boats themselves. The British merchant mariners, and those of other nations, too, were later astonished by the proficiency which they acquired in formation sailing.

Until the last few weeks of the war, the British directed and commanded all the American cargo convoys, including the convoys of ships carrying supplies to the A.E.F. We organized the American troop convoys ourselves from the very first expedition; we grouped the troopships, laid down the rules for their protection, escorted them across the ocean, and protected them in the submarine zone. But the convoying of our cargo ships, whether those ships carried naval or civilian crews, we left to hands more expert in ocean shipping than ours. In 1917 there was just one institution on earth competent to conduct such an immense undertaking as the administration of world marine traffic as a unit, and that institution was the British admiralty. For many months, U.S. participation in the management of convoying consisted in sanctioning the plans of the admiralty and furnishing armed protection for the ship groups. The U.S. cruisers and destroyers assigned to the service received their orders from British officers.

Such an arrangement could not be permanently acceptable to the United States.   .

☆   (Crowell and Wilson, *How America Went to War*, 456)

And so late in the war the U.S. Navy was ready to start implementing its own system of convoy management for U.S. merchant ships. It demanded organization, planning, attention to detail, and luck.

☆

Before a group sailed, the master of every cargo ship in it received oral notification of any special procedure to be followed during that voyage; and all masters were also rehearsed in the standard rules of convoying and of self-protection, until the group commodore was convinced that every mariner under his command was thoroughly indoctrinated in them. This instruction was given in that marine institution of notable memory, the convoy meeting.

The convoy meeting was held on the morning of the day before a group was to sail. All masters of merchant ships assigned to the group, and also the commanders of the naval vessels in the group's escort, met at the office of the port convoy officer. On the wall hung a large blackboard. On this the convoy officer diagramed the group formation, placing each ship in it just as it was to proceed at sea, so that each mariner present might see with his own eyes exactly what vessels were to be in front of him and what ones behind, and where he was to sail in relation to his neighbors to starboard and port. Each captain received a sealed letter containing the group route instructions. This he was not to open unless he became hopelessly separated from the group; but in that event he might open it and attempt to reach the destroyer rendezvous with the group. He also received a slip of paper telling him the hour and place for the group to assemble for the voyage.

Officers of the embryonic U.S. convoy office sat in the convoy meetings to look out for the interests of American vessels and to make sure that all American ship masters in the group were familiar with the procedure.

The chief radio operators of the ships in the group also attended the convoy meetings. To them the full radio procedure at sea was read and thoroughly explained, no matter how familiar it was to every one of them. The system took nothing for granted. Several radio codes and ciphers were used. The merchant ships in the convoy used the code of the so-called mercantile tables. If, however, any merchant ship wished to communicate with a naval officer or vessel, it used another secret system known as the convoy cipher. The rules required each commodore to carry with him always a small library of war manuals, consisting of the various code books and maritime instruction books, and to be familiar with the contents of these documents. Each mercantile captain was ordered to have with him at sea a copy of the mercantile convoy instructions, the Allied signal manual, the wireless instructions for merchant vessels, and the mercantile code tables. Masters of British vessels carried, in addition to these documents, a publication called *War Instructions for British Merchant Ships.* The U.S. Navy issued to all U.S. ship captains a document almost identical in text and illustration, entitled *War Instructions for United States Merchant Vessels.*

The governments took unusual precautions to prevent any of the secret convoy publications from falling into the hands of the enemy. The printed *War Instructions* were bound in sheet lead covered with buckram. The lead cover would sink the book if it were tossed overboard. Every copy of the *War Instructions for United States Merchant Vessels* was registered and numbered, and every man who received one was required to return it to the Navy Department or give good evidence that it had been completely destroyed. After the armistice the Navy Department incinerated all copies of this document except one, which [was] retained for possible use in some future submarine war.

Each master was expected to provide for his ship a canvas bag to contain all confidential books and papers. This bag was weighted with lead at one end and was perforated with eyelets to ensure rapid sinking; moreover, it laced shut, so that there was no cover to open and allow secret papers to float out. U-boat commanders sometimes boarded captured ships or searched the surface of the waters to discover anything of value. Therefore the *War Instructions* forbade ships' officers to write down any confidential information on their vessels' logs. If a ship were fatally torpedoed or about to be captured, it was the master's first duty, and a duty not to be delegated to anyone else, to burn the sealed letter containing the group route instructions.

These and many other matters of operations were rehearsed at the convoy meetings. Indeed, our government regarded the convoy meeting as so important a part of convoying that it permitted no U.S. vessel to sail in a group unless its master had attended the meeting or unless a convoy officer had personally instructed and examined him in the procedure to be followed at sea.

☆   (Crowell and Wilson, *How America Went to War*, 469–71)

However, by the time all the procedures were in place and masters were beginning to get reasonably comfortable in following them, the war was over.

U-boats and mines were hardly the only threat to Allied war cargoes. Germany's surface raiders worked serious damage on merchant ships from the beginning. They were playing exactly the same game as the Confederate raiders, notably the CSS *Alabama,* played in the Civil War— indeed almost retracing the wakes of those Rebel raiders.

The lot of the captured mariner almost always included boredom, often camaraderie with fellow-captives, terror perhaps as often, and at least occasionally comedy.

As noted in chapter 13, the first U.S. freighter sunk in World War I, the four-masted ship *William P. Frye,* was done in by a raider. In January 1915 the *Frye* was southbound off Brazil, en route to Australia, when she encountered the *Prinz Eitel Friedrich,* a passenger liner converted into a commerce raider. The *Eitel Friedrich* had rounded the Horn into the Atlantic after working the South Pacific off Chile. When the raider encountered the *Frye,* laden with wheat and bound for Australia, its boarding crew set out to dump her cargo and let the windjammer proceed. But $300,000 worth of wheat proved too much to shovel overboard, so the *Frye* was sent to the bottom.

A few months and many sinkings later, the *Eitel Friedrich* was in need of repairs and entered the neutral U.S. port complex at Hampton Roads, where she was promptly interned. When the United States seized interned German ships after declaring war in 1917, the *Eitel Friedrich* became the auxiliary cruiser USS *De Kalb.* Exactly the same fate befell another raider a few weeks later when the *Kronprinz Wilhelm,* also a converted liner, sought repairs, was interned, and later became the auxiliary cruiser USS *Von Steuben.*

The *Karlsruhe,* a German cruiser, was one of the most dreaded raiders and had sunk seventeen Allied ships in the South Atlantic when her magazines exploded mysteriously off Barbados and destroyed the ship. The

The German raider *Emden*, shown here in Manila Bay after the war, sank sixteen U.S. merchantmen in the Indian Ocean. (Photograph by P1C J. L. Highfill, USN, from National Archives, RG 19N, JN 5046)

cruiser *Emden* roamed the Indian Ocean, sinking sixteen cargo steamers and two light warships, in addition to conducting the damaging bombardment of a number of shore targets. She stopped but released one U.S. freighter carrying an obviously neutral cargo. Another Indian Ocean raider, the *Königsberg*, was discovered by Allied warships at the mouth of an East African river, where she was penned up for the duration.

The *Möwe* (Gull), under the dashing nobleman *Graf* (Count) Nikolaus Paul Richard zu Dohna-Schlodien, sank fifteen Allied merchantmen on her first cruise in 1915 and went back the next year to sink six more in the North and South Atlantic.

Two other major surface raiders of the Kaiser's navy are the subject of this chapter. The skipper of the less important militarily was, like Dohna-Schlodien in his *Möwe*, both titled and dashing and gallant as well. Indeed he was briefly assigned to be Dohna-Schlodien's gunnery officer on *Möwe's* second cruise when fate or luck switched him to a dream assignment, command of a sailing ship that was to be a German raider.

The man was *Graf* Hugo von Luckner, once almost a ne'er-do-well, and the heir to a distinguished title from the time of Frederick the Great. He had run away to sea as a lad, in the days of sail, and later steadied a bit, studied, and became a lieutenant in the German Navy, a *Kapitänleutnant*.

His ship, to become the fabled *Seeadler* (Sea Eagle), was an old iron-hulled windjammer with a history of switched nationalities that was almost comical. A three-master built in Scotland, the 245-foot *Pass of Balhama* had sailed the seven seas in the British merchant navy for a generation. A U.S. shipping company bought her and in the spring of 1915 loaded her with cotton and sent her off to Russia's arctic port of Archangel.

The *Pass of Balhama* encountered the British naval blockade off Norway, and the boarding officer, despite papers showing she was destined for the Russian ally and not the German enemy, declared her a British prize. Over the protests of her master, the windjammer was sent, under guard, to the Orkney Islands off Scotland's northern tip.

On the way there the next day, the German submarine *U-36* stopped her. Because her papers declared her cargo as destined for Russia, which was at war with Germany, the U-boat seized her as a German prize. She was a sturdy vessel, and the Germans decided to make a raider of her by reinforcing her, refitting her completely, and arming her. Her holds were converted into extensive sleeping accommodations, and a powerful auxiliary gasoline engine was added that could propel her into the wind at ten knots. Her sails and rigging were replaced and augmented as necessary, and a crew that had trained in sail was gradually assembled.

The *Pass of Balhama* was rechristened the *Seeadler,* and with Luckner in command, put to sea disguised as an innocent Norwegian sailing ship (Luckner spoke Norwegian). She ran the British blockade successfully and escaped to the Southern Hemisphere, where the count roved across the sea lanes of the Pacific and Atlantic, astonishing his early victims by baring his well-disguised 4-inchers and firing a shot across the bows of his prey.

Luckner's fame spread quickly, mostly because despite the ubiquitous Allied propaganda about the brutality of the German Huns and barbarians, he was conspicuously courteous to his captives, even gallant to the point of flamboyance. He was chivalrous. And his picturesque exploits made "good press." The U.S. news media made him famous as "the Sea Devil."

After the war, Luckner wrote an autobiographical account of his experiences, which was edited and translated into breezy English by Lowell Thomas, the author, lecturer, and pioneer radio commentator. President

Wilson sent Thomas to Europe after the war at the head of a mission to compile a history of the Great War, and there he struck up a lifelong friendship with the Sea Devil.

In the book, the count recalled a somewhat twisted tale of romance that resulted from one of his captures. It is reprinted with the kind permission of Lowell Thomas Jr. from his father's *Count Luckner, the Sea Devil.*

☆

We captured three American ships in these waters, the *A. B. Johnson,* the *R. C. Slade,* and the *Manila.* Our prisoners numbered forty-five men, one woman, and a pet opossum. The captains were not half so astonished and bewildered as the former captains when we unmasked ourselves as a buccaneer. They knew that the sailing shipraider was abroad. So we were deprived of some of our former amusement of astounding and befuddling officers and crews by suddenly hoisting the German flag, unmasking our cannon, firing a machine gun into their rigging, and similar pleasantries. Everything went off according to routine. However, we ran into a most intricate complication. We had expected the complications of war and piratical strategy. That was part of the game. But now we were faced with a new and tender complication, a romantic complication.

"He's got his wife along," Boarding Officer Preiss informed me.

He referred to the captain of one of the ships. Indeed, we had noticed a woman aboard the captured ship.

The skipper in question presently introduced me to his helpmate, and a knockout she was, pretty, petite, and—well, just a bit roguish.

"By Joe," I thought, "the skippers of these days are marvelous fellows. Where do they get these swell-looking wives? When I was in the forecastle, it was different."

In those days, the skipper's wife was something to run away from, usually fat, usually savage, and always sloppily dressed. I thought of all the windjammer captains under whom I had sailed, and I couldn't think of one who had a wife that looked like a chorus girl. Well, times do change! There was the captain we had captured in the Atlantic who had such a pleasant little bride, and now here was this skipper and his sprightly beauty. . . .

Aboard the *Seeadler* we greeted the pretty little lady with great cordiality. Our former fair company had been so pleasant that we anticipated another similar brightening of the dull monotony aboard. The monotony was indeed broken somewhat! But in a decidedly different way than we had expected. The captain had not been long aboard before he took me aside and made an awkward and somewhat embarrassed confession. He had been thinking things over.

"Count," he said, "in your reports you may say something about my having my wife along."

"Yes," I replied.

"Well, by Joe," he continued, "I wish you wouldn't say anything about it. Don't say anything about my having a wife along. My real wife might find it out, and then there would be hell to pay."

"Oho," I exclaimed, "so that's the way the wind blows, eh?"

"I said she was my wife," he continued lamely, "because I thought it might help to save her from your sailors. But I don't want my wife to find it out."

"All right, Captain," I said, "I won't report it, and I won't let my officers or crew know anything about it. That will be best. Treat the girl as your wife. I will keep my mouth shut, and you keep your mouth shut."

It was a difficult point of morals aboard ship. If the sailors found out that the girl was not the captain's wife but only a kind of stowaway, they would lose all respect for her, and there was no telling what they might try to do. Sailors are not angels, but usually, in fact, a lot of rogues, but they are highly respectable. They have a very fine code of honor, and a woman who is off the line is simply off the line to them. Certainly, I did not want them to know that the captain's wife was not the captain's wife.

After the *R. C. Slade*, the next ship we captured was the *Manila*. Her skipper turned out to be a friend of the captain of the . . . and all of his family.* I told him that the captain of the . . . had his wife along and introduced him to the girl. He laughed so hard he nearly fell over. He wanted to tell the joke all around. It was awkward for a moment, but I got the two men aside and talked earnestly to them.

"We must be gentlemen in this matter," I said. "She is a girl. We are men. We must protect her. The sailors must not know about it. You must both keep mum and tell nobody."

They both promised.

---

*Count Luckner omitted the name of the philandering captain's ship.

Everything went all right until the second captain took a shine to the girl, too. It was funny business. She kind of liked him. I kept an eye on the whole affair and saw what was happening. Here was more worry and trouble. I took the two captains aside and said to them: "I don't care what arrangements you two fellows make with your fair playmate, but it has got to be kept quiet. The sailors must think that she is the wife of the captain of the . . . and that the captain of the *Manila* is only a friend of the family."

They made some kind of change, I believe. I never could figure just how it was. I never was much good at mathematics or at figuring out anything, for that matter. At any rate, they kept it quiet. The captain of the *Manila* was married, too, and he didn't want anything of the complicated romance to get around either.

I had come to expect my captains to be good company. Our former captains' club had been one of the most delightful social organizations ever formed. These two sentimental skippers, however, were not much good for comradeship. It was difficult to get together with them for a pleasant chat or game of cards. They were always thinking about the girl, and, although they were old friends, their feelings toward each other had become slightly strained. There is something about the air down there in the South Seas, I guess.

★　　　　　　　　　　　　　　　　(Thomas, *Count Luckner*, 218–21)

Count Luckner was captured in 1918 and sat out the remaining months of the war in New Zealand. He was the object of considerable worldwide opprobrium for a time when he was accused of having sunk the SS *Wairuna* with all her passengers and crew. In truth, the ship had been sunk by the steam raider *Wolf*, under *Kapitänleutnant* Karl Nerger. And Nerger, after his fashion, had taken the *Wairuna*'s entire complement safely aboard the *Wolf*.

Nerger's 5,000-ton raider destroyed a total of Allied shipping in excess of 150,000 tons during the war, hanging mainly in southern latitudes and cruising endlessly. He logged a record 64,000 miles without venturing once into any port. He drew his coal and food and all necessities from his victims. He took their crews on board the *Wolf* and held them until circumstances permitted him to set them adrift near a neutral shore.

Sometimes this took many, many months. Such was the fate of the

American bark *Beluga* and of the men, woman, and little girl that sailed aboard her from San Francisco six weeks after the United States declared war on Germany. Her master, Capt. John S. Cameron, related his family's remarkable adventure as captives of Nerger and for a long time of his brutish lieutenant. Major agents of their eventual escape, improbably enough, were the little girl's wails and a misplaced kewpie doll.

(The story appeared in four installments in *Sunset* in August–November 1918. With the generous cooperation of that magazine, it is abridged here.)

☆

The Sea Wolf*'s Prey*

BY CAPT. JOHN S. CAMERON

We sailed from San Francisco in the little bark *Beluga*, on 15 May 1917, with a cargo of 15,000 cases of benzine, for Sydney, Australia. Seldom have I gone to sea under more favorable circumstances. A tight little vessel, a good deep-water crew of Scandinavian sailor men, plenty of good wholesome provisions, and a cook who knew his business. Added to this was the pleasure of having my wife and our little 6-year-old Juanita along. My wife, an Australian by birth, had not been home for ten years and she was naturally in the highest spirits. . . . We all settled down for a quiet and uneventful passage. . . .

[Crossing the equator west of] the Fiji Islands, I was hoping that when I ran out of the southeast trades I would get a favorable wind and cut close by the southern end of New Caledonia. . . . Two days of favorable wind and this story would never have been written. But unfavorable conditions forced me to the southward and into the regular sailing vessel route. . . .

On 9 July, I was having some work done aloft on one of the masts. About four bells in the afternoon, Fritz, a Norwegian sailor who was working aloft shouted down: "Smoke, oh, on the port beam. . . ." On the horizon to the south I could make out the smoke of a steamer . . . coming in our direction. . . . I shouted down the cabin skylight to my wife.

"Mamie," I called, "come on deck and see the steamer. . . ." My wife and Juanita scampered on deck and watched the other vessel with interest. It soon became evident that the steamer was going to pass close to us.

"Is there a chance of her speaking us?" [she asked].

"It's just possible," I said.

"Then we're going below to change our frocks," said she. "It won't do for Juanita to meet strangers at sea in her overalls, looking like a boy. . . ."

Mr. Buckert, my chief officer, came along to where I was standing. "Can you make her out?" he asked.

"She's either a British or a Jap tramp," I answered. "Have a look," and I handed him the binoculars. After studying her for a while he said: "By God, captain, I don't know her nationality, but she carries the largest crew I've ever seen!"

I snatched the glasses out of his hand. Sure enough; by that time her rails both forward and aft were black with men in the regulation men-of-war jumpers. . . .

Suddenly she changed her course, heading to pass directly under my stern. At the same moment she broke out the German imperial navy ensign at her jackstaff aft. At her signal yard amidships she showed the letters "G-T-E," [international signal code meaning] "Heave to and I will send a boat on board." I was given time, perhaps two minutes, to read this signal. Then the steamer dropped her bulwarks forward, uncovering her guns, and fired a shot across the *Beluga's* bow. . . . Not till then did I fully understand that my little vessel had been stopped by a German raider in the South Pacific, almost 15,000 miles from the war zone. . . .

Against the wheelhouse my wife was leaning, her arms around Juanita, her face as white as their fresh dresses. . . . I knew she was thinking of what she had read concerning the German atrocities in Belgium, the barbarities practiced on women and children in the invaded regions. . . .

Alongside was a small motor launch crowded with heavily armed German bluejackets. A young lieutenant came to the quarterdeck, saluted, and asked in excellent English, with an American accent: "Are you the captain of this vessel?"

I replied affirmatively. After another question or two about ports of departure, time of passage, and similar matters he formally took charge of the ship, had his men haul down the stars and stripes—they saved the flag and the company's burgee as trophies—and had our crew searched for weapons. The raiders had brought twenty pairs of handcuffs with them, but they were not needed. Neither did they use the bombs they had brought to blow the ship to pieces with.

They intended to blow up the *Beluga* immediately, but when the nature of the cargo was wigwagged to the commander of the *Wolf*, which was the name of the raider, he decided to take three hundred cases of the benzine for use in the hydroplane the raider carried. . . .

[The Germans searched the vessel, listing everything worth taking to the *Wolf*. Captain Cameron found Lieutenant Zelasko a decent chap, who had served on merchant vessels, including one Cameron had sailed in. He had won the Iron Cross at Antwerp. He assured the captain that his family would receive the best care possible aboard the *Wolf*. Learning that the raider was manned by ex–merchant mariners cheered the Camerons considerably. Captain Schmell, chief officer of the *Wolf*, told the family, "We are not the Huns you probably think we are."]

"I am very sorry that the *Beluga* had a woman and child aboard," [Nerger said later]. "Had I known that such was the case I would have passed right on. But, once my vessel had revealed herself to you as a raider, I had to protect myself. We are now compelled to keep you prisoners until we can land you at a place where your release will not jeopardize the safety of our vessel and crew. In the meantime I will endeavor to make you as comfortable as possible under the circumstance."

Our proposed quarters did not suit him. He ordered that we three be given one of the officer's staterooms on the berth deck, remarking that we would have the freedom of our side of the deck so long as I continued to mind my business and did not talk to the sailors. Otherwise I would have to join the other prisoners in their quarters, well named the "Hell Hole."

The Spectacular End of the Beluga

Late that afternoon the man who later was my orderly came in with cotton batting to put in our ears, as the *Beluga* was to be sunk by gun fire. I was granted permission to watch her sink.

They fired nineteen shells at her and eighteen of them were clean misses—rotten shooting, as the target was only two and a half miles off. The nineteenth shell hit her amidships. The *Beluga* burst into flames, and the benzine cargo exploded, making one of the most wonderful sights I have ever seen. The calm sea for miles around was covered with burning petrol, an occasional cat's paw of wind causing this flaming oil to run in various directions, opening paths of black water here and there in the red flames. When the spars fell out of the ship, the splash threw the blazing oil high in the air in great sheets. Even the Germans were impressed with the spectacle. For some time the beauty of the sight caused me to forget that it was our little home that was burning.

There were a great many satisfied "a-ahs" from the German crew as the ship disappeared; a general feeling of satisfaction among them. For myself, I am afraid there was a tear in my eye, and all that I can wish these destroyers of good, honest ships is that sometime when they are standing around with empty bellies waiting for a chance to earn a living as a sailor, they may think of how they smiled when they sunk these ships. I can understand a landsman sinking a ship and thinking it a joke, but a sailor, to my mind, should feel sad at seeing the end of an honest vessel, whether she belong to friend or enemy. . . .

✩   (Cameron, "The Sea Wolf's Prey")

The *Wolf* was formerly a freighter of the Hansa Line, of 6,728 gross tons, single screw, equipped with wireless. She had two Sampson posts on the poop and four sets of cargo booms, one pair of which disguised a gun. There were three lifeboats. Painted all black, she had no distinguishing marks.

The *Wolf* carried two 6-inch guns, one forward and the other on the poop, and four 4.7-inchers, two forward and two aft. The rails at the guns were hinged to drop down before action. She was further armed with four torpedo tubes, two forward and two aft, and four machine guns on the boat deck that could control the decks and the prisoners' quarter aft.

Her crew of 375 men included the commander, one lieutenant commander, three senior and six junior lieutenants, two surgeons, and twelve warrant officers. She had mine experts, plus wireless and signal men, and a code expert. She seemed to have mechanics representing almost every trade and apparently an inexhaustible supply of materials for making repairs or new additions to her equipment.

The hydroplane which the raider carried, "the Bird," met with an accident that demolished wings and pontoons and cracked all six cylinders. The *Bird* appeared a total wreck, but after a few days the mechanics had her ready for duty again.

The *Wolf*'s triple-expansion engine was very fuel-efficient, and gave her a top speed of 11½ knots per hour, while consuming only twenty-eight tons of coal per diem.

☆

The commander of the *Wolf, Korvettenkapitän* Nerger, of the Imperial German Navy, was a man of probably thirty-five years of age, of moderate height and slim build. He was immaculate in all things pertaining to his person and a strict discipliniarian. I was in Commander Nerger's quarters one day. I had visited him to thank him for the courtesy he had extended to my family and to myself and found him a very agreeable man to talk to, a thorough gentleman and apparently anxious to do anything he could to make our lot bearable. . . .

Yet Commander Nerger was a man "all alone." He kept absolutely to himself; he took no man into his confidence. No man ever knew an hour ahead what his plans were. . . . On the 15-month cruise of the *Wolf*, Nerger was in full charge and ran his vessel as a one-man ship. . . . In the five months I was on the *Wolf*, I do not think I saw him on the berth deck more than a dozen times and then only on an inspection trip of some kind. He always had the appearance of having just stepped out of a band-box, he was so immaculate in his dress. I was told by his officers that Nerger never gets excited, always remains cool under all circumstances. They tell a story of his being in command of a light cruiser in the battle off the Dogger Bank, and throughout this engagement he calmly passed back and forth on the bridge, with a cigar in his mouth, giving his orders as calmly as if at some gun practice or maneuver. His officers and men respected him, which to my mind is a good enough recommendation. . . .

One afternoon I asked Commander Nerger for permission to talk to some of the men.

"It isn't healthy," I told him, "for a man to sit around all day and part of the night and not say a word to anybody."

He laughed. "One can get used to it," he said. I knew he referred to himself. "But you needn't be so lonesome. You may walk around and talk some to the men on deck. But on no account are you to talk to any of the prisoners taken before you came aboard. . . ."

Thereafter I could hold short conversations with a good many members of the crew, and before long I had practically the run of the ship. But I had been on board for some time before I got a chance to sneak down below aft and see what the prisoners' quarters were like and manage a talk with some of the men. What I saw that day fairly sickened me, and I'm not squeamish. I had been fearful for the treatment that would be given my wife and child. Now I saw that they had been the means of saving me from cruel hardship.

Prisoners' Quarters: The Hell Hole

The prisoners' quarters on the *Wolf* were located aft in the main cargo hold, . . . reached by means of a narrow ladder only, [built so] that not more than two persons could pass up while one came down, thus guarding against . . . escape.

Over the entrance . . . was strung a heavy iron hatch or cover, in such a manner that it could be dropped into place instantaneously by one of the guards, [effectively closing] the only exit from the quarters where there were two hundred prisoners confined. Also the closing of this hatch would cut off nearly one half the air supply, so [when] the *Wolf* was passing through some kind of danger, the suffering in the hold, from lack of air, was intense.

Even under normal conditions the air supply was inadequate. It was probably 8:20 P.M. when I was there, and I would judge the temperature to have been between 118 and 120 degrees Fahrenheit, and the reek of breath and bodies was something awful. . . . I should judge that from one-quarter to three-eighths of an inch of sweat was on the floor, and when the vessel rolled there would be a thin scum of liquid running from side to side.

The walls and ceiling were literally running water, which was caused by the moisture drawn from the bodies of the men and by the hot iron sides of the ship and the deck overhead. Combine stale tobacco smoke with this atmosphere, and it was a wonder to me that a human being could exist in it.

At this time everybody was herded into the one compartment—captains, mates, engineers, foremen, sailors, cooks, and flunkies, all together. There were niggers, Turks, Greeks, and Japanese. At night everybody slept in hammocks and during the day these hammocks were "made up" and piled away in one corner, this leaving enough room for several rough plank tables and benches to be set up.

There were no lockers or any compartments where a man could put his spare clothing or shaving gear. Therefore no man's gear was safe from theft. A man who didn't have a shirt would steal one from a man who had two; this made it impossible for a man to have any more clothes than what he stood in. Later on, many of the men were given empty cases or boxes and would fix them up to keep spare gear in.

Certain squads of men would take turns in keeping these quarters clean, the whole place being thoroughly scrubbed out three times a week. I mean "thoroughly" in every sense of the word. Everything movable excepting the clothing boxes would be taken on deck, then the room scrubbed with heavy brushes and sand; next the table and benches would be scoured with sand and canvas, the hammocks scrubbed, and the various tin dishes used for food would be scoured bright. After everything was dry they would be put back in place, and the prisoner officer would make an inspection. It was very seldom he found anything to complain of, as the men seemed to welcome this housecleaning; it gave them something to do and occupied their time. Reading material was very scarce, so the time passed very slowly.

There was supposed to be a regular daily routine, but owing to the many interruptions—such as gun practice, fire drill, boarding drill, and drills with small arms—this routine was not always carried out. At 5:30 A.M. the prisoners were awakened and by 6 o'clock all the hammocks were made up and stowed away. Then the tables were set up and the table laid for breakfast. At 7 o'clock the squad flunkies would get their gear ready, and promptly at 7:20 breakfast would be ready.

Immediately [afterward] they would wash the dishes and give the quarters their regular daily clean up. Usually during the forenoon, after their work was done, the prisoners would be allowed to go up on deck and enjoy the fresh air. Dinner at 12:30 noon, coffee 3:30 P.M., and supper at 6:30. Very seldom was anybody allowed on deck after coffee. At 8:00 P.M. all lights were extinguished excepting three, one over the steps at the exit and two at the back of the quarters.

The distribution of the fresh water was also very poor. Each prisoner was allowed one-third gallon per day for washing, drinking, and bathing purposes. This amount, properly conserved, will answer the purpose, but unfortunately the method of distribution was so poor that all did not get their regular allowance, and the loss of water caused the unfortunate ones great inconvenience, especially during the time that the *Wolf* was in the tropics. Many of the men used tea to brush their teeth. . . .

[One time the mine officer, Lieutenant Dedrick, a humane officer, came down into the "Hell Hole" and got one good lung full of the rotten atmosphere. He went immediately to the commander and reported conditions. Commander Nerger at once called both doctors and accompanied them aft on a tour of inspection. The next day everybody was chased on deck, and the "Hell Hole" below was cleaned out and better ventilation arranged for; it was also painted. Also, the captured captains and ships' officers were given quarters to themselves, while the whites and blacks were separated. On the whole the conditions for these two hundred men were improved 100 percent. The prisoner officer was confined to his room for five days for allowing such conditions to exist.]

When we arrived at the southernmost end of New Guinea, we stopped and lay to for a couple of days. . . . One of the German sailors told me that in another day or so we should have plenty of beer—that they had picked up a wireless message stating that the Australian steamer *Matunga* would soon arrive in Rabul with five hundred tons of coal and three hundred tons of foodstuffs, so many hundred cases of beer, etc., for the government. Sure enough, on the morning of 4 August, I was awakened by my orderly with the usual supply of cotton batting for our ears. Shortly thereafter there was a bang from one of the cannons, and the *Matunga* stopped. Lieutenant Rose and the prize crew went on board and took charge. . . . The cargo and coal of the *Matunga* were transferred to the *Wolf;* also nine passengers who had been allowed to remain upon the steamer. . . .

On 25 August . . . the *Matunga* was sunk by three bombs. Her officers and crew . . . were in the "Hell Hole" of the raider, but the nine passengers were given quarters on the same deck where we were. There was [an Australian] colonel and a major, with his wife, [three captains, three civilian planters], and the stewardess of the *Matunga*. . . .

[One night a Japanese cruiser was seen nearby, cruising without lights, as was the *Wolf,* and the raider's crew prepared for battle, but] fortunately, the Japanese cruiser did not see us. In a few minutes the signal was given to swing the guns in. The danger was past, but there was a mighty nervous crew of men on board the *Wolf* that night. . . .

[The following night the tantalizing sight of the lights of Singapore was plainly visible from the portholes.] We were less than ten miles offshore, and we were there for a purpose, for the *Wolf* was . . . a minelayer [as well as] a raider. Locked in my room for two hours, I could count the "eggs" as they were being laid. The mines would come up out of no. 3 hatch on an elevator and were conveyed aft to the chute on a small rail car which had a flat wheel, and I could hear it bumping along the deck. I estimated that ninety-eight mines were thus laid in about one hour and forty minutes.

[In the Indian Ocean, the *Wolf* encountered a big Japanese liner, the *Hitachi Maru*, which Nerger hoped would be useful in several ways: to supply the raider with coal and fresh food, to decrease crowding on the *Wolf* by supplying ample prisoners' quarters, and by taking home to Germany as a prize. The coal and the accommodations were supplied, but the meat was ruined when a shot from the raider destroyed the liner's refrigerator.

Before long], we were transferred from the *Wolf* to the *Hitachi* along with all the rest of the "top side" prisoners, including many of the original passengers on the Japanese vessel. Our quarters on the *Hitachi* were splendid. The Camerons fell heir to the bridal suite. It seemed mighty good to sit down to a regular table with a white cloth and napkins again.

I shall never forget my feelings as we sat there for the first meal, waiting for the white-coated Jap waiter to bring on the food. I could feel myself getting up from the table with that satisfied, contented feeling amidships. Soon the waiter came and set before us each a plate containing two ordinary soda crackers, or ship's biscuits, with a poor, lonely, godforsaken sardine stranded on the top. This, and a cup of the regulation "near" coffee, comprised our first evening meal on the luxurious *Hitachi*.

For the following morning's breakfast, we had porridge with kerosene spilt on it—absolutely uneatable. For dinner, rotten meat with good potatoes, water—or soda water, if you had money to buy it with—and in the evening canned crab and crackers. In the meantime, Lieutenant Rose, the commander of the prize crew now in charge of the captured vessel, was having a series of banquets in his room with his brother officers. . . .

The German chief engineer and chief mate used to eat at the same table as we did . . . and one night the chief engineer took the matter up with Rose and told him a few truths. Rose said that it was "too bad," that he did not know anything about it before, but now he would straighten it up. The engineer told Rose that if he cut out his private champagne suppers and looked into what the rest of us were getting it would not be necessary to make these complaints.

This is a condition that could not exist on the *Wolf* because there we were under the charge of a gentleman and an officer, and we got square treatment; but [in Rose] we were under a sublieutenant, a snob, and a man who did not know the meaning of the word "gentleman."

[The *Wolf* hoped to find a vessel loaded with enough coal to get both the raider and the *Hitachi Maru* "home" to Germany, but this hope proved vain, and on 7 November 1917 the Japanese liner was bombed and sunk. Off Ceylon just three days later the *Wolf* captured a small Spanish freighter, the 6,558-ton steamer *Igotz Mendi* that was loaded with coal. The prisoners were transferred to the *Igotz Mendi,* still under Lieutenant Rose, while the *Wolf* went her own way in search of further captures.]

Christmas Blues on the Igotz Mendi

I had the blues worst of all on Christmas Day. . . . Bright and early Lieutenant Rose was around, wishing us all a merry Christmas. . . . My wife wanted to stick a hat pin in him as he said it. . . . We were all terribly depressed—all but Juanita. Her faith in Christmas had been justified, no matter what the rest of us felt about it. One of her friends on the raider was the officer of the "bird," and he brought gifts to Juanita on Christmas day, trinkets, evidently from the loot of the *Hitachi Maru.* He had been up, he told her, and had met Santa Claus flying across the world with only a few things left in his pack, but he had got something for her and even a little gift for her baby sister at home.

On New Year's Eve we all sat up to see the new year in. . . . One or two of us worked up enough enthusiasm to make a little noise, [but the situation] was too depressing; the effort subsided into deeper gloom. Meanwhile the Germans were holding high carnival in the engineers' mess. . . .

On 20 January, the weather being very fine and the sea exceptionally smooth, the raider came alongside and we transferred some eight hundred tons of coal to her. . . . The *Wolf* then left us, after arranging a final rendezvous at a point . . . southwest of Iceland. Four days later . . . my wife came to the door.

"Stan," she said, bursting with suppressed excitement, "oh, Stan, there's a cruiser with four funnels ahead of us." I thought of course she was kidding. . . . Looking up at her, I saw that she was white as a sheet. [I jumped out of the bunk as] one of the prisoners put his head in at the door, his eyes staring.

"By God, Captain," he cried, "a cruiser at last!"

I ran out on deck. There, just on the edge of a rain squall was what appeared to be a four-funneled cruiser. Just about this time the Spanish second mate, who was on the bridge, discovered her, and a sailor ran into Lieutenant Rose's room, calling him to come on deck. As soon as I looked at the vessel through my glasses I saw that instead of being one four-funneled cruiser, it was two American army transports, both of them heavily armed with what appeared to be big guns. There was great confusion among the Germans.

I remember how sorry I was that the *Wolf* was not along to get the benefit of those guns. They were not needed for the harmless little *Igotz Mendi*, but I certainly would have liked to see them busy with the raider, even if we stood some risks before we were hauled up on good American territory on board the transports.

Two Germans, armed, chased us into our rooms in no uncertain manner. And as we obeyed we grinned at them in no uncertain manner. Meanwhile, as we found later, Rose and the other officers, in a bad state of fright, ran to their quarters and put on their good clothes in anticipation of being the guests of the U.S. government. At that moment Rose must have had a whole lot of regrets about the way he had treated us, especially certain favorite remarks about the "star-spangled banana. . . ." We, in our cabins, after hoping and praying and building on running across a cruiser, not for days but for months . . . we were trying to keep our happy hearts from choking us.

The Germans altered the course of our vessel in such a manner as to pass under the stern of the two transports. They were less than a mile from us when they crossed our bow. They passed calmly on, not even signaling and asking who we were. They paid absolutely no attention to us, and in a few minutes they were swallowed up in the drizzling fog. . . .

When you give up hope and then suddenly have it revived in a way that takes your breath out of you, only to lose it again when it seems yours for keeps, it is almost too much to bear. And then to have to sit at table and see Rose sitting there with that "Chessy" cat smile on his ugly Prussian mug and to hear his remarks about the "star-spangled banana." He used to laugh at the U.S. soldier, saying we were crazy to imagine that we could take a man and make a soldier of him in a year; at best our men could only be cannon fodder, for Germany had proved it takes three years to make a soldier. Our submarines were mere toys, he said, and as for defense against their U-boats, just as soon as we figured out some Yankee patent to protect our ships, the Germans would invent some other way to destroy them. . . . To sit at the same table and hear an enemy slam America and the Americans and hold my tongue . . . was pretty hard. . . .

The statement has been made repeatedly in papers in Europe that on the *Igotz Mendi* the prisoners had the same food as the German commander and crew. . . . In reality, eleven of us sat down at the first table, with Rose at the head. The one platter started with him. He first helped a special friend on his right, very generously, then himself likewise, then passed the platter to the man on his left. This man was a glutton, all appetite and no shame. These three persons got very nearly, and often fully, half the contents of the dish. What was left was divided among the remaining eight, comprising five men, two women, and a six-year-old child. . . . If the food had been equally divided and we had all shared alike, it would not have been so bad, but under the heads-I-win-tails-you-lose division we got up from the table hungry. It is an awful sensation to realize suddenly that you actually covet the food your neighbor is eating. . . .

[We met the *Wolf* again on February 5th, when] Lieutenant Wolf, Division Lieutenant of the *Wolf*, [came] on board to assist Lieutenant Rose. Wolf took over control of the food and the cook's department and made an honest effort to better things. . . . After his arrival favoritism was abolished, and we all got a square deal.

The next day the *Wolf* parted company and was not seen again. The *Igotz Mendi* tried twice to round Iceland to the north but was forced by ice to try the southern route, risking an encounter with the British blockade. The *Wolf*, a radio message revealed, got safely through the blockade into the North Sea and home to Germany.

The *Igotz Mendi* made it around the south of Iceland and successfully penetrated the blockade between Iceland and the Faeroe Islands, picked up the Norwegian coast, and headed for the Skaggerak on the way to the Baltic Sea. Captain Cameron's wife, fearing long imprisonment in Germany for her husband, urged him to swim for neutral Norway, close at hand: "I'm not afraid. They won't hurt [Juanita and me], they don't want us . . . two more mouths to feed. . . . Better be separated now and united later than leave you there in a prison camp."

She was very earnest about it and kept begging me to make my getaway while there was a place to get to, but I couldn't bring myself to do it. . . .

Igotz Mendi *"Smells the Bottom"*

The day we crossed from Norway to the northern end of Denmark, Jutland, it set in foggy, and Lieutenant Rose was strutting around with a smile on his mug saying: "Just the weather I want; made to order; I am all right now." I didn't argue the point with him, as I thought he was right. About 3:30 in the afternoon we picked up a fog whistle ahead, of the character we call a "blatter" on the Pacific Coast. I was standing on deck just under the bridge, talking to Rose. I nodded my head toward the signal and asked him what it was, and he said, "Oh, that is the lightship." I thought at the time it was a peculiar character for a lightship but dismissed the thought. . . .

I stood looking out into the fog, as gloomy as my thoughts, when I noticed, by the bearing of the fog signal, that we had altered our course, and knew that Rose wanted the pass the lightship close aboard.

Suddenly I felt an astonishing thing. I turned to the wife.

"Holy Poker," I cried out, "I thought I felt her smell the bottom!"

No sooner had I said these words than the *Igotz Mendi* ran slap-bang on the beach, about 350 yards offshore and less than half a mile from that fog signal.

Rose's mistaking the lighthouse signal for the lightship's signal was a lucky piece of business for us, because I knew for an absolute certainty when I felt the *Igotz Mendi* had taken the beach that it would require the assistance of a powerful tug to get her off again.

I guess we all realized just how much this stranding meant to us, and the very nearness of freedom kept everybody quiet and busy with his own thoughts and plans. I know that, for one, I had decided to get over and swim for it, provided the vessel should give any indications of getting off the beach. This was a different matter from swimming ashore on Norway while the ship went on to Germany. Here I could get warning to the authorities and put an end to the prize crew's voyage.

Right after the stranding, the weather being foggy, we were allowed out on deck. One of the neutral sailors, a Dane named Jensen, identified the spot where we were ashore and gave me the good news that the little town of Skagen was only about two miles distant, and that one of the best lifesaving crews in Europe was stationed there. Sure enough, in about an hour a lifeboat drew up alongside. We were all chased inside again. Rose invited the captain of the lifeboat on board and took him into the chart room just above the saloon for a drink and talk.

The Ladies Rise to the Occasion

Our lady prisoners immediately rose to the occasion in a truly feminine way, and I confess it was their clever trick that saved us after all. They commenced at once to play "Button, button, who's got the button?" laughing and talking at the top of their voices. It certainly seemed like a fine case of hysterics all around. Nita was delighted at this sudden reversal of form and didn't bother to ask why.

But suddenly, in the midst of her joy, her mother made a dive at her and boxed her ears soundly. The astonished child burst out with such loud wails that they must have been heard all over the ship. Then my surprise gave way to appreciation. That lifeboat captain, taking a drink in the chart room just above us, must have wondered what on earth women and children were doing on what was supposedly a German merchantman, running the British blockade, a boat absolutely without accommodations for such passengers. So the louder poor little Nita bawled the broader I smiled, which only made the abused child cry the louder. Shortly Rose came down with a black scowl on his face. "You people can cut out the noise now," he said, "the stranger has gone ashore."

"Why didn't you introduce us to your friend?" asked somebody, unusually bold.

Rose answered savagely, "What do you think I am, a fool?"

Nobody went on record with an opinion, so the matter was dropped.

Lieutenant Wolf had gone ashore to arrange for a tug for his "German merchant ship." The salvage company manager ordered his largest tug to the scene but with orders not to put a line on the vessel until the manager had investigated. Rose was tickled at this news. But the head of the salvage company, talking with people gathered at the lighthouse, sensed something rotten in Denmark and called the Danish navy. About midnight the Danish cruiser *Diana* arrived. Its commanding officer, Lieutenant Lagoni, being a gentleman and also a shrewd, wide-awake officer, took his chief officer on board the *Igotz Mendi*, telling him that he, the commander, would keep the captain of the *Igotz Mendi* busy answering questions in the saloon while the chief officer should have a good look around and gather what information he could.

As soon as the Danish commander arrived on board we were all pushed and shoved into our rooms, and the doors closed. Rose led the way to the chart room above. Lieutenant Lagoni did not follow.

"It is not customary, Captain," said he, "to entertain the commander of a cruiser in the chart room. Let us go into the saloon."

Thus they came into the saloon before there had been time to hustle us all out of sight. Rose's face was red with vexation, but the Danish officer made no comment. Now began again the campaign of the women's signal corps. One of them would call down the hallway in a voice like she was calling to the lighthouse.

"Oh, Mrs. So-and-so, won't you come in my room a minute?"

Another shrill voice would come back: "No, I don't dare to. I'm afraid they wouldn't like it."

"Don't be frightened," the first voice would call back, "it's a Danish officer, and he won't hurt us." And so on, back and forth, until Lieutenant Lagoni must have wondered what sort of a party it was.

Juanita's Kewpie Doll

In the meantime, the Danish chief officer was wandering around the *Igotz Mendi* taking notice of all he saw. Strolling through the bunkers, he came to [a bunker where a temporary warm place had been made for the Cameron family when the arctic cold was too much to bear in their unheated cabin]. Here he stopped and looked at something lying on the floor. It was Nita's kewpie doll.

There were men standing around through all these quarters. Suddenly the officer turned toward one of these and said: "You are not a German." "No, sir," answered the man, "I am a Dane."

"Well, what are you doing here?" was the next question. It was Jensen, the man who had told us where we were. He now told the officer everything, how he was from the *Wolf* and was working on the *Igotz Mendi*, and that there were U.S. and British prisoners on board, including some women and children.

After completing his rounds, the Danish officer went on deck and told Lieutenant Lagoni that he was ready and, calling him aside, told him what he had found out. Lieutenant Lagoni then gave orders to disable the wireless plant and told Rose that the tug could not assist him off the beach, and that at the end of twenty-four hours the vessel would be interned, providing she was still under the German flag; he advised him to land any prisoners he had.

[Of course we prisoners had no idea what was going on. My wife and I lay] on the bunk with our clothes on and listened to Rose on the bridge ringing the [engine] telegraph and working his engines in an attempt to get his vessel off the beach. I supposed of course the salving tug was on the job. And at the last minute my chance to swim for it was gone. A feeling of complete despair took hold of me. I did the best, the only thing I could—I went to sleep.

At 6:30 A.M. of 25 February (will I ever forget the date!) I was awakened by one of the German seamen named Hans knocking at my door and saying: "Kapitän, Kapitän, wake up and get ready to go ashore in the boats." I'll bet we broke all speed records getting on deck. Rose asked me to get into the lifesaving boat first, as the Danish crew could not speak English, and then I could help the [other captives] as they came down the ladder. I got Juanita firmly on my back and climbed down into the boat.

There was a large sea running, and as the *Igotz Mendi* was stationary on the bottom and the lifeboat was riding on the seas, one moment it would be even with my feet and in another it would be fifteen feet below. The idea was to jump the instant the boat was even with me. This was easy enough with myself and my wife, who understood such things and had had previous experience, but . . . it was hard to make [the other passengers] let go at the right time. . . . In some cases it was necessary absolutely to tear the passengers off the ladder by main force. However, we finally got all the women, children, and men into the boat, and we started for the beach. When we got into the breakers and the seas would wash clean over us, many thought it would be a case of swim or drown, not reckoning on the kind of lifeboat we were in or the class of men that manned it. . . .

I have seen various lifesaving crews . . . but these old Danes . . . were in a class by themselves. On entering the breakers they dropped a kedge anchor with a long line on it and literally slacked the boat through. A gigantic comber, one of those curling ones, just commencing to break, would rush us; up would go the stern of the boat, and at just the instant I would expect her to go end for end, the old "Sinbad" tending the anchor line would check her, and in another instant we would rush for the beach, just as the Kanakas ride the surf on a board at Honolulu. When we finally grounded, the men from the beach ran out and seized the women; the balance then ran the boat higher up on the beach.

The natives must have thought we were a bunch of raving maniacs, the way we carried on, getting our feet on good "terra firma" again. We danced, we shouted, we cheered, and made blame fools of ourselves generally; but to my mind the situation warranted it. What a fitting climax to an adventure of this kind, after nine months prisoner on a Teuton raider, to be set free at the very gates of Germany, at the eleventh hour and fifty-ninth minute. . . .

We were taken to the nearby lighthouse, where the keepers and their families did everything possible for us—drying our clothes and giving us hot coffee to warm ourselves. About midday we went into Skagen, two miles distant where our various consuls took us in charge and sent us to Copenhagen, where we separated, going our several ways.

Lieutenant Rose and the prize crew left Skagen just ahead of us for a detention camp. I had a glimpse of Rose under Danish military guard. I noticed him just long enough to favor him with a "Chessy" cat smile, which he didn't return. And now [November 1918] that the friendly holiday season is coming 'round again, I must not forget to write him at his stopping place in Denmark and wish him "many happy returns of the day."

★   (Cameron, "The Sea Wolf's Prey")

Epilogue

☆

The war ended—with our huge projected [ship]building just getting under way. Of the 1,741 steel emergency ships contracted for, not one was launched in 1917. By the Armistice in November 1918, only 107 steel, 67 wooden, and 4 composite vessels had been finished. There was talk of stopping the building, but the pressure of builders—making profits—and of laborers—earning big pay—was too strong. Contracts for 941 were canceled, to be sure, but much of the construction continued. Not only were partly completed ships finished, but keels were laid for more than a third of the shipping board's fleet after the Armistice was signed. Almost four years after our entry into the war, the last ship was launched in late February 1921.

The United States had returned to the seas with a vengeance. In 1920, the nation's registered shipping reached its all-time peak of 9,924,000 gross tons, almost ten times what it had been in 1914. For the first time since 1863, half the tonnage entering U.S. ports from foreign countries flew the Stars and Stripes. All that tardy tonnage was more than the merchant marine could absorb. The surplus became as serious as the deficit had been! For a while after the war, the business of feeding Europe, and bringing home the army and its stores, kept many vessels well employed; but then the tide began to ebb.

Seagoing vessels became a drug on the market. Many Hog-Islanders and others of the better ships, to be sure, were operated with government subsidization on strategic trade routes to many parts of the world, while the new tankers were proving highly useful. But hundreds of others were held in less esteem. Some of the new steel ships, which had cost two hundred dollars a ton to build, were sold for as little as five dollars a ton. Ford bought 149 of the lake-built steamers for about eight dollars a ton to be broken up for scrap. Nearly two hundred more emergency freighters were laid up at anchor in rusting, desolate groups that swung with the tide year in and year out along the coasts. Half of them would still be there when the next war started.

☆   (Albion and Pope, *Sea Lanes in Wartime*, 332–33)

World War II

FOR FIVE YEARS ACROSS THE SEVEN SEAS THE U.S. merchant marine played the greatest role in its history. Overcoming shortages of ships, men, guns, convoys, and escorts. Transporting the monstrous bulk of supplies needed by U.S. and Allied forces across the oceans of the world. This war was the last in which control of the seas was a large and absolutely vital issue. Pearl Harbor introduced the formal war to the United States—seven months after the first U.S. merchant ship was sunk by a German submarine.

The most famous vessel produced in America's emergency shipbuilding program of World War I was the "Hog Islander," the first of which was launched less than three months before the Armistice. That was the SS *Quistconck,* and like many another she was still in active service at the start of the next war. The first U.S. ship sunk in World War II was a Hog Islander, SS *Robin Moor.*

Albion and Pope describe the product of the Hog Island shipyard at Philadelphia:

> Its celebrated Class A [freighter], measuring about five thousand gross tons, [was] almost double the size of the average submarine victim of [World War I]. These Hog Islanders were far from beautiful, but unlike some of their jerry-built contemporaries

which "spat rivets all over the seven seas," they proved tough.
Designed to eliminate curves for greater speed in building, they
were wall-sided, flat-bottomed, blunt-bowed, and square-sterned.
Durable and satisfactory products of honest workmanship, they
became the backbone of the new merchant marine.

(Albion and Pope, *Sea Lanes in Wartime,* 330)

But the ships arrived too late to carry more than a minor fraction of
the war supplies they were designed to haul. The *Quistconck* did not
actually get into service until three months after the end of World War I.

The record next time—for all its inescapable faults—was dramatically
better. As European tensions increased in the late 1930s and the prospect
of a new major war became more likely, U.S. legislation replaced the old
shipping board with a U.S. Maritime Commission, which set out with
commendable vision to examine the economics of the shipping industry,
to develop modern, standardized cargo ship designs, and even to order a
substantial fleet of such ships.

The new C-ships (C-1, C-2, and C-3) could be powered by steam or
diesel engines and were larger, faster, and more efficient than the best of
the old order. The C-2, for example, could cruise at 15.5 knots burning
the same quantity of fuel as the older ships at their maximum speed of
11 knots.

The British, meanwhile, began to feel a shipping crunch, particularly
after the fall of France in 1940. "From the start of the war," writes Rene
De La Pedraja,

Britain had made the potentially fatal mistake of underestimating
the cargo-carrying capacity needed to supply the island . . . [and]
found after June 1940 new obstacles, not the least of which were
the conversion of French ports into U-boat bases and the closing of
the Mediterranean to British shipping. . . . As the fastest solution, in
October 1940 the British established a Merchant Shipping Mission
in the United States that placed orders in shipyards for 60 ships of
identical design to speed up delivery.

(Pedraja, *Rise and Decline,* 139)

These became, in effect, the prototype for the U.S. Liberty ship,
and over the strenuous arguments of the maritime commission and

its chairman, Rear Adm. Emory S. Land, the Roosevelt administration announced early in January 1941 that the United States would build two hundred similar ships for its own merchant service. The commission was, in Pedraja's phrase, "overruled . . . on the argument that speed in delivery was more important than speed in steaming."

The design essentially copied the old British Sunderland type of tramp steamer, but the hull was welded instead of riveted. Its power plant was an old-fashioned, triple-expansion, reciprocating steam engine delivering 2,500 horsepower—and whose peculiarities could be quickly mastered by green engine-room crews.

By the fall of 1940, however, as the new program got under way, 177 of the C-ships had been ordered, and 47 of them were already afloat. One year later, the first Liberty ship, SS *Patrick Henry,* was launched—ten weeks before Pearl Harbor. And only fifteen weeks after that she was unloading 10,000 tons of war cargo in Egypt. It took thirty-five weeks to build the *Patrick Henry*—and just six to build the last of the 2,710 Liberty ships that were built (though the last was not actually delivered until two months after V-J Day).

"Born of the emergency," Allan Nevins writes,

> the Liberty ships met that emergency so well that long before the conflict ended it was possible to turn to newer, faster designs; to ships of a type that would have greater postwar utility. As 1944 opened, therefore, the Maritime Commission announced that thereafter it would place its emphasis upon fast and highly efficient cargo ships and tankers. The last Liberty ship contracts were let in the summer of 1943. Already shipyards were then being converted to a new design—the Victory ship. This new vessel, which came into production late in 1943, was slightly larger than the Liberty ship, possessed finer lines, and made better speed. It was driven by geared turbine propulsion machinery instead of reciprocating engines. Yet, though it had these superior features, it also was adapted to mass production methods. To make it, the great shapes and frames that came from the fabricating shops, often fifty and seventy-five tons in weight, ranged in as orderly a sequence as the automobile parts in a factory, were lifted into place by giant cranes. It also could be turned out at need by a few weeks of intensive labor.

The first Victory ship was delivered in February, 1944, and by the beginning of November that year, eighty-two of them had gone into commission.

(Nevins, *Sail On*, 94–95)

But the Liberty was the quintessential ship of the World War II merchant marine. First dubbed the "ugly duckling," she actually was prettier than that, and she—"the Lib"—is cherished still by many a mariner (of those who survive) who made her his home on peril-filled seas.

I have one final observation for the reader, as we turn to the events of World War II. This book consists largely of passages from the books of others, and here in part 5 appear the only extended quotations that have never seen the light of day in public print. They are extracted from official logs and voyage reports, mainly of gunnery officers on merchant ships. Those records have been thoroughly combed by historians and other writers, seeking facts, dates, and details. This of course was my motive for seeking them out in the National Archives.

But again and again I have stumbled across beautiful writing in those mandatory reports on routine matters both bloody and prosaic. In the pages that follow, watch for these occasional jewels and pause to savor them—the words of young men, now old or dead, who in their gallant and valorous youth recorded moments of heroism or gruesome violence and death with the eye and voice of a poet.

17 ★★ Who Were the Merchant Marine?

Who were the merchant marine of the second world war? A handful of prewar seamen—whom the fastidious saw as the scum of the earth—manned the small merchant fleet in 1941. As emergency shipbuilding programs rushed new vessels off the ways, urgent recruiting programs sought crews to man them.

The early crews were augmented by a swelling flood of old men, boys, retired seafarers, draft rejectees—"slackers and suckers," *Time* magazine once called them in a story on the U.S. Maritime Service's training program (21 December 1942). They were motivated, variously, by a search for adventure, patriotism, sense of duty, money, envy, frustration.

Crash training programs of the government and the marine unions made seamen of the vast inexperienced majority of them, and off to war they went. Without military discipline, uniforms, or spit-and-polish, they were civilians all and volunteers to a man.

And they died. From torpedoes, aerial bombs, collisions, shell bursts and machine-gun bullets, frigid seas, flames, exploding cargoes. From drowning trapped below decks or from freezing or starving adrift in oarless lifeboats. Their casualty rate in World War II was exceeded only by that of the U.S. Marine Corps. (Merchant marine deaths were 2.74 percent; 2.9 percent of marines were killed in battle, and the rate rose to 3.6 percent when nonbattle deaths are included. The overall armed forces death rate was 1.05 percent.)

Shipping was slow at the eve of the war. In port cities, idled sailors lounged in and around the hiring halls of the various maritime unions. When "respectable folk" thought about merchant seamen at all, the images that came to mind were seedy and shabby: waterfront radicals, bums and brawlers, hangers-out in down-at-the-heels bars, reeking of rotgut booze. They were seen as malcontents stirring up quickie strikes that tied up passenger liners at principal ports on Atlantic, Pacific, and Gulf Coasts. And for what?

As the maritime chronicler and second-generation seafarer Felix Riesenberg put it sardonically, their motivations were seen as "extra sheets, special safety gear, or the firing of some second cook." Many a traveler believed these inconvenient work stoppages were fomented by agitators who

☆

came aboard from some gin mill or brothel, and held "communistic" crew meetings. . . . Citizens were amazed that a few men could flout authority and disrupt luxury transportation. . . . [Newspaper readers] sympathized with shipowners who asked for "responsible leadership in the sea unions" and a guarantee [against breaking work agreements]. . . .

But the new union sailor, remembering when the boot was on the other foot, replied, "If we let the bastards get away with the small things, we'd soon see everything go by the board."

☆   (Riesenberg, *Sea War*, 22–23)

The War and the Unions

The maritime unions had changed things to a massive degree from the early 1930s when jobs were scarce and pay was low. An able seaman— the seasoned AB, rough and ready and able to rise to any emergency at sea—was the mainstay of the deck department's unlicensed crew. He could earn $32.50 a month before the unions' bitter and expensive strikes of the mid-1930s—and twice that after the strikes.

While the captains of great ocean liners were significantly better off than ordinary seamen and ABs, merchant marine officers in general ranked hardly higher than seamen in public esteem. The master of a freighter or tanker, with a quarter century of experience sailing the oceans of the world, could earn almost $350 a month. As Riesenberg observes, "They usually owned one uniform—for sailing day—and considering their responsibility were the poorest-paid executives in the country. . . . [They] had no access to various government concessions, no pension, and no paid-for insurance" (Riesenberg, *Sea War*, 25).

Shipowners and seafarers existed in a maelstrom of hostility and mutual suspicion, which poisoned attitudes and convictions on both sides. Two organizations—indeed two men—dominated the dozen or more maritime trade unions.

The West Coast was the turf of Harry Lundeberg, the tough, rough-hewn, Norwegian immigrant, and his SUP (Sailors' Union of the Pacific). It was the union of the deck department, originally established in 1891, that became an affiliate of the American Federation of Labor when the AFL was founded. By the late 1930s the Seafarer's International Union (SIU) had been set up as an umbrella organization with which SUP, along with the early Marine Firemen, Oilers, and Watertenders–Pacific, the union of the black gang, also was affiliated. Lundeberg was the primary influence and spokesman for the lot.

The East Coast heavyweight, Lundeberg's bitter rival, was Joseph Edwin Curran, an Irish-American slum kid whose father died when he was two and who quit parochial school after fifth grade. Joe Curran went to sea at age sixteen in the miserable conditions of the 1920s and was a leader in both the seamen's rebellion against the corrupt International Seamen's Union (AFL) and in the founding of the NMU. The NMU became part of the CIO.

Other major unions at the time of World War II represented licensed officers. The MMPA (Masters, Mates, and Pilots Association), founded in 1887, is still in business. Engineers were represented by the Marine Engineers Benevolent Association (MEBA), which a generation after the war merged with the NMU as MEBA/NMU. Smaller unions of the 1940s included MCS, or Marine Cooks and Stewards, and rival radio unions, the American Communications Association (ACA) and the American Radio Association (ARA).

Lundeberg was a militant anticommunist; Curran was a militant left-winger but no communist. Ever since Lenin's day radicals of every stripe had propagandized seamen—anarchists, syndicalists, communists of various factions, stoking and trying to harness the resentment left by genuine, cynical, often brutal exploitation. The Communist Party influence on seamen (and longshoremen) was substantial but neither universal nor overwhelming. However, the clamor of the real leftists, claiming to speak for seafarers everywhere, had a profound effect on public opinion.

The war (and the looming likelihood of U.S. involvement in it) and labor union activities in the context of wartime needs sharpened the focus of the press on the two dominant maritime labor leaders, Lundeberg and Curran. Many columnists and editorialists ascribed maritime union militancy to Communist Party influence, and this rhetorical sleight of hand resonated widely in the white-collar world.

Then came the Japanese attack on Pearl Harbor. Long-idled Hog Islanders were being made seaworthy again. Shipyards were booming. The first of a new breed of freighter had already come down the ways. But the great fleet abuilding could sail nowhere without solving the ultimate problem: Where could crews be found to sail the new ships?

The maritime unions, in large and small strikes of the previous decade, had won the right to control the hiring of all unlicensed personnel manning U.S. merchant ships. The prospect that all the unions feared most was that war necessity might erode or demolish—or might be manipulated to erode or demolish—all the gains they had won for their members in years of bitter strikes and struggle.

These gains were nothing to scoff at. The strikes had prevailed over ghastly conditions: meager and often rotten food; no mess hall; drafty forecastles crowded with skimpy, vermin-ridden bunks and bedding; filthy toilets; crude cold-water spigots; and buckets for lavatories. The strikes also had won massive increases in compensation.

There was no realistic possibility of a reversion to the scabrous working conditions of yore, but the fear of losing some of the hard-won gains in pay was realistic enough. If the merchant marine were absorbed into the navy, the merchant seaman's greatly improved pay scale was a certain loser. So was the relatively relaxed discipline that prevailed on merchant ships.

By the winter of 1941–42, the two dominant unions—NMU and SUP—had prospered mightily. They were not only militant, they were tight ships indeed: well-run, well-advised organizations, with their own newspapers and pamphlets produced by accomplished writers, and millions of dollars in the bank—$300 million for the NMU and half as much for SUP. Moreover, they were solidly supported by the great political muscle of the umbrella organizations: CIO for the NMU, and AFL for the SUP.

The Navy and the Merchant Marine: A Takeover?

Newspaper stories in the first week of April 1942 told of the sinking by German submarines of ten U.S. merchant ships, including one whose crew came under fire while abandoning ship. And the *Washington Post* issued the first of what became a rash of stories in major papers anticipating a U.S. Navy takeover of an insubordinate merchant marine: "The navy has charged that there has been a failure by cargo vessel crews and officers to obey navy orders and that the discipline of the crews, afloat and ashore, is inadequate" (cited without date in Riesenberg, *Sea War*, 95).

The unions saw this as an ominous portent indeed. The SUP paper, *West Coast Sailors*, told its member-readers that authorization for a takeover had progressed as far as President Roosevelt's desk and awaited his signature. Actually, there had been earlier speculation and reports. Samuel Eliot Morison, no adoring devotee of the merchant marine, puts the move at least two months earlier.

☆

Relations between the navy and the merchant marine have always been somewhat delicate, and the presence of the Naval Armed Guards on merchant vessels created a new point of friction. The National Maritime Union, most powerful of the seamen's unions, had recently been struggling for better wages and conditions on board merchant ships. Joseph Curran, its president, nailed the slogan "Keep 'Em Sailing" to the masthead of his journal, the *Pilot*, prevented strikes by his men in wartime, did his best to get rid of "performers" (drunkards, troublemakers, etc.), and displayed the most ardent patriotism. This union also showed a good example to the navy, which it did not follow, in abolishing the color line and encouraging Negroes in every way. But it was unduly concerned lest the government or the shipowners put something over. . . .

At the beginning of the war, trouble or friction with merchant seamen on board was reported by about 30 percent of the Naval Armed Guard officers. Naturally the presence on board ship of military personnel who were neither under union control nor interested in pay, bonuses, and overtime was galling to many of the seamen and to their union officials. Relations gradually improved. By the fall of 1943 "incidents" had become rare, and the ships' crews very generally cooperated by passing ammunition or otherwise helping to serve the guns. Nor were the licensed personnel (the ships' officers) uniformly cooperative. In the merchant marine there is a sturdy independence which in time of war becomes a fault; certain masters and mates were resentful of gold braid, although given the right to wear a uniform almost indistinguishable from that of the navy. Proper orders of an armed guard officer in the interest of security—such matters as blowing tubes and dumping garbage after dark—were sometimes ignored because they disturbed the master's routine or disobeyed because he regarded them as unnecessary.

The trouble between naval seamen and merchant seamen had its root in totally different attitudes. Any ship in which a bluejacket serves is his ship, his country's ship, to be defended with his life if need be. But to the union-indoctrinated merchant seaman the ship is the owner's ship, his class enemies' ship, to whom he owes nothing and from which he is morally entitled to squeeze all he can. The navy principle "Don't Give Up the Ship" did not appeal to merchant seamen.

Into this large and controversial subject, it is impossible to enter at length; but the writer, after giving it considerable study and doing his best by conversations and by reading the *Pilot* to understand the merchant marine point of view, wishes to express his emphatic opinion that if and when another war occurs, the merchant marine should either be absorbed by the navy or made an auxiliary service under military discipline—like the Naval Construction Battalions, the famous Seabees. Certain high-ranking officers of the navy recommended this about 1 February 1942, but it was not done.

☆   (Morison, *Battle of the Atlantic*, 298–300)*

Admiral (and Professor) Morison's comments here require some analysis. His acknowledgment of the patriotism of Joseph Curran and his NMU is not inaccurate but is hardly wildly enthusiastic. Every wartime issue of the NMU weekly newspaper, the *Pilot*, prominently displayed the "Keep 'Em Sailing" motto, and its articles reinforced the point constantly.

The union's "encouragement of Negroes in every way" is immediately evident to any reader of wartime issues of the *Pilot*. Hardly an issue appeared without photographs and/or articles reporting heroic or otherwise outstanding conduct of black seamen, and several monthly issues gave extensive coverage to the first naming of a Liberty ship after a black

*From *History of United States Naval Operations in World War II*, vol. 1, by Samuel Eliot Morison. Copyright © 1947 by Samuel Eliot Morison; © renewed. By permission of Little, Brown & Company.

man—Booker T. Washington. The union also clamored successfully for black skippers. The NMU's vigorous actions against racism were decades ahead of their time.

Morison's assertion of "union-indoctrinated" class warfare between seafarer and owner is close to the mark, even though its effect runs counter to the "Keep 'Em Sailing" exhortation. Curran, and Lundeberg as well, and their principal aides (and writers) dipped deeply into the rhetoric of class warfare. Both the NMU *Pilot* and the SUP's *West Coast Sailors* reflected attitudes the whole labor movement inherited from the days of the IWW (International Workers of the World—or the "Wobblies").

The papers did not exactly echo the language of old-time union organizers, with their waterfront harangues about goon squads, finks, scabs, and stool pigeons. That old labor standby, "phoney," however, was ubiquitous. (Phoney, now usually spelled phony: a noun or an adjective connoting sleaziness, hypocrisy, dishonesty, sham, falsity, flimflam, pretension, and much else, all bad.)

Inculcating an underlying hostility to management was certainly an intent of union management, but its expression in action by union membership at large was no more universal than the greed and indiscipline Admiral Morison so casually attributed to the merchant seaman.

The canard that merchant seamen disdained the navy sailor's principle, "Don't Give Up the Ship," is myopic at best. There were indeed mariners who abandoned ship prematurely or otherwise demonstrated cowardice and self-preservation over duty and loyalty to shipmates. Several such shameful instances are related in these pages, and they were at least as offensive to most merchant seamen as to the magisterial historian. Similarly of course, and rarely, bluejackets also embarrassed naval tradition by disgraceful conduct (though no such cases fall within the scope of this book).

The Morison work describes the presence of armed guard crews on merchant ships as "a new point of friction" in relations between navy and merchant marine. This it was in part, but by no means universally. A few days spent perusing the voyage reports of armed guard commanding officers will reveal occasional tensions and, rarely, real hostility. From time to time criticism of the difficulty or incompetence of a particular officer appears. More frequent are expressions of appreciation for teamwork and cooperation between the civilian merchant seamen and their navy ship-mates—under fire, in lifeboats, in day-to-day life at sea, and ashore.

Interestingly enough, in a number of cases merchant crews pooled contributions to make a fraternal gift to gun crew members, to augment their relatively meager pocket money to spend in port. (The first such instance I learned of was a $20.00 gift to each member of the gun crew of SS *Arizona* by her merchant crew, reported to the *Pilot* [5 June 1942] as a thank-you by one of the navy men. This was by no means unique; the paper reported such incidents from time to time.)

Troublemakers and ne'er-do-wells in merchant crews had no harsher critic than the seagoing unions, which waged an unceasing campaign to weed out drunks, brawlers, and other "performers" whose conduct gave all merchant seamen a bad name. Sometimes crews would cite miscon-duct by ship's officers—for example, a complaint published in the *Pilot* (5 March 1943, 5) about the skipper of SS *McKeesport*, who despite con-voy blackout orders incessantly lit cigarettes on the bridge at night. (In an apparently unrelated incident on her next voyage the *McKeesport* was torpedoed and abandoned.)

Professor Morison does rebut the often-heard slander that procom-munism was what moved merchant seamen to dare the dangers of the Murmansk run (see chapter 21). But this grace note is warped by his recurring "explanation" that greed was the only motive.

☆

An officer of a ship detained there eight months said that he had never heard one seaman, bluejacket, or officer evince the slightest interest in the Soviet system; the poverty and drabness of life in North Russia were a sufficient deterrent. Merchant seamen, as on less dangerous routes, were mainly interested in their pay and bonuses, which were enormous. In addition to the base pay of $100 per month for a 44-hour week, war bonus of the same amount, and overtime for work on Saturday and Sun-day, a common seaman drew $5.00 a day for each day's detention in North Russia, $125 for every air raid to which he was subjected after March 1943, a 17 percent bonus for handling ammunition, and, on top of that, a $100 bonus from the Soviet government—until "Uncle Joe" got on to the fact that he was tipping marine plutocrats, and stopped it. For one round voyage that included several months' detention in North Russia, the least pay anyone received on a certain American merchantman was $3,200.

★ (Morison, *Battle of the Atlantic*, 374)

That Rarity, an Objective Comparison

In his unique study of laws affecting the legal status of U.S. merchant vessels in time of war, *Merchantman? Or Ship of War*, Charles Dana Gibson presents a strikingly objective comparison of relative long- and short-term benefits of navy and merchant marine personnel in the context of World War II. It is a letter from a top administrator in the maritime service training program, Telfair Knight, seeking to put to rest just such misconceptions as Professor Morison's monumental work repeatedly advances.

Knight is addressing the national commander of the American Legion in October 1943, who had stated the legion's opposition to including merchant seamen on local legion-sponsored honor rolls of men and women "in war service," on grounds that, among others, merchant marine service was equivalent to home guard or civilian defense service. But such activities, Knight wrote, "have few casualties directly attributable to enemy action, as has the merchant marine. The casualty lists show that the percentage of casualty in the merchant marine is at least three or four times the percentage for any of the armed forces" [N.B., in late 1943].

★

We believe it particularly unfair to compare the highest-paid merchant seaman to the lowest-paid member of the armed forces, as is done so often. . . . You mention that the gun crew on board merchant vessels draw from $50 to $80 per month. For your information, all navy personnel assigned to navy gun crews are at least seamen first class. The base pay for this rate is $66, with a 20 percent sea-pay bonus, bringing this to $79.20, which is the very smallest pay drawn by any member of the armed guard.

The ratings for other members of the armed guard range up to petty officer second class, the base pay plus allowances for that grade being $115. The above, of course, is minimum and applicable only to single men without dependents. If he is married or has dependents to whom he allots $22 per month from his pay, the government pays to his dependents further allowances:

Wife	$50	Child, no wife	$42
Wife and child	$80	Divorced, wife	$42
Each added child	$20	Divorced, wife and child	$72

Plus various additional categories. Thus, a married man with two children serving in the armed guard will be paid from $157.20 to $193.20, depending on his rating.

This compares with a base pay of $72, which, with 15 percent special emergency raise, is $82.50 for ordinary seaman . . . plus a bonus ranging from 40 percent to 100 [percent]. For able seamen the base pay is $82.50, with a 15 percent special emergency raise, bringing it to $100. The merchant seaman, therefore, gets [a total base pay of] between $115.50 and $200 per month.

Overtime pay averages about 30 percent of base. No allowances are granted for dependents. Every man serving aboard a merchant vessel, with the possible exception of the master and chief engineer, could earn more money ashore in a shipyard or defense plant without taking the chance of being killed by bombs or torpedoes.

You also mentioned that the navy gun crew cannot quit their ships. This is, of course, true; but it is also true that in return they are paid for twelve months per year, with thirty days' leave allowed per year, with pay. They are also paid during periods of transfer and stand-by. The merchant seaman is paid only when serving aboard ship and has no leave pay, except in a few isolated instances. He can, however, take a specified maximum leave between voyages without pay.

A merchant seaman's pay starts only after signing on a ship and stops as soon as the ship is paid off in its home port. He is paid for an average of ten months per year, while the navy man is paid for twelve months per year. From actual payrolls of ships on various runs, the War Shipping Administration has determined that the average monthly pay for ordinary seamen is $197.50; and for able seamen, $231.25. All this is subject to income tax. This includes wages, voyage bonuses, and overtime. [Table 2] shows a comparison of average gross income received by four men, each with a wife and two minor children. Two are navy men paid for twelve months, and two are merchant seamen paid for ten months.

★   (Gibson, *Merchantman? Or Ship of War*, 147–48)

TABLE 2. Comparison of After-tax Income of Merchant Seamen and Navy Enlisted Men

	USN S1c	MM OS	USN PO2c	MM AB
Per month	$ 157.20	$ 197.50	$ 193.20	$ 231.25
Yearly (N = 12 mos., M = 10 mos.)	1,886.40	1,975.00	2,318.40	2,132.50
Less USN tax exclusion	1,500.00	0	1,500.00	0
Gross income	386.40	1,975.00	818.40	2,312.50
Less personal exemption	1,900.00	1,900.00	1,900.00	1,900.00
Surtax net income	0	75.00	0	412.50
Less earned income credit	188.60	197.50	231.81	231.25
Normal tax net income	0	0	0	181.25
Victory tax net income	386.40	1,975.00	818.40	2,312.50
Less exemption	624.00	624.00	624.00	624.00
Taxable balance	0	1,351.00	194.40	1,688.50
Est. surtax (13%)	0	9.75	0	53.63
Est. normal tax (6%)	0	0	0	10.87
Est. Victory tax (5%)	0	67.55	9.72	115.62
Total tax	0	77.30	9.72	180.22
Gross income	1,866.40	1,975.00	2,318.40	2,312.50
Less total tax	0	77.30	9.72	180.22
After-tax income	1,866.40	1,897.70	2,308.68	2,132.28

Source: Gibson, *Merchantman? Or Ship of War,* 149.
Note: The figures assume that each man is married and has two children. I have reversed columns 2 and 3. —Ed.

Telfair Knight then reviewed major differences in indirect compensation. Permanent disablement: merchant seaman (any grade), lifetime maximum of $7,500; navy petty officer third class (the median armed guard rating), $58.50 per month for life (if thirty years, e.g., a total of $21,060). If killed in action, a merchant seaman's dependents would receive a lump sum of $5,000; the dependents of a petty officer third class would receive base pay for six months ($468), but would be eligible for lifetime pension payments monthly, roughly $50 for the wife, $20 for the first child, and $10 for each additional child. A widow and two children would receive $80 monthly ($480 yearly) as long as the children were dependent, then $600 a year until death or remarriage. He concluded by reviewing such additional navy benefits as purchasing insurance at lower rates and coverage while ashore, medical benefits, and clothing allowances, plus the career navy man's retirement benefits—none of these available to the merchant sailor.

And he appealed to the legion commander to "help dispel this myth [that merchant seamen are paid too well] by advising all posts of the true facts" (Gibson, *Merchantman? Or Ship of War,* 151).

Manning the Merchant Fleet

The threatened naval absorption of the merchant marine that so alarmed the unions did not come to pass. Construction and delivery of the great new fleet of freighters and tankers was under way. There were berths to be had in union hiring halls, and men began to file through the halls, looking to fill them. But it was obvious from the outset that voluntarily returning retirees and other former seafarers could not begin to command and operate the enormous oceangoing fleet that was starting to appear.

A Merchant Marine Cadet Corps had been created at Kings Point, Long Island, under the U.S. Coast Guard in 1938, and now had schools on Gulf and Pacific Coasts as well. The Kings Point school later became the U.S. Merchant Marine Academy; the others were located at Pass Christian, Mississippi, and San Mateo, California.

But turning out even barely qualified deck and engine officers from raw recruits took nearly four years: basic training, a year's sea service as cadets, plus two more years of advanced training. The first graduates—fewer than one hundred—graduated in 1942.

On-the-job training could enable almost anyone to function as an ordinary seaman, wiper in the engine room, or messman; seaman's papers were easily obtained. Training centers also had been established where experienced ordinary seamen could qualify as able seaman and wipers as oilers or fireman-watertenders.

In February 1942 President Roosevelt established the War Shipping Administration and moved Admiral Land over from the maritime commission to head it. Seamen's wage scales were cranked up substantially from their low prewar levels to attract prospective crew members. The commission immediately created a recruitment and manning organization directed by an educator and former Justice Department official, Marshall E. Dimock.

A publicity campaign was launched to persuade former merchant seamen to give up lucrative jobs ashore and return to sea. Recruiting teams were assigned to seeking out exmariners who had been forced ashore by the shipping drought after World War I. In Felix Riesenberg's phrase, they were "flattered, embarrassed, and cajoled into shipping out again." Many of them did so. A number of the candidates had been drafted into the army, and a handful of them, at the request of the recruitment and manning organization, were released to return to sea.

Five coastal states operated schools to train merchant marine officers: California, Maine, Massachusetts, New York, and Pennsylvania. From all these sources, at last the manpower pipeline began to fill.

A Mississippi boy named Jac Smith responded to the recruiting campaign and entered a seamanship training program at Pass Christian. He did well, learned fast, worked at the school as an instructor for a time, and decided he was ready to ship out. His story was told long after the war by a fellow Mississippian named Thomas E. Simmons, a businessman author who had served on the National Maritime Council.

☆

Seamen were hired out to man merchant vessels through their union and [seamen's hiring] halls. A shipping company needing a crew for a certain vessel . . . called the halls and requested the number of men of such-and-such qualifications required. [Men wanting to ship out registered for jobs, and those on the list the longest] went first, always on a "destination unknown" basis. Jac was told that Philadelphia was a good place to be hired on quickly. Crews were desperately needed for the T-2 tankers being turned out by the Sun Shipyard.

It was a long train trip from St. Petersburg to Philadelphia and was as far as Jac had ever traveled from home. When he got there, he found Philadelphia awash in navy sailors and merchant seamen. The naval yard and all docks and shipyards in the area were crowded with ships of every description and in every stage of building, repair, outfitting, and loading. The arcs of welding torches flared brightly day and night. Trucks lined the streets waiting to load or unload at the docks. Cranes hefted cargo of every description aboard ship. There was one message in the air: *Hurry.* Europe has fallen, England is in peril, Hitler is at the gates of Moscow— *Hurry.*

Jac checked in at the seaman's hall to await ship assignment, then hastened out to buy his outfit. Merchant seamen furnished their own clothing, and he had a long list: wool shirts, wool pants, long underwear (no insulated longjohns in those days), warm leather boots, rubber sea boots, foul-weather gear, a heavy sheepskin coat, gloves, and mittens. That list completed, he loaded up on what medical supplies he thought he might need.

The only ones available aboard most merchant ships at the time were iodine, castor oil, and cotton. Whatever ailed you, you used iodine or castor oil—it was a real incentive not to get sick. The captain or the officer in charge of the naval armed guard usually had a sea chest equipped with morphine, splints, sutures, and other supplies for serious wounds or injuries, but with ordinary ills you were pretty much on your own. A merchant ship's "designated hospital" might be a paint locker or other storage area used mostly for on-going poker games. When a ship had a real sick bay, it was often requisitioned as quarters for the naval armed guard or as a place to store clean linen until it was needed.

☆　　　　　　　　　　　(Simmons, *Escape from Archangel*, 31–32)

☆

Life at Sea

[Life on shipboard, in the long intervals of boredom between episodes of terror, was described succinctly by an armed guard commanding officer on a Liberty ship.] The monotony of nearly two weeks at sea was also punctuated by the regular predawn general quarters, "3:30 A.M. Coffee Time," cleaning guns, tidying up the crew's fo'c'sles, and interminable chow downs with unending rivers of java at all hours.

This Liberty, presumably like others, spoiled its voyagers with a culinary largess: bacon and eggs or hotcakes for breakfast; steak and a variety of meat for dinner, the midday meal, with vegetables; an entrée again for supper, and always lots of potatoes and fresh-baked breads, plus pies, puddings, and other desserts. The already stocky among us augmented their avoirdupois.

Nonetheless, the gun crew maintained a more or less constant undertone of grousing, in spite of the provender and adequate living spaces.

The men slept in mattressed bunks instead of yesterday's hammocks. When sailors stopped complaining, a commanding officer should commence worrying—an age-old wisdom of the sea.

Most dwelt amidships within the main superstructure. A small fo'c'sle, for both crews, was located on the fantail above the throbbing propeller. The men drew lots for the some half dozen berths there. In them they whiled away the long off-duty hours playing cards, Chinese checkers, cribbage, dominoes, even darts, and listening to the tinny whine of a portable phonograph—all part of an entertainment kit provided to every gun crew by the navy.

Paperback books, which met with indifferent reception, were on loan from the American Merchant Marine Library Association and distributed by the purser. The latter was a true jack-of-all-trades, even ship's doctor. When one of the older gunners was hit by a painful gallstone attack, I called on the purser to give him a morphine injection.

Often, representatives of the American Red Cross or other charitable organizations and church groups were at dockside to bestow little keepsakes or goodies on the two crews, from candy and cigarettes to writing paper, pencils, and Bibles. I opened one of the Bibles to find the donor had inscribed on the front pages: "In my Father's house are many mansions; if it were not so, I would have told you. I go to prepare a place for *you*" (John 14:1–2). It was scarcely an encouraging bon voyage.

☆   (Hoehling, *Fighting Liberty Ships*, 38–39)

Medical emergencies beyond the purser's capability were met by luck on ships running alone; but convoys usually had qualified surgeons on board navy escort vessels. One armed guard CO (at least) lamented the absence of a pharmacist's mate aboard his ship. The voyage report of an armed guard commanding officer, Ens. Harold Unterbert of the SS *Argon*, had a practical recommendation. The *Argon* was the only one of four U.S. merchant ships to survive in a homebound convoy in April 1943, ONS-5.

☆

A pharmacist's mate should be attached to each navy gun crew. During the voyage two cases of venereal disease (one a chancroid in which the glans burst) and one case of acute appendicitis clearly evidenced the need of trained medical personnel. This pharmacist's mate would also be able to assume gunnery duties.

☆   (National Archives, Voyage Reports, *Argon,* 1–3)

☆

One September, a convoy was heading from New York to Guantanamo Bay, and among her escorts was the destroyer U.S.S. *Broome.* That day, a distress call came from the SS *Genevieve Lykes,* one of the ships in the convoy, and *Broome* responded. A medical officer was wanted.

Lt. Harold W. Fleischer was the medical officer of the *Broome,* and he was quickly transferred to the merchant ship. There he found Steward John Lance in considerable pain. Lance was suffering from appendicitis; on examination, Fleischer ascertained that the appendix had burst about twelve hours earlier.

The situation was serious. Unless something was done, Steward Lance would soon be dead. But the merchant ship was no place for an operation. The medical officer decided it would have to be done aboard the *Broome.*

They took the patient back to the destroyer. Usually, in such situations, the ship would be stopped but not this time. *Broome* was in submarine territory, and she had an obligation to continue her patrol and protection. So she moved at 25–30 knots, and the doctor would have to work out his procedures accordingly.

Lieutenant Fleischer took his patient into the wardroom and strapped him to the table. Only one other man aboard, a chief pharmacist's mate, knew anything about surgery. Several of the others would have to learn in short order.

So men were enlisted for the operation. The engineering officer became chief anesthetist, and Fleischer's nurses were a chief commissary steward, a ship fitter, and a mess attendant. The sterilizer for the instruments was the big copper kettle from the galley.

In the heat of the badly ventilated destroyer wardroom, Lieutenant Fleischer and his assistants worked. He made the incisions and removed the ruptured appendix. Peritonitis had already set in, he observed gloomily, as he sewed the patient up.

"Operation successful. The patient will die," was the prognosis, unless heroic measures could be taken.

Steward Lance was thirty-six years old and had been in good health. Now he was dehydrated and suffering from massive infection. He must have immediate aid in the form of glucose to restore the body liquids and sulfanilimide, the most effective treatment then known against infection. The captain of *Broome* broke radio silence and told the Norfolk navy base what was needed. Eight hours later, a PBM (medium-sized flying boat) bomber circled the convoy and came in. *Broome* sent out a launch, and the PBM dropped a parachute that landed nearly on target; all the supplies were in the package, and not a bottle broke on impact.

Lieutenant Fleischer and his "nurses" worked on Lance for hours. They tended his glucose drip. They made sure he had the sulfanilimide. Still he seemed to be sinking. Preparations were made for a burial at sea; a piece of canvas was brought out and the sewing begun.

Then, as hope seemed lost, Lance began to rally. But the glucose was nearly gone. So another call was sent to Norfolk, and another mercy mission was flown by a PBY. Steward Lance survived the convoy and was delivered alive to the Guantanamo naval hospital.

Then, on the way back, with a rough storm kicking up off Hatteras, the SS *R. H. Colley* signaled the destroyer that she had a sick man aboard. Lieutenant Fleischer got on the voice radio. It was a case of appendicitis again.

This time, the storm was raging so fiercely that no man could be transferred, even by breeches buoy. So, for twenty-four hours, Fleischer radioed treatment instructions, and the men of the merchant ship gave the sick man the treatment. The next day, he could be moved, and he was taken over to *Broome*.

The seaman had been packed in ice, and Fleischer believed that this treatment had been successful. But, in a few hours the man began to show signs of extreme distress, and Fleischer knew another operation was in order.

The whole procedure was repeated: strapping the patient down on the wardroom table, the scrubbing and instructions to his voluntary staff. The "nurses" were full of themselves this time and bragged to one another about their "technique."

When Fleischer made his cut, he saw with satisfaction that the appendix had not ruptured, although it was very near to that point. Carefully, he extracted it, powdered the cavity with sulfa, and sewed up the incision. The man was on his feet before the convoy reached New York.

☆   (Hoyt, *U-Boats Offshore*, 207–08)

The treatment accorded John Lance and the patient from the *R. H. Colley*, while out of the ordinary, was not quite so unusual as that received by a navy gunner on the MS *Arriaga*, an Esso tanker sunk in the Caribbean Sea on 7 June 1942. After missing a shot at the sub from her stern gun, the crew abandoned ship, and the *Arriaga* sank slowly. The lifeboat the tanker's captain was in drifted astern of the wreckage as the submarine surfaced nearby, and the sub signaled the lifeboat to approach.

☆

[After ascertaining the *Arriaga*'s name and destination, the submarine's skipper asked her master, Gunnar Gjertsen,] if we had any injured men. One of the U.S. Navy gunners, suffering from a strained back and also from oil in his eyes, was helped aboard the submarine and treated in the conning tower by her surgeon. A few minutes later he was helped back into our boat and the commander bade us farewell and wished us good luck. Before that he had given us five packs of German cigarettes and ten boxes of French matches. He told me the course and distance to the nearest shore.

☆   (Standard Oil Company, *Ships of the Esso Fleet*, 311)

Performers: Trouble at Sea

If the maritime union jargon of the World War II era were searched for its single quintessential term, that word might be "performer." Surely hardly an issue of the NMU *Pilot* or the SUP *West Coast Sailor* appeared without denouncing performers—drunks, thieves, card sharks, shirkers, barroom loudmouths, brawlers, and mischief-makers in general. The unions hated performers for sapping crew morale and making life at sea difficult and unpleasant—and possibly even more so as lightning rods for journalist detractors of the merchant marine and for antilabor voices in government and the press.

Ironically, one of World War II's classic tales of the mischief performers can do is set in a ship with an accomplished black captain and a racially mixed crew. It is ironic because of the generally successful racial integration of merchant crews in the war and perhaps especially in the light of the navy's foot-dragging on that front. As noted earlier in this chapter, Samuel Eliot Morison cited approvingly the role of the National Maritime Union in breaking down the color barrier to employment at sea. And indeed the NMU under Joe Curran was aggressive and effective in that role. The union's 1967 "autobiography," *On a True Course,* proudly discusses its leadership in race relations. Absent union pressures, mixed-race merchant crews would have been extremely rare. In fact they were relatively common.

Most such crews got on reasonably well, and in the case of the SS *Frederick Douglass* this was true in a special sense. The performers in her crew, black and white, were thick as thieves. Another irony is that both of the ships involved were named for great figures in the history of American race relations. The other vessel was the *Theodore Dwight Weld.*

Theodore Dwight Weld was a famous New England abolitionist who was involved in the founding of the American Anti-Slavery Society. Frederick Douglass was an escaped slave, a brilliant orator, a highly effective abolitionist, an advisor to President Lincoln, and much more. His namesake ship was commanded by a black master whose skill and integrity were remarked widely. Nonetheless, a disgraceful episode played out when a U-boat picked off both his ship and the *Weld*—side by side in convoy.

The story of the torpedoing is told in chapter 20, but the outrageous behavior of several officers and merchant crew members on the *Douglass* related there—smuggling a woman stowaway on board, insubordination, stealing the captain's whiskey, drunks in a lifeboat—illustrates elegantly why both the NMU and the SUP criticized "performers" with such anger and scorn. That such seafarers were a disgrace to U.S. mariners may have been the only matter on which Joe Curran and Harry Lundeberg, those quintessentially irascible and antagonistic union leaders, could agree.

18 This Is War, But . . .
★★

The first U.S.-flag submarine victims in World War II were torpedoed long before the United States was formally at war, and their ship went down far from home. In March 1941, President Roosevelt promised "all aid short of war" to the British. The next month, as they were fighting Axis desert troops in Libya, he removed the Red Sea from the list of war zones where U.S. merchantmen were forbidden to sail. This offered U.S. ships an alternative to the increasingly threatening German submarine traffic in the North Atlantic by opening an eastern route for delivery of Lease-Lend supplies the British sorely needed in North Africa. This proclamation opened a route romantic in the telling, if less so when actually sailing in the punishing heat. Down the South Atlantic, around the Cape of Good Hope, up the Indian Ocean, northeast through the Arabian Sea, west through the Gulf of Aden, and finally northwest up the Red Sea, or even into the Gulf of Suez. (The Suez Canal was still off limits.)

German submarines immediately adapted to this dodge and began stopping U.S. ships heading for the eastern South Atlantic, demanding their destinations and a look at their cargo manifests. On 21 May, near the Cape Verde Islands off Dakar, the *U-69*, her conning tower adorned with the caricature of a laughing cow, halted the SS *Robin Moor*, a Hog Islander operated by the Moore-McCormack Lines.

She was one of the last U.S. vessels carrying on routine, peacetime trade with various West African ports. She had aboard a handful of passengers and a diverse mix of general cargo including breakfast cereal and brassieres, coffees and candies, golf clubs and adding machines. And, alas, a small shipment of steel rails, which the U-boat skipper, Kapitänleutnant Metzler, concluded were contraband of war. By blinker he ordered the *Robin Moor* not to use its radio, and (at 4 A.M.) gave crew and passengers twenty minutes to get dressed and into their lifeboats.

Then he sent the ship to the bottom with gunfire. Pearl Harbor was six and a half months in the future.

The *Robin Moor*'s boats—its passengers subsisting on emergency rations of biscuits and water—drifted apart after a week. Both were picked up, the first, after thirteen days, by another freighter bound for Brazil. The other, after nineteen days, was rescued by a ship headed for South Africa. News of their fate only reached America when the Brazilian contingent of survivors landed first.

That September another German sub caught the Isthmian Lines freighter *Steel Seafarer* in the Gulf of Suez. The U-boat's case this time was clear-cut; the *Steel Seafarer* was loaded to the Plimsoll line with patently military supplies for the British.

On 7 December the Japanese attack on Pearl Harbor removed all ambiguities. On 10 December a Japanese submarine northwest of Hawaii sank the Matson Line freighter *Lahaina.* Five days later in the South Pacific a sister ship, SS *Manini,* was torpedoed shortly after nightfall. The Lykes Lines ship *Prusa* was off Honolulu on 19 December. Accounts of the lifeboat experiences of their survivors appear in chapter 24.

The morning after the sinking of the *Prusa,* another Japanese sub sank the tanker *Emidio* within two hundred miles of San Francisco. There were a few other encounters in the general area, but then submarines effectively disappeared from the Pacific Coast of the United States. They never approximated the early reign of terror imposed on the Atlantic Coast by the German U-boats.

It should be noted here that occasional reports of German brutality, such as shooting men in lifeboats, often are either exaggerations or misinterpretations. The NMU *Pilot* reported several instances of this in the early months of 1942, though it does not suggest that they were either frequent or typical. One careful scholar, Michael Gannon, makes this point in an endnote in his *Operation Drumbeat:* "It bears repeating that the shooting of survivors in lifeboats was not a common German practice. . . . Suggestions that inhumanity of this kind occurred off the U.S. mainland appeared first in Morison, *Battle of the Atlantic,* p. 130 and n., and most recently in John Terraine, *U-Boat Wars 1916–1945* (1989, p. 498); but in the absence of documented evidence it is hard to credit these statements" (Gannon, *Operation Drumbeat,* 460, n. 77).

On the other hand, Japanese brutality of this stripe is thoroughly documented in many instances, a number of which are discussed in these pages.

Drumbeat on the Atlantic Coast

Immediately after Pearl Harbor, Adm. Karl Dönitz, with Hitler's approval, ordered his U-boat forces to initiate Operation *Paukenschlag*—or "Drumbeat"—on the U.S. coast, a furious roll of the drums to serve notice on the Americans that they faced a dauntless foe. Because of submarine commitments elsewhere, only five *Unterseebooten* could be spared at first—the *U-66*, *U-109*, *U-123*, *U-125*, and *U-130*—and within a week this first installment began heading west from their French bases on the Bay of Biscay. Reinforcements would follow from the flourishing German submarine-building program.

"For six or seven months," Winston Churchill wrote, "the U-boats ravaged American waters almost uncontrolled, and in fact almost brought us to the disaster of an indefinite prolongation of the war. . . . Their success was immediate" (Churchill, *Second World War*, 4:109).

One of the lethal quintet of early arrivals sank seven merchantmen alongshore in the second week of January. In that early concentration on the Atlantic Coast, tankers were a favored target. They were the last remnant of a once-flourishing coastwise trade, and their cargoes brought gasoline to the whole Eastern Seaboard from Gulf Coast refineries.

The *Paukenschlag* U-boats had hardly gotten their bearings when one of them, *U-123*, under the German ace Reinhard Hardegen, sank a British freighter off Cape Cod on 12 January 1942, a big Norwegian Panamanian-flag tanker off Nantucket on the fourteenth, and a British tanker off Long Island the next day. Then the subs turned to U.S. targets.

On Sunday, 18 January, the unarmed Standard Oil tanker *Allan Jackson* was beating north off the North Carolina coast with 79,000 barrels of Colombian crude oil for New York, when she became a statistic. The master, Capt. Felix W. Kretchmer, was resting at 1:35 A.M. when he felt the first torpedo.

An instant later, a second explosion broke the ship apart and set her on fire. Burning oil poured out of ruptured cargo tanks and spread across the surface for half a mile around the sundered ship. The blast threw the captain out of bed, across his cabin, and onto the bathroom floor. Flames were coming into the bedroom through the portholes and doors. He was able to crawl through the bathroom porthole to the boat deck.

☆

I started up the ladder to the bridge. The decks and ladders were breaking up and the sea was rushing aboard. As the vessel sank amidships, the suction carried me away from the bridge ladder.

After a struggle I came to the surface, on which oil was afire a short distance away. I never saw any member of the crew or any lifeboat afloat at any time, but later I distinctly saw a large submarine emerge, some distance away.

With the help of a couple of small boards I was able to keep afloat until I was picked up, about seven hours later, by the destroyer USS *Roe*. I was almost completely exhausted and hardly regained consciousness until I was landed at Norfolk and placed in the Marine Hospital.

☆   (Standard Oil Company, *Ships of the Esso Fleet*, 77)

Boatswain Rolf Clausen was amazed that the captain managed to survive. "He clung to two pieces of wood so small that when he was rescued I couldn't see how they kept him up," he said. Clausen and two others had managed to launch the only lifeboat—no. 3—that got away from the ship. Davits damaged by the explosion prevented the mates and several others from swinging out no. 2 boat, and approaching flames forced them to jump overboard.

This and similar failed launching experiences led to the 13 April 1942 order to all port directors by Rear Adm. Adolphus Andrews, commander of the Eastern Sea Frontier, that all merchant vessels keep lifeboats swung out and ready for lowering. The order also required lifeboats to be equipped with day and night signaling apparatus and stocked with emergency provisions.

The outboard half of the *Jackson*'s no. 1 boat was blown off, and flames prevented launching no. 4.

The boatswain's boat was lowered into a small area cleared of flames by the discharge from the *Jackson*'s condenser pump. By the time the oars were manned, Clausen said, "the boat was being sucked toward the propeller. [Its blades] hit the boat a number of times before we [cleared] it by shoving with oars against the ship. Again we were saved from the surrounding fire because we were in the backwash of the propeller, which made a clear lane through the flames. Not a man in that boat would have lived except for two elements of luck—the condenser discharge and the propeller's backwash."

Searching for survivors, they heard several calls in the darkness, and managed to pick up the radio operator. After sighting the submarine's light, low over the sea, they put up sails and headed west toward shore. Two and a half hours later they saw a light that turned out to be the USS *Roe*, which they signaled with a flashlight.

The *Roe*, aware of the U-boat trick of lurking near lifeboats for a shot at would-be rescuers, was cautious, but boat no. 3 passed the destroyer's quiz and was picked up. Other survivors clung to floating wreckage and were found by the *Roe*, which also recovered several bodies and eventually found Captain Kretchmer. All thirteen survivors—five seriously injured—were landed at Norfolk about nine o'clock that night. The other twenty-two perished (Standard Oil Company, *Ships of the Esso Fleet*, 76–78).

Originally six submarines had been assigned to the first wave of Operation *Paukenschlag*, but the sixth, *U-128*, was delayed and did not show its presence on the American side of the Atlantic until the night after the *Allan Jackson's* survivors were landed. Then, twenty miles off Florida's Cape Canaveral, it sank the 8,200-ton tanker *Pan-Massachusetts.*

☆

[One crew member told the NMU *Pilot* that nobody would have gotten off alive but for the first assistant engineer, who] was off watch when the torpedo hit. The ship burst into flames. They shot down the alleyways, through the ventilators and everywhere else. The first rushed below, threw the ship into full [speed] astern, then turned everything off. This stopped the ship. As long as the ship was moving, the flames were being swept aft, where the crew's quarters were.

When the ship stopped, the flames spread and we had a chance.

Even so, the heat was so intense on the boat deck aft, where almost the entire crew gathered, that the skin was running off one man's back like water.

☆   (*Pilot*, 27 February 1942)

By chance a veteran editor of the *Pilot*, Fred Fitzgerald, who had left the paper to return to sea, was one of those lost on the "*Pan-Mass.*" On the eve of his last trip he had mailed a long letter to an old crony, the NMU's New York port agent, Blackie Merrell, reflecting on some of the realities of being a U-boat target.

☆

It's the dark of the moon now so we can expect little trouble until the 22nd [February], when the first quarter will be here. From then till the ninth of March—it's full moon on the 2nd—we can look for trouble.

No fooling, though, it's a queasy feeling to be shadowed by those bastards. One of them tried to decoy us with signals off St. Augustine, by flashing "P," which means to show your lights. The old man [skipper] zigzagged to hell-and-gone, and most of us were kidding each other about the false alarm when the *Pan Amoco* reported sighting a sub off Jupiter [Florida, above Palm Beach]. Our incident occurred the previous night, sixty miles away. We stopped kidding then.

[Fitzgerald's account of his last previous trip told of a sighting off Cape Henry, Virginia. The temperature] was 12 degrees with a strong northwest wind and heavy seas. Every damn thing on the ship was covered with ice, and the boat falls were useless. . . .

Just as the moon was going down the second mate happened to make the big circle with his binoculars and spotted the sub in a perfect silhouette. It was also seen by Sparks, the Old Man, and the man at the wheel.

First thing I knew was the ordinary on watch giving me the shake. "There's a Jerry on our tail," he said. "All hands get dressed, with life belts, and stand by in the messroom for an alarm. The moon's gone down so he probably won't take a bearing on us till dawn but be ready."

I got up there, all right, but nothing happened. Later that day the same sub got the *India Arrow* and the *China Arrow*, just a few miles away from where we were.

What burns you up is no guns. You can't fight the bastards back. Luckily, this crate is fast, and the steering gear is in good shape so we can get going, but on those old Socony crates, especially the *Arrow* boats—and I've been on nine or ten of them—there isn't a damn thing you can do except call the sub commander an old meanie or something. Later, it comes as something of a jolt to discover that fellows you knew well, and were shipmates with, are gone for good. Worst yet, without a fighting chance.

☆   (*Pilot*, 27 February 1942)

One of the *Paukenschlag* U-boats encountered a Standard Oil tanker, SS *W. L. Steed*, on 2 February, about eighty miles east of the Delaware Capes. It was not the first such encounter of her master, Capt. Harold G. McAvenia, though it would be his last.

Captain McAvenia had commanded the tanker *R. G. Stewart* in 1939 when she was accosted by a U-boat on 11 September, en route from Le Havre to Caripito, Venezuela. The submarine ordered the *Stewart* to stop, but was distracted by the approach of an Irish-flag tanker, SS *Inverliffey*, which tried to flee but was easily overtaken. The submarine's captain summoned the master of the gasoline-laden tanker, concluded that she was owned in London and thus fair game, and announced that he would sink her. He gave the crew time to take to lifeboats, then blew up the ship.

The sub took the *Inverliffey*'s crew aboard, then returned to the *R. G. Stewart*, which the German captain asked to take the survivors aboard. The *Stewart* did so, later transferring them to a Belgium-bound U.S. freighter. The *Inverliffey*'s master told Captain McAvenia that the sub captain had mentioned that he had a surface speed of 18 knots and 10 knots submerged.

Captian McAvenia concluded his report on the incident with a modest and deadly accurate observation: "I realize that meeting one submarine does not qualify me as an expert. However, I would venture a guess that the chance of escape for the average merchant vessel of less than 13 knots speed is nil" (Standard Oil Company, *Ships of the Esso Fleet*, 25–26).

Two and a half years later Captain McAvenia was transferred to another tanker, the *W. L. Steed*. Built in 1918, the *Steed* had a triple-expansion steam engine that would propel her at 10.2 knots. She was unarmed and had a crew of thirty-eight. On 2 February 1942, carrying a load of Colombian crude oil, she was torpedoed without warning. Only four men survived, but most of the thirty-four lost took a long time to die.

The *Steed* had stopped at Key West for sealed navy orders; only Captain McAvenia knew her destination, but she proceeded north through the Florida straits. Several times beginning 30 January, the ship spotted submarines but was not attacked—until 2 February at 12:45 P.M. Then, despite the tense vigilance of her lookouts, an unseen U-boat put a torpedo into her no. 3 starboard tank. The ship was about eighty-five miles

A torpedoed ship, her bow resting on the shallow bottom off Banana Island on Florida's east coast in June 1942. A diver is at work at extreme left. (National Archives, RG 80-CF, 1055F6)

off the Delaware capes, in wicked seas, with heavy snow in a northwesterly wind limiting visibility to two miles.

All four boats were launched and got safely away, heading northwest in dangerous seas into the wind and snow. The sub surfaced, then a second submarine that proceeded to shell the after end of the stricken tanker until she blew up. During the long, bitter-cold night of 2 February the lifeboats lost sight of each other.

Second mate Sydney Wayland, who was on watch when the torpedo hit, was in boat no. 2. "Everybody in the boat was suffering from the cold," he said, "due mostly to lack of clothes. The men in lifeboat no. 2 died one after another until February 5, when chief mate Nilsson and I were the only ones alive in the boat." They were picked up by SS *Hartlepool* on

6 February, landed at Halifax three days later, and hospitalized. The chief mate died the next day.

Boat no. 3 lost its sea anchor, improvised another from a broken water keg, and ignited a distress flare, which was answered by a flare from another boat. The five men in the boat rowed in that direction, vainly. Able seaman Ralph Mazzucco recalled that "a big sea came over our boat and washed overboard all but three of our oars, also carrying away our rudder, tiller, sails, and boat hooks, and filling the boat half full of water. Using our buckets and scoop and even drinking cups, we proceeded to bail the boat out. By this time we were all wet to the skin. . . . [The men then crawled] under the canvas boat cover for protection from the heavy spray and strong wind . . . talking and joking through the night . . . to keep up our morale."

One man went to sleep on a life preserver and never awoke. Another became delirious and died the next day. Mazzucco and the others made a fire in a water bucket using bits of wood they chopped up and oil from a broken lamp. The surviving trio spotted a Canadian navy cruiser the next day, signaled wildly, were approached warily, and eventually picked up and landed on 7 February at Halifax.

One boat was never heard from. The fourth was found about three hundred miles east of the torpedoing on 12 March by a British freighter, the *Raby Castle,* bound for Cape Town. It carried the *Steed's* second assistant engineer, Elmer Maihiot Jr. and three dead bodies. Maihiot died three days later and was buried at sea (Standard Oil Company, *Ships of the Esso Fleet,* 86–87).

Spectacle on the Jersey Shore: Fire and Icy Death

Able seaman John J. Forsdal was on watch at the bow of the tanker *R. P. Resor* when she was torpedoed off Barnegat Light on the night of 26 February 1942. He and one of the nine-man navy armed guard crew, Coxwain Daniel L. Hey, lived to tell the story.

It was a fine, clear evening, with a half moon brilliant in a cloudless sky. "I could easily distinguish the individual lights on the New Jersey shore," Forsdal said. He spotted a dark, indistinct object on the port bow. As he was walking toward the bell to report what he thought might be a fishing boat, she turned on her navigating lights. Within a second or two, he said later, "I rang two strokes on the bell and then reported by voice to the bridge, 'Small vessel about two points on your port bow, sir!' The bridge answered, 'Aye! Aye!' . . . Thinking that she was a fishing boat because of her small outline and not realizing that a submarine would venture so close to shore, I resumed my lookout without giving further thought to the vessel."

Within a minute or two there was a violent explosion on the port side. With a fraction of a second the *Resor* was aflame from her bridge aft and debris was hurled high into the air. Forsdal was thrown to the deck, dazed, but as debris began raining on him he crawled under a platform built for a future bow gun. When the fall of fragments ceased he went down to the foredeck, and by the light of the burning *Resor* saw the sub heading toward shore.

☆

The fire was too severe to venture aft toward the boat deck.

I released the portside life raft, found a line hanging over the side, and lowered myself into the water, which was icy cold.

When [I was] swimming in heavy oil, I heard a second violent explosion. Looking over my shoulder I saw that the oil floating on the water in the vicinity of the ship was afire. I had to swim out to sea at least twenty minutes to get away from the burning oil. [He heard two voices nearby, and swam toward one. It was the radio operator, Clarence Armstrong, on a small raft. The mass of flames from the tanker grew steadily worse.] Covered with more and more oil, I struggled hard to reach Armstrong, answering him each time he shouted. In the light of the flaming *Resor*, after a period of time I cannot estimate, I arrived at the raft, [about half a mile] from the ship. Hooking my arms around the lifelines, I rested for ten minutes or so in a state of exhaustion. Sparks was hanging onto a lifeline on the other side of the raft.

I was heavily weighted down with cold and clinging oil; the exertion of climbing up on the raft taxed my strength so seriously that I was unable to do anything but lie down. The cold and heavy oil seemed to be paralyzing my body.

[A Coast Guard patrol boat approached, put a searchlight on the raft, and threw a life ring on a line to the raft.] I managed to get my arms through the ring, but as the vessel went ahead I was hauled off the raft into the sea. Then the patrol boat's headway pulled the life ring from my grasp. I managed to return slowly to the raft, but as I felt warmer in the water, I did not attempt to climb aboard it.

☆ (Standard Oil Company, *Ships of the Esso Fleet*, 108–10)

Meanwhile, Sparks had died on the raft. A small boat went over to Forsdal, secured a line to his body, and passed it to a picket boat, which had already rescued the only other survivor, navy Coxwain Hey.

The picket boat that rescued Hey and Forsdal was commanded by Chief Boatswain's Mate John W. Daisey. Forsdal, he said, "was so coated with thick congealed oil that we had to cut his clothes and his life jacket off with knives. They were so weighted with oil that we couldn't get him aboard. Even his mouth was filled with a blob of oil."

Horror-stricken crowds along the Jersey shore gathered to stare at the oily black clouds rising from the *Resor* until, under tow toward shallow water by a navy tug two days later, she capsized and went to the bottom.

Wartime radio communication with merchant ships generally was limited to radiotelegraphy using international (Morse) code of dots and dashes. Within a convoy, especially later in the war, very high-frequency (VHF) voice transmission began to be available. On ships with only one or two radio operators, where 24-hour radio watch could not be maintained on the universal frequency for distress signals of 500 KC (kilocycles, now termed kilohertz, or KHz), an automatic alarm system was used.

To activate the autoalarm on such a ship, before sending a distress signal, if circumstances permitted, the radio operator was required to transmit twelve four-second dashes one second apart. The autoalarm of every ship within range, usually several hundred miles, would then set off a piercing clangor in the radio shack and the operator's quarters, bringing him running to receive and log the distress message, which he would then relay to the bridge. The autoalarm also sounded if the radio power supply failed.

That was the situation aboard the tanker *E. M. Clark* at 1:35 A.M. on 18 March 1942. The ship was off Cape Hatteras and bound for New York with a cargo of heating oil. The autoalarm ringing madly was the first thing Earle J. Schlarb, the sole operator on the *Clark*, heard when he awoke to find himself thrown halfway out of his bunk. He rushed into his clothes, and as he burst into the radio room next door he smelled "the sharp, acrid odor of burnt powder."

☆

[His flashlight illuminated] chaos. Parts of the apparatus, the filing cabinet, the spare-parts locker, table, and racks were in a tangled heap on the floor. The typewriter had been flung across the operating chair and table and had crashed into the receiver-battery charger. The door leading to the boat deck had been blown off, and part of the bulkhead was gone.

Feeling lucky to be alive, I pulled the autoalarm switch and stopped the clamor of the bells. Then I heard the captain saying, "Sparks, get on the air!"

There was no ship voltage; that was why the alarm bells rang. . . . Immediately I threw in the battery switch for the emergency transmitter power supply. It worked! Then I connected the antenna transfer and telegraph key switches and "sat on the key," sending and repeating SSSS.* But there was no radiation on the dial. Had the main antenna been broken?

Going outside to the boat deck, I stumbled in the darkness over more wreckage. A flash of lightning showed the damage done by the torpedo; the lifeboat was a blasted heap of torn-and-twisted metal and splinters; a jagged hole yawned in the sagging deck. Awning and stanchion bars were smashed off or hanging loosely.

When the lightning passed, inky blackness shut in tightly. I could not see whether the mainmast was still standing. Feeling my way by flashlight, I bumped into the first assistant engineer, who was coming up from aft. I asked him whether the mainmast was down. "Damned if I know," he said, "but the deck is full of wires. Your antenna must be broken."

☆   (Standard Oil Company, *Ships of the Esso Fleet,* 145)

The starboard lifeboat was being readied to launch, and Schlarb returned to the radio room, donned his life jacket, grabbed the tangled coil of spare antenna wire (a stranded copper cable), and backed out on deck uncoiling it and trying to figure out where to rig it. From the distance a

---

*SSSS was the wartime substitute for the universal distress signal SOS, to be used in case of a submarine attack (or hitting a mine) at sea. The comparable signal for a surface raider was RRRR, and for an aircraft attack, AAAA.

yellow searchlight played over the *Clark* as the U-boat inspected the damage.

The tanker's master, Hubert L. Hassell, and the second mate, Richard Ludden, approached in the dark, and Sparks explained the problem. Both pitched in, pulling and twisting the wire, as Schlarb clambered up to the bridge wing and fastened his end to a broken awning bar.

Back on deck Captain Hassell told Schlarb the lead-in was free, and he and the mate hauled the wire taut while the radio man connected it to the radio shack.

☆

[As Schlarb started for the room to transmit his SSSS] the ship leaped and shuddered . . . as the sound of a dull, heavy explosion reached our ears. Hit again! This time it was up forward, in the way of no. 1 tank and the dry cargo hold. The torpedo had apparently gone deep inside before detonating.

The ship's whistle jammed and sent forth a steady roar. Broken steam lines hissed loudly. . . . The second mate ran to starboard to see if no. 1 lifeboat was still intact.

I thought it had started to rain but . . . the "raindrops" were . . . cargo heating oil . . . blown high in the air . . . falling in a fine spray! It seemed a miracle that the ship had not caught fire. The explosion had ripped down the spare antenna we were working on, and part of it could not be seen.

The second mate came back, holding the rail as the ship took a list to port. "Captain," he shouted, "she's going down fast!"

Captain Hassell looked at me. "How long will it take to repair this and send an SOS?" he asked.

"At least fifteen minutes, maybe more," I replied.

Captain Hassell said calmly, "I doubt if we have fifteen minutes."

☆   (Standard Oil Company, *Ships of the Esso Fleet*, 145–46; this gripping account was written by radio officer Earle J. Schlarb for the Esso history, augmented by subsequent interviews)

The captain was right. Two lifeboats were launched; one had been destroyed. Within minutes the *Clark*, her whistle still roaring, slipped beneath the waves. The twenty-six men in one boat were rescued by a

Venezuelan tanker, and Sparks, Captain Hassell, and a dozen others were picked up the next morning by a U.S. destroyer. One was presumed killed in his bed near where the first torpedo hit, and three were gravely injured. All forty returned to sea, one to his death on his next trip, and eight who survived torpedoing on other ships.

Unflinching courage, heroism, gallantry, altruism despite great personal risk . . . these qualities are rare in human affairs, but when one reads the accounts of life and death of men and ships in wartime, they come to seem almost commonplace.

Three days after the *Clark* went down, at almost the same place and time and with the same cargo, the *Esso Nashville,* bound for New Haven, was hit once, then all but thrown on her beam ends by a second torpedo. When she righted she was in the shape of the letter V, sinking amidships with bow and stern in the air. The ship parted the next day, and her after section was towed to a drydock where a new forward section was built onto her.

So much for the tanker. The tales of courage and generosity focus on two men, the master and a humble oiler.

Capt. Edward V. Peters was credited with the survival of all hands in part because of the rigorous boat drills he frequently conducted without warning. Also, well before the navy ordered the practice, Captain Peters had issued a standing order that all lifeboats be kept swung out and ready for launching. The *Esso Nashville* was abandoned quickly and virtually without mishap once the order was given.

The only mishap was that the captain's leg was fractured when lifeboat no. 2 crashed against the hull as he was trying to board it. "The ship had changed position to windward," he said later, "and the crew members in no. 2 were experiencing great difficulties in handling their boat and keeping it away from the ship's side. Seeing this and fearing trouble for them in case the ship sank, I shouted to them to get away and pick me up later if they could."

When they managed to get clear of the rigging, in which they were entangled, and pull away, the chief mate said they yelled for Captain Peters but got no response. They rowed all night and got three or four miles away from the ship. Captain Peters had started to swim away but made no headway because of the thick carpet of oil coating the water and pain from his fractured leg. He decided to swim back to the ship, which was still afloat.

As the captain recalled, "I boarded her . . . where her deck was awash, and after considerable effort I got aft to the engineers' quarters. After resting in the second assistant's room and bandaging my leg which had badly swollen, I fastened a white sheet to the rail on the windward side and ran up the ship's ensign upside down on the flagpole on the poop deck."

At daybreak, the captain sighted three navy vessels picking up the crew from the lifeboats, and as one of them approached the *Esso Nashville*, he got back into the water, swam toward it, and was rescued. His heroism was recognized fourteen months later when he was awarded the American Legion Medal by the Robert L. Hague Post of the Legion at ceremonies at the Maritime Exchange in New York City.

Duty and a Brave Old Man

It was third assistant engineer Henry H. Garig who told the story of the unsung hero of the *Nashville*'s sinking, an oiler named Leonard E. Mills.

☆

A man fifty-six years of age, Mills was in the navy in the First World War and had since then served many years in the fire department of Akron, Ohio, until he retired on a pension. Feeling it was a patriotic duty regardless of his age to go to sea in time of war, he signed on as an oiler on the *Esso Nashville*, 4 March 1942, the day before we sailed from New York on this voyage. When the men were getting into no. 4 boat, Mills appeared in a life jacket, but on that cold night in the drenching rain he was clad only in his trunks. When one of the younger men standing nearby yelled for a life preserver, Mills took his off and gave it to him. I at once told Mills to take his life jacket back, but he told me he could swim better than the younger man.

[The boat was overcrowded with twenty-one men aboard, and those at the oars (trying to pull away from the ship) did not have enough space to row. Garig, who was in charge of the boat, asked those wearing rubber lifesaving suits, to get into the water and hang onto the boat, and he and the others did so at once. But Mills, wearing only trunks,] jumped in before we did, and he stayed with us, hanging on in the cold water for three or four hours. When we got back into the boat he was suffering from the cold, and I offered him my rubber suit. Refusing it, he wrapped himself in a blanket and took one of the oars.

☆   (Standard Oil Company, *Ships of the Esso Fleet*, 157–59)

The gallant oiler survived this sinking, promptly shipped out again, and was lost in the torpedoing of the tanker *R. W. Gallagher* in the Gulf of Mexico on 13 July 1942.

Tanker operators had been pleading with the navy for armed guard guns and crews, and eventually their pleas led to action. The *Resor* (discussed above) was one of the first ships armed—but it never had a chance to fire a shot. So also was the brand-new tanker *Gulfamerica*, whose guns never came into play.

In 1990, the historian Michael Gannon published the fruits of his research; what started out as a footnote in an earlier book eventually became an exhaustive portrait of German submarine operations in the Atlantic, largely through the eyes of one submarine, *U-123*, and its captain, the ace Reinhard Hardegen, and crew.

The *U-123* tragically ended the maiden voyage of the *Gulfamerica* on 10 April 1942. The following excerpt from Gannon's work *Operation Drumbeat* begins as the submarine has just launched one of its last two torpedoes at the U.S. tanker, and Hardegen and his number one watch officer, Leutnant Horst von Schroeter, are watching the ship through their periscope, counting off the seconds and waiting for the explosion.

☆

Both men stared at the large fast-moving shadow now sharply outlined against the brilliant Jacksonville Beach lights . . . the western sky suddenly erupted in a blinding red-and-yellow explosion! . . . He watched the tanker torch break apart in the middle and its photoflash illumine the beach as brightly as though it were noon. In the incandescence he saw people on shore pour out of their hotels, homes, and places of entertainment. "A rare show for the tourists," he wrote in the KTB, "who probably were having supper now." It was 10:20 P.M. local time, which was a little late for American supper, but the bars, dance halls, drive-ins, and amusements were still going strong [because] it was the end of the week and the beaches were crowded with sailors from the training base, Jacksonville NAS, twenty miles inland from Mayport on the St. Johns; soldiers in basic training from Camp Blanding in the interior; and high-spirited youths and civilians of all walks and ages to whom Friday night in Florida was party time.

Not satisfied that the tanker with its compartmentation would sink when its cargo burned out, Hardegen ordered the deck guns manned and approached the broken vessel with the intent of holing her fatally with artillery. When he saw the large number of spectators on shore, however, and noted the proximity of the beach homes to the point of attack, he worried that the shells he fired from seaward might overshoot and hurt innocent people and their property. He therefore made a turn around the victim's stern and came up on its shoreward, or port, side, where any errant shells would pass harmlessly out to sea. The tactic created four problems for him: one, U-123 was silhouetted against the fire's glare and thereby became vulnerable to any onshore weapons; two, the shallow depths in which he now swam forced Hardegen to take a position only 250 meters from the fiercely blazing target; three, as he closed the target he saw that it was equipped with a 4-inch gun on a platform aft, though for some reason it was not yet manned; and, four, when U-123's forward gun crew pulled the lanyard on the first shot the muzzle flash ignited the sea of spilled oil around them! Only the fortunate circumstance of a wind blowing away from the boat prevented the gun crew and bridge watch from being roasted alive. At point-blank range every shot was a hit, and soon the target hull was aground. There was no return fire. Two large concentrations of oil now burned independently, giving the appearance of two ships ablaze. Hardegen began a fast withdrawal south on a course of 165 degrees. He wrote: "All the vacationers had seen an impressive special performance at Roosevelt's expense. A burning tanker, artillery fire, the silhouette of a U-boat—how often had all of that been seen in America?"

On shore, it was true, frivolity quickly turned to horror as the shocked revelers beheld the funeral pyre at sea and the U-boat itself bombarding the fiery corpse. Their faces red from the glare, the witnesses stood in stupefaction, endeavoring to comprehend how a war they considered so officially remote from their daily lives could suddenly appear in front of them. By telephone they spread word of the experience to family and friends in nearby communities, including Jacksonville, Florida's most populous city at the time; and soon the highways to the beach were clogged with the automobiles of the curious. Most were stopped and turned back by military police.

. . . On the ocean highway where there was no barrier . . . the tanker [could be seen] spitting twisted red columns like a volcano. Other, smaller, oil-fed conflagrations rode the waves. A pall of black smoke rubbed out the stars.

The curious were not alone in racing to the scene. No more than five minutes after the torpedo struck, PBY-3s from NAS Jacksonville were over the area dropping magnesium flares in an attempt to sight the U-boat. They were quickly joined by North American B-25 Mitchell bombers armed with MKXVII depth bombs from the Army 106th Observation Squadron, based at the Jacksonville Municipal Airport. No attacks were made using bombs, but the constant use of parachute flares and star shells enabled rescue craft to locate survivors. These vessels came from Mayport. Too small to have been spotted by Hardegen when he passed by the St. Johns, they were Mayport's total fleet of two converted yachts, one the 125-foot *Tyrer*, which had rescued survivors from *Esparta* two nights before, one minesweeper, and two Yippies. The vessels made trip after trip to bring in survivors and bodies. Emergency medical care was given in the base administration building, which was transformed into an emergency sick bay. The dead were placed on the lawn outside. Many were charred beyond recognition. George W. Jackson, a reserve ensign commanding Yippie YP-32 (which had been a World War I subchaser), remembers reaching into the burning water to rescue a seaman only to have the man's flesh come off the arm as he seized it. For him and his twelve-man crew it was the grisliest experience of their young lives.

SS *Gulfamerica* at 8,081 GRT was not quite the monster that Hardegen supposed but was still a good-sized, spanking-new vessel. Owned by the Gulf Oil Company, she was steaming toward New York on her maiden voyage from Port Arthur with 90,000 barrels of fuel oil when she had the misfortune to encounter Reinhard Hardegen. Forty-one merchant crew and seven naval armed guard formed her complement. Oscar Anderson, the master, had her on course 352 degrees true, speed 14 knots (higher than von Schroeter's estimate), all lights out, radio silent, two lookouts on top of the pilothouse and two more, from the gun crew, on the poop deck. At 2022 EWT a torpedo approaching at 35 degrees from stern to starboard exploded in the after-bunker no. 7 tank, which blew oil skyward and caused an immediate fire. Anderson, like all the other survivors, would report that a second torpedo, quickly following the first, struck in the engine room at after mast about ten feet below the waterline. This must have been a secondary explosion, perhaps of the boilers, since only one torpedo was launched. Anderson ordered engines stopped and abandon ship. Radio operator William M. Meloney, who had been torpedoed on another ship thirty days before, put out distress calls on 500 KC, while Anderson threw confidential codes overboard in a weighted bag; those members of the crew who were capable lowered the lifeboats. Abandonment was orderly until the U-boat began shelling from the port side, and elongated red trails of machine-gun tracer fire curved overhead seeking the mainmast and radio antenna. In the confusion that followed twenty-five men threw themselves overboard, many of whom were lost, and no. 4 lifeboat capsized. Two other boats made it safely down the falls. One of the last men to leave was 57-year-old Chief Engineer Vasco R. Geer, a native of nearby Jacksonville, who with Second Pumpman Glen W. Smith and Third Mate Oliver H. Gould lowered the no. 2 boat on the starboard side. The three circled to the port side looking for men in the loathsome-smelling water but had to withdraw when oil flames threatened to engulf them. Geer saw the men from one boat go overboard while the U-boat was firing, in the apparent belief that the Germans would shoot at the lifeboats. But, he reported, "there was no attempt to shell or molest survivors in the boats." Rescue craft picked up twenty-four (including the master, with a shell splinter in his arm, and the radio operator) of the forty-one merchant crew, five of the seven-man armed guard, and twelve bodies. Geer told USN interrogators, "I only wish we had a chance to use the gun against them [the Germans]." No explanation is given in the records for the failure of the armed guard to use either the 4-inch or the two .50-caliber machine guns with which *Gulfamerica* was one of the first U.S. tankers to be equipped. The U-boat's position was clearly revealed by muzzle flashes and tracer fire when it began its surface attack. The official USN Armed Guard report reads: "The 4″ after gun was manned and loaded but no defensive fire was offered." Perhaps the 4-inch could not be trained because of list. Perhaps the gun crew obeyed the abandon ship order before it had a chance to sight the U-boat on the surface. Or perhaps the gun crew panicked. The navy's public announcement stated simply, "The crew had no opportunity to fire at the attacking submarine."

Realizing that backlighting from the Jacksonville Beach shore had

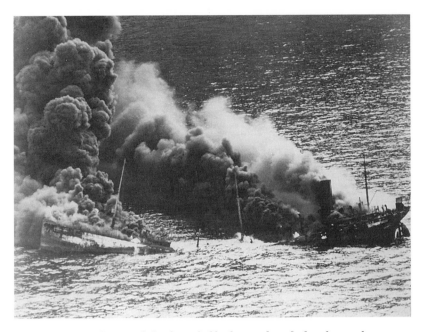

Torpedoed ships frequently broke in half. This unidentified tanker in the Atlantic in early 1942 is crumbling amidships from the heat of her burning cargo and settling toward the bottom. (National Archives, War and Conflict Collection, 1316)

enabled the U-boat to sight its target, Florida governor Spessard Holland on 11 April declared a "screenout" of all lights showing to seaward in coastal and beach communities. The regulations and their enforcement would never be adequate, however, to prevent silhouettes at sea. . . .

On 16 April *Gulfamerica,* which had settled by the stern with a 40 degree list to starboard, finally rolled over, bubbled, and sank from view, her maiden voyage now completely ruined.

On the same day COMINCH issued an order halting all further oil tanker traffic on the East Coast. Molasses could travel from the gulf ports to Port Everglades. But as far as oil was concerned Hardegen's attack on *Gulfamerica* had been the last straw. No oil would move in tanker bottoms for the remainder of the month. The Allied war effort would have to live off its capital.

☆   (Gannon, *Operation Drumbeat,* 362–66)

19 Inside Battles
☆☆

While torpedoes and tankers were exploding in the Battle of the Atlantic, the explosions of an even more consequential battle going on in Washington, D.C., and between Washington and London, were rhetorical. This was a battle of debates in Washington, with and within the U.S. Navy, over protecting merchant ships from the submarine scourge that was devouring them.

Should the merchant fleet be armed? Should it be convoyed? If so, where were capable escort vessels to be found? By diverting them from other vital tasks? Similarly, where would air cover come from?

In January 1942, transatlantic convoys were escorted as far as a mid-ocean meeting point where British escorts took over. But merchant traffic along the coast from Canada to the Caribbean, and in the Caribbean and the Gulf of Mexico, was on its own. In the first six months of 1942, 154 Allied merchant ships were lost along the East Coast and in the northwest Atlantic, and 167 in the Caribbean and the Gulf. In the convoyed transatlantic traffic, losses were a minor fraction. In January alone submarines sank fifty-eight merchantmen in the north Atlantic, but only three of them were picked off in convoy.

Although the British had been using convoys effectively since 1941, it was two years before President Roosevelt managed to coerce his navy chief, Adm. Ernest J. King, to authorize U.S. convoys. FDR was responding to pressures from Churchill and Stalin and from astronomically mounting cargo losses in the bloody sea lanes.

☆

Admiral King was an extraordinary figure, with a varied background in cruisers, battleships, and submarines. He learned to fly at the age of forty-seven and became captain of the aircraft carrier *Lexington* in June 1930. Later, as chief of the Bureau of Aeronautics, he was central to the selection of the aircraft with which the navy began World War II. His wide experience made him one of the first to develop the concept of separating the battleships from cruisers and aircraft carriers, knitting the latter two into hard-hitting task forces.

He was a man of powerful and generally unpleasant personality; he disliked and distrusted almost everyone, with the British at the top of his list. His attitude was universally reciprocated by all but the most extreme loyalists on his staff; over time he battled all comers, confident that he alone knew not only what was right but also what was morally correct.

Nonetheless, while full credit must be given King for the masterful way in which he put heart and punch back into the Pacific fleet after Pearl Harbor (the battles of the Coral Sea and Midway were going on at the time of the German U-boat thrust on the East Coast), he nonetheless must bear the responsibility for the total failure to anticipate the German submarine incursion and for the six long months it took to combat it. Because he had not provided sufficient smaller ships for escort duties, King refused to institute convoys, insisting that a weak convoy was worse than none at all, despite clear evidence from the British that this was not so.

The result was slaughter on a scale that no one could have imagined, least of all the incredulous German submariners, who found the richest, safest hunting of their careers.

☆   (Boyne, *Clash of Titans,* 97–98)

The outrageous toll, especially of tankers, on the Atlantic Coast during the first months of the United States' active participation in the war was wrought by five German submarines. That tiny fleet was reinforced before long to a strength of twelve—never more. Its depredations quickly grew to enormous proportions.

Four problems affecting the merchant marine at war were aggravated by Admiral King's foot-dragging. First, merchant ships, being sunk whole-sale and without notice, were unarmed and thus completely defenseless. Second, air patrol of the sea lanes close to shore could be conducted by volunteer private pilots of the Civil Air Patrol (CAP); their very presence and their ability to alert air corps or navy attackers could keep U-boats submerged, at least in daylight. Third, merchant ships sailing alongshore were sharply silhouetted against the brilliant outdoor lighting of resort areas and highways along the shore; this made the coastal strip a backlit

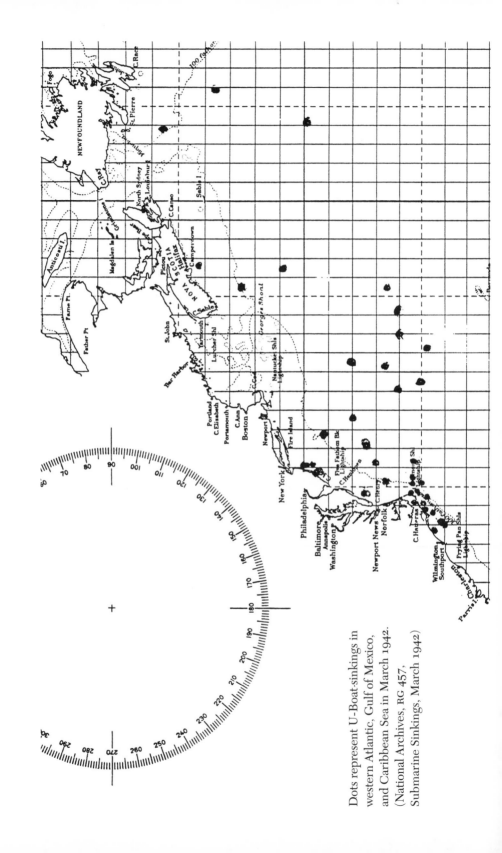

Dots represent U-Boat sinkings in western Atlantic, Gulf of Mexico, and Caribbean Sea in March 1942. (National Archives, RG 457, Submarine Sinkings, March 1942)

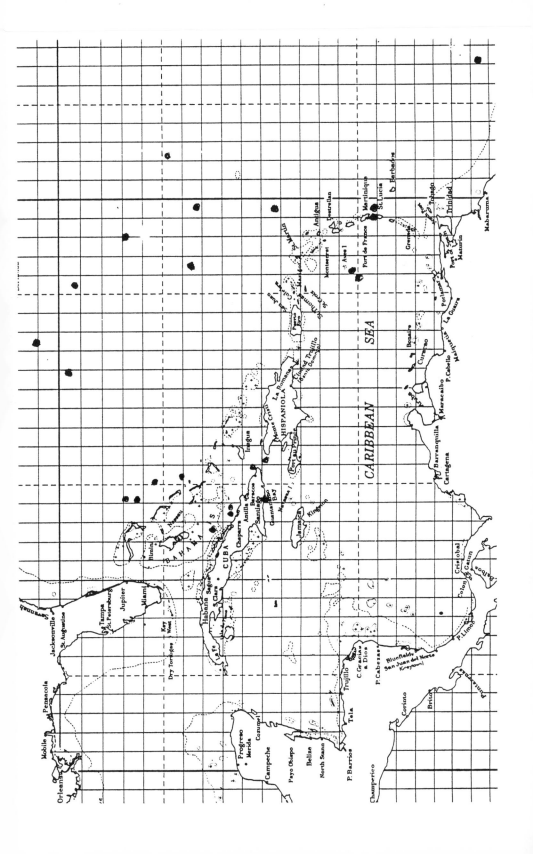

What a torpedo can do to steel deck plates. The SS *Aurora* (running empty) was hit twice off New Orleans in May 1942 (photographed here while under tow). The ship was repaired in drydock and went back into service. One of the explosions blew a full-grown porpoise, intact, onto the bridge. (National Archives, RG 80-CF, 1055E2)

shooting gallery for U-boats. And finally, there was no provision for a convoy system, grouping freighters and tankers under the active protection of armed escort vessels and aircraft.

As tanker losses mounted early in 1942, the first three of these problems were addressed by an emergency committee formed by the oil industry.

☆

[It made] numerous positive suggestions for improving the situation, chief among which were: (1) swinging guns aboard all tankers, as the British had done, and crewing them with highly trained USN armed guards; (2) engaging the services of the Civil Air Patrol, private pilots with their own light airplanes, to force down U-boats in the sea lanes (an idea endorsed by Admiral Andrews); and (3) suppressing bright shore lights showing to seaward against which it was obvious U-boats silhouetted their targets. (These eminently sensible suggestions, be it noted, came from laymen.)

☆   (Gannon, *Operation Drumbeat,* 343)

Problem 1: Arming the Ships

The navy agreed to consider the proposals and acted promptly on arming the ships. In November 1941, after the sinking of the *Robin Moor* and shortly after the sinking of the U.S. destroyer *Reuben James* with the loss of a hundred navy men, Congress removed a legal difficulty. It repealed the most restrictive elements of the Neutrality Acts of 1939, and this opened the way to arming merchantmen. The navy had enough guns and gunnery training capacity to provide weapons and armed guard crews for a hundred ships a month.

The first ship armed was the freighter SS *Dunboyne,* which was about to depart for north Russia and was outfitted with a 4-inch 50-caliber gun (please see the glossary under "Caliber" for a definition of this gun), a pair of .50-caliber machine guns, and seven .30-caliber (or light) machine guns. A navy armed guard crew (no. 1E) was put aboard. The *Dunboyne* gave an excellent account of herself. Ens. Rufus T. Brinn reported on the freighter's stay in Murmansk.

☆

We were frequently bombed by enemy planes and manned our anti-aircraft guns fifty-eight times. Gun Crew #1E shot down two enemy planes, helped bring down a third, put one rear gunner out of action, and hit several others causing slight damage. . . . 31 March . . . 1500 [ship's time] A.A. guns manned, approximately ten German bombers (Junkers 88) dropped bombs in Murmansk. Tracers from starboard .50-caliber manned by Hoban, E. C., GM3c, were seen to enter enemy plane that was brought down. (The American naval observer Commander Frankel, USN, informed armed guard commander to credit gun crew 1E with plane.) . . . 2100 . . . German 4-motored Focke-Wulfs bombed dock area heavily for two hours and one-half. During entire raid gun crew was continually firing. Dixon, T, J., GM3c, manning the port .50-caliber hit one of these planes heavily, and the gun crew also received credit for it. A third plane that was brought down was claimed jointly by gun crews on SS *Dunboyne* and SS *Eldena*. . . . Gun crew of the *Dunboyne* and the gun crew aboard the *Eldena* were verbally commended for their effective A.A. barrage by both the Russian military authorities and the U.S. naval observer.

☆   (National Archives, Voyage Reports, *Dunboyne*, 1–5)

As noted earlier, the new and ill-fated tanker *Gulfamerica* was one of the first tankers armed. Soon after launching she was given a 4-inch 50 and a pair of .50-caliber machine guns and an armed guard crew. Her story, told at the end of chapter 18, shows that arms and gun crew alone are not always enough. But as many of the stories in this book amply demonstrate, the armed merchantman is far likelier to survive.

Problem 2: Air Patrol

Admiral King's response to the oil industry suggestion on air patrols was unspecific and irascible: too many "operational difficulties." Later, under important pressures, he retreated from his initial position. But from the outset the Army Air Corps, which was the principal participant in air searches offshore, welcomed the help proffered by the civilian volunteer pilots of the CAP.

By April, army and naval air forces had 170 planes and the first of the navy's antisub blimps assigned. It was a start, though (in Walter Boyne's phrase) "hardly sufficient for a danger area that extended from Canada to the Caribbean and beyond."

Problem 3: Coastal Lighting

The third element of the oil committee's suggestions was reducing the nighttime backlighting of coastwise ships by shore installations and traffic. Again Admiral King issued a foot-dragging and ineffectual response.

As Michael Gannon points out, President Roosevelt, in Executive Order 9066 of 19 February, authorized the services to control "all lighting on the seacoast so as to prevent the silhouetting of ships and their consequent destruction by enemy submarines." But both army and navy vacillated.

☆

Their reluctance to take action came principally as a result of intense pressure exerted by such coastal business interests as beach resort operators who did not want to "inconvenience tourists." In the meeting of 4 March it was decided by the military representatives that control of coastal lights was "a Navy function." Accordingly, five days later—and two months after the date when, it might be argued, he should already have acted decisively and on his own initiative—Admiral King sent out a halfhearted "request" to Andrews in New York: "It is requested that the Commander Eastern Sea Frontier take such steps as may be within his province to control the brilliant illumination of Eastern Seaboard amusement parks and beaches in order that ships passing close to shore be not silhouetted and thereby more easily exposed to submarine attack from seaward." An additional five days later, on 14 March, King made it clear that what he was requesting was not a blackout but a "dimout"; blackouts "were not considered necessary" since only the glare of the brightest lights posed a danger to shipping. This tragic misjudgment, repeating an error that Andrews had made on 10 February . . . would lead by omission to further loss of lives and treasure.

On the very day that King was rejecting blackouts, the 7,610-GRT American freighter SS *Lemuel Burrows* was torpedoed and sunk by *U-404* (Korvettenkapitän Otto von Bülow) off Atlantic City, New Jersey. Twenty crewmen died. The second engineer, who arguably had a better picture of the situation from his lifeboat than King had from his desk, reported that the lights of a New Jersey beach resort doomed his vessel and that they would "continue to cause daily torpedoings until a blackout is ordered along the coast." The engineer added: "We might as well run with our lights on. The lights were like Coney Island. It was lit up like daylight all along the beach. . . . We're going to lose boats every day if they don't do something about it." On 19 March Third Naval District advised the Commanding General, Second Corps Area, U.S. Army, that even with dimout, vessels were silhouetted as much as ten miles out to sea against the sky glow cast from ground light on haze or low-lying cloud banks. It recommended "a complete blackout of all communities within approximately five miles of the coastline," but this would never be done. Tests at sea in April found that patrol boats twenty-five miles out could discern the New York glow even with dimout. In May, army studies concluded that dimout was still so dangerous to shipping that "like targets in a shooting gallery our ships are moving in off a backdrop of hazy light." And as late as 7 July when the 8,141-GRT British freighter *Umtata*, under tow, was torpedoed and sunk off the south Florida coast (at 25-35N, 80-02W) by *U-571* (Kptlt. Helmut Möhlmann), the *Umtata's* second officer blamed the sky glow of Miami ten miles to the northwest. "We could see the loom of Miami 35 miles out to sea," he reported. "The glow of light is just what those subs want." The glow came from street and automobile lights, resort and house windows, dog tracks, and other amusement areas. On 8 July the Miami *Herald* reported that motorists on the Overseas Highway between Homestead and Key West were driving with high beam lights, and, in a related story, cited the experience of a U.S. naval vessel that found the loom of Key West so clearly visible from thirty-one miles at sea that it silhouetted any ship that passed before it.

During the time of slaughter no general blackout was ever declared on the U.S. East Coast. While the British and German coasts, which were quiescent in the same period, practiced total light elimination, the endangered U.S. littoral remained lighted. Dimout and shielding was as far as King would go. The army concurred. So did the general public, which wanted business and pleasure as usual. Civilian avarice and carelessness must take their places on the list of agents accountable for the U-boat triumphs.

✮   (Gannon, *Operation Drumbeat,* 344–45)

The Ultimate Problem: Convoys

Even if the oil industry committee's suggestions had been followed immediately and completely, the most crucial problem of all would have remained—and did remain: convoying. The question of convoys was not only urgent but ancient.

✮

Convoys are not new; the British used them as early as the thirteenth century to protect their cross-channel shipping. Some of these early convoys consisted of two hundred sail, escorted by up to two dozen men-of-war, and directed by two King's officers: the commodore of convoy, in charge of the merchant vessels; and the escort commander, in command of the warships. But even at that early date, merchant sailors and the shipowners were reluctant to sail their ships in convoy, and Edward III had to forbid independent sailings by royal edict.

In the sixteenth century, the losses of galleons between their overseas colonies and Spain became so serious that the Spanish also instituted convoys. Covered by powerful warships, known as the Indian Guard, these convoys were so effective that privateers were never able to capture the convoyed treasure ships. They did, however, succeed in taking many vessels sailing independently.

The Anglo-Dutch wars of the seventeenth century saw both sides using convoys, covered often by the main fleets, and the attempts of the British fleet to interfere with Dutch convoys led in nearly every instance to major actions.

Convoy was an accepted practice in the Napoleonic wars and was obligatory for all English ships; Lloyd's would not insure those sailing independently. The huge convoys were conducted in accordance with carefully developed instructions and procedures, many of which were still applicable a century later. The necessity for convoys was unquestioned by naval officers as the Napoleonic era ended in 1815.

For nearly one hundred years after that, no major sea wars were fought, and with the possible exception of the threat occasioned by a few Confederate raiders against Union shipping, the need for convoys never arose. In the absence of an immediate and compelling threat, convoys—with their inconveniences and the connotation of a defensive strategy—slipped into an undeserved disrepute. . . .

The opponents of the convoy system, and this included the majority of naval officers in the years immediately before the First World War, had developed a number of arguments to support their views. Some were difficult to refute, for the long years of peace had precluded the acid test of new naval theory—combat at sea.

Arrival of large numbers of ships at one time would, they maintained, overcrowd port facilities, resulting in congestion and long delays. Convoys sail at the speed of the slowest vessel, and faster vessels would have to dawdle wastefully along with the others. Finally, few naval planners of the era thought that a sufficient number of warships could be mustered to adequately escort the large number of convoys that would be required.

Because of the loss of revenue, the shipping companies themselves were reluctant to accept the slow speeds and long periods in port awaiting the makeup of convoys. Merchant seamen—an independent group jealous of their prerogatives—resisted being subjected to naval discipline and the many demands and constant alertness required during a convoy operation. Everyone desired a system of protection that would keep the merchant vessels moving as in peacetime with a minimum of interference from both their own and the enemy's navies.

In such an atmosphere, it was natural that the concept of patrols "keeping open the sea lanes" by sweeping the oceans should be quickly accepted, not only by the merchant marine but by naval officers, who naturally gravitated to an "offensive" concept rather than one in which warships were tied down to the unglamorous task of defending slow-moving convoys. In dealing with submarines such a concept ignored the fact that after the warship on patrol had swept through an area of ocean the water was as unprotected as it had been before. Few would admit that, despite the patrolling ships and the distant presence of the main fleet, such a system offered no direct protection to a merchant ship.

[The coming of the submarine invalidated this new strategy even before it was applied, but the anti-convoy school of thought refused to acknowledge the changed situation.] Because of its desire to avoid trouble with the neutrals, Germany until the end of 1916 did, in fact, observe many of the principles of the Hague Convention. Most merchant ships sunk by U-boats were stopped on the surface and the crew allowed to abandon ship. Yet, even under these restrictions, a relatively small number of U-boats had succeeded in sinking over 1,300 ships by the beginning of 1917. Thousands of Allied warships, blimps, and aircraft patrolling the sea lanes in offensive sweeps during the same period had managed to sink only four submarines. The failure of such tactics to blunt the U-boat offensive was painfully clear, but merchant shipping losses were still in the acceptable range and enough supplies were still arriving in Britain to postpone a crisis.

With an intensified building program, and few losses, the U-boat fleet by 1917 had been increased to one hundred operational U-boats. Finally, on 1 February 1917, all restrictions were removed, and an all-out campaign began in order to starve Britain into submission. The result for the Allies was catastrophic.

In the three months after the start of unrestricted U-boat warfare, eight hundred ships totalling two million tons were sunk. In the black month of April 1917, a total of 420 ships of 881,000 tons were lost. The grain reserves in the islands were down to six weeks, and the government put the limit of endurance as 1 November at the latest. . . .

Despite the critical situation, and the obvious success of the two convoy routes already in operation, the admiralty refused to extend the system. It remained for Prime Minister Lloyd George, armed with information supplied by junior officers at the admiralty, to force the issue. He advised the first sea lord that he would come to the admiralty for a discussion of the matter, and the note left little doubt as to his intentions. The admiralty had a change of heart, and when the prime minister arrived, recommended widespread instigation of the convoy system.

The results were dramatic. Losses in convoy promptly dropped to 10 percent of those suffered by independent ships. By the turn of the year, though much hard fighting was ahead, the crisis was past.

The lessons of seven hundred years of sea convoys had been reaffirmed and were not quickly forgotten again. In 1939, convoy plans were ready and were quickly implemented on the outbreak of World War II.

But Allied planners had almost completely disregarded the tremendous benefits to be derived from aerial protection of convoys. Of 257 ships sunk in convoy in World War I, only five were lost when aircraft augmented the surface escort. Despite the obvious conclusions to be drawn, World War II found the Allies unprepared to provide long-range air coverage for convoys, and hundreds of fine ships and thousands of seamen were lost due to this lack. Not until 1943 were the necessary aircraft provided, with startling results. . . .

One of the most successful British escort commanders of World War II stated: "Convoy is the essence of offense, for instead of dispersing your forces in search of an enemy whose object is to avoid them, it forces the enemy to scatter his forces in search of your shipping and when he finds it either to fight on your own ground and your own terms in order to reach your shipping or to remain impotent." . . .

Not even the most daring U-boat commanders desired to attack strongly escorted convoys, for the risk was too great. The top aces, such as Kretschmer, Schepke, and Prien, made most of their kills against ships sailing independently or in weakly escorted convoys.

No one realized this difficulty better than Adm. Karl Dönitz, Flag Officer, U-boats, and himself once a top-flight combat U-boat commander. Describing his experiences in World War I, he said:

In the First World War, the German U-boat arm achieved great successes; but the introduction of the convoy system in 1917 robbed it of its opportunity to become a decisive factor. The oceans at once became bare and empty; for long periods at a time, the U-boats operating individually would see nothing at all, and then suddenly up would loom a huge concourse of ships—thirty or fifty or more of them—surrounded by a strong escort of warships of all types. The solitary U-boat, which most probably had sighted the convoy purely by chance, would then attack, thrusting again and again and persisting, if the commander had strong nerves, for perhaps several days and nights, until the physical exhaustion of both commander and crew called a halt. The lone U-boat might well sink one or two of the ships, or even several, but that was a poor percentage of the whole. The convoy would steam on.

☆ (Waters, *Bloody Winter*, 2–9)

But this was a lesson Admiral King had not learned. In high U.S. naval circles the import of this lesson was slow in getting through to the top. The British had learned it the hard way. The Soviets knew it, and both urged the point on Roosevelt. And FDR finally squeezed King and the navy hard enough.

Many navy people below the very top understood it, especially Adm. Adolphus Andrews, commanding the Eastern Sea Frontier. It was understood by an acute, young army "brigadier general in charge of war plans," as Gannon observes. Dwight D. Eisenhower had confided to his diary three months earlier, "One thing that might help win this war is to get someone to shoot King."

It was 19 June 1942 before Army Chief of Staff Gen. George C. Marshall addressed King on the subject. He dispatched a memo to his chief of naval operations reading, in part: "The losses by submarines on our Atlantic seaboard and in the Caribbean now threaten our entire war effort."

He went on to cite statistics just brought to his attention: the War Shipping Administration had allocated seventy-four ships to the army for the following month (July); seventeen of them had been sunk by mid-June. Tanker tonnage was being sunk at a monthly rate of 3.5 percent (an annual rate of 42 percent!). Marshall went on: "We are all aware of the limited number of escort craft available, but has every conceivable improvised means been brought to bear on this situation? I am fearful that another month or two of this will so cripple our means of transport that we will be unable to bring sufficient men and planes to bear against the enemy in critical theaters to exercise a determining influence on the war" (*Marshall Papers*, cited in King and White, *Fleet Admiral King*, 455).

Admiral King responded with alacrity but not without some dissimulation. Two days after Marshall's memo he fired off a voluminous and detailed response, in which he ardently embraced convoys for merchant ships—with no reference to the fact that his inaction had delayed escort for coastal traffic for months: "If all shipping can be brought under escort and air cover our losses will be reduced to an acceptable figure. I might say in this connection that escort is not just *one* way of handling the submarine menace; it is the *only* way that gives any promise of success" (King and White, *Fleet Admiral King*, 457).

This was true enough and was not the point of King's nearly ruinous failure. The admiral believed in convoys—but only if the escort were at optimal strength. He clung stubbornly to his mistaken belief that an understrength escort was as bad as none, or even worse. In fact, any escort was better than none.

Earlier in his memo, King had answered Marshall's plea for improvisation by not only endorsing the idea but claiming that he had been improvising on a large scale right along—citing as examples some of the very approaches his foot-dragging had long delayed: "We took over all pleasure craft that could be used and sent them out with makeshift armament and untrained crews. We employed for patrol purposes aircraft that could not carry bombs, and planes flown from school fields by student pilots. We armed merchant ships as rapidly as possible. We employed fishing boats as volunteer lookouts. The Army helped in the campaign of extemporization by taking on the civil aviation patrol" (King and White, *Fleet Admiral King*, 456).*

Marshall may have been somewhat incredulous at the admiral's seeming about-face—or perhaps at his dissembling. Nevertheless, when it

---

*Admiral King adopted and slightly elaborated these claims in his published collection of wartime reports to the Secretary of the Navy in 1946, *U.S. Navy at War*.

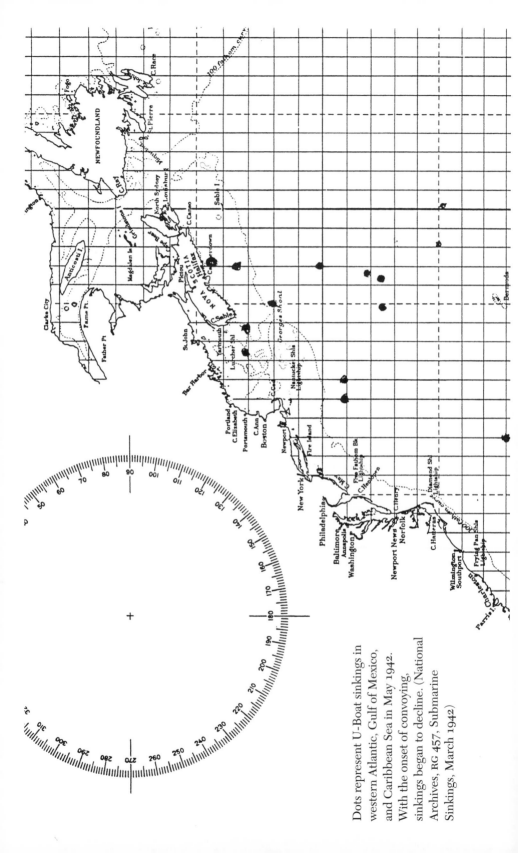

Dots represent U-Boat sinkings in western Atlantic, Gulf of Mexico, and Caribbean Sea in May 1942. With the onset of convoying, sinkings began to decline. (National Archives, RG 457, Submarine Sinkings, March 1942)

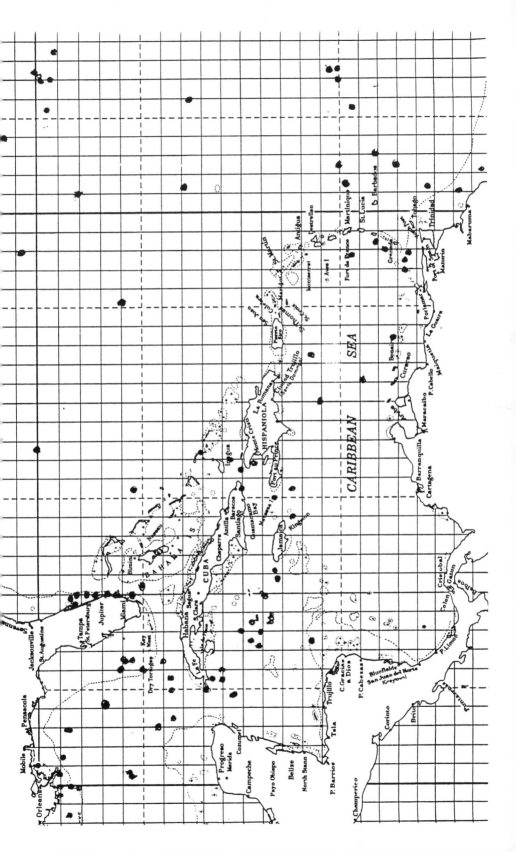

did move, the navy really swung into action. As Michael Gannon, no fan of Admiral King, observes, within little more than a month "King and the navy performed creditably in the creation and operation of an anti-submarine force that became so formidable, sophisticated, and well trained that, in concert with the British during the following year, it overwhelmed the U-boats in every quadrant of the Atlantic" (Gannon, *Operation Drumbeat,* 391–92).

As soon as the first American coastal convoy was organized in mid-May the dreadful toll began to decline. Immediately, President Roosevelt noticed the difference between losses in convoyed ships and those sailing alone. His comment to Admiral King was tart: "I think it has taken an unconscionable time to get things going."

July saw the last sinking of the year in what had been the incredibly happy hunting grounds of Dönitz's undersea fleet. Whatever it had taken to pry open his eyes, Admiral King had seen the light at last.

His conversion was welcome, and it came not a moment too soon. Gannon put it deftly: "The Pacific Pearl Harbor lasted two hours and ten minutes on a Sunday morning. The Atlantic Pearl Harbor lasted six months" (Gannon, *Operation Drumbeat,* 389).

20 "Wolf Packs" and the Battle of the Convoys

★★

Once the convoy system was adopted merchant ship losses dropped dramatically and at once. The wily head of Germany's U-boat operations, Admiral Dönitz, had realized this would happen; he had drawn this lesson from the previous war. He was ready with a response, which he called *die Rudeltaktik*, the tactic of the pack, as in wolf pack: a large concentration of submarines waging a mobile, coordinated onslaught on a single convoy. Individual subs in the pack would seize opportunities to sneak between escorts and pounce on tankers or freighters on the inside, or launch torpedoes through momentary openings in the protective screen of destroyers.

An antidote to the wolf pack tactic had to be found, and was found, and at last was able to end the German field days in the vital North Atlantic sea lanes. March of 1943 would be the last month of wholesale destruction of merchant shipping there.

★

Both the Germans and the Allies, of course, had been keeping close watch on the statistics of the fluctuation, spread, and impact of that struggle, upon which even ultimate victory might depend. Now those statistics were swiftly confirming the new situation. In contrast to those disastrous figures of the ten months since July 1942 (989 sinkings, with 686 in the North Atlantic), the following ten months, from May 1943, showed the overall total of Allied losses dropping to a total of 359 ships. Of these, only ninety were in the now less hazardous North Atlantic! Conversely, the German record, now no longer tinged with hopes of victory, was closely linked to that change. In those first ten months, only 59 U-boats had been lost, but the numbers jumped to 219 in the following ten months.

In this spectacular drop in Allied sinkings and the increased toll of U-boats, various elements had been responsible. The United States and

Britain had worked together and would continue to do so in joint operation. The credit for success belongs to each of them in different ways. The British had the longer and heavier share of the gruelling patrol and convoy work so vividly pictured in Nicholas Monserrat's *The Cruel Sea;* they sank more submarines than did the Americans; and their merchant seamen suffered far heavier casualties. But in the spring of 1943, probably the most important contribution consisted of the new developments in several fields, largely by the United States. In particular, there was a very effective combination of antisubmarine-warfare (ASW) tactics and devices.

The new "hunter-killer" tactics were probably the most potent element in the latest Allied successes. These utilized in particular two new types of vessels as well as several original scientific devices. The ships, the Destroyer Escort (DE) and the Escort Carrier (CVE), differed from their prototypes, the Destroyer (DD) and Carrier (CV), mainly in their lessened speed. The latter had never been used in connection with convoys as the DDs had been. In the new tactics, the planes of the Escort Carriers could cover the convoys all the way across the Atlantic, unlike the land-based aircraft from Britain, Canada, or Iceland. The Escort planes did not stay with the 10-knot convoys but swept the seas through which a convoy would pass. The particular purpose was to catch U-boats on the surface. Until nuclear craft began to appear a decade later, the submarine was essentially a surface vessel, which now and then could submerge to avoid detection. Its electric batteries were able to keep it submerged for only a relatively limited time before it had to surface to replenish them. When the scouting planes sighted a surfaced submarine—unless they could bomb it themselves—they directed the attendant destroyers or escorts where to go in for the kill. The latter, if not in position to depth-bomb the submarine, would try to keep track of it until it would have to surface.

An example of the typical "hunter-killer tactics" has been described by Rear Adm. Daniel V. Gallery, whose Task Group 23 was based around the CVE *Guadalcanal* early in 1944:

> We prowled through our assigned area with the carrier 3,000 yards behind a bent screen of five destroyer escorts, using our airplanes to scour the ocean for about one hundred miles on each side of our base course and 160 miles ahead. With four turkeys (planes) you could, during a four hour flight, cover an area of roughly 20,000

A definite kill for the Coast Guard cutter *Spencer,* escorting an Atlantic convoy whose ships can be seen in the background, on April 17, 1943. The depth charge she projected off her bow destroyed the *U-175,* whose oily smoke and debris is erupting dead ahead. (Photograph by W/O Jack January, USCG, from National Archives, War and Conflict Collection, 970)

square miles. In round numbers, this is one-third the area of the New England states. . . .

Aircraft can't find a submerged U-boat . . . Our destroyers could find them submerged with their sonar gear, but the maximum range at which we could get an echo off a sub was about 2,000 yards. Even with five destroyers sweeping a path ahead of us all day long we only searched 3,600 square miles with sonar—about three percent of the area the planes covered.

While on that duty, his task group performed the unique feat of boarding and capturing the *U-505* and then brought it home to be an exhibit in a Chicago park.

The Destroyer Escort was needed badly not only in those "hunter-killer" tactics but also for regular convoy duty. The regular destroyers' expensive equipment for their high speed of 33 knots was wasted in convoy duty, even had there been enough of them to go around. Their faster mobility, moreover, was essential to operations elsewhere. Convoys averaged barely 10 knots. To the uninitiated, the DE looked little different from the DD. But the DE made less of a demand upon critical materials and precious construction hours; it could be built more quickly; and with its lower speed was far cheaper, at about $5,500,000, than the wartime DD at about $8,000,000. Yet the DE was nearly as large, and its 20 knots were sufficient for chasing submarines away from the slow convoys and keeping up with the CVE in the "hunter-killer" group. It could, moreover, stand the gruelling work of the North Atlantic, for which the old 110-foot subchaser and the newer 175 patrol craft were too small.

Unfortunately there was shameful delay in producing DEs, which can be laid at the doors of the navy's policy advisers in Naval Operations and the General Board. For years there had been a vague realization of the need for some sort of escort vessel, cheaper than the fast destroyer, yet tough enough to stand Atlantic gales. But now with ships being sunk by the hundreds out in the Atlantic, the masterminds of the navy, moved by considerations of perfectionism and economy, turned down one proposal after another. Later Admiral King was to say angrily that they were "bickering about details of displacement, speed, and armament, and behaving as if time were of no consequence." Action finally came through Capt. (later Vice-Admiral) Edward L. Cochrane, a naval constructor, who would become the head of the navy's whole construction program. He designed the DE; and the General Board turned it down. Thereupon he pulled enough wires to have the British request a hundred of them. With a strong push from Under Secretary James Forrestal, Cochrane's bold action ultimately led to the first of the DEs in February 1943. In 1940, the navy had only 225 DDs, but by the end of the war, there were 373, and 365 DEs in addition.

Whereas the Destroyer Escort represented in general both a type and function long in use, the function of the Escort Carrier was the new concept of giving continuing air protection to convoys. This made it of prime importance in the "hunter-killer" tactics of the antisubmarine warfare, particularly in the deadly "Greenland Air Gap." The British had already been experimenting with converted vessels, and now the United States followed a similar course with the Escort Carriers. Known popularly as the "baby flattop" or the "jeep carrier," the CVE was a far cry from the big CVs of the *Essex* class, which were developing an important new role in the Pacific warfare. The CVE measured some 7,880 tons to the 27,000 of the *Essex;* carried only 28 planes to 103 on the *Essex;* and its speed was 17 knots as against 33. The big ships, needed for the new "fast carrier task forces" in the Pacific, simply could not be spared for Atlantic anti-submarine work.

In 1940, one lone CVE, the *Long Island,* was launched, but not until the summer and fall of 1942 did these new "jeep carriers" begin to join the fleet in force. Four of them had been converted from four-year-old tankers and appeared in August and September. They were followed closely, also from the Seattle-Tacoma yard, by the *Bogue, Card,* and *Core,* which were to be the first CVEs in U.S. action in the North Atlantic. The planes of the early Escort Carriers were the Avengers and Wildcats.

In the meantime, scientists had been rushing to complete some valuable new devices in connection with antisubmarine warfare. Probably the most significant was the small microwave radar for search planes. At any rate, Hitler and Admiral Dönitz blamed it for the sudden reversal in their U-boat successes in the spring of 1943. Radar itself was almost a complete novelty when the war started, and it had taken a while to overcome the initial skepticism. Besides, the early plane radar equipment had given off certain emanations, which the Germans had ingeniously been able to detect, giving their submarines the chance to evade aerial searchers. But that new 10-centimeter (4-inch) microwave radar did not betray its presence, and the unsuspecting surfaced submarine had little chance to escape the search plane swooping down through the clouds.

While that microwave was aiding the CVE planes, further developments of sonar or asdic, as the British called it, enabled surface vessels, DD or DE, to follow the movements of submerged U-boats but not, of course, over as wide a range as the search planes.

A further device, already in use, but in process of being improved, was the shore-based High-frequency Direction-finder (nicknamed Huff-Duff). This device was able to plot the bearings from distant submarines. Then daily from Washington and London warnings went out to the convoy commanders of the presence of enemy U-boats in their vicinity. The

Germans, too, maintained remote control over their submarine movements. Admiral Dönitz could even take over the direction of a wolf-pack attack from his headquarters in a chateau at Lorient in France. So much depended in this war on the efficiency of scientific devices, that the competition was close and strenuous in the laboratories of both Germany and the Allies. When the Germans, for instance, invented an acoustic torpedo that would track down the sound of a ship's propeller, the Allies quickly countered with the "Fix," strips of metal towed behind a ship so noisily that the enemy torpedo would be attracted to them and not to the propeller.

The new "hunter-killer" tactics and the searching devices were to be most effective against the U-boats from the Germans' first encounter with them, when their "wolf packs" were raiding what seemed to be easy convoy targets in the Greenland Air Gap. This action on 5 May 1943, called "the climax of the Battle of the Atlantic," proved the tide had turned against the Germans. The CVEs were not yet at hand, but the combination of the new radar, and the "Huff Duff" enabled seven convoy escorts, aided by the arrival of two Antisubmarine Support Groups, to drive off an attack of fifteen U-boats which had threatened to annihilate that convoy. Before the month was out, forty-one U-boats had been sunk.

With such North Atlantic losses, Admiral Dönitz decided to change his scene of operations to safer waters.

☆   (Albion and Pope, Sea Lanes in Wartime, 344–50)

The developments in strategy and technology that eventually won the Battle of the Atlantic for the West were worked out against a tapestry of gallantry and devastation. The battle pitted convoy against wolf pack.

A convoy is arrayed in a broad rectangle of ships in rows and columns. There may be five or six rows, spaced five hundred yards apart, and ten to fifteen columns, eight hundred to a thousand yards apart. Each master must keep his ship in its proper station in relation to the others, and each ship is numbered by its column and row. The ship on the left front corner of the convoy is in column 1 and row 1, hence its station is 11. Column 2 row 2 is 22, and so on.

Problem ships are "rompers," which sail ahead of the convoy; if possible, escort vessels bring them back into line. "Stragglers" usually fall behind because of fog or stormy weather; "lame ducks" drop out with engine trouble, which leaves them at the mercy of the enemy, for the convoy cannot and will not stop to wait for them.

Once the United States adopted convoying, getting crusty old merchant skippers to follow the rules and maintain their stations—which many cranky old salts pronounced impossible—was an arduous and tricky task. Each convoy was under the command of its commodore, a retired navy officer recalled to duty, and a vice commodore on another ship took over if the commodore were sunk.

Not all the skippers were old cranks; a considerable and growing number of them were relatively youthful recent graduates of the maritime service's officer training programs, and they treated regulations with more respect than many of the old-timers.

The day before sailing, an all-important convoy conference is held. Samuel Eliot Morison attended the conference for Convoy UGS-21 (US-Gibraltar Slow, number 21). The speed of a convoy is necessarily limited to the speed of its slowest ship—a maximum of 11 knots for a Liberty, sometimes as slow as 8 knots or even less.

For UGS-21, a New York section and a Chesapeake Bay section will rendezvous off New York to make up the convoy. Morison sits in on the conference for the Chesapeake Bay section, which is held in the afternoon before sailing, in a large room at the Norfolk navy base.

☆

Escort commander, convoy commodore and vice-commodore, port director, the president of the Virginia Pilots' Association, and every master or first officer of a merchant vessel must be there. The first three are in naval khaki (or blues if the day is nippy); a few masters wear the new merchant marine uniform, but most are in civilian suits and flannel shirts without ties. A varied-looking lot they are, of all ages from twenty-one to seventy, and of several nations; some recent graduates of King's Point, crisp and taut; others stooped, bewhiskered, and weather beaten; but almost every man lean and serious, with the eyes of a sailor used to long-distance gazing.

Here are the writer's notes taken at one of these conferences:

(The mimeographed convoy instructions are first distributed.)

PORT DIRECTOR: Are ye all ready for sea?

A MASTER: I have to sign on some crew at Newport News.

TWO MASTERS: We haven't cleared ship yet.

A FOURTH MASTER: I have three men yet to come aboard.

PORT DIRECTOR: Well, hurry up and get yer business done.

CONVOY COMMODORE: The signal for departure will be given at 0500 tomorrow morning by one prolonged blast of my whistle. Each ship must hoist the convoy signal number. When ye enter the Med., no more zig-zagging, no balloons, show all yer lights, and any submarines you encounter are friendly. (*Sensation among the masters!*) Get yer mates familiar with the contents of the convoy instructions. Give 'em authority to turn on signal light at night, after passing Europa Point, whence you will all proceed independently to your destinations. Columns 1 through 4 will consist of the vessels joining us from New York. Watch yer green officers; see that they keep closed up five hundred yards to the ship ahead.

ESCORT COMMANDER: When an escort comes alongside steer the steady convoy course. If you see lights in another ship, signal him by whistle, one blast for forward, three for amidships, two for aft. Three of our escort vessels have surgeons on board who can be transferred to you by boatswain's chair if you have any serious cases on board.

CONVOY COMMODORE: Use blue stern light and dim running lights in visibility so poor that you cannot make out other ships.

PILOTS' ASSOCIATION PRESIDENT: I will have thirty-seven pilots available to take you through the swept channel. The first thirty-five ships to sortie should have anchor cables hove short, engines in stand-by, and ladder lowered on the port side.

CONVOY COMMODORE: Good sailing!

PORT DIRECTOR: Beer in the rear—Good luck—Scram!

(*One of the masters, an Oriental by his looks, asks me, "Does that mean the blue stern light?" Fortunately not; it means free beer in the rear of the room!*)

The conference disperses after a few handshakes and backslappings. Motor lifeboats take the members on board, and precisely at 0500 next morning anchors are weighed and the convoy stands out of the Capes, through the swept channel in a single column twenty-five miles long, forming up outside while a blimp maneuvers overhead and land-based planes slice across the sky.

☆   (Morison, *Atlantic Battle Won,* 10:155–56)

An Ammo Ship in the Next Column

An ever-present dread of seafaring men in convoys, nearly always unspoken but never far from the surface, is that a tanker with aviation gas or an ammunition ship in the next column will sustain a direct hit and go off like an enormous bomb. Or worse, that one will find oneself aboard such a vessel at the moment its luck runs out.

One major contributor to that legendary fear was the SS *Mary Luckenbach*, which was vaporized on 14 September 1942. She was on the way to Murmansk in Convoy PQ-18, the first resumption of the North Russia convoys after the awful destruction of PQ-17 (which is treated at some length in the next chapter). Reports from the armed guard officers of eleven ships hard by the *Luckenbach* when she went heavenward—or was blown to hell—describe the cataclysm. Each of those reports was a hair-raising adventure story of its own, but two in particular are told in compelling detail from different physical perspectives.

Lt. (jg) Wesley Norton Miller, commanding the armed guard aboard SS *St. Olaf*, filed a brief report at first and an amplified one, exquisitely written, a couple of weeks later. He had had his hands full from the day before.

☆

[13 September 1942]. . . . The British freighter, Empire Stevenson . . . was hit and exploded in one towering sheet of bright yellow flame that reached to the sky. After two minutes time the flames subsided to a mere flickering on the waves. Not a trace of that unfortunate ship could be seen. It was sickening. Not one man survived. I saw above the flames as the explosion occurred, the wings of an airplane flying through the air. I believe that the explosion got the German plane that torpedoed her.

In the column next to us (position #41), another British freighter, the *Empire Beaumont*, was blazing amidship and listing to port. A few members of her crew floated by on a raft while others were floating in the water. It was pitiful to hear their cries for help. The Hurricanes had driven off the enemy by this time, but I shall always maintain that they were caught napping on this attack.

As I gazed around me, I saw the bow of the Panamanian ship, *Macbeth*, slide down and out of sight like a tired fish. Four U.S. ships were sinking also. They were the *Oregonian* with only thirteen survivors; the *Wacosta;* the two Liberty ships *John Penn* and the *Oliver Ellsworth.* Another Panamanian ship, the *Africander,* was lying on her side—finished. It was a discouraging sight to see ten of our forty merchant ships go the first day of the attack. . . .

At 2100, just as darkness was settling down, twelve torpedo planes came sneaking in from the starboard quarter. We were waiting for them. The entire sky was aflame from our gunfire. Tracers cut fantastic figures on the dark curtain above. . . .

[14 September] . . . Two German pilots came floating by on a rubber raft, close to a Russian freighter in the first column. The Russians killed both of them with machine gun fire. I watched this horrible sight through my glasses.

At 1315 a seemingly unending line of torpedo bombers came toward us from dead ahead and on the starboard side. I counted up to thirty-five and got too busy to continue counting. They came in low, not more than thirty feet above the water, zigzagging; they rise and drop continually to make themselves difficult targets. There are Heinkel 111s and Junkers 88s among them.

Again, ten Hurricanes roar out to meet them. The enemy splits and a great number swing around toward our port beam. They are definitely cautious about coming into our curtain of gunfire. Finally one Junkers 88 rises to a higher altitude and heads across our bow about two hundred yards ahead. My 3″50 gunner burst a shell under him. The motor of this bomber began blazing. I watched all my men around our 3″50 gun dance around and clap their hands. On fire and losing altitude, this bomber headed toward the fourth and fifth columns. I watched him carefully to see him crash.

It was then that I saw a sight never to be forgotten. The pilot of this plane, undoubtedly knowing that he was doomed, deliberately dove his flaming bomber with its cargo of death onto the mid-decks of the U.S. ship *Mary Luckenbach.* There was one great boiling mass of greyish-black smoke and flame, which must have reached a thousand feet in height, as the *Mary Luckenbach* was literally blown to atoms with all her crew. The smoke was so thick for a few minutes that the two U.S. Liberty ships, *Virginia Dare* and *Nathaniel Greene,* were completely blotted out from view. I thought surely that they were gone too.

In five minutes all is quiet again. No other ships are hit. We sail on silent, perhaps white-faced, but determined. Overhead a brave Hurricane begins to smoke around its motor. Filled with admiration for the bravery of these pilots . . . I watched this [one] literally push his failing plane to a higher altitude, barrel-roll over, and bail out in a perfect parachute leap. He slowly floated down and was picked up by a destroyer. His plane crashed into the sea.

A Junkers 88 dove like a streak for the carrier. Every gun in this area, including ours, streamed bullets at him in an effort to save our precious carrier. We breathed again as the carrier swerved beautifully and the three huge bombs crashed harmlessly far ahead. The bomber limped off badly damaged.

☆   (National Archives, Voyage Reports, *St. Olaf,* 29 September 1942)

The crew of the *Nathaniel Greene,* immediately ahead of the *Luckenbach* and in the next column to her left, thought its own ship had blown up. The *Greene's* armed guard CO was Lt. (jg) R. M. Billings. His day on 14 September went like this:

☆

At 0035 CVT a British tanker was torpedoed by a submarine off our port hand, somewhere near the middle of the convoy. At 1337 CVT upwards of twenty-five torpedo planes attacked the port flank of the convoy and some of them went for the aircraft carrier. At about 1355 CVT a swarm of torpedo planes were sighted near the water in front of the convoy, on the starboard side. We fired an eight second fuze-nosed projectile at them from the 3-inch gun. Luck was sitting in the pointer's seat for we got a direct hit on the leading plane, and it blew up. The planes circled and came in between columns seven and eight. About fifteen planes came in directly at us, and we opened fire with everything we had. The planes split up right off our bow (port side) and some of them passed in front of us (at not more than one hundred feet), and the rest went down the port side. One plane crossing our bow received a direct hit from our 3-inch gun and crashed in the water. Two more planes on the bow were shot down with our machine-gun fire. Two more planes were shot down by our machine-gun fire as they went down the port side, and another plane was shot down on the starboard side with the machine-gun fire. The planes were so close you couldn't miss with a machine gun. A parachute was dropped off our port side by one of the planes. At that time the ship experienced a terrific explosion. My helmet and phones were blown off, and much debris was dropping around all over the ship. I had seen four torpedos dropped by planes off the bow and thought we had been torpedoed. Boat stations was sounded by the Captain. The wounded and injured were brought to the boats. The second mate ordered my men to let go the two forward life rafts, which they did. The engines had been stopped by the master. The first assistant engineer came up from below and said that everything was all right in the engine room. I ordered my men back to their guns. Two of my men had been wounded, five of the merchant crew had received injuries, and one of the merchant crew was lost overboard. The British destroyer G04 came alongside and took off the above injured. Several of my men had small wounds that were treated aboard ship. We then resumed the place in convoy that we had temporarily vacated. The captain, George A. Vickers, should be commended for his ship handling and coolness during the attacks and explosion. He dodged four torpedos that I saw and never gave orders to abandon ship. The rafts were dropped into the water, and the no. 2 lifeboat was lowered on unauthorized orders given by the second mate. My two wounded men; Hyams, N. E. Cox, USNR 632 22 86, and Marihugh, C. H., S2/c USNR 612 24 09, acted in a very commendable manner. Although shot, each kept his station until I ordered them to board the destroyer. Marihugh never even mentioned his injuries (a bullet in his left shoulder and shrapnel in his right leg) until after the planes had left. The First Asst. Engineer Calvin H. Hand (suffering from an internal hemmorage) also showed great courage and coolness with handling of the injured, insisting that we should not abandon ship and carrying out his duties in the engine room. He was the first one back into the engine room after the explosion and got the ship under way by himself. Another of my men, Walters, C. E., S2/c USNR 662 18 59, showed very admirable qualities. He had a piece of shrapnel in his left foot that cut into two toes. He pulled it out of his foot and kept to his station. The wound was not serious but would tend to be most unnerving. We discovered, upon returning to the convoy, that the SS *Mary Luckenbach* had blown up about two hundred yards off our starboard quarter. I believe that this explosion plus the object on the sighted parachute exploding was responsible for all our damage. All the cargo boxes on deck were smashed by the concussion. About ten doors and some bulkheads were blown down and smashed. The inside of many rooms (mine included) was a shambles. The cast-iron venilators buckled. Shrapnel and scraps were covering the deck. A piece of angle iron penetrated my starboard 4-inch ready box and went through a shell, missing the primer by less than an eighth of an inch. Glass ports were smashed. The hospital aft was practically demolished. The compasses were all out of adjustment. The pointer's platform on the 4-inch gun had completely disappeared, and the pointer's sight was nearly ruined. A side plate about two feet square was found on deck. Bullets were picked up all over the deck (both tank ammunition from the *Luckenbach* and bullets fired at us by the planes). Every splinter shield on the ship had bullet marks in it. Every gun station had been marked by shrapnel and bullets. The ship's hull held up, and as far as we now know, no leaks were sprung. How everyone topside was not killed or injured seriously I don't know. It is impossible to put into words the force of the explosion or the amount of debris that hit the ship. A cup grease fitting on my port Oerlikon had even been shot off. The ship and the crew, including my navy men held up 100 percent. If we would have actually abandoned ship, I believe that the planes would have come back to finish us off as they had been doing to others. My men never showed the least sign of cowardice. Although scared stiff (and who wasn't?), they obeyed my orders to the letter and kept fighting. No man could be more proud of a group of men than I am of my navy men and the men who were assisting them at their gun stations. The commodore sent us a message complimenting us on our gunnery.

★   (National Archives, Voyage Reports, *Nathaniel Greene*,
                                              24 September 1942)

The usual navy memorandum for file ("Summary of Statements by Survivors") in this case noted the "violent explosion and disintegration of the ship" and extracted relevant details from the voyage reports (VRs) of other neighboring ships. It concluded with a handwritten note:

There were no survivors from the *Mary Luckenbach*. All armed
guard personnel were reported missing as of 9/14/42 and were
presumed dead as of 14 Sept. 1943 under section 5 of Public
Law 490 as amended.

                                              /s/ Edward C. Cleare
                                              Captain, USNR
                           (National Archives, Memorandum for File)

When the *William Moultrie,* in column immediately behind the *Luckenbach,* steamed over the spot where that ship had been, her "crewmen could not spot a single bit of wreckage from the unfortunate vessel—not even a board or a shattered piece of life raft" (Bunker, *Seafarers,* 15).

Other Perils: Collision

Any deck officer or quartermaster (the helmsman, the able seaman who stands the wheel) is apprehensive about collisions in convoy, and in fact collisions were a major cause of sinkings and near sinkings throughout the war. Zigzagging, or suddenly ordered changes of course, or evasive action to avoid a torpedo, all enhance the prospect of collision.

Fog carries a perennial threat of collision. Fog buoys (spars towed by every ship in a convoy, designed to throw up a spray of phosphorescent water behind the ship) help, but the spray is not always phosphorescent, and the fog is often too dense to see anything at all. The radio operator of the tanker *G. Harrison Smith* counted twenty-one collision reports in a ten-minute period when a fog-bound convoy off Greenland had to change course to avoid icebergs.

The full extent of collision damage was not always apparent. Undetected structural damage from an earlier collision may have contributed to the instantaneous breakup of a homebound Liberty in September 1943. The ship was the *Theodore Dwight Weld,* which on her eastward voyage had seriously damaged her bow in colliding with the Norwegian freighter SS *Santos.* The *Santos* sank immediately.

After repair work, the *Weld* was bound for New York in Convoy ON-202, having left Avonmouth below Bristol, England, on the fourteenth. She was in position 21 (second column, first row). Next to her to port was number 11, the *Frederick Douglass,* another Liberty in ballast. A German submarine, U-238, lined up these two vessels and two others in her sights and launched four torpedoes at them from her bow tubes.

Two targets were missed. The *Douglass* was hit at 0736 GMT, the *Weld* one minute later. The torpedo caught her amidships in the fuel settling tanks; there was no explosion for fifteen or twenty seconds, and then her engine room blew up. The stern sank instantly, its open forward end first. There was no time to launch lifeboats. The bow remained afloat until after the convoy lost sight of it. Nineteen of the *Weld's* merchant crew and thirteen from her armed guard were lost.

The survivors—twenty-two merchant marine and fifteen navy— jumped or were blown or thrown into the sea. This was an ordinary enough incident for the North Atlantic in the fall of 1943. What was extraordinary was the performance of some of the survivors of the ship next door, the *Douglass.*

Other Perils: Performers

The torpedo caught the *Douglass* in her no. 5 hold (farthest aft), opening that hold and the shaft alley to the sea. The hold was filled with sand ballast. The explosion blew the hatch covers off but fortunately did not detonate an adjacent ammunition magazine. The ship began to settle slowly in the water, stern first, but was still afloat when the convoy passed out of sight.

The crew's response was a wild mix—perhaps three parts of responsible emergency behavior and one part monumental irresponsibility. The miscreants in the crew gave a classic demonstration of why both NMU's Joe Curran and SIU's Harry Lundeberg despised "performers." The merchant marine component of the *Douglass's* company was racially integrated, as were both its elements, responsible and irresponsible.

(Most mixed-race merchant crews got on reasonably well. A particular irony in the *Douglass* debacle is that both she and the *Weld* next door bore names that resonate in the history of race relations. Theodore Dwight Weld was a famous New England abolitionist who was involved in the founding of the American Anti-Slavery Society. Frederick Douglass was an escaped slave, a brilliant orator, a highly effective abolitionist, an advisor to President Lincoln, and much more.)

On board the *Douglass,* immediately upon impact, the black gang (who were mixed as to color) abandoned the engine room so fast that no one shut the watertight door separating the shaft alley from the engine room, as is standard procedure in a torpedoing, to prevent the engine room from flooding in case of a hit aft near the propeller.

The (black) master, Capt. Adrian Richardson, left the bridge at this point to go below and assess the damage. As soon as he was out of sight, two white officers—the chief engineer and the second mate—without authority to do so, issued orders to abandon ship.

This rascally pair had drawn copious attention from neutral observers in the ship's complement. Ever since joining the ship, the chief had declared repeatedly that he had been torpedoed three times on the Murmansk run, and if it happened again he would be the first man off the ship.

The *Douglass* carried secret antitorpedo equipment, and crew members had heard the mate blather about it in stateside bars before departure. At sea, he would engage the helmsman in protracted discourses while on watch. The captain was so apprehensive about this constant distraction of the AB steering the ship that he made it a point to be on the bridge whenever the second mate was on watch. The armed guard commanding officer on the *Douglass*'s eastbound trip detailed his irresponsible behavior in the section of his official voyage report headed "Recommendations for Improvement of the Service."

While Captain Richardson was below investigating the torpedo damage, the rogue elements of the crew, black and white, were having a field day. The report of the armed guard CO on the homebound trip, Ens. John Roang, details it succinctly.

☆

Immediately after we were hit, two lifeboats on the starboard side were taken over by the second mate and chief engineer without definite orders to abandon ship. Whiskey was stolen from the captain's quarters by several men and while in the lifeboats they proceeded to get real drunk. When they arrived on the [English rescue vessel that picked up survivors, RS] *Rathlin* they began fighting among themselves. The ship's boatswain had a Negro woman aboard, which I knew nothing about until I boarded the rescue ship. [Other evidence indicates that the (black) boatswain and the (white) ship's carpenter were joint participants in the matter of the woman stowaway. When the captain returned to the bridge, three of the four lifeboats had already been launched.] After we had been hit the ship's carpenter and several others began rummaging through my room and the ship's officers' rooms. After boarding the *Rathlin*, the SS *Frederick Douglass*'s merchant crew broke into the *Rathlin*'s clothes stores and stole clothes, most of which were later retrieved. The merchant crew's messman, in an argument about a dog, stabbed the chief cook in the hand. All the while we were on the *Rathlin*, there were continuous arguments between the merchant crew. They were always kicking about the way they were treated and never satisfied. Aboard the *Rathlin,* after the stealing of the clothing, I posted a watch on guard in the store room, plus gunnery watches with the English gunners.

★   (National Archives, Voyage Reports, *Frederick Douglass*)

Several survivors from the *Weld,* which lost thirty-two men, were bitter that lifeboats from the *Frederick Douglass*—which remained afloat for hours—made no effort to come to their aid as they bobbed in the ocean in their life jackets. Only boats from the *Rathlin,* and the rescue ship itself, carefully maneuvering close enough to individuals to haul them aboard, did so, while the drunks partied on in the *Douglass's* boats. The entire company of the *Douglass,* merchant, navy, black, white, stowaway, and all, survived.

Even worse conditions prevailed on SS *El Oriente* in convoy from Loch Ewe, Scotland, to Murmansk in January of 1943. Indiscipline in the merchant crew spilled over to some of the armed guard crew, though evidently not impairing its gunnery, which brought down one attacking plane. In port in Murmansk, however, which was under virtually incessant air attack by individual planes and small groups, and where the *El Oriente* took one direct hit from a bomb, it was "necessary to take drastic measures in restraining the actions" of two of the navy crew. The skipper, according to the armed guard CO's report,

★

was continually drunk with most of the ship's officers, and particularly when at anchorage. . . . As a result . . . there is absolutely no discipline among the merchant crew and extensive waste of food and materials [and] breakage of . . . dishes and glasses in drunken brawls in the mess halls. There is also no cleanliness aboard the ship. . . . The crew's toilets are in such a state that both the merchant and navy [crews] have had either body lice or scabies at one time or another.

The chief engineer has either been drunk or under the effects of alcohol ever since I joined this ship. On occasions at sea when he has been called to the engine room he has not been able to make it because of his condition.

[This and similar conduct by other officers led the gunnery officer to] respectfully [recommend] that merchant officers of ships owned by the U.S. Maritime Commission be restrained from the use of liquor when at anchorage or at sea. . . .

☆   (National Archives, Voyage Reports, *El Oriente*)

A modest request. Excessive access to the demon rum was not a universal problem, but it was not exactly rare. Indeed, the author was chief radio man on a T-2 tanker, SS *Sappa Creek*, sailing at night from Birkenhead, Liverpool, to join a homebound convoy. The master was drunk on the bridge. Down the Irish Sea we went, the skipper ordering "What ship?" challenges blinkered at every tug or fisherman we encountered. Until the soporific effect of the alcohol (and deft intervention by the young chief mate) led the potted captain to bed.

Other Perils: Straggling

U-boats often followed convoys, waiting for "lame ducks," ships with engine trouble, to fall behind,

☆

or for stragglers separated from the brood by fog or stormy weather, a frequent occurrence in the North Atlantic.

The *William Pierce Frye*, a lame duck in convoy HX230 from Halifax to England on 28 March 1943, was hove to making engine repairs when two torpedoes missed her by a matter of feet. Repairs were hastily concluded and the *Frye* started off at top speed, with the submarine paralleling her course several thousand yards away. Heavy seas were running and this, plus evasive action, enabled the *Frye* to evade the U-boat, but the next night two more torpedoes hit her and set off the cargo of explosives. She sank so quickly there was time to launch only one lifeboat. Some men jumped overboard, climbed into an LCT that was being carried on deck and floated off when the ship sank and were picked up five days later by HMS *Schikuri*. Only seven men out of sixty-four survived.

The commodore of convoy HX230, on 31 March, radioed to Commander-in-Chief, Western Atlantic: "*W. P. Frye* torpedoed when straggling. Do not intend detaching ships to search unless situation improves. U-boats shadowing all last night in spite of sweeps. Straggler *John Eaton* rejoined." Stragglers and lame ducks had to take their chances; *Eaton* won, *Frye* lost.

☆   (Bunker, *Liberty Ships*, 87)

(The *William Pierce Frye*, incidentally, was a namesake of a schooner sunk in World War I, as related in chapter 16.)

In action with the enemy, merchant ships in the convoy are not to slow or to maneuver in order to pick up lifeboats or men in the water, nor, ordinarily, may their escort vessels. When a convoy has the luxury of rescue craft sailing with it—as was the case increasingly with the passage of time—they plucked bedraggled seamen from the waves and saved many a life. But whatever the chances of rescue if sunk, the straggler's lot was not a happy one.

The Liberty *Henry Bacon* was leaving northern Russia in February 1945 with the 34-ship convoy RA64 bound for England.

☆

[She carried] thirty-five Norwegian refugees—men, women, and children—who had fled to Russia during the Nazi invasion and were being sent to England.

The convoy cleared North Cape and started down the Norwegian coast. On 18 February a violent storm with sixty-mile-an-hour winds whipped up turbulent seas and completely scattered the ships. By the time the escorts had rounded up the strays, several freighters had been torpedoed by U-boats. The British escort sloop *Bluebell* was sunk by *U-711*, with only one survivor.

Four days later another storm scattered the fleet again. Some ships hove to, while others ran before tremendous seas that rolled a British escort carrier 45 degrees and nearly sent her aircraft over the side.

Again the escorts rounded up all the strays except the *Henry Bacon*, which had lagged some fifty miles behind because of trouble with the steering engine. It took the engineers several hours to make repairs, and by the time the ship resumed her course she was a tempting target for planes or U-boats. Capt. Alfred Carini backtracked up the course for an hour hoping to find the other ships but with no luck. By that time he had not slept for forty-five hours and kept awake by pacing the bridge and drinking black coffee.

At 1415 on the afternoon of 25 February, the lookout in the crow's nest reported: "Airplanes. Sounds like a lot of them."

Even against the whine of the wind, Carini could hear them and sounded the general alarm. Men tumbled out of bunks and grabbed helmets, lifejackets, and extra clothing for protection against the wintry blasts of wind on the open deck. The steward mustered his cooks and messmen to break out bandages, splints, and anesthetics, covering the wardroom tables with blankets in preparation for battle casualties. Below decks, all the black gang could do was listen—and wait.

Gunners jerked the canvas covers off the guns none too soon. Big, black Junkers 88s broke out of the overcast, flying thirty feet above the wave tops. There was no need for the armed guard officer on the bridge to give the order to fire. Every gun that could bear went into instant action.

Carini counted twenty-three planes. Twenty-three bombers against one ship. Heavy odds for even a cruiser or a battleship. Aircraft carriers had been sunk by fewer planes than this. There was no nearby ship the *Henry Bacon* could call for help.

A bomber dropped a torpedo five hundred yards away on the port quarter, and Carini yelled, "Hard a port!" The helmsman spun the wheel hard over, and the torpedo just missed.

Another plane started a torpedo run several hundred yards off the bow, and the 3-inch gun blew it to bits. Pieces of flaming aircraft fell into the sea just off the bow.

Another plane flew into a wall of 20-millimeter shells that sliced it in two and sent the pilot's compartment cartwheeling into the sea.

So many planes had only to persist to be successful against one ship. A torpedo finally hit the *Henry Bacon* in no. three hold on the starboard side, forward. The vessel shuddered as a 50-foot column of water shot up above the bulwarks. The spray was still falling along the deck when the second torpedo hit. Carini ordered abandon ship. If he waited any longer, a third torpedo might send the vessel down without a chance to launch the boats.

"Refugees first," he called to the mate. "Get the passengers on the boat deck as fast as you can. Tell them to bring lots of clothes."

The German bombers, seeing that their target was doomed, broke off the attack and withdrew, with one bomber skimming the wave tops as black smoke poured from an engine.

The *Bacon* carried four lifeboats, plus a number of rafts, but men on a raft would have little chance of survival in winter seas. Carini maneuvered the ship to provide a lee for lowering the boats. They would be lucky to get even two boats safely into the water.

The first boat lowered away successfully and pushed off. When the second boat was safely overside, Third Mate Joseph Scott counted the passengers. "I can take six," he shouted. "Six more . . . and hurry." Several merchant crewmen and navy gunners climbed down into the boat as it rose on the crest of a wave. The ship was settling and waves were breaking over the bulwarks.

Chief Engineer Donald Haviland looked up at a young navy gunner on deck. The boy couldn't have been more than seventeen years old. "Put me alongside," he said to the third mate. "Let that kid have my place. It won't matter so much if I don't get back."

Haviland climbed back to the deck while the sailor scurried down the scramble nets into the boat, which pulled quickly away. The ship was going down soon, and they didn't want to be sucked under with her. A raft with several men on it bobbed some distance away. The wind and waves were taking the lifeboats away from the ship, and no pulling on the oars would bring them close enough to pick up the men on the raft.

Men in the boats saw Haviland, Boatswain Halcomb Lammon, and several other seamen on the foredeck, probably making a raft out of dunnage. Captain Carini waved from the bridge. The boats drifted off into the mist as the *Henry Bacon,* her ensign snapping proudly at the gaff, settled slowly beneath the sea.

By the time convoy escorts arrived to look for survivors there were only a few boards and crates to mark where the *Henry Bacon* and twenty-two of her men went down.

Said the maritime commission: "It was a splendid defense by a merchant ship against overwhelming odds and of discipline of the highest order amongst the ship's company." The men of the *Henry Bacon* had added a gallant chapter to the history of the U.S. merchant marine.

☆   (Bunker, *Liberty Ships,* 77–79)

21 The Murmansk Run
★★

The defining horror of World War II for merchant seamen was and remains the Murmansk Run, a savage arctic gauntlet into and within the
Arctic Circle of German U-boats, heavy cruisers, scout planes, torpedo
bombers, dive-bombers, and icebergs. Soviet troops desperately required
munitions and all other supplies to prevent a Nazi triumph in the north.
The Baltic Sea was closed. The only route lay along and around the Norwegian coast, studded with German airfields.

The port of Murmansk itself, nine hundred miles from the North Pole,
was under constant air attack. Winter brought night—and ice-choked
seas. In summer the pack ice retreated—and night never fell. Each convoy through this frigid hell was more deadly than the last.

A ship bound for Murmansk would join her transatlantic convoy at
Halifax or Sydney, Nova Scotia. The skippers—many of them retired
masters, often of sailing ships, who had returned to sea as a patriotic
duty—would attend the convoy conference. Their resentful demeanor
and sour looks identified the crusty ones who had no tolerance for wartime restrictions. Their vessels were positioned in the last row, where
failure to keep station only imperiled their own ship.

The U.S. Navy escorted these convoys half-way across the Atlantic, to
the MOMP, or Mid-Ocean Meeting Point. There the Royal Navy took
over and shepherded the flock to Scotland. Loch Ewe on the northwest
coast, at about the latitude of Juneau, Alaska, was a usual departure point.

On departure the convoy sails northwestward for Reykjavík on the
southwest coast of Iceland, where the escorts refuel for the 2,000-mile
trip to Murmansk. West now, along the "bottom" of Iceland, then northeasterly through the Denmark Strait separating Iceland from Greenland,
up and across the Arctic Circle, around lonely Jan Mayen Island, north to
beyond 75 degrees north latitude, east past Bear Island, whose northern
half is never free of ice, holding a course through the Barents Sea as far

north as the pack ice will permit, then suddenly far south to Murmansk, 125 miles north of the Arctic Circle.

Most of the humans found in these regions during World War II were in ships, and like the few hardy mammal species native to the region, were either hunters or the hunted. Those in the American merchant ships on the Murmansk Run were definitely the latter.

Before the United States entered the war, there were small convoys including U.S. ships running from Scotland to Murmansk, and they saw relatively little German opposition. Then Hitler realized that he could not topple the Soviet Union with his first blow, and that he must stop the flow of supplies from the West, which were arriving via Murmansk and Archangel, on the White Sea, farther east and south.

In the spring of 1942 the first of twenty submarines moved into the northern waters. Northern Norway, already under Nazi control, became host to Luftwaffe bases all along the northwestern coast. In addition, fearing an Allied invasion of Norway, the Führer ordered his new battleship *Tirpitz*, five heavy cruisers, and every destroyer that could be spared to Norwegian waters. And he agreed that in the absence of an active threat of invasion this formidable fleet could be used against Allied convoys.

The Going Gets Tough: PQ-15

The Murmansk Run suddenly became infinitely more deadly. Convoy PQ-15 (PQ designated Murmansk-bound convoys; returning, the symbol was QP) had fourteen U.S. merchant vessels among its twenty-three ships. It left Halifax on the first day of spring 1942 and sailed directly into heavy gales and snowstorms, which persisted all the way across. The third day out it was attacked by a wolf pack—which was driven off by heavy, sustained fire from the escorts and merchant vessels alike.

On the last leg of the trip a German long-range patrol plane picked up the convoy three days out of Reykjavík, on 30 April. The next day they came within range of torpedo planes from the North Cape of Norway and were under continuous air and submarine attack for the six days it took to reach Murmansk.

Some of the U.S. freighters had been given extra guns at Gourock, Scotland, where members of the merchant crew were trained to handle them, augmenting the small armed guard crews—five men in the case of SS *Expositor*, whose cargo was 10,000 rounds of artillery shells and 5,000 cases of TNT. The merchantmen gave a good account of themselves.

☆

Several enemy planes were shot down by the concentrated fire of the merchant vessels during the frequent attacks. On 2 May an enemy submarine was sunk by fire from a merchant vessel. The merchant ships succeeded in landing the bulk of their much-needed cargoes in north Russia. While the ships of Convoy PQ-15 were in port at Murmansk there were numerous bombing attacks and it was reported that more than 250 enemy planes took part in one of the attacks.

☆   (National Archives, Memorandum for Commander in Chief, 25 November 1944, in *Deer Lodge* file)

Although the convoy lost several ships, including the (British) commodore's, all the U.S. vessels reached port. One of them was the SS *Deer Lodge*, a World War I freighter of 6,187 gross tons. Her armed guard officer had groused about the discipline and performance of the merchant crew on the way over, but in port it was a different story.

The United States maintained an assistant naval attaché's office in Archangel because of the remoteness of the north Russian ports and the prolonged stays there of navy and merchant ships and personnel. It was headed by Cmdr. Samuel B. Frankel, who had praise for all hands. In a memorandum to the U.S. Maritime Commission, he briefly summarized the *Deer Lodge*'s adventures.

☆

1. On 18 May 1942, while at anchor in the Kola Inlet near the city of Murmansk, USSR, the steamer *Deer Lodge* suffered a near miss that resulted in extensive damage to the after part of the vessel.
2. The ensuing two months [was] a period of extensive enemy air activity in that area; the officers, merchant crew, and armed guard unit stood by their vessel and not only defended themselves against enemy aircraft but assisted materially in the defense of the port.
3. Through the initiative and untiring efforts of the master, chief engineer, and the officers, the ship was successfully repaired on a mud flat

in spite of the technical and physical difficulties involved. In this they were ably assisted by the entire crew.

4. It is strongly recommended that suitable recognition be made of the fact that, without the excellent spirit of cooperation and bravery of the ship's complement and armed guard, she would have remained an abandoned hulk at Murmansk.

5. The following are deserving of special recognition:

   a. The master, Alexander S. Henry, for his leadership and success in saving his ship.

   b. The chief engineer, Frank F. Townsend, for the brilliant application of his technical knowledge and his mechanical ability.

   c. The chief steward, Kal Petersen, for his ingenuity in stretching the limited food supply and his important part in maintaining the high morale.

   d. The armed guard officer, Ens. Thomas E. Delate, USNR, for his defense of the ship, the courage he inspired in his men, and his coolness under fire.

6. The conduct and morale of the officers, crew, and armed guard of the SS *Deer Lodge* have set a high standard and have earned the admiration of the harbor officials at Murmansk and of this office.

[The near miss which Cmdr. Frankel laconically described was a bomb explosion hard by the vessel's stern, which was] lifted bodily out of the water while the vessel went through a series of violent buckling movements. She settled instantly by the stern. The chief engineer meanwhile rushed below and closed the watertight bulkhead door leading from the shaft alley, from which water was rushing, thereby saving the vessel.

☆   (National Archives, Commendation, 9 September 1942 and 20 December 1942, in Summaries of Survivors, *Deer Lodge* file)

A diver found a gaping hole about ten feet square on the port side aft, but the bulkhead forward of it was intact. With ingenuity, cooperation, and hard work, the ship was leveled, temporarily moored in five fathoms of water, and later beached on a mud flat where she was repaired. During an air raid while she was moored temporarily, the stern mooring parted and the *Deer Lodge* swung around with the tide—just as a stick of three bombs exploded on the very spot she had just vacated.

As can be seen in chapter 22, this vessel's remarkable luck and her courageous crew (with one exception) could not last.

Robert Carse and PQ-16

Robert Carse (1902–1971) was a newspaperman and a prewar seafarer as a boy, and later the author of many books on his wartime experiences, none more evocative and natural and gripping than his first account of a profoundly perilous voyage. He was an able seaman (AB) in Convoy PQ-16 on the Murmansk Run. This was the largest Murmansk convoy yet and the second-worst ordeal of them all. His ship, incidentally, the *Alcoa Banner*, had a navy armed guard crew of two and the pop-gun armament of five .30-caliber machine guns, one of which Bob Carse manned. The story told here comes from his 1942 book *There Go the Ships* (published by Morrow).

Because it was written and rushed into print in 1942, under conditions of censorship that later were relaxed somewhat, Carse could identify the ships in his narrative only as "the So-and-So." I have substituted the actual names of the ships, which I identified from a little modest detective work in the armed guard CO's voyage reports in the U.S. National Archives and from later books that touched on Convoy PQ-16.

The ordeal of PQ-16 began in the last week of May. No longer did the sun set at 1:00 A.M. but shone day and "night." Before departure there was one last liberty, and Carse and his Scottish shipmate Wee Wullie spent it in Edinburgh, a moment of homey counterpoint to war in the icy seas. A war, be it noted, that they would fight with pitifully inadequate weapons, mere .30-caliber machine guns where even 20-millimeters should have been merely supplementary to 5-inch 38s and 4-inch 50s.

☆

Chapter 4: There Go the Ships

It was a riot down in the cabin of the steamer that took us out to anchorage. Almost every guy had a bottle, and they got passed quick and slick from hand to hand. What we'd heard ashore here let us know that the run to Russia was an extremely difficult and dangerous one, and, as certain as we sat there, some of us wouldn't be making the trip home again.

THE MURMANSK RUN 253

So we whipped the whisky neat, and, when we pulled in alongside the various ships, we gave a hand to the drunks, hoisted their tails up onto the ladders, or passed lines around them and got them safe aboard. . . .

We got our guns there, eight of them, four double-mount Marlin .30-caliber pieces. They were old U.S. pieces, of 1918 issue, given by the States to the British for use in planes and equipped with an automatic trigger on the top of the receiver plate above the breech. But for us they had been refixed with finger triggers and safeties, with steel tube side and shoulder handles with rubber grips. They were good for seven hundred rounds a minute out of their khaki web belts, the Royal Navy armorer told us when he instructed us in them. He wore a long, hooded duffle coat as he stood by the hatch and broke down the piece for us, showed us the mechanism, how to clear jams, and handle them on target. We were to be our own gunners, the skipper had just made us to understand, and we were a quiet, intent group of men as we watched the armorer handle the piece.

Most of us had never seen a machine gun to put our hands on it before in our lives. None of us had ever had any real machine-gun instruction or practice except the second assistant, who'd served in the destroyers in the last war, but he would be busy below. It was up to us deck men, the mates, the ABs—any man who was competent—to go on them and serve them in battle.

The twin pieces, mounted behind a long and heavy steel shield, were placed one on each side of the wheelhouse topside, the highest place of immediate vantage in the ship, and on each side of the mooring bridge on the poop. That was our armament. With that we were to go out and fight the Luftwaffe or anything we met with .30-caliber tracer bullets fired by a crew whose only actual fire practice was a pair of rounds let go out the scupper port into the loch to get the feel of the guns.

But we talked about the guns a lot and studied them after the red-faced old armorer had finished his pert and snappy half-hour's instruction and pushed off to do his act on the other ships. There was a circular hole in the middle of the gun shield, and that was where you started firing at a target making three hundred knots. Inside that were two concentric rings in a regular steel ring sight, each of them a hundred knots a part; inside that the vertical and horizontal crossed bars that meant you were right on and keep it there. "Lead off of Jerry," the armorer had told us in his heavy Cockney accent. "Don't try to put it up his ass. Throw it ahead of him. This 'ere's all tracer fire. Let 'im see the stuff. 'E's no f———n' superman. 'E wants to live the syme as you and me. When it's too close for 'im, 'e'll run. I know. I was out against 'im, and we met the *Graf Spee* on Christmas day."

"Lead off," we kept telling ourselves, scanning the skies, watching the British planes overhead to accustom ourselves to distance and speed and altitude. Hold your fire. Wait for him. That was going to be tough, we knew, although we didn't say so aloud to each other. Waiting with the Nazis jumping down on you with TNT under your feet would take some little self-control.

We tried out our rubber lifesaving suits up there in that beautiful, spring-warm water. They were big affairs, starting at the bottom with regular seaboots to which were soldered rubber suits of about the same thickness and material texture of a good raincoat. A light kapok life jacket was worn under them, and the wrists of the sleeves fitted very tight. There was a belt about the middle, and the neck was secured by a double lanyard that was pulled fast and secured as the final act in putting on the suit. Above the suit and really a part of it, affixed to the collar, was a yellow rubber hood—yellow so that it might be seen in the water—and this fitted close about the face to keep out sprays and spindrift.

The men who jumped over the side wearing the suits made out all right in them, although, of course, they found them bulky for swimming. We felt better about the suits, then, and kept them, as we had been instructed when they were issued to us in our home port, neatly folded down over the boots and in the ready position right beside our bunks.

We were eager to go now, eager to get under way and make that run around the North Cape. The nervousness was growing on us. We'd waited long enough, and if we had a nasty job to do, let's do it. But there was going to be one weekend left before we sailed, we found out, and "Mac" and "Wee Wullie" and I took off for Edinburgh. . . .

"Wee Wullie" had served his apprenticeship in Edinburgh, knew the city well, and loved it. We found it slam-bang full of troops and that just that afternoon there had been a great parade, the first of such for Allies Week.

There on Princes Street, we met the Free Polish, and the Free French, soldiers and sailors, Free Norwegians, Free Greeks, and, of course, Scots from the crack regiments. Punjabis in their shorts and tall, sharp-peaked turbans—every sort of outfit in the British services—and men of the British Merchant Navy—Hollanders and Norwegians and Greeks and Yugoslavs among them. Those men, the merchant navy lads, had paraded in ranks with the troops that afternoon, and they'd carried the merchant flag, for in the United Kingdom they're fully recognized as fighting men and rate as such ashore.

We talked about that—"Wee Wullie" and "Mac" and I—as we had a couple of throws of whisky, a little ale, and some food in a big restaurant bar on Waterloo Road. It kind of saddened us to think that here on a foreign shore we were treated better—one hell of a sight better—than at home. Here we weren't a bunch of bums, the waterfront scum, or the lousy seamen with radical ideas who are out on strike all the time or drunk and diseased in the gutter. Here we were men who knew our job and did it, and more than two thousand of us were already at the bottom with the ships they'd tried to bring home. . . .

We found some fine old public houses, better, "Mac" was forced to admit, than his regular boilermaker hangouts in Jersey City. But we were quiet at times as we stood there at the softly shining mahogany bar, because in our heads was the knowledge that this was the last weekend, the last piece of shore leave. . . .

The nostalgia was on "Wee Wullie" when we left there at closing time. We walked the streets in the darkness, looking up at the black and stark loom of the castle on its crest, the stars whitening the sky, and a moon coming up over toward the Firth of Forth. The chimney pots showed dark, distinct against the sky's pallor, and all about us was the clack-click-clack of the British army's boots, and then, occasionally, on Waterloo Road, in front of some fish-and-chips joint, the quick, blue glim as a constable flashed on his electric torch and cleared some knot of people on their way.

We didn't talk much, the three of us, but all of us were thinking of home and whether we'd make it out and back, because in that quiet, ancient city, man had the impulse to reflect, to cast up the balance of his life and what it meant to him. . . .

We turned in then, away from the moon and the soft, pale sky, and made up our bunks on the schoolroom floor with the fine, white woolen blankets they gave us. Around us, during the night, with the quietness men learn, a sailor here and a soldier there got up as he was called by the watchman, packed his kit, picked up his rifle, mask, and helmet, and shoved off for the station. His leave was done; he was going back at it. Lying there, sleep still away from me, I watched their faces and their eyes, and they were sad men, sad to be forced to go out and kill; yet they were calm in the going, and, somehow, they were steadfast.

"Wee Wullie" went home to his folks in Midcalder in the morning, and "Mac" and I roamed Edinburgh from the castle down through the Canongate to Holyrood House Palace and back again. The girls were bonnie, and "Mac" laughed aloud sometimes at the fashion of their talk. It was sunny and splendid, this early May Sunday, and there was a band concert in the afternoon in Princes Gardens. We went to sit among the yellow of the crocuses and the tawny green of the lawns beside the band shell as the band of the First Polish Rifle Brigade played, and, then, strutting the gravel smartly underfoot, the pipe band of the Royal Scots paraded.

That was fine then, very fine. The tightness was out of our brains and our hearts, and here we were with the fighting men, guys like ourselves. But as darkness came we saw the women carrying their children and their dogs in their arms against the possibility of a raid during the night, and along Princes Street, before the railway station, the faces of the women walking beside the men going back from leave made you want to weep. . . .

Then we went and turned in down in the great, steel-and-concrete main sleeping room of the Servicemen's Home. Early in the morning they roused us out, and we grabbed the train back for the ship and the sea. But always, always way down in me will be that memory of Edinburgh, the most beautiful and the most friendly city I have ever seen in any country and at any time.

Chapter 5: There Go the Ships

We sailed at eight o'clock. This time of day we still—out of habit—called evening; but for us, for several months, there would be no more night. Outside, where we formed we found that we were a big convoy. Our escort was superb.

British cruisers were with us, a big converted merchantman that we called the "flak" ship, destroyers, and minesweepers. Our commodore's ship, *Ocean Voice*, a big British freighter, carried a Spitfire fighter on the fore deck. We felt pretty confident leaving Iceland.

For the next thirty-some hours we ran along the coast, past the murky fjords, the bitter, snow-clenched mountains. Orders had been passed by the commodore, and each ship now dragged astern of it on rope or wire a heavy, white wooden contrivance with a brass hood at the end which kicked up a three- or four-foot crest of water. These were our fog buoys, and by them we steered and kept on station and in column. . . .

Alongside of us, stepping fast, came a British destroyer, her white, red-crossed ensign stiff with the wind of her speed. She gleamed as she stepped the sea behind her high, silver bow wash. Men were at all her gun stations; her conning bridge was full with them.

She stood close aboard us on the port hand, and we could see her skipper, a red-faced, keen man in a long khaki duffle coat. "What ship, please?" he asked over the loud-hailer system. . . .

"*Alcoa Banner*," our skipper told him, out in the bridge wing with his megaphone lifted.

"Your number, please?" the high, clipped, Royal Navy voice came back.

"Thirteen," our skipper said.

"Thirteen!" the loud-hailer took up from the destroyer skipper's voice. "Ha, ha, ha! Something of a number, eh? Jove. Rejoin convoy now. There's danger of surface and aerial attack out here as well as the subs. We'll be right alongside you. Here's your course. . . ."

Our lookouts were already sighting ice. It lay electric green, grotesquely shaped and chiseled, on the uneasily rolling sea. This was floe ice, some of the pieces twenty, thirty, and forty feet above the waterline. They took the shapes of polar bears and seals; one that passed close aboard us—we could feel the penetrant, stinging chill from it—had exquisite, fluted columns—a lost, weird, and gelid temple in this arctic sea.

We steered along those floes hard over with the wheel and back again, quick with the spokes, for we must keep station and columns, never lose the formation of our convoy. Our fog buoys, trailing astern, scraped and jerked and leapt over the floes, sometimes fouled aboard and parted from their towlines. But we gave only the barest necessary attention to that. The signal hoist meaning that aircraft was coming was up on the commodore's ship. The Nazi planes had sighted us. . . .

For nine days and nine nights they were with us, forever there in the sky. We followed them with our glasses and with our straining eyes. We hated them, we cursed, asked them countless times to come in and jump us, give us a chance at them.

That, though, wasn't their job. They were there to give our position to the faster and more deadly of their swastika-marked brothers on the shore, to talk to the land bases by radio telephone. . . .

Our time came on Monday afternoon with clear sun, perfect visibility, and only small cirrus horizon clouds and fragments of altocumulus toward the zenith.

The signal hoists on our commodore's halyards were swiftly replaced and the last one was: Fire.

The cruisers in the center of the convoy, the flak ship and the destroyers and the minesweepers were already letting go. The Nazis came out of the South, from Norway, and high. . . .

There were several squadrons of them that we could count, our hands jerking shut in nervousness, the breath quick in our throats, that hard, violent knotting of muscles in the pit of our stomachs that is the real feel of battle.

Then, from around four thousand feet, the first squadron of them started down on the center of the convoy. They were after the cruisers and the flak ship. They came down the stairs one by one, too far from us, where we were stationed over in the outboard port column, to use our .30-calibers.

The motor sound was no longer a gathered droning. It was a whine, a scream, a thunder. The gun sounds were wham-wham, the deep 5- and 4-inchers, the doubled, quicker slam of the 37-millimeters, above that the rap-rap-rap-rap of the 20-millimeter Oerlikons and the concatenations, treble against those deeper sounds, of the pom-poms and the Chicago pianos, the multiple-mount antiaircraft .50-caliber machine guns.

Bursting shells had another sound, slower than the guns at first, so that you heard the guns first, then the crack and rend and c-rang of the shells. Then, as the fire concentrated, got faster, gun and shell sound were one hell's melee of detonation.

Goddamn, we shouted to each other, our boys are tough. Then the Messerschmitt 110 squadron leader got it. To us, it seemed that he had been a very long time in his dive, would be sure to make his target. But he only got about halfway down the stairs. The yellow shell explosions against the blue sky and the white cloud were closer, closer to the stabbing silver streak of the plane. Then a salvo bracketed him on each side.

He went with that. There was a third yellow blooming up there between the other two as his bombs exploded. He came twirling, twisting, slanting down the sky, hit crumpled and already a wreck far over on the starboard side . . .

Now our side of the convoy was getting it, and they were all around and over us. Bombs were close in the air. We heard them, the very faint, very thin, first whistling, then the louder hirpeling sound that was a whine that deepened, deepened, deepened until to yourself you whispered, "Christ, this one's for us." You waited then, crouched, your feet set wide, your head bowed, for it to hit. Hear it burst, you thought, and you'll know you're alive. If you don't, they've got you.

That was my two-hour spell on the wheel at that time, and I was glad to be there, with the familiar smoothness of the teak wheel spokes in my hands, the skipper up in front of me at the forward windows, conning the ship, giving me "Left a bit," "Now check her; steady," as they came whipping down the columns. It was best there on the wheel or at the guns, for then you knew you were doing something, were actually taking her through; but to stand there, just to wait, that was very hard.

The two pairs of pieces on our wheelhouse topside right overhead were going now. They jarred us slightly in the room below with their running throb of concussions. Their empties hit the steel deck with a brassy, rapid rattling, and the skipper had to raise his voice to make me hear.

But we were lucky. Jerry was missing us, . . .

Then one of the Messerschmitts jumped the *Alamar* right astern. He came slithering in from the port sky, hurdling over the flaming skirt of fire from the escort on that wing. He gave it to the ship astern; we could hear him give it to her.

That bomb caught her on her fore deck, between no. 1 and 2 hatches, stove a great hole in her fore plates. Then, as she reeled out of line, he came straight on, up column, for us.

The third mate and the fourth mate on our after guns on the poop gave it to him. They let him take all they had. They put it right into the leading edge of his wings, their pinkish-flaring tracers winking right into the yellow-green wink of his 9.7-millimeter guns as he whanged at them so he could get over and give us the business low.

They drove him off, those two young men who never before in their lives had fired more than two rounds out of a machine gun. Their fire whaled him off his straight run for us, and he veered yet came close in, driving up forward along our port side.

He was no more than thirty feet off the shipside and at the height of the bridge. The gunners of the struck ship, those of them who had kept their feet, were still firing up his tail. The navy gunners on the next ship to starboard were slapping in their share with their machine guns. And when our third and fourth mates had to cut out because they didn't want to fire through our mainmast shrouds, our second mate and our "Flags" took it up with their pieces on the wheelhouse.

They had him, those two, like you'd had a bucket on a boathook. They just slung it into him, and you could see those pink tracers and the dark khaki ordinary slugs streaking into his guts. The black, white-bordered iron crosses on his side showed a yard big to us, he was that close, and we could see the white whip of his stationary gun fire in the sea alongside, the yellowish-green jetting of his gun flame, the pilot slumped over in his bucket seat, his head, his goggles, and his shoulders.

Those two forward gunners of ours ripped him for seconds. They put a double zigzag of punctures all along his silver hide and then up the hump of his back and the jerky line of his tail as he hunkered past us. He climbed when he was away from us, while the other ships in our column ahead gave him what they were there to sell.

Our forward guns were still. His motor sound was out of our ears, and we shook ourselves and moved our feet, feeling the stiffness flow out of our nerves and bodies. On the wheelhouse topside, "Flags" and the second mate were whanging each other across the shoulders and shouting, and the skipper let a holler out of him like a college kid at a football game.

That Messerschmitt had just slung into the sea about a mile and a half forward of us on the port bow. He hit with a great big, white clatter, and his back broke and he sank.

We had got one, our old merchantman with her little pop-gun thirties. An enormous exhilaration took us then; we laughed at each other and cursed jeeringly at the few remaining Nazis in the sky. . . .

Fog closed some hours after that, bringing obscurity and a kind of fulginous darkness. Allen and I were in our bunks in our room at 2:30

when blond Olë and "Sensation," the wild-eyed ordinary, came running to the door. "Get up on deck," they said, the same note of shock and horror in their voices. "The *Syros* has just got it. She's sinking."

We grabbed our shoes and coats and ran for deck. The *Syros* was over on our starboard hand, two columns away from us to the inboard. Fog was close about her, dimming her, but her hull still showed black against the gray shoulders of the sea.

That hull was in two pieces. She had broken in half 'midships, was sinking. The explosion we had dully heard as we ran up the companion ladder was her cargo of TNT, and she carried a lot of the stuff. Vapor in a low and white and then broad and high cloud rose from her as her cylinder tops and boilers gave.

She sank, and those two black halves went into the sea like swiftly withdrawn fingers. We stood there, the wind hard against us, the fog clammy on our faces and coat collars, the deck slightly areel under us, but firm, shaken only by the strong turning of our screw. We didn't speak. The horror and the sorrow were too great. They were dead, and we were alive, and our brains could take no more.

The *Syros* had been old "Uncle" Charley's ship. "Uncle" Charley was the broad-bellied and gray guy who in our last port had laughed in a tremendous shout as "Two-Gun" had taken his cap and plugged a pair of forty-five holes through it. "Uncle" Charley had been drunk then and singing "The Halls of Montezuma." Now he was dead.

We were sure of that. Olë and "Sensation" had happened to be up there on deck when the *Syros* got it. It was a torpedo fired from a submarine, they said, and hadn't gone far past our stern. Then it had made the *Syros*. There were two explosions: the torpedo, then the TNT. She'd sunk in two and a half minutes, broken as we had seen her go.

"Uncle" Charley was the kind of skipper to be on the bridge during a time of fog like this. He was also the kind of skipper to stay on the bridge until there was no more chance for her. We were glad that in port he'd been drunk and that we'd been with him when he was.

We returned to our room, Allen and I. The hooded light showed it neat, clean, comfortable. There was our desk, our settee, our lockers and books, our gear piled ready for when they called us for the watch. We had soogied this place until it was spotless, swept it out and arranged it every time we came off watch. It was our home, and we were proud of it. But to us, before, it had always seemed solid, permanent. As we lay in our bunks, above us was the thump and turn of the steering engine as the man forward at the wheel gave her a spoke or two. Through all this part of the ship was the majestic vibrance of the propeller turning that sent us on, on, on. Outside, the sea ran, slapping, whispering, rustling, sometimes heavy booming. The steel plates were strong against the sea; the port deadlights were tightly secured. We had, until now, considered ourselves safe from the sea in this room. Danger, the edge worn from it by constant presence, had retreated from our thoughts.

Yet aboard the *Syros* there had been rooms like this one. Men had slept and sat and talked and dressed in them, read and laughed and fixed their gear. Now, not a mile from us, the *Syros* was at the bottom—deep, far gone in the Arctic Ocean—and floating in the room among the mass of wrecked junk were what had been warm, live, and strong men.

"But we can't think that way," Allen said, his ruddy Danish face sober in the hooded light. "We've got our own job to do; we've got this one to bring into port, if we can. Maybe we won't get it, like them. That's how we have to figure, anyhow."

He turned out the light then and said goodnight to me, this twenty-one-year-old New Jersey boy who was serving his first year at sea and his first long voyage on deep water. Lying there in the bunk staring into the dark, I pondered on such as Allen, and I wondered why the world didn't have more of them. If the world did, I knew it would be a better place for all hands, and peace and freedom would exist for all of us. Thinking so, restored by the thought, I fell asleep.

That next day, in snow squalls and a rising wind, the Nazi squadrons came out for us from Norway again, and once more we fought them. This time it was all day long.

Chapter 6: There Go the Ships

Raid after raid was made on us. The Messerschmitts were back, the jobs that had been on us yesterday and the same type that had done so much damage to London and the other cities in the Battle of Britain. But today, too, we had the Heinkel 111 K's, the twin-motored medium bombers that here were being used as aerial torpedo carriers.

They slanted down from the low ceiling at us through the snow and the sleet, and we hardly had our guns on them before they'd released their torpedoes and were up and away again. Those torpedoes they carried had a 21-inch warhead and weighed half a ton. In the air, they held the speed of the plane, 274 knots per hour. In the water, they made a speed of 35 knots, were fired from an approximate distance of 500 yards.

Our commodore had warned us against them. We crouched tense watching for them, knowing just one would finish everything. The Heinkels came in a roaring dive, straight in the first part of it in the fashion of the dive-bombers. But then, as they released the torpedoes, they made a peculiar upward, flipping motion, and from under their broad wings the torpedoes took the sea.

There was a white splatter of spume as the torpedoes rushed into the sea. Then they went beneath the surface to leap and broach at intervals, porpoise-wise, as they raced toward the ships. We swung with hard right helm, hard left helm back and away from them. Our gunners, waiting, waiting, let go at the Heinkels just in that moment when they executed that upward-flipping swing.

Visibility was bad, though, and it was hard for us to see our enemy; the same for them. There were a lot of near misses that day from torpedoes, from bombs, and from the floating mines the Nazi planes dropped, but all of our ships came through safe. Tuesday was another good day for us. We had done all right. Yet the Nazis had discovered one major fact that a lot of us overlooked as we sat in our messroom after the "All Clear" was given: the cruisers were no longer with us. Our fire power was greatly reduced, particularly at high altitudes.

The snow and the sleet squalls passed. Wednesday gave a clear cerulean sky, a blue and gleaming sea, very little horizon or zenith cloud. This was their day, the Nazi's, we knew. We dragged our ammunition cases closer to the guns; got ready as well as we could.

They came early: the Heinkels, the Messerschmitts, the Stukas, the Junkers 88s, and all told there were 105 of them over us during that day's fight that was to last twenty hours. They used everything: 1,100-pounders, 550s, 250s, aerial torpedoes, mines, their cannons, and their machine guns; while outside, always trying to get in, their submarines rushed our escort.

That was hell. There is no other word I know for it. Everywhere you looked aloft you saw them, crossing and recrossing us, hammering down and back, the bombs brown, sleek in the air, screaming to burst furiously white in the sea. All around us, as so slowly we kept on going, the pure blue of the sea was mottled blackish with the greasy patches of their bomb discharges. Our ship was missed closely time and again. We drew our breaths in a kind of gasping choke.

At about half past ten that morning, the long-shanked fourth mate and I were on the after guns on the poop. Two Messerschmitts came after us, off the bank of broken cirrus cloud on the northern horizon. Since Monday, the Messerschmitt squadrons had given our ship a lot of attention, no doubt remembering their pal that we had nailed.

This pair came down in one-two formation, the aftermost perhaps three hundred feet behind his partner. At the start of their direct dive on us they had about two thousand foot altitude.

It was my first time to fire at them, and, eager and excited, I shot too soon. My tracers curved off; I was out of range, so I cut the guns. But they kept on coming, bigger and bigger in the ring sights, their wings growing from thin lines to thick fierceness from which lanced gun flame. We could see the bombs in the racks; we could see the bombardiers. Together, the fourth mate and I cut in at them.

We were leaning far back, knees bent, hands hard on the rubber grips, fingers down on the triggers, eyes to the ring sights. We were no longer conscious of the empties clacketing out underfoot, of the cold, the trembling motion of the ship as the other bombs burst. Here was death, and we were throwing death back to meet it.

The aftermost plane peeled off, banking toward the ship astern. The other kept on, right into our fire, smack for us. Then he dropped it, a 550-pounder. He was gone, away from our fire, and, hanging to the guns, all we could do was look up at that bomb.

It fell, slanting with the pull of the plane's speed. It whirled, screaming and howling in the air directly overhead. We could very clearly see the cylindrical khaki shape, the fins, even the white blur that was the serial markings on the side. This was for us, we thought. This was death. Even should it miss, the concussion will take the TNT.

There was nothing to do but hang on tighter to the gun grips. We said good-bye to each other, but the bomb held our ears, the sound of it seemed to possess all sound.

Then in some sudden and not-yet-strong gust of wind it veered a bit. It struck the sea no more than twenty-five feet astern of us. There was the impact of passage into the sea, an immense, rushing smack, then the detonation. My wife's image was before my eyes. I stood there waiting for the TNT.

Water went tumbling over me in a dousing, blinding column. The ship rose and fell, groaning, terribly shaking. Empty cartridges jumped under the shock, pitched off into the sea. Beneath my feet, as the ship still jarred from that awful violence, the deck seams opened, and the oakum lay loose.

Water dripped from my helmet brim into my eyes. I was soaked from the collar of my sheepskin coat to my felt-lined boots. Beside me, still at his station between me and the fourth mate's guns, was old Ben. He was the oldest AB in the ship; Ben, a Baltimore man, who in the last war had seen service at the front in France. He might have run as that bomb fell, taken out forward for the lifeboats on the boat deck, anywhere away from the bomb. But he stayed there; he just bent his knees and set himself and waited, empty-handed and where he belonged.

For that moment of steadfastness, I loved Ben, and I always shall. We looked staring, shaking, just about conscious, into each other's eyes, and as the frightful tightness gave from our stomachs and lungs, spoke to each other. I forget what we said, and I guess it doesn't matter. We talked as shipmates, that was all.

Allen, my partner, was the next man up there. He had been coming up the companion ladder from the fo'c'sle below, and the shock had all but hurled him back down the steps. He helped me dry and reload my guns, and we tried them and they were all right. The ship was still going on, good. The air, the sea, were full of death. So many aerial torpedoes were in the water that the destroyers and the corvettes let go depth charge after charge at the minimum depth to crack them before they tore into the ships.

Our ship trembled, rocked, shook. A constant vibration went through her that we had to compensate as we fired, or loaded belts, cleared jams, even lit a cigarette, in the few minutes we had free. The sea was shattered into great pillars and columns and waves of explosive-tortured water. The air was bitter with gun smoke drifting gray and yellowish down the slight wind. On the deck around us and into the sea alongside, spent bullets and shrapnel fragments kept constantly hitting with a keening little whicker and slash. Among the dunnage planks piled behind us and in the deck cargo were German machine-gun bullets. Those Nazis that dived us fired as they came.

We were afraid, so afraid that we were almost physically sick from it. The impulse was to run and hide any place safe from those steadily pulsing and sweeping silver planes in the sky. But we couldn't hide, not us guys who had the guns. Our job was here, with the pieces in our hands. . . .

But here, all about, was destruction. Our column leader had just been struck by a bomb on the fore deck. It rent down through the port side a gaping hole twenty feet high and ten wide. Her skipper and her wheelsman kept their heads. She fell neatly off station, out of column to port, let us keep on in line.

We stared aside and then astern at her, hoping that her men would make it safe. One boat went over and a couple of rafts. The men were going down the ropes and davit falls all right. Another boat was in the water; she was slowly sinking, but they'd make it.

Then she was jumped. The Messerschmitts and the Junkers gave it to her. One bomb went square through a boat. Another got the ship and her explosive cargo this time.

There was a great, a horrible, blast. She went in fifteen seconds, a blazing upward sheet of carmine, scarlet and yellow that had a bite of acrid heat we could feel like a blow. The Nazis came back, low, right over the boats and rafts that somehow had lived to get away from what had been the ship.

They machine-gunned those men. They tore those boats and rafts with 9.7-millimeter and 2-inch cannon fire. The men lay helpless, hunched. There was nothing they could do except keep still and die. Our gunners, all the gunners whose pieces could reach, poured it at the Nazis. We cursed them, yelling wild with a rage that burns my throat right now as I write this.

At last we drove them off, but not more than a very few of our own were alive out there.

Bombs had caught the commodore's ship, *Ocean Voice*. A stick of four hurled the water all around her. Then one struck fair on the fore deck. She's gone, we thought. They've got her, too. But although she fell out and back, she kept on coming. She made Russia, too. . . .

Our time was next. Our ship had suffered near hits 'midships on both sides, off the port beam and the starboard bow. Plates bulged inward three feet and more in the fire and engine rooms. Water was gaining against the pumps in the shaft alleyway, and the propeller shaft had a grinding thump as it turned. The ammonia tanks in the engine room, secured in huge blocks of concrete, were loose in their frames, leaking. Ammonia fumes filled the engine and fire rooms. The main fuel lines were leaking, smashed. Our skipper gave the order to abandon ship.

We put no. 2 and no. 3 boats in the water. The double black ball, signal of distress, was run up on the bridge halyards. The mate pitched the code and signal books into the sea, passed down to me in no. 2 boat his sextant. The little chief cook, numb with horror, was in the boat, and a couple of others. One of them was calm and steady Juan. Juan kept the boat off the shipside as I rigged the tiller, got the boat ready to push away.

Then we were ordered back aboard, although right overhead, within fifty feet of our mainmast truck, a pair of Messerschmitts passed to bomb hell out of the next ship. Our chief engineer had gone back down alone into our engine room.

He had put on his gas mask against the ammonia fumes. Then, in his careful way, he had moved from valve to valve, opening and shutting, testing. He found fuel lines that would work, and pumps. He got oil through the hot-well to the furnaces. Steam could be put back on the boilers, be fed into the turbines. We could proceed.

We were dizzy with weariness, just able to stand as we heaved the two boats back up the falls into their chocks on deck. The chief cook, spent, lay inert in the boat until Allen went down and rove a bowline about him, sent him up on a line. Then the chief took men below with him, a man went to the wheel, the black balls came from the halyards, and we went back under way.

The rest of that day was sheer horror, and all the next, for it kept fair, and they kept bombing us all the time. We were wearing our heavy rubber lifesaving suits now, and inside them, thick, double clothing. It took tremendous effort just to lift your feet, your hands. In the dark gloom of the port passageway in the main house, all the galley and messroom force except Juan, our messman, and Charley, the second cook, lay supine on the pipe covers. They were lost men, lost in their heads and hearts, and there were more like them clustering the 'midships deck and the saloon. Their faces, pale, gauntly terrible, were shown by the wild-staring glare of their eyes as we passed back and forth to our duties and the guns.

Juan, who lacked a helmet, brought us coffee on the fo'c'sle-head and poop. He walked out, dark-headed, smiling, with the steaming pitcher in one hand, mugs in the other. Shell fragments, spent bullets were cracking all around him. He would grin at that. "How you making out, commodore?" he would ask us, standing there with his feet broadly set to the deck.

"OK, commodore," we would say, grinning, for there isn't anything else you can do but that with a man like Juan.

Olë and Charley and Allen, Jersey City "Mac," were taking their turns at the guns now, because we needed every pair of steady hands and eyes. The skipper stood in the bridge wing and fired his .32 revolver at the dive-bombers and the Heinkels when they came close, flipped his cap at the bombs. We were half off our heads from battle shock and exhaustion; still, by God, we were sailing our ship.

Thursday it was a lot of the Heinkel 111s with their aerial torpedoes. At the wheel it was agony, because the skipper was forced to give one rapid command after another. You'd catch the wheel down at the bottom spoke, gasping as you bent, your body stinking and weak inside the strangulation of the rubber suit. Then you'd spin her, your teeth closed to keep strength. The spokes whirred creaking, the brass telemotor gears ahead of you went rapidly clicking up and down, and the ship took helm, put over. That torpedo missed; the next one, the next one. Jesus Christ, you'd whisper. Jesus, this was hard. . . .

Thin-faced Barney, the navy wireless man, brought us coffee there at the wheel. His face was emaciated by the last days, but he could grin and give you a funny word as he poured the stuff. Barney was like his partner, "Red," a real navy man.

But by late Thursday afternoon nearly all the ships were very low on ammunition, some of them completely out. Our skipper stood in our starboard bridge wing and talked back and forth during one of the lulls with the skipper in the next ship.

"How are you, you old horse?"

"All right. These boys of mine can throw it up there good. But we've got no stuff left. We've been using our P.A.C. rockets the last couple of times on them low-diving bastards. What'd you think—we going to see Olga furl her drawers in Russia?"

"Sure," our skipper said. "If they haven't got us by now, they probably won't."

★   (Carse, *There Go the Ships*, 41–96)

Slaughterhouse: The Bloody Debacle of PQ-17

The largest of the PQ convoys, number seventeen, with thirty-six freighters and tankers, sailed from Reykjavík on 27 June 1942, after waiting for several days in hopes of a weather forecast that would promise snow or fog. Well they might hope for poor visibility, for Adolf Hitler himself had ordered a massive attack force assembled to destroy the next convoy.

Operation Rösselsprung, the knight's move in chess, would appear from nowhere and pounce on the convoy. The plan called for the Luftwaffe to assemble enough aircraft to keep two hundred planes in the air at once. The white-painted submarines of the Northern Seas Flotilla were in place. The battleship *Tirpitz*, the heavy cruisers *Hipper, Lützow,* and *Scheer,* twelve destroyers, and flotilla of submarines were positioned. Nazi scout planes combed the sea lanes for the convoy this formidable armada had been created to destroy.

The Allies expected massive attacks on the convoy and assigned it an escort more numerous than the merchant ships convoyed, including HMS *Duke of York* and USS *Washington,* and two squadrons of US cruisers and their accompanying destroyers. The battleships and heavy cruisers were to accompany PQ-17 as far as their cruising radius would permit. They were far from their bases, whereas the Germans were on their home turf in the waters and airspace of occupied Norway. Six destroyers, two "flak ships," or antiaircraft ships, and two destroyers were to stick with the convoy all the way, along with associated corvettes, minesweepers, trawlers, and rescue ships.

Late at "night" on 1 July, in the Greenland Sea sixty miles east of Jan Mayen Island, general alarms sounded throughout the convoy, and the doubled lookouts spotted reconnaissance planes hovering just out of range.

The next day the hoped-for fog arrived, with intermittent snow, but on 3 July the weather began to lift. Planes could be heard just above the thinning cloud cover. On the fourth—U.S. Independence Day—PQ-17 got its sardonic moniker: The Fourth of July Convoy. A flight of Heinkel torpedo bombers came roaring in at masthead height, right through the AA barrage from the ships. Four ships were hit on that first pass. Another flight of Heinkels attacked from another angle. JU-88s dive-bombed the convoy, their guns strafing the ships as they leveled off after releasing their bombs.

The commodore signaled a 45-degree turn with a red flare. The sky was black with aircraft and antiaircraft shell bursts. An ammunition ship was vaporized. The planes regrouped, and small formations selected target ships by radio and bombed and strafed in simultaneous coordinated attack. As ships were sinking and burning all across the convoy, the commodore signaled again with a succession of pistol flares, red and green: "Scatter fanwise and proceed utmost speed."

As the convoy broke up, its escort had been ordered to withdraw, and the U-boats moved in for the kill. Like the planes, they decided by signal exchanges which sub would sink which of the fleeing merchantmen. One of the dispersed freighters was the SS *Daniel Morgan*, which at 1500 on 5 July was zigzagging in intermittent fog, on a southeasterly base course, making for the Soviet island of Novaya Zemlya far to the east. The *Morgan* had been followed by a German observation plane, and now a trio of JU-88 dive-bombers appeared high overhead. SS *Fairfield City* emerged from a fog bank nearby, and the bombers hit her and sank her.

Three more planes joined the first trio and now turned their attention to the *Morgan*. "Nine sticks of bombs were dropped on this ship during the next hour," her armed guard officer, Lt. (jg) Morton E. Wolfson, reported,

☆

resulting in no hits or near misses. The ship was kept swinging and all AA guns were firing at a maximum rate. [The *Morgan* was armed with a 3-inch 50 forward, a 4-inch 50 aft, and four .50-caliber machine guns amidships.] The forward gun crew was firing at a rate of thirty per minute. The men were beginning to show signs of physical exhaustion and eyestrain, having been at quarters for more than twenty-eight hours.

There was a short interval of about fifteen minutes between attacks, giving us time to load ready boxes before another group of five JU-88s came into view. The planes [climbed into the sun and then] started their dives. The first plane was hit after releasing its bombs and left over the horizon with flames coming out of his engine and the forward part of the plane on fire. This plane dropped two large bombs that missed to starboard by a good fifty yards. The second . . . also was unsuccessful. . . . The third plane made its dive and was also set afire by the shells from the 3-inch 50 gun, [and] hit the water about three miles to the west of the ship.

[Bombs from the fourth plane] fell close on the starboard quarter. The fifth plane . . . dropped two large bombs alongside the ship on the starboard quarter, rupturing the plates between no. 4 and no. 5 holds.

☆   (National Archives, Voyage Reports, *Daniel Morgan*)

The *Morgan* started taking water, listing to starboard, and settling aft. A shell stuck in the breech of the bow gun, overheated by its sustained rapid fire. After the ship was abandoned, and when the three boats safely launched were some distance away, the ship was hit by torpedoes from two submarines, one to port and one to starboard. The *Morgan* sank stern first at 1730.

At 0200 the next morning, the Soviet tanker *Donbass* was sighted and took the *Morgan*'s crew aboard. They were cordially received, and the sharpshooters of the U.S. gun crew manned the Soviet tanker's forward gun, a 3-inch 50. They stayed at their gun until 0130 on 8 July, when the *Donbass* reached a naval anchorage in the White Sea. The next day they made port at Molotovsk, and the exhausted crew of the *Daniel Morgan* were taken to Archangel, their original destination, where they were hospitalized for two weeks.

"Without the splendid cooperation offered by Captain George T. Sullivan, Master of the *Daniel Morgan*," Lt. Wolfson wrote, "in furnishing men, providing food at the guns, etc., the fine work shown by the gun crew would not have been possible. Many drills were held and all members of the merchant crew were assigned to battle stations" (National Archives, Voyage Reports, *Daniel Morgan*).

Ten U.S. ships were among the twenty-four merchantmen sunk from this doomed convoy of thirty-six. Some sank before a boat could be launched; there were more than fifty lifeboats and rafts in the Barents Sea after the convoy was destroyed, some of them adrift among the ice floes for several days.

All the survivors were eventually repatriated in U.S. warships, but the month or more they spent in Archangel was no picnic. The cuisine was black bread and barley soup for breakfast, lunch, and dinner. Such amenities as cigarettes—or shoes and clothing—were not available. Still it was better than the icy, watery grave of the hundreds of shipmates they had lost.

The high price in ships, cargo, and men paid by the Fourth of July Convoy demonstrated that convoys to north Russia could not be sailed during summer's 24-hour daylight. With one exception, PQ-18, which sailed in September at the insistence of the Soviet Union, they were put off until December, when the sheltering night lasted twenty-four hours. (That convoy had an aircraft carrier in escort, and some high drama as related in chapter 20.)

22 War in Warmer Climes
★★

Away from the murderous cold of the arctic, all the other horrors of war at sea prevailed. From late 1942 and the Allied assaults on North Africa through most of 1944, Allied shipping in the Mediterranean Sea was subjected to a concentration of hostile arms similar to the German domination of the route to Murmansk in the spring of 1942. Only icebergs and subfreezing temperatures were lacking.

"The Med": Every Peril in a Small Sea

Every inch of "the Med" was vulnerable to land-based aircraft from bases in Occupied France, Italy, and along the North African coast. The South of France was not cleared of Luftwaffe bases until October 1944. German and Italian submarine and air attacks were a daily occurrence. Minefields abounded; a safe channel from the western Mediterranean to Suez was not cleared until the spring of 1943. German "E-boats," fast and light torpedo boats, harassed Allied vessels.

"Human torpedoes" wearing scuba gear and riding a torpedo like a horse would fasten the device—equipped with a timed detonator—to the hull of Allied ships. Often these were placed by swimmers or divers working under the cover of the universal port phenomenon of the "bumboat," small craft looking to sell wine or trade anything of value for U.S. cigarettes or currency.

Standing instructions to U.S. merchant ships were to warn any approaching bumboat to depart at once, with a shot across her bow for emphasis. If this warning was not heeded promptly, an antipersonnel depth charge was to be dropped. These charges were not strong enough to damage the ship, but up to a range of fifty feet or so they could blow a diver out of the water.

Despite blackout regulations, ships anchored off Gibraltar were advised by harbor authorities to maintain an all-night watch with flashlights around the perimeter of the vessel at the waterline, looking for air bubbles—which would signal the presence of a diver or human torpedo. Any bubbles observed were to be greeted by a barrage of antipersonnel depth charges, and the nearest patrolling picket boat was to be hailed at once. A diver from the picket boat would inspect the hull where the bubbles had been seen to remove whatever explosive device had been placed.

Observation by German aircraft and reports of spies kept the Nazis well informed of the arrival of convoys at Gibraltar, and their English-language propaganda broadcasts would inform any listener of their knowledge and intentions. In January 1944 the master of the U.S. Liberty *Edward Bates* was listening to one of these broadcasts as his ship, one of a convoy of fifty-four bound for Italy, cleared "the Rock."

There was news of his convoy: "A 54-ship convoy is now passing Gibraltar. It will be attacked in a few hours."

Indeed it was, and the *Bates,* on her first day in the Med, was one of the victims (Bunker, *Liberty Ships,* 125).

The Mediterranean coast of Africa between Egypt and the Atlantic—the Barbary Coast of notorious memory—was thick with Axis spies who kept the enemy informed, by various means, of Allied ship movements—often at night with a parade of bonfires lit on the sea cliffs, marking a convoy's progress eastward. Allied efforts to supply the North African and Italian campaigns were hotly contested in every dimension.

Most ships did get through, of course—otherwise the outcome of the war, or at least its duration, would have been different. Luck played a role, but better still was luck aided by courage, determination, and endurance.

In preparation for the vital effort to defeat Germany's Afrika Korps, guns and ammunition and bombs had to be landed in Algeria. So did gasoline, often transported in dry-cargo ships in barrels and tins, ready when landed to be trucked into the desert to fuel thirsty tanks and other vehicles.

All these staples of war were among the cargo of the Liberty ship *Daniel Huger* in the harbor of Bône, Algeria, one night in May 1943 when a flight of seventeen German bombers raided the harbor. Shrapnel from

Landing craft offload drums of gasoline from freighters and soldiers roll them up the beach at Luzon. (U.S. Coast Guard photograph from National Archives, War and Conflict Collection, 857)

two bombs that barely missed the ship itself raked her decks, killing the third mate and a navy gunner on the bridge. Other fragments started a fire in the no. 5 hold aft, where drums of gasoline awaited unloading. They began to explode, spraying burning gasoline everywhere, with flames surging at least two hundred feet in the air. Ammunition at the gun positions was thrown overboard, the magazine was flooded before the fire could reach it, and the captain ordered abandon ship.

After all hands had gotten safely into the boats, the navy's port fire brigade arrived alongside, and the decision was reached to try to extinguish the fire. Volunteers went aboard and took a fire hose into the adjacent hold, playing a steady stream on the bulkhead next to the fire to prevent the overheated steel from spreading the flames. Meanwhile, the fire brigade filled the burning no. five hold with foamite, extinguishing the fire and saving the ship with no further loss of life.

Earlier in 1943 another Liberty, the *William Wirt*, was part of a small convoy bound for Philippeville, Algeria, about fifty miles west of Bône. John Bunker describes her approach to the port, in which the *Wirt* seemed to have as many lives as the proverbial cat.

☆

On 7 January German reconnaissance planes shadowed the convoy but were chased away by British Hurricanes. Two hours later Junkers 87s started torpedo runs on the convoy, and at the same time a flight of dive-bombers attacked. The *William Wirt*, carrying 16,000 cases of aviation gasoline, was the first ship in the convoy to open fire and before the attack ended had sent four bombers into the sea. One of the planes shot down by the *Wirt* put a bomb into a hold filled with drums of gasoline, but it failed to explode. Another one shot down by the *Wirt* flamed into a Norwegian freighter astern of her and set it on fire. That ship exploded and sank. At the same time the British ship *Benalbanach*, carrying American troops, was torpedoed. She exploded and sank within a few minutes. Many soldiers jumped overboard from the burning ship only to be killed by depth-charge concussion. Another plane set on fire by the *Wirt's* fighting gunners pulled out of a dive and stalled just above the bridge of the ship, then crashed into the water. Two bombs near-missed the ship and a third hit and flooded no. four hold, but she stayed with the convoy.

On 19 January, the *Wirt* was in convoy only six miles from Philippeville when three waves of torpedo bombers and high-level bombers staged a 70-minute attack. Again the *Wirt* escaped damage. Several hours later a submarine was forced to the surface by depth charges, and the *Wirt's* gunners opened up on it, along with an escorting destroyer. They saw its bow point skyward, then slip back into the sea.

That night as the convoy neared Algiers, torpedo planes and bombers attacked again, and the *Wirt* knocked one down. Two hours later there was another air attack. The *Walt Whitman* was hit but made Algiers under her own power. Again the *Wirt* was lucky. The ships sailed from Algiers that night under another air attack in which one ship was bombed and sunk. The attack was so intense that three of *Wirt's* gunners had their ear drums ruptured. The *Wirt* was undamaged.

Finally, as the *Wirt* steamed past Gibraltar on 7 February, homeward bound, the Germans tried once more. That time the concussion of near-miss bomb hits knocked the propeller shaft out of line and the ship had to go to Liverpool for repairs.

☆   (Bunker, *Liberty Ships*, 112–13)

The Allied invasion of Sicily began on 10 July 1943, and at virtually every anchorage along the southern and southeastern coasts of the island merchant ships were discharging cargo and troops into landing craft. At Avola, on the Ionian Sea south of Syracuse, the *Timothy Pickering* was unloading her material cargo of ammunition and her human cargo of British troops.

☆

Because of the coastal terrain, it was possible for enemy planes to sneak in over the surrounding hills and attack before anyone knew they were coming. In such an attack, two Stuka dive-bombers hit the Avola anchorage before the alarm could be given. The *Will Rogers*, which had just arrived, got in a few bursts of 20-millimeter fire, as did some other ships, but the planes were gone within a minute. One plane put two bombs into a hold full of ammunition on the *Timothy Pickering*, which had arrived with the *Will Rogers* and still had most of her troops aboard. The *Pickering* vanished in a mushroom-shaped cloud of smoke and fire that towered a thousand feet into the air. Some of the burning wreckage hit a

Ammunition ship *Robert Rowan* explodes at Gela, Sicily. A hit by a German bomber started a raging fire while she was unloading ammunition and Eighth Army troops. Firefighters tried to stop the blaze, but she blew up twenty-two minutes after the last man was safe ashore. (Photograph by Lt. Robert Longini, USA, from National Archives, War and Conflict Collection, 1023)

nearby tanker, which also blew up, and bits of that ship killed several men on the *O. Henry*. Of 192 men aboard the *Pickering*, the only survivors were twenty-three men blown overboard in the initial explosion.

☆   (Bunker, *Liberty Ships*, 114)

The next day, "around the corner" on the Mediterranean coast and some fifty miles to the west, the SS *Robert Rowan,* another Liberty ship, was discharging U.S. Seventh Army troops and a cargo of ammunition. At 1540 she was hit by a bomb and set afire. While the troops continued to disembark firefighters tried desperately to bring the flames under control. After more than an hour it was evident that the effort was doomed, and all hands got ashore safely and in good order. Twenty-two minutes later, at 1702, the *Rowan* blew up, the remains of her hulk burning through the night.

The *Paul Hamilton* Vanishes

Nine months after the tragedy of the *Pickering,* it was dwarfed by what befell the SS *Paul Hamilton,* another American Liberty in a large convoy in the western Mediterranean, running east along the Algerian coast. Off Cape Bengut, a half hour after sunset, the convoy was attacked by a flight of German torpedo bombers, flying low to avoid radar. A plane in the first wave was hit and set afire by gunners on a British tanker. But before it crashed it managed to launch a torpedo at the *Hamilton.*

Immediately there was a colossal blast, and the *Hamilton* disappeared in a towering cloud of black smoke, debris, and dust. Her cargo had been bombs and other high explosives, and she carried 498 Army Air Corps passengers as well. All were lost, including the merchant marine and armed guard crews, who swelled the death toll to 580. The vaporizing of the *Hamilton* was the costliest Liberty ship "sinking" in all of World War II.

Ironically, a similar catastrophe did not occur a few months later off the Philippines. A Japanese dive-bomber scored a direct hit on another "Lib," the *Augustus Thomas,* loaded with ammunition, tins of gasoline, and troops. The bomb set the *Thomas* afire, but she did not explode, and her entire complement of 548 men survived.

In August 1943, after Allied forces completed the occupation of Sicily, the U.S. tanker *Esso Providence* was at anchor off Augusta, on the Ionian seacoast, fueling three British warships during an air raid. A 250-pound, armor-piercing bomb hit the *Providence* aft, angled through a cargo tank, and exploded in the opposite tank, opening a 40-foot hole in the hull along the waterline.

She did not sink or catch on fire, and when a berth opened up she was docked and cargo in undamaged tanks was discharged. It was decided to bind the wreckage with cable and sail to Malta for temporary repairs. While the *Providence* was in port at Valletta, an unexplained fire broke out in the after ammunition magazine. Powder bags for the 5-inch stern gun ignited and blew the magazine door open. This vented the expanding gases and forestalled a confined explosion that could have wrecked the entire stern. However, the intense heat was setting off 20-millimeter shells and threatening to detonate the shells for the 5-inch gun.

The fire was detected at 1:30 P.M., and the second mate sounded the general alarm. The chief mate, Leslie H. Winder, was supervising a work crew forward. He dashed to the boat deck to open the flood valve to the magazine. Second Mate John D. Hall, joined on the fly by Capt. Walter Andrews and the third mate, Douglas L. Masin, ran to rally the crew and get fire hoses to the magazine. The first assistant engineer, Steve English, instantly started the fire pump.

But the ferocious heat at the magazine made it impossible to connect hoses to the closest valve, and extra lengths of hose had to be run from a valve amidships and rushed aft to the magazine. All this happened within 180 seconds of the alarm.

When the chief mate got to the magazine, 20-millimeter shells were exploding by the hundreds, their projectiles banging into the magazine walls and other cases of ammunition and hurtling through the open magazine doors. The lid of the steel box housing the valve to flood the magazine was red hot, and it was padlocked. Chief Mate Winder grabbed a hatchet from the nearest lifeboat, smashed off the lock, and pried open the lid. With his hands he grabbed the valve wheel, also red hot, and opened it, flooding the magazine—and severely burning both hands.

The powder bags had been consumed and the 20-millimeter ammunition expended, but the flooded magazine and the hoses subdued the fire before the charges in the 5-inch shells could go off. Only then did the chief mate head for the medicine chest to treat his seared hands. He returned to the magazine to see whether anything else needed to be done.

The *Providence* never did get to Taranto. Eventually she was patched up at Gibraltar and permanently repaired later at New York. There an interviewer asked the laconic chief mate for an account of his recent trip to the Med.

"Nothing interesting happened on this voyage," Mr. Winder replied. "There was a fire and it was put out" (Standard Oil Company, *Ships of the Esso Fleet*, 491).

As the Allied campaign proceeded up the Italian mainland, supplies were landed on both the Mediterranean and Adriatic coasts. On the night of 2 December a flight of 105 German JU-88s attacked the Adriatic port of Bari, just above the heel of the Italian boot. The harbor was brightly lit and packed with shipping.

The gun crew on the U.S. Liberty *John Bascom* was the first to spot the raiders.

☆

The *Bascom*'s guns let go, and in a second or so half a hundred guns poured shells into the sky as the first stick of bombs hit the Norwegian freighter *Lom*. She rolled over and sank with her crew of twenty-three men. The *Samuel Tilden*, which had just arrived at Bari, had a bomb go down her stack and explode in the engine room. Incendiaries set fire to her cargo of gasoline and ammunition. Men went overboard to escape the flames.

Direct bomb hits made raging infernos of the *John L. Motley* and *Joseph Wheeler*. Crewmen on the *John Bascom* tried to fight fire on the *Motley*, until the *Bascom* had a stick of bombs walk up her deck from stern to bow, with hits in no. 5 hold, the boat deck, and no. 3 hold. Officers and men rescued the wounded, got the only serviceable lifeboat into the water, and pulled away. By that time the harbor was filled with wreckage and flaming oil burned many men as they tried to swim away from wrecked ships.

Just as the *Bascom* boat reached the quay, the *John Motley* and the *John Harvey* both exploded. The terrific blast lifted the stern of the nearby *Lyman Abbott* out of the water and rolled her on her port side with decks ripped open. The *Joseph Wheeler*, hit at the same time as the *Motley*, blew up next, and the British *Fort Athabaska*, beside her and carrying two captured 1,000-pound German rocket bombs, caught fire, blew up, and sank. Forty-four men out of her crew of fifty-six were killed.

By that time, ships still afloat along the quay were burning fiercely, and violent explosions shook the air every few seconds. The little British freighter *Devon Coast*, untouched during the battle, had a stick of bombs miss her, and as she rolled and pitched in the resulting explosion, a last bomb made a direct hit. She went down, and the attack was over.

The battle at Bari lasted twenty minutes. Seventeen ships were sunk or damaged beyond repair, [five of them American, all Liberties.] Searchers probing [those five the next day] found 38 bodies; 150 men were missing. . . . The only man to survive out of the *Joseph Wheeler* crew had been ashore when the battle began.

☆   (Bunker, *Liberty Ships*, 122)

The relatively narrow confines of the Mediterranean Sea had made it an early shooting gallery for German submarines and airplanes. As the Allies gradually won air and sea superiority there, it became a death trap for Axis submarines, and in the second half of 1944 not a single U.S. merchantman was sunk there. The wider reaches of the seven seas, however, still offered choice hunting to the U-boats.

U-Boats in the South Atlantic

From time to time, a U-boat skipper would show some consideration for the safety of a victim's crew. One example was the sinking in the South Atlantic that marked the beginning of World War II for the U.S. merchant marine. Then the *Robin Moor*'s passengers and crew were given time (twenty minutes) to take to the boats off the bulge of West Africa in the spring of 1941 (see chapter 18).

Twenty-one months later, off the tip of South Africa, the target was the SS *Deer Lodge,* which had survived two months of continuous air attack at Murmansk (chapter 21). On this voyage—her last—she carried general cargo plus four railroad locomotives and three trucks on deck. Of her merchant and armed guard complement of fifty-five, only the chief engineer, Frank Townsend, had served before this trip.

About 2:30 A.M. on 17 February 1943, the *Deer Lodge*'s second mate was on watch and had gone atop the wheelhouse, where he was peering into the darkness trying to spot the coastal light at Great Fish Point. The navy lookout beside him spotted a submarine surfacing a mere twenty yards off the starboard bow. The mate immediately sounded the general alarm, the U-boat crash dived, and the 17-man armed guard crew ran to battle stations. The master, Capt. Irving D. Jensen, got to the bridge before the submarine dived. Despite an intensified watch it was not seen again.

In conformity with standing orders, the captain immediately ordered a zigzag course. But after a half-dozen turns the crotchety old steering mechanism of the World War I–vintage ship broke down. The captain ordered her put in manual steering and went aft to examine the steering engine. At 2:55 there was a loud explosion forward. A torpedo had struck on the port side forward, breaking beams, bending decks, flooding no. 2 hold and blowing off its hatch and the three trucks lashed to it.

The captain sent the first assistant engineer to secure the engines and returned to the bridge, on his way shouting to men gathering on the boat deck to abandon ship. He gave the radio operator the ship's position to transmit with the SSSS distress signal and issued the general order to abandon ship. He assembled his confidential papers and sank them in a metal box, as required.

Up to this point all accounts of the sinking agree. An AB was fatally injured by a swinging davit when the boats were launched, the steward was missing and presumed dead, and two men were seriously injured.

Almost everything else that happened was seen differently through different eyes, as in the movie "Rashomon," in which a series of brutal events is remembered differently by different characters.

The Captain

The captain remembered reaching the boat deck as the last lifeboat (no. 1) was going down with two men in it. He looked around and saw that his orders were being obeyed and climbed in. "After I got the boat into the water, I picked up four men from no. 3 boat, which had been damaged and was hanging by the after fall. I then pulled astern . . . about three hundred to four hundred yards."

The submarine surfaced nearby and the captain answered the questions of its commander. The sub fired a second torpedo into the *Deer Lodge*, and she sank two hours later. "I stayed in the vicinity until daylight to pick up any men who had been thrown clear or jumped overboard," the captain said. "I picked up six men. . . ." The boats and a raft were rescued the following day. (National Archives, Voyage Reports, Master's letter, 22 February 1943, *Deer Lodge* file)

The Chief Cook

Chief cook Abraham Morrison, remembered the captain ordering him and the deck cadet to pull away from the crippled ship—the first boat to leave—while a few yards away four men floundered in the water from boat no. 3, which was wrecked in launching. The cook persuaded the captain to wait long enough to pick up the quartet from the water, and then they pulled away.

The Deck Cadet

Gordon Holmes, the deck cadet, remembered the captain ordering him to steer while the captain "curled himself up in the bow, threw a blanket around him, and prepared to sleep," interrupting his slumbers only to answer the questions of the U-skipper. He left navigation, sailing, and safety to Cadet Holmes.

The Armed Guard Officer

Ens. J. Kenneth Malo remembered rushing to the bridge when the alarm sounded, consulting with the captain, and dashing aft to his battle station at the ship's only heavy gun, a 4-inch 50. He and his gun crew waited for an attack but could see nothing except "many shadows on the heavy swells."

Meanwhile the port lifeboats, nos. 2 and 4, were in trouble, fouled in the launching and tangled together in the water. The chief mate and AB Leslie Morrison slid down the falls to free them as Chief Engineer Townsend, after securing the engines from the controls on the boat deck, stayed aboard holding a light for the mate and the AB in the water as they worked to clear the boats. At last they were free, and other men in the water clambered in.

Forty minutes after the first torpedo hit, the second exploded in almost the same place as the first. The *Deer Lodge* took a heavy port list and settled by the bow. Ens. Malo and his crew stayed at their gun twenty minutes more looking vainly for the sub. Just before the ship went under, the coxwain, John Rusconi, and the pointer threw over a doughnut raft and all went over the side as the *Deer Lodge* sank bow first.

It was Malo who noticed—later confirmed by the others—the humane conduct of the U-boat's skipper.

☆

He was evidently quite gallant and had some degree of mercy, as he could have killed at least a score of men with his second torpedo. After the first torpedo struck, both starboard boats were gone, a good part of the merchant crew were still aboard trying to get away in the port boats. The boats were both in the water, but were tangled in the net sling and falls;

several of the men and the first mate were down in the boats working feverishly to untangle them. The chief engineer was on the saloon deck holding a light and other members of the crew were on deck helping. The sub commander must have seen the confusion before he fired his second torpedo, as it struck well forward of the men and boats in no. 2 hold again.

☆ (National Archives, Voyage Reports, 7 April 1943, in *Deer Lodge* file)

Although the lifeboats were separated during the night, apart from two men lost in the sinking, all were rescued the next day. After the sinking of a merchant ship the Office of Naval Intelligence reviewed all available documentation of the event and the performance of the officers and men involved and prepared a report entitled "Enemy Attacks on Merchant Ships." The *Deer Lodge* report, filed at Baltimore on 14 June found "outstanding service . . . beyond that expected in line of duty" on the part of some crew members.

☆

Gordon Holmes, the deck cadet in the captain's lifeboat who rigged its sail, navigated by the stars, whom the others in the boat credited with their safety.

Frank Townsend, chief engineer, who had served on the ship with conspicuous bravery and skill in the arctic, secured the engines after the third assistant deserted his post, held a light for the chief mate and the AB as they cleared fouled lifeboats, and was the last man off the ship.

Ens. Kenneth Malo and his gun crew stood by their guns until the ship was almost submerged.

Coxwain John Rusconi of the armed guard threw a line to men who had jumped overboard, saving several of their lives, disregarding his own safety and solely interested in saving the lives of the men in the water.

[Others were singled out for commendation—and two for reprehensible conduct.] Capt. Irving Dana Jensen, one of the first in the first boat launched and first to pull away; sleeping in the bow, unconcerned with the safety of the boat or its twelve other passengers.

Ralph Roosevelt, the third assistant engineer, who after the first torpedo left his post in the engine room and ran to his quarters to don his uniform, standing in water up to his knees. After all, he explained, it had cost sixty dollars.

☆ (National Archives, "Enemy Attacks on Merchant Ships," *Deer Lodge*)

Persian Gulf and Arabian Sea

✩

[On a sultry June evening in 1942, the Liberty ship] *Henry Knox* was attacked by submarines in the Persian Gulf. A torpedo exploded part of her cargo of war supplies. In less time than it takes to tell it, the vessel was ablaze from stern to stern and listing 20 degrees to port.

Cadet-Midshipman Maurice W. Price of Tulsa, Oklahoma, made his way calmly to his assigned lifeboat. He found it afire so he climbed in to fight the flames. Just then the forward ropes burned through, and the boat was left dangling over the sea. The cadet clung to a seat until, a few seconds later, the after ropes also burned through and the lifeboat fell into the sea.

As the boat dropped, Price's leg became entangled in one of the lifelines. Freeing himself, he dropped into the water between the boat and the ship. The lifeboat swung in, striking the cadet on the right arm and chest, crushing his ribs, fracturing his right arm and shoulder, and injuring his back. Nevertheless, he managed to climb into the boat and, as ranking survivor, took command and picked up fellow crew members who were clinging to bits of wreckage. The master, Capt. Eugene M. Olsen, was rescued by Price's boat.

"Two Japanese submarines surfaced and stood by the wreck of the *Henry Knox* until it sank," declared the cadet-midshipman in a report that he forwarded to his supervisor. "Then they prowled the surface, seeking survivors. No. 1 lifeboat was stopped. The Japanese took the sails, mast, charts, flashlight, and rations, broke the oars, and departed. One of the subs came within seventy-five feet of our boat but the men hid under blankets and the submarine passed by."

"We were in the lifeboat eleven days before we reached safety."

✩   (West, *Down to the Sea*, 123–24)

✩

[Even more sadistic treatment awaited another Lib, the SS *Jean Nicolet*, the following month.] She was homeward bound down the Arabian Sea on 2 July 1944 with a merchant crew of forty-one, an armed guard contingent of twenty-eight, and an army and civilian passenger list of thirty, many of them men returning home after two or more years in the Persian Gulf.

The first torpedo hit in no. 2 hold and the second in no. 4. The vessel took a heavy starboard list. All hands abandoned ship safely in four lifeboats and two rafts.

The submarine soon surfaced and began shelling the deserted hulk. After firing ten or twelve rounds at the ship, the raider circled around the wreck to the rafts and lifeboats, and an officer on the conning tower shouted to them through a megaphone: "All come here!"

The first boat to approach the submarine contained about twenty-five merchant seamen, navy gunners, civilians, and soldiers. As they climbed aboard their life preservers were snatched from them. Japanese sailors also took their watches, wallets, and shirts and shoes.

The survivors were then prodded with bayonets onto the forward deck, where they were ordered to kneel and their hands were tied behind them with wire, lines, and strips of clothing. William Musser, a messboy who did not kneel fast enough, was shot in the back and thrown over the side. So began a night-long orgy of torture and murder.

One by one, the boats and rafts were ordered to the submarine. A machine gun was trained on each boat as it came alongside. Men were clubbed with lengths of pipe and cut with knives and bayonets.

When Lieutenant Deale, the navy armed guard officer, and five of his gunners tried to paddle away on a tiny doughnut raft, the Japanese turned on a searchlight and then opened fire. A man was hit and fell over the side, but the others flattened themselves on the raft, and the searchlight was soon cut off—the Japanese evidently assuming they had been killed.

The men lay as still as they could while the submarine circled the slowly sinking ship and listened to the screams and cries of their comrades. As the night wore on, men succumbed to wounds and beatings and were shoved off the submarine into the sea. Others were forced to run a gauntlet of clubs, pistols, knives, and pieces of pipe. When Charles Pyle, the first assistant engineer, hesitated, a sailor hit him on the head with the butt of a pistol. Another kicked him in the back and sent him reeling through the line of yelling, flailing seamen, until he stumbled over the side into the sea. The cold water revived him, and he paddled away, struggling to free his hands. He was about to give up when AB Stuart Vanderhurst hoisted him head first onto a floating hatchboard.

Vanderhurst had slid off the bow of the submarine and swam away unnoticed earlier in the night. His wrists had not been tightly fastened, and he freed them with a clasp knife the Japanese had overlooked.

By then the submarine was almost indistinct, marked by the glow from its hatches and lights carried by crewmen as they moved up and down the deck. The cries of the captives gradually diminished as they were beaten unconscious, one by one, or kicked overboard.

About dawn, when a distant aircraft was heard, the submarine hurriedly submerged, leaving several survivors still on its deck to flounder in the sea and drown but for a navy gunner who, like Vanderhurst, had secreted a knife in his trousers, cut his own bonds, and then freed the others who were still afloat.

Minutes later, a Catalina patrol plane flew overhead, made a few lazy circles and left. It returned several hours later to drop life preservers and food. Some thirty hours later the frigate *Huxac* of the Indian Navy picked up the twenty-three survivors of the ninety-nine men on the *Jean Nicolet.*

☆   (Bunker, *Liberty Ships*, 135–36)

A touching counterpoint to the brutality encountered by many torpedoed seamen in the Arabian Sea and environs is one of the war's many dog stories. Masters' rules—and their observance—for pets aboard ship varied widely, but many seafarers brought or smuggled a dog or cat aboard. (The author had a kitten aboard the *Sappa Creek* on several North Atlantic trips.)

Most of the dogs starring in wartime canine adventures were simply mutts, strays picked up here or there and adopted, but this one was a fine specimen of Persian deerhound, bought by Harold L. Myers, the ship's clerk of the tanker *E. G. Seubert*, at Abadan.

At the great refinery there the *Seubert* took on 79,000 barrels of admiralty fuel destined for the Mediterranean to support the Allied invasion of Italy. On 6 February 1944 she sailed down the Persian Gulf for Hormuz to join a convoy heading for the Gulf of Aden, the Red Sea, and the Suez Canal.

The first four days in convoy were uneventful, but on the afternoon of 20 February they sailed through waters littered with packing cases and other debris from sunken Allied freighters. The next night the hulls reverberated with the hollow booms of depth charges detonating nearby, and at 3:30 A.M. on the twenty-third, a torpedo opened the *Seubert's* port quarter, and she sank in twelve minutes. Two more ships of the twenty-one in the convoy were sunk before daybreak.

On the *Seubert*, the exploding torpedo awakened Harold Myers by hurling him out of the bunk in his room in the midship house. As parts of the heavy, wooden bulkhead of the room splintered and fell around him, he heard his dog whimper. He pushed through broken pieces of wood, to release the trapped hound, donned his life jacket, put the dog's collar around its neck, and reported to the bridge. Capt. Ivar Boklund ordered him to help launch boat no. 1, so he put the dog in the boat and bore a hand with others at the falls.

The ship was sinking fast, and a couple of feet before the boat reached the water the *Seubert* lurched, and the boatswain yelled, "There she goes!"

✩

I took a flying leap and grabbed a man rope The lifeboat came up to me, and I dropped into it. [But it was too late for the boat to clear the falls.] I grabbed the dog's leash and pulled him overboard with me to avoid going down when the ship sank. As the dog and I swam for our lives, he went ahead of me, and I followed as best I could with the leash wrapped around my wrist. Swimming was difficult in the layer of oil, several inches thick, which covered the sea for a considerable distance. [Fuel oil or crude congeals into a viscous mass on contact with cooler sea water. Swimming through it is difficult in any clime; in frigid seas it is impossible, as the oil becomes a thick carpet with a texture almost like polystyrene foam.] When I went under, the fuel oil filled my eyes and ears. I tried unsuccessfully to wipe it from my eyes; more oil, running down from my forehead, practically blinded me. I knew I could not see a lifeboat or raft or hear voices that might be calling. My leg hurt badly. I did not know where I was going or whether there was any chance of rescue. My feeling of suspense, mingled with determination, fear, and hope, was indescribable. Somehow, sympathy for my dog and the desire to save him helped me to carry on.

I had no idea whether the dog could see or hear any better than I could. The night was clear but very dark. He may have heard men talking on one of the life rafts, which, unknown to me, we had neared to within a few yards.

In any event, someone on the raft heard the dog panting and gasping when we were only a few feet away and pulled him aboard. I felt the leash tighten and instinctively shouted for help. The next instant I was hauled up on the raft.

We rescued other survivors. It was not long before I found I could not bend my legs; one of them was badly swollen.

When we were put ashore at Aden I went to a hospital where I stayed for nine days, receiving fine medical attention. After that I was sent to an army camp for a month, until repatriated on a troopship, the *Solomon Juneau,* which sailed on 30 March. Meanwhile, my dog had been treated at the hospital for two weeks. I was permitted to take him with me on the transport, and on arrival in New York, on 11 May, after a voyage of 18,000 miles, I sent him to my mother in St. Louis. Feeling that he had saved my life, I did not want him to go to sea again during the war.

☆   (Standard Oil Company, *Ships of the Esso Fleet,* 498–99)

The Far Pacific: Sadism and Suicides

For the torpedoed seaman, the Pacific Ocean in World War II was a place of vast cruelties as well as vast distances. While certainly not routine, atrocities virtually unknown in the case of German or Italian submarines were disturbingly familiar and thoroughly documented on the part of Japanese subs. It seemed that nearly everyone who put to sea in that war had a shipmate who had survived an attack on lifeboats, or had lost a friend that way.

☆

On 30 October 1944, the Liberty ship *John A. Johnson* was steaming from San Francisco toward Honolulu with food, explosives, and a deckload of trucks. That area of the Pacific was not considered particularly hazardous then, and the ship was running alone, although lookouts were posted and the gun crew was ready for action. The weather was clear, with scattered clouds, heavy swells, and a three-quarter moon.

No one saw the submarine, or the torpedo that struck at no. 3 hold. The ship was making a heavy roll at the time, and the explosion at the turn of the bilge was fatal. The crew abandoned ship, and as the last man left the ship she broke in two.

All hands escaped safely in two lifeboats and a raft. About half an hour after the ship was abandoned, the submarine surfaced and began shelling the two sections of the wreck, by then about a quarter of a mile apart. After a few rounds, the forward section blew up in a thunderous blast, with flames shooting hundreds of feet into the air. The after section was set on fire.

Finished with its target practice, the raider then turned on the lifeboats. One boat, with twenty-eight men on board, was about two hundred yards from the submarine when it surfaced. It was a big one—at least three hundred feet long—with several U.S. flags painted on the conning tower. The captain was dressed in a white uniform, and the crewmen were laughing and shouting as they fired into the wrecked ship.

When the submarine headed toward the boat, with the evident intention of ramming, the men jumped over the side and swam out of the way. A searchlight was turned on, and several Japanese fired on the survivors with pistols and a machine gun. After the raider passed, the men could hear a number of their shipmates crying for help, but there was nothing they could do.

They climbed back into the boat but jumped out again when the submarine made another try at ramming, the sailors shouting "Banzai!" as they went by. This time, however, there was no firing. When the submarine finally headed off toward the other castaways the men climbed back into the lifeboat, but several of them had been shot or drowned.

The raft, with seventeen men aboard or clinging to grab ropes, was silhouetted by the burning ship and provided a perfect target for the gunners on the submarine. A machine gun fired several bursts at it and the submarine tried to ram, but twice a heavy sea rolled up just in time to carry the raft free. The third time the submarine sank the raft. Three men were killed by machine-gun fire as it passed. Then, after one attempt to ram the other boat, the submarine disappeared into the darkness.

Survivors were spotted the next morning by a Pan American Airways clipper, which directed the USS *Argus* to the scene. Ten men were killed by gunfire or drowned during the night of terror.

★ (Bunker, *Liberty Ships,* 155–56)

There were abundant other perils in the far Pacific. Early in the war Japanese air power devastated Allied shipping in the region. "In February of 1942 at Port Darwin, Australia, the SS *Admiral Halstead* . . . was the only ship of twelve . . . to escape being sunk, discharging her cargo of gasoline and ammunition for Australian troops, and escaping the Japs to participate in more Pacific action" (Bunker, *Seafarers*, 31).

The *Halstead*'s survival was due to more than luck. She was armed with two machine guns—puny weapons against bombers—but manned determinedly by six men of her merchant crew. Their valor was recognized by the award of the merchant marine's Distinguished Service Medal.

In the last year of the war the kamikaze dive-bombers appeared. In Leyte Bay, gunners on the SS *Thomas Nelson,* a Liberty ship loaded with gasoline and ammunition and 630 army troops

☆

blasted a suicide plane which made a run at the ship, but the Jap hit his target nonetheless, his two exploding bombs turning the freighter into an inferno of flame, with 213 soldiers killed, wounded, or missing.

Gunners of the Liberty ship *Matthew P. Deady* (SUP) bagged two Jap planes at Leyte, but the ship was bombed and set afire with considerable loss of life. . . .

In December of 1944, a convoy of ammunition-laden ships, including the Liberty *John Burke,* was attacked by kamikazes. One hit the *Burke* square on, blowing her up with the loss of every man aboard. Not a bit of wreckage was left to mark her place in the convoy. . . .

In the invasion of Leyte . . . the Liberty ship *Adoniram Judson* won a special niche for herself in the annals of war, by not only delivering vital landing mats and 3,000 barrels of high octane aviation gasoline for the captured airfield at Tacloban but by providing the principal air protection there for several days.

☆   (Bunker, *Seafarers*, 31)

The tanker *Esso Rochester* arrived in the Philippines in December 1944 with 114,000 barrels of bunker C, or navy fuel. She rendezvoused with a Liberty tanker at Leyte, where the U.S. army was fighting to retake the island. Her orders were to transfer her cargo to the Lib, and she stood by while it finished refueling two destroyers.

With her cargo booms and nets, SS *Peter Cooper Hewitt* discharges cargo onto a pontoon pier built by SeaBees at Los Negros, in the Admiralty Islands off New Guinea. (National Archives, RG 80G, 254892)

"Suddenly a Jap bomber attacked these vessels," the *Rochester*'s skipper, Capt. Frank Pharr, related, "and we opened fire with our 3-inch gun. Our gun crew claimed that we put a few shells into the enemy plane, which swerved and dived into an LST."

A week later, after fueling fifteen navy ships, the *Rochester* joined a departing convoy. That night a kamikaze plane dived toward her. The merchant ships had been warned not to fire at night lest their tracer bullets reveal their position. "But our escorts, with their radar-controlled antiaircraft guns, hit the oncoming bomber in the nick of time," Captain Pharr said. "It crashed into the sea about 100 feet short of our stern."

The next day another kamikaze attacked the ship. The *Rochester*'s guns, with six or seven merchant crewmen assisting the armed guard crew, started firing as the plane approached. The 3-inch gun scored a hit, which did not slow the attacker, but one or both of the 20-millimeter guns on the starboard bridge wing hit the kamikaze's starboard motor, which erupted in flames. It plunged into the sea hard by the port bow, and sank at once.

The navy, which had a sort of institutional conviction, not unreasonable, that more aircraft kills were claimed than made by armed guard gun crews, later confirmed this one by letter.

★

NAVY DEPARTMENT
Executive Office of the Secretary
Office of Public Relations
Washington 25, D.C.

February 16, 1945

Mr. M. G. Gamble
Assistant General Manager
Standard Oil Company
Marine Department
30 Rockefeller Plaza
New York 20, N.Y.

Dear Mr. Gamble:

The Navy Department takes great pleasure in confirming the report of the destruction of a Japanese airplane by the *Esso Rochester* on 21 November 1944.

The attacking enemy plane was a twin-engined medium bomber known as "Sally." The Japanese aircraft had already dropped a bomb near one of the LSTs in the convoy. The *Esso Rochester* opened fire with its 3-inch gun; as the "Sally" came closer, the 20-millimeter guns went into action. The first burst caught the bomber squarely, and the starboard engine burst into flame. Seconds later the plane struck the water and sank almost instantaneously.

Sincerely,
Harold B. Say
Commander, USNR
Officer in Charge
Review Section

★ (Standard Oil Company, *Ships of the Esso Fleet,* 386)

23 Mulberries, Gooseberries, and Bombs

★★

Operation Overlord was the code name for the Allied invasion that would rout Hitler from Western Europe. The huge armada that would deliver the soldiers, artillery, ammunition, and supplies to do the job had to land them somewhere.

The Cotentin Peninsula running west from Le Havre was only a hundred miles south of Brighton and Portsmouth. Its channel coast, in Churchill's phrase, was a "fifty-mile half-moon of sandy beaches." The ideal ports of Le Havre and Cherbourg were heavily defended by the Germans, who knew full well how badly the Allies needed them.

Large-scale landings on the beach were rendered especially difficult by the fact that the entire length of the beach in that section was backed by bluffs on which German guns—75-millimeters, 155s, and the especially lethal 88s—were emplaced. Moreover, the tide rose and fell there by twenty-one feet.

After much planning and debate this grinding problem was addressed with a building program that got under way late in 1943. At London's East India Docks and at other locations on the Channel coast, curious structures began to take shape. There were long sections of highway bridges, narrow, steel assemblages two hundred feet long, and what appeared to be scores of huge, windowless warehouses or factories six stories high and nearly a block long.

The weird structures of this top-secret project were so vast and so strange that their existence could not be hid from German reconnaissance planes (and spies), but their purpose remained obscure. The best speculation seemed to be that they were to be towed into French harbors and sunk to block them.

Meanwhile in Scotland, in the Firth of Lorne off Gourock, a growing fleet of superannuated freighters and a few decrepit men-of-war began to

Phoenix breakwater units, prefabricated and towed from England , being positioned for sinking end to end. They formed the western breakwater at the U.S. Mulberry harbor at Omaha Beach. On the lee side of the completed Phoenix, seven Liberty ships could be moored for unloading their cargoes into landing craft for transfer to the beach. (Office of Strategic Services photograph, from National Archives, RG 80-G, 285129)

These battle-scarred freighters, firmly sunk off Omaha Beach, were the seaward anchor of the Gooseberry line of blockships on the east end of the American Mulberry harbor, sheltering it from the stormy English Channel. A similar British instant port was created a few miles east at Gold Beach. (Supreme Headquarters, Allied Expeditionary Forces [SHAEF] photograph, from National Archives, RG 80-G, 285149)

assemble. One of the latter was a long-decommissioned British dread-naught that had been disguised as an active battleship to fool the Italian navy. The ship was HMS *Centurion,* and the disguise was a favorite trick of the privateers of the seventeenth and eighteenth centuries, painting long logs black to look like cannon.

Operation Mulberry

Coordinating these bizarre endeavors was a monumental task, but over a span of five days beginning on D-Day plus one, it eventuated in the emplacement on the Normandy coast of two complete prefabricated harbors, each the size of the Royal Navy's port at Gibraltar.

This was Operation Mulberry, and within ten days its instant harbors would land the men, tanks, guns, trucks, and supplies that would open the Normandy invasion. The U.S. Mulberry was situated off Omaha Beach at St. Laurent and the British one a few miles east off Gold Beach at Arromanches.

The strange objects whose purpose had puzzled German intelligence analysts were five in number. Their fabrication occupied more than 20,000 British workers from late 1943 to their deployment.

OPERATION PHOENIX

The seeming windowless factories were code-named Phoenix, and there were a hundred of them. They were monstrous caissons, each a floatable section of a prefabricated breakwater that could be towed into position—end to end next to another Phoenix—and sunk in place by opening flood valves. For its self-defense, both off Normandy and while being towed there at three miles per hour, each Phoenix was topped with a gun plat-form for 20-millimeter antiaircraft guns.

Each of the Mulberry harbors had a row of Phoenixes more than a mile long, set on the bottom nearly a mile offshore from the high-water line and roughly parallel to it. When emplaced, the landward side of this long row stood in five fathoms of water at low tide, deep enough for ocean-going vessels to tie up to it. The top of this breakwater stood thirty feet above the sea at low water and at ten feet at flood tide. Seven Liberty ships at a time could be moored there to discharge their cargo into land-ing craft or other small vessels.

Operation Gooseberry

The line of Phoenixes protected the west half of the U.S. landing area of Omaha Beach. Extending the breakwater to the east along the three-fathom curve was a line of sunken ships—part of Operation Gooseberry. Twenty-five vessels from the rust-bucket fleet that had been assembled at Gourock stretched more than a mile, nearly to the far end of Easy Red, the easternmost sector of Omaha Beach. The combined breakwater of Phoenixes and Gooseberries sheltered a harbor more than three miles long from the turbulent waters of that stretch of the English Channel.

All the ships selected for Gooseberry were near the end of their useful lives. Once they had discharged their last cargoes in a British port, explosive charges were positioned in their holds that, on signal, would blast out their bottoms. Then they were loaded with sand ballast and sent up to Gourock to wait.

Manned for their last trip by volunteer crews of merchant seamen, who knew their mission would come under intense attack from air, sea, and shore, the battered old ships sailed down the Irish Sea and through St. George's Channel late in May, anchoring off the Isle of Purbeck to await their final sailing orders and to await also a break in the foul weather that was delaying the start of Operation Overlord.

On D-Day plus one the first three of these blockships were nudged into position and scuttled. (The first was a Liberty battered in the Mediterranean campaign, the *James Iredell.*) Two days later the last of them was in place.

The positioning did not go without a hitch. On D-Day plus two the tugs were nudging the Liberty *George S. Wasson* into her spot—under simultaneous attack from dive-bombers and the German 88s on the bluffs. At the right spot the dynamite charges in her hold were detonated, and the *Wasson* started to settle, but the swift incoming tide pushed her shoreward as she was sinking. She wound up too close to shore, and the Gooseberry line had to be wrapped around her. Another blip in the line of hulks detoured an old Hog Islander, the *Matt W. Ransom,* which suffered a similar fate.

At the U.S. Mulberry, the west end of the Gooseberries, on the bottom along the three-fathom line, was about five hundred yards closer to shore than the east end of the Phoenix breakwater on the five-fathom curve.

This gap was the entrance to the port from the English Channel. At the east end of the sunken blockships was a short row of Phoenixes extending in toward shore, to damp the strong crosscurrent that ran like a river along the shoreline under some circumstances.

Simultaneously, similar lines of Gooseberries—but not the Phoenixes—were being sunk off the Americans' Utah Beach to the west and the three British beaches to the east—Gold Beach, the closest, was the site of the British Mulberry harbor. At the others, Juno and Sword, as at Utah Beach, the purpose of the Gooseberries was to shield LCIs (landing craft–infantry)—and other small vessels ferrying supplies to the particular landing areas.

The impact of the breakwaters was apparent immediately. Even the leading marine salvage expert of the day, Capt. (later Adm.) Edward Ellsberg, USNR, who played a major part in planning and carrying out the scheme, was amazed at the effect of "the Gooseberry and Phoenix breakwaters on unloading. Gone now were the waves in the inner harbor and with them were gone also the surf and the breakers pounding the beach" (Ellsberg, *Far Shore,* 311).

LOBNITZ PIERHEADS

The strangest looking of all the prefabricated harbor elements was the Lobnitz pierhead. In the shipyard, it looked like a vertically shortened version of the Phoenix, but from each of its four corners rose a tall black tower looking something like a chimney. These towers were huge steel legs, on which the floating pierhead would eventually rise and fall with the tide. This enormous contraption was designed to solve a single problem of the utmost importance: the speedy unloading of LSTs (landing ship–tank) at the beachhead.

Ten Lobnitz units were made for the two Mulberries. When each was towed to the desired position, its gangling legs were driven firmly into the bottom of the bay. Thus framed within the vertical members like an elevator in its shaft, the floating landing surface rose and fell with the tide so it was always at sea level, always at the right height for LSTs to unload.

The LST was a seaworthy ship three hundred feet long. Deep inside its capacious hull, open at the top, was a flat deck a few feet above sea level that could accommodate a large cargo of tanks, mobile artillery pieces, fully loaded trucks, or any other bulky, heavy wheeled objects. This vessel was loaded and unloaded through great doors at its bow. It would nose up to a suitable landing area, its bow doors would yawn open, and a drawbridgelike ramp would be lowered to the landing. Then the cargo would be driven aboard or ashore.

But the Normandy coast, with its 21-foot tides, battering seas, and constantly shifting sands at the shoreline, made unloading LSTs a tricky business. There was a real danger that in attempting a landing this invaluable ship could break its back in the violent surf. So as soon as the breakwaters were up and until the Lobnitzes were ready, LST's were unloaded inside the harbor onto LCTs, whose far smaller size and shorter draft enabled them to beach and unload tanks safely—but slowly.

As soon as the breakwaters calmed the waves, combat engineers began leveling and smoothing the beach sands with bulldozers. This sped the process of unloading smaller landing craft and also paved the way for another improvisation. The army set up such a howl over the delay in getting tanks and self-propelled guns ashore that, over navy protests, LSTs were discharged directly at the beach by an expedient made possible by the great height of the flood tide. The ship would nose into shore at high tide and offload its tanks or trucks in less than an hour.

That was the good news. The bad news was that by that time the tide had already receded enough to leave the LST, always in short supply and great demand, aground for nearly twelve hours, until the next high tide. However, by nightfall on D-Day plus nine the Lobnitzes were in place, and the next morning, 16 June, they were in operation.

WHALE CAUSEWAYS

Whale was the code name for a steel pontoon causeway running from the Phoenix to shore. Its sections were what in English shipyards had looked like spans for highway bridges. They too were towed into place on barge-like pontoons, which to some resembled beached whales. One end of the causeway was secured to the Lobnitz pierhead and the other firmly implanted inland at the high-water mark. Over them 38-ton tanks—and self-propelled guns and trucks, whether loaded for combat or bearing ammunition or any other supplies, were driven directly ashore.

BOMBARDONS

The last element of the Mulberries was the farthest from shore: the Bombardons, steel floats functioning as supplementary offshore breakwaters. They were narrow structures two hundred feet long, with a keel nine feet deep; when they were moored offshore, they were positioned so as to give the Phoenixes some protection by breaking up the incoming long, coastal waves or rollers that wash the beaches of Normandy.

Operation Corncob: Getting It There

Getting all these devices in place on schedule was itself a massive undertaking. Operation Corncob, as it was code-named, involved a fleet of 176 towboats under many flags, a company of 800 U.S. merchant seamen—all volunteers—coordination among U.S. and British navies, armies, and civilian mariners, and a large infusion of luck.

Consider what was undertaken: moving the Phoenixes into place entailed assembling them at a staging area, sinking them there until D-Day, then refloating them, towing them, and sinking them in position—all 600,000 tons of them; moving the doomed merchant ships to their last resting place off Normandy—in effect burial at sea with full military honors for ships that already had given their all; landing 630,000 troops in a dozen days, and 95,000 vehicles and 200,000 tons of supplies in the same period; and enemy attack at almost every stage from some combination of shore artillery, dive-bombers, submarines, mines, and speedy E-boats on the surface.

As soon as the Phoenixes were in place, and while the rest of the harbor was abuilding, incoming freighters tied up there and began to discharge into landing craft. The first merchant ship lost in the Normandy invasion finished doing that in the nick of time. The *Charles W. Morgan* was a Liberty, an ammunition ship, and she had been under attack from the big guns on the bluff as well as dive-bombers trying to get past Allied air cover, as they did from time to time.

They missed the *Morgan* for a day and a half, but on 10 June one of the bombers dropped one in her no. 5 hold—just after she had finished unloading and was preparing to return to England. The harbor and the channel outside were swarming with tempting targets, but when the Allies achieved clear air supremacy the air war on shipping virtually subsided.

The English Channel approaching the Cotentin Peninsula was still a maritime mob scene. Merchant and navy ships arriving in the Mulberries at Omaha and Gold beaches to unload found themselves in a crush of landing craft and other small vessels swarming like ants in an anthill.

One merchant skipper who arrived soon after the Germans had been driven back from the beachfront bluffs, Capt. Heinrich Kronke of SS *Cyrus H. McCormick,* described the scene: "The Channel is the busiest thoroughfare in the world. Craft of every description are traversing it day and night and often there doesn't seem to be enough room to squeeze another ship through. The astonishing thing is how it all can be done in such safety, for we all feel that we are as safe as we would be walking up Market Street. Now and then there are planes making a fuss, but they do not hit anything" (Bunker, *Liberty Ships,* 165).

When the harbors were complete, the commander-in-chief of Allied naval operations, Adm. Sir Bertram H. Ramsay, sent his compliments to the U.S. War Shipping Administration.

☆

Operations in which thirty-two U.S. merchant ships participated have been brought to an extremely successful conclusion. This reflects the greatest credit to the officers and men who manned these vessels. Particular praise is due to the engine room staffs for their tenacity and devotion to duty; especially in the case of those ships which had to be positioned under enemy shellfire. The result of their efforts is already bearing fruit, and the shelters they provided are of great benefit to the army.

It is requested that you will convey to all the officers and men concerned my high appreciation of the valuable services they have rendered to the Allied cause.

☆   (Bunker, *Liberty Ships,* 165)

The Great Storm of 19–22 June

The U.S. Mulberry was in operation well before the British version, but its location made it distinctly more vulnerable to an intense storm from the wrong direction. That was exactly what Mother Nature had in store beginning on D-Day plus thirteen (19 June). Soon after dawn a 30-knot northeaster blew in and continued for three days. It demolished the Mulberry at Omaha Beach and severely damaged the British one at Gold Beach. When it was over, the U.S. harbor was good for nothing but repair parts for Gold Beach.

The first night anchored landing craft inside the harbor began to drag their anchors, and their soaked engines would not start. At Omaha, a U.S. salvage barge out of control and six runaway British LCTs crashed into the whale causeway of the Lobnitz at Omaha Beach—the LCTs literally picked up by the sea and hurled onto the roadway. Before dawn the harbor was beyond repair.

At the outer row of breakwaters, the Bombardons began to break loose and the 200-foot steel sections were tossed and blown against the row of Phoenixes, hammering them repeatedly until they began to break up. This fury continued for two more days and nights, wrecking structures and vessels with wild abandon. Hundreds of small craft were pounded to pieces against the beaches. On the fourth day the storm began to blow out at last. "The American Mulberry lay," in Felix Riesenberg's words, "in sea-washed ruins except for the blockships. Viewed at a distance the old ships looked much as they had at sea— freighters hull down, making heavy weather of it, yet withstanding all the fury of the oceans. The lee they provided for landing craft was all America had until Cherbourg fell on June twenty-sixth" (Riesenberg, *Sea War*, 254).

Snickers among Latter-day Critics

Not many military historians have addressed Operation Mulberry more than in passing. Among the exceptions are Walter Scott Dunn Jr. in *Second Front Now*, Edward Ellsberg in *The Far Shore*, Guy Hartcup in *Code Name Mulberry*, and Max Schoenfeld in *D-Day 1944*. Modern revisionists scoff at its value, sharply criticize its cost in money and in preemption of the scarce resource of steel, and pooh-pooh the strength of the four-day gale that wrecked the U.S. Mulberry.

These are the ones so aptly characterized by Max Schoenfeld as "later critics with the benefit of hindsight and without informed first-hand knowledge of the situation in Britain in 1940–44." To this one need add only: "or on the Normandy coast on 19–22 June 1944" (Schoenfeld, "Navies and Neptune," 90).

Most of the historians have observed that Operation Mulberry's primary value may have been in convincing British doubters from the prime minister on down that (with it in place) the cross-channel invasion could succeed. Therefore they allowed it to be executed.

Churchill's Inventions

To this there is an intriguing sidelight.

Small wonder that Operation Mulberry should win the approbation of the prime minister. Sir Winston had virtually invented it more than thirty years before.

In 1917 he had returned, after active military service, to the cabinet of David Lloyd George, as minister of munitions. Without expert collaboration he drew up a plan for invading two of the German-occupied Frisian Islands to use as a naval base. It revolved around "tank-landing lighters" with "a drawbridge or [sloping] bow," enabling the tanks to land under their own power.

Further, he suggested preparing "a number of flat-bottomed barges or caissons, made . . . of concrete," towing them to a selected site, and sinking them by opening their seacocks. This would create "a torpedo- and weather-proof harbour, like an atoll . . . in the open sea."

He even observed that while the Germans would surely observe their construction, his 1917 Phoenixes would be thought "intended for an attempt to block up the river mouths" (Churchill, *Second World War,* 2: 244–45).

In 1942, now heading his own government, Churchill returned to the topic and proposed a pontoon causeway from shore to a "particularly well moored" pierhead that, he noted by hand, "*must* float up and down in the tide."

Lord Mountbatten had endorsed the suggestion of an aide that "block-ships [be] brought to the scene by their own power and then sunk in a prearranged position." Churchill added this to the plan, and thus Gooseberries came to be. "The whole project was majestic," he concluded and declared that he "was now convinced of the enormous advantages of attacking in the Havre-Cherbourg sector, provided these unexpected harbours could be brought into being from the first and thus render possible the landing" (Churchill, *Second World War,* 5:72–74).

Churchill was somewhat daunted by the four-day gale, "the like of which had not been known in June for forty years," and which delayed the push beyond the beachhead area by twelve days (Churchill, *Second World War,* 6:20).

24 Life and Death
★★ in Lifeboats

For thousands of seafarers lifeboats lived up to their name. For many—as in the case of the luckless *W. L. Steed* related in chapter 18—they did not. Many lifeboats sailed, rowed, or drifted for up to six weeks or longer. In scores of cases the men in the boat died one by one until one or none was left. A baby was born in a boat from a ship sunk while repatriating consular employees.

Masters and messmen were crushed between boat and ship in failed launchings. Boats sank and burned and were swamped by gigantic seas. More than one swimming seaman, blinded by oil, was guided to a lifeboat by a stray dog he had befriended ashore and taken aboard. Men went mad and responding to siren voices strolled or leaped overboard. Others revealed incredible heroism. The infinite variety of lifeboat experiences is fairly reflected in what follows.

Three days after Pearl Harbor, the Matson Lines' SS *Lahaina* was stopped northwest of Hawaii by a warning shot from a Japanese submarine, which was followed by a succession of shots that shattered the starboard lifeboat, set the ship afire, and left her slowly sinking. The entire crew of thirty-four got away in the remaining boat and stood by overnight.

In the morning several officers returned to the still-burning wreck and were able to retrieve some meager provisions. How meager was recorded in a lifeboat log kept by Third Mate Douglas McMurty, and the list was reproduced later in part by the NMU *Pilot*. Typical menu excerpts were:

Dinner: 1 raw egg and ½ cup of water
Breakfast: 1 raw egg, 1 biscuit and ½ cup of water
Dinner: 1 carrot and ½ lemon

The master, Capt. Hans O. Matthiesen, set a course for Hawaii, some seven hundred miles away, and they set sail. The next day the *Lahaina* was still in sight as she heeled over and sank. They heard a plane and fired a Very pistol flare—in vain. The second cook had become ill, and he died on 19 December.

The next day, after threatening weather overnight with heavy seas and swells, a gale developed. The boat was shipping water, and all hands were bailing. The boat was swamped, and the bailing grew frantic. The wind tore the sail to flapping shreds. Two of the crew drank sea water and soon became ill, then delirious.

The last of the eggs, beginning to go bad, were consumed. One of the sick men, an AB, went overboard and was immediately swept away. On 20 December, they caught sight of Hawaii's volcano Mauna Loa. The other delirious man, an oiler, went overboard. That night another AB died—four and a half hours before the boat landed on Maui.

The *Lahaina*'s sister ship, SS *Manini*, was sunk five days later in shark-infested waters of the South Pacific. Two boats were launched successfully, and the crew "played dead" by staying below the gunwales while the Japanese sub probed the night with its searchlight. The submarine left the scene, but the two boats became separated.

They were alternately cheered and desolated as aircraft passed overhead—but did not see their signals. The heat was extreme and their thirst intense. Ten days after their sinking, they celebrated Christmas by feasting on an extra half cup of water. Finally, after another ten days, one of the boats was spotted by an airplane, and surface rescuers dispatched. Both boats were found, but one man, a messman, died of exposure and thirst and was buried at sea.

2,700 Miles in an Open Boat

The Lykes Lines freighter *Prusa* was torpedoed without warning before dawn on 19 December, a hundred miles off Honolulu. She went down in less than ten minutes with nine of her crew trapped below. The ship's deck cargo of mahogany logs broke loose and shot to the surface, thrashing and bobbing in heavy seas. All four boats were launched but two of them were quickly torn apart by logs and seas.

One of the two that got away was picked up by the Coast Guard after twelve days. The other made landfall thirty-one days later at Nikunau in the Gilbert Islands, after a voyage of 2,700 miles. On board were the master, all four mates, the chief and second assistant engineers, the chief steward, an oiler, a fireman, and an AB.

The boat had been battered and holed, and they plugged the leaks with clothing—again and again, for tiger sharks tore out the plugs several times. The sea anchor was carried away, and another was improvised from a bucket—which was smashed into the bow by seas and opened another leak.

They had emergency rations but only thirty gallons of water. On and near the equator for days, their tongues swelled in the daytime heat, and

Consular personnel and their families evacuated from Nairobi were aboard SS *City of New York* when she was torpedoed and sunk. This infant was born in a lifeboat, delivered by the consular physician, who was injured in the explosion. Here Jesse Roper Morohovicic is in the arms of a nurse as he landed at Norfolk. (National Archives, RG 80-CF, 103D-1)

they shivered in the nighttime chill. The first mate soon died from exposure and hunger, and the second died a few days before they sighted land.

The *Prusa* was an NMU ship, and the *Pilot* interviewed the men when they eventually reached San Francisco some three months later, and food was a major topic. Some of the sea biscuits were fresh, but most were moldy. "We ate them," said the AB, Floyd McWilliams.

☆

"Bad ones too, and called 'em good! And they were good, when you don't have anything else to eat."

"After we got past the real hunger stage the first ten or fifteen days we didn't care anymore what we ate. The second assistant like to drive me crazy talking about steaks, how delicious they were, how they could be fixed this way and that, broiled with mushrooms. The chief engineer would chime in, too." But the closest to steak they got was a couple of seagulls. One of them landed at night on the captain's head. "He just reached up and grabbed it. We wrung its head off and we ate it. . . ."

[Pounding seas kept opening new cracks in the boat, and the engineers worked constantly to keep them packed with] "rope yarns, cotton, anything we could use. It was pounding like hell, and at one time we thought she wouldn't last more than a day or two. Then two more cracks appeared in the after end, leading away from the main hole. It started us to thinking."

Their only answer was bailing. "We kept bailing day and night, never let up bailing, every man kept at it. . . ."

Flapping of the sail when the wind got low down around the equator almost drove the men crazy. "It kept flapping and flapping and you start thinking about how you got to get somewhere to land and you know you're slowly starving," was the way [oiler James C.] Higgins described it.

[They sighted land one morning, and] the wind played out, and they took to the oars and rowed 'til about three in the afternoon. Their hands blistered from rowing steady. They voted to take her through the breakers even though the tide was coming out. "We didn't care whether we lived or died," McWilliams said. They just wanted to get to dry land. They tried taking the boat through the lowest spot in the breakers but she turned over on a coral reef. Waves were crashing around them. "It's a wonder some of us didn't drown." From the reef they could walk ashore. Some could walk and some just dragged themselves.

[The men were helped ashore by a native, then aided by a swarm of others, who gave them coconuts and helped them fish.] The steward fixed it up American style—and it was good. [After six weeks a vessel, contacted by radio from a nearby island, took them to Fiji, and they were repatriated from there.] "Most of the guys want about a month's vacation and then they're going right out again. Ask any of them what they're going to do now and they snap back, 'Ship out again, of course.'"

★   (*Pilot*, 1 May 1942)

On 3 June 1942, the tanker *M. F. Elliott* was off the Caribbean island of Trinidad, in ballast, and heading for the Venezuelan oil port of Caripito. At 3:58 that afternoon she was torpedoed without warning and sank in six minutes, with the loss of thirteen lives.

The master, Capt. Harold L. Cook, was on the way to the bridge when the torpedo hit aft, and it was obviously a mortal blow. He ordered Sparks to get out an SOS and all hands to lower the boats—though the blast had wrecked no. 3. Oil from the ship's bunkers blew into the sky and rained down on the ship for a full minute, which, with a kind of bucking motion the ship was going through, made footing difficult.

"Suddenly," the first assistant engineer, Charles K. Helton, recalled, "the ship settled by the stern very rapidly with the bow coming high in the air, capsizing the lifeboats and throwing all hands into the water in every direction." The suction of the sinking ship pulled many of them under water, but most were able to struggle to the surface.

★

Fortunately, all four life rafts had been launched, and twenty-seven of the survivors, including the seven navy gunners, were able to reach them or were pulled aboard. . . . The men on the rafts lashed them together. Early in the evening a plane appeared and signaled by blinker that help was coming. About 6 A.M. 4 June, the destroyer USS *Tarbell* arrived and picked up the twenty-seven men on the rafts. [She] also rescued two . . . who had drifted all night in their life belts, [retrieved the body of another, and later in the morning picked up first assistant Helton].

He had been thrown into the water without a life jacket and was one of those sucked under. He was too weak to swim after he got back to the surface. He was able to cling, overnight, by his fingertips, to a floating

55-gallon drum. About ten the next morning he was sighted and picked up by the *Tarbell*. These men were landed in Trinidad on 4 June. Helton was hospitalized for ten days. The boatswain liked Trinidad so well he decided to stay; the others were repatriated by various routes.

✩ (Standard Oil Company, *Ships of the Esso Fleet*, 236–37)

A Visit to a U-Boat

AB Raymond Smithson and Ordinary Seaman Cornelius O'Connor, after their ordeal ended, told interviewers what happened after they crawled onto a makeshift raft they assembled out of floating debris. They could see boats rowing around picking up men still in the water, but they were too far away for the boats or rafts to see or hear them. Three planes appeared, and one dropped a float with a flag by the ship's rafts, but did not see Smithson and O'Connor.

That night, cold, tired, and still soaked with oil, they were about to give out when, O'Connor recalled, "All of a sudden a big black shape loomed up—it was the submarine. We began to cry for help with all our might. She seemed to be heading for the rafts, but our shouts were heard and she turned in our direction. We kept yelling and after about five minutes we were sighted. Two seamen in the bow threw us a heaving line and pulled us to the sub."

Smithson observed that they were too slimy with oil to hang onto the line but clambered aboard as best they could.

✩

[According to O'Connor, the submarine commander] could speak perfect English. We asked him to take us to the rafts, and he agreed. The U-boat started in that direction, but when we could see the rafts three hundred to four hundred yards away, a flare suddenly went off directly above them. In the bright glare I saw an airplane overhead but did not get a chance to see anything more, as we were shoved down the hatch of the conning tower. I went down almost head first, with all the Germans right behind me. The commander bellowed out some orders in German and the U-boat submerged.

We were told to sit down on the floor in the control room near the conning tower ladder. They gave us water, hot tea that tasted like sassafras, and bread and cheese; the bread and cheese were not very good. They also gave us rags to wipe off the oil.

The commander came in and asked us the name of the ship again. We told him *Elliott* but he did not seem to understand this. Then I said, "M. F. *Elliott*," and he said, "Oh, oh, *M. F.*" He went to the navigator's desk and looked in a little black book, then turned around and said, "Six thousand," to his aide. One of the officers asked me, "What do the people in America think about the war?" I told him after a little hesitation that they thought they would win. He laughed and asked, "What do you think about it?" I said, "Well" about a dozen times and then said, "In time we should win." He laughed again and said, "Germany is stronger than you think." I said nothing and he asked, "How old are you?" I told him, "Eighteen" and he said, "You are very young."

[Smithson said the sub surfaced for a few minutes, then dove again.] The commander grabbed my head and turned my left cheek to the light as if looking for a mark of identification.

We were then blindfolded and taken to the torpedo room, where they washed us in petrol to remove some of the oil and fed us graham crackers and water.

[O'Connor:] We were in the torpedo room about an hour and a half. The men with us could speak no English, but they were very kind and kept feeding us water and graham crackers.

We were then taken back to the control room and the blindfolds removed. The commander said "We are going to give you our lifeboat and water and bread. Row six miles south and you should find your comrades. If you do not, keep heading south and you will reach land. This is war, and it is all that I can do."

The submarine having surfaced again, we said goodbye, shook hands, and went on deck. We had been aboard the U-boat three hours.

[Smithson:] We found their 12-foot dinghy in the water. They gave us four gallons of water in petrol cans and a day's ration of hardtack. We rowed south until we were sure we had covered the six miles. Then we saw a flare shot from the rafts, but due to the rough sea we could not go in that direction, though we did our best. At daybreak we saw another flare, and, after sunrise, a plane which appeared to be taking off from that direction.

All that day and all the next—4 and 5 June—a plane was circling around. It seemed unbelievable that he could not see us because at times he seemed to be within three miles.

[O'Connor:] The first night we took turns rowing and bailing. Every now and then a big wave nearly swamped us and we had to bail to keep afloat. I got seasick and vomited into the sea all I had eaten on the submarine.

In the morning of 4 June we took an oar and lashed it upright with some strips of canvas which we found in the boat. We tied both of our shirts to it for a sail and tried to head southward but could not because of the wind and current.

On the night of the fifth of June I accidentally dropped the bailing can over the side. We had eaten a little of the hardtack, and it was salty and not very good. We threw it overboard and used the can for a bailer.

The same night I thought I saw a light, but I couldn't have, we were so far from land. The third day—6 June—we tried to kill a seagull with the idea of eating it raw, but we were unsuccessful. That day Smithson thought he saw some little boats, but by that time we were beginning to imagine things. The fourth day, we tried chewing some of the cork from my life preserver.

★   (Standard Oil Company, *Ships of the Esso Fleet,* 238–39)

A flying boat passed within a couple of miles, flying low, and never saw them. A submarine surfaced nearby but did not see them and sailed off. The fourth day they were too weak to row, and they lay passively on the bottom of the dinghy, drowsy, just drifting. O'Connor, who was wearing only his shorts, was so badly sunburned that his skin stuck to the boards when he tried to sit up. They would wake up when a wave would dump water into the boat.

★

[Simpson:] I was keeping a record of the days with notches cut on the thwart, and at about noon I had just cut the fifth notch. As I stood up to return the knife to my pocket, I sighted a ship not far off and told O'Connor. At first he merely lay there and grunted, but soon jumped up. We started beating the water cans with the oarlocks; we whistled and waved. It appeared at first as if the ship would pass us by.

[O'Connor:] Suddenly the vessel turned around and started toward us. She hove to nearby, and we rowed alongside. They threw a life ring with a heaving line bent to it and pulled us up the side of the ship. The bos'n, a big Brazilian, grabbed me by the arm and pulled me up on deck. The ship was a loaded Brazilian tanker, the *Santa Maria.*

☆   (Standard Oil Company, *Ships of the Esso Fleet,* 239)

A couple of the crew spoke English, but all of them treated the survivors kindly—a drink of rum and some welcome hot cereal at first. They bathed them, treated their sunburn and blisters in the ship's hospital, gave them cigarettes, clothes, "and everything else [they] wanted." They were landed at Santos, Brazil, on 1 July, and a week later, by ship, plane, and train, made their way to Rio de Janeiro, Miami, and home to New York (Standard Oil Company, *Ships of the Esso Fleet,* 239).

Another lifeboat–sub encounter figured in the sinking of the new Liberty ship *James W. Denver.* When she was torpedoed in the central Atlantic on the night of 11 April 1943, two of her lifeboats got away safely. On the third night after the sinking, a big U-boat surfaced directly in the path of one of them. As the lifeboat scraped against the sub's hull, an officer shouted from the conning tower.

☆

"Where are you from?"

"Brooklyn!"

The German laughed. "That's where the baseball comes from," he said in good English.

As *Denver* was stencilled on the lifeboat equipment, they answered up readily enough when the officer asked the name of their ship: "*James Denver.*" The German laughed again so the men guessed this was the submarine that had sunk them.

"Well, well," he said. "You are from one of the new Liberty ships." A German sailor handed them a carton of cigarettes. From the bridge, the officer shouted a course for them to steer, and the U-boat moved off into the night on the hunt for more victims.

In another boat, some unidentified man, probably First Mate Andy Del Proposto, kept a log of their 23-day ordeal.

[Excerpts from the log follow.]

12 April: Lost sea anchor 11 A.M. Rig up new one and put over side 12:05. Mounting sea. Sea anchor out all night. Men living on one cracker, two ounces water.

13 April. 6:00 A.M. Hoist sails. 6:30 A.M. Take sails down. Sea too rough. Put sea anchor out again. Boys feeling fair. Still living on two crackers, four ounces water. Found out had no flares. Cans empty. No chocolate in food containers. Drifting southwesterly. Out forty-eight hours.

14 April. 5:30 A.M. Hoist sail, heading south. Wind NNE. Medium sea and swell. Men living on two crackers, four ounces water. Sun came out for first time today. 9:45 A.M., chop sail. Sea too large. Put out sea anchor. Wind force 6. Lost sea anchor at 6:53 P.M. Had to rig up another from two oars. 9:45 P.M. cleared up a little. Hoisted sail. Head south. Wind during night. All men have wet clothes now four days. . . .

Friday. 16 April. Raining. All calm. Try to catch water. No luck. Went to three ounces of water, two crackers and pemmican also one malt milk tablet. Twelve noon approximately six hundred miles from coast. Try fishing. No luck. Fish all around. Won't bite. Air stirring a little. 5 P.M. Breeze freshing to NNE. Making a little time. Sun out. Maybe we'll dry out. Everyone's clothes damp. Getting on everyone's nerves. All snapping at one another. Set regular watches. Five men to watch. 5:30 A.M. Men talking of food and water and what they like to have. Also talking of religion. Rain during night. Try to catch water. No luck. . . .

Palm Sunday. Clear NWly breeze. Continued sailing easterly course. Men got four ounces of water but not eating much. 12 N. Still sailing easterly course. Small following sea. Making good time. 3 P.M. gave men extra two ounces water. Wind change to westerly. Have not see a thing yet. Men feeling pretty good. Doing a little singing. Now and then a man is a little seasick. Have not eaten since in boat. Given extra two ounces of water. First ass't. and lieutenant pretty sick. Given extra water. Deck cadet feet swelling. Can't get in shoes. Clothing starting to dry out a little now, but with night everything wet and cold again. 11 P.M. continued on easterly course. 4 A.M. rain squalls. Still heading easterly. Wind westerly. Following small sea. . . .

Friday, 23 April. Overcast. Beam sea. Fresh NE breeze. Not making any time. Men pray now before breakfast and after supper. Not a thing sighted as yet. Still have hope. Body starting to ache. Damp clothing. Can't keep them dry.

Saturday, 24 April. Overcast and cloudy. Cold NE winds. Heading south. Tide to west. Large, rough, choppy, quarter seas. Shipping sea occasionally. Must bale frequently. Everybody's nerves on edge. Still living on six ounces of water, crackers and pemmican. Now and then men will talk of home and what they would like to be doing or different food and wine. Worst part is you can't lay out straight. Always cramped up. No wonder we ache.

Easter Sunday, April 25. First time and hope it is the last I ever spend Easter in a lifeboat. Not sure of your position or anything. Day started clear. Put up sail. Wind from east, force 3. Large swell. Shipping water occasionally. Heading south. Twelve noon. Men got treat. Half can of pemmican, ten ounces water. Nothing in sight. Still have hope. . . .

Tuesday, 27 April. High mountainous beam sea. Wind northeasterly. Force 4. Shipping water. Temperature 72 degrees. Everything damp. 12 N. Cut down on rations again. Can't see anything. Must make food and water last. Try fishing. Nothing bites. Have no bait. Let's hope we see something soon. Men's feet swelling at joints and every word a complaint. Hoping to hit mainland or Cape Verde Islands. Strong westerly winds and sea. Small swell. Making fair time. Heading SE.

Thursday, April 29. Daybreak clear. Had prayer and breakfast. Small sea. Easterly swell. Wind NE heading SE. Made app. fifty miles yesterday. Men starting to break. Sure wish I was in my ap't, with my wife and baby. Hope I can keep up my courage and stop thinking of home too much. Made fair time last night. . . .

Saturday, May 1. Second assistant passed away during night. Gave burial at sea this morning 7:20 A.M. Men feel bad. 12 N went in swimming for a bath. Water felt good. Wind force 3. Making good time.

Sunday, May 2. Daybreak cloudy. Wind force 2. Small sea and swell. Force 1, making little headway. 11:25 A.M. sighted plane. . . .

Monday, May 3. Daybreak clear and calm. Drift SW. Losing quite a bit of distance covered. Small sea and swell. Sight seven whales at 10:05 A.M. Close enough we could have hit them with a stone. Sighted raft at noon. Boarded it to look for food and water. No luck. Found some marine growth so ate that. No sign of life yet. Looks like plane did not see us yesterday. . . .

Tuesday May 4 (position 21 degrees 55 minutes north. 17 degrees, ten minutes west). Sighted smoke on horizon, but too far away to signal. Makes one feel low to see help so near yet so far. Daybreak clear. Wind strong NE. Heading SEly. Sighted fishing vessel 10 P.M. Sent up flare. They sighted us and picked us up. We were thirty miles from African coast. Fed us and wined us in style. Now heading for Lisbon. Will be there in five days. Treat us like gentlemen. Gave us clothes and washed ours. Fed us again. Gave up their bunks so we may sleep. They keep feeding us everytime we open our eyes. They really are wonderful people. They just can't seem to do enough for us.

Wednesday, May 5. Aboard the *Albufeira*. Daybreak clear. Making 10 knots. Had fish for breakfast and soup and wine. Then a nap. Feel like a million. Now supper. Cabbage and beef noodle soup, beef and potatoes. Abeam Canary Islands now. Only three days to Lisbon. Had spot of tea before going to sleep. These men give you their bunks and sleep on deck. Too bad there is nothing we can do in return.

☆   (Bunker, *Liberty Ships*, 89–91)

On the evening of 12 May 1942 the general alarm sounded on the SS *Esso Houston*. Capt. Trafton Wonson returned to the bridge he had just left, as Third Mate Boris Voronsoff ordered the helmsman to keep the wheel hard right because a submarine had been sighted crossing the bow from starboard to port. At that moment a torpedo hit on the port side amidships, ripping open the deck and spraying the ship with oil and fire.

The *Houston*'s back was broken. Abandon ship and an SOS were ordered. After the survivors were in the boats a second torpedo hit. The captain's boat picked up several men out of the water.

☆

[The captain said,] Suddenly we sighted the submarine approaching our boat. . . . She came close and an officer asked in English, with a strong German accent, if the master was in the lifeboat. . . .

[The chief engineer, who was also in the boat, recalled that after the routine questions as to name, destination, etc., the German officer] inquired as to our welfare—"Have you a steering compass? Do you need any food, water, or medicine?" When Captain Wonson had replied the

Survivors of the torpedoed tanker *Esso Houston* were covered with oil by the explosion. They were picked up two days later, still oil-soaked, but happy. This photograph was taken aboard the Norwegian ship that rescued them, SS *Havprins.* (Courtesy of SeaRiver Maritime, Inc.)

voice said, "It's the war, Captain. Pleasant voyage." Then the U-boat disappeared. It returned about ten minutes later, Captain Wonson said. I was informed that one of our boats was in a sinking condition about 60 meters astern of the ship. After thanking the officer I proceeded to the place indicated and found our no. 3 lifeboat badly damaged and full of water. All hands were transferred to our boat, and we used no. 3 as a sea anchor to keep us in the vicinity until daylight.

☆   (Standard Oil Company, *Ships of the Esso Fleet*, 213–16)

The captain's boat made land on the island of St. Vincent four days later. Boat no. 4, with eighteen survivors, rowed seaward away from the ship and lay to for the night. On the morning of 13 May they set sail heading west by south and were picked up the next morning by the Norwegian motor tanker *Havprins,* bound for Africa. The next day the Norwegian ship encountered a United States–bound Latvian steamer, SS *Everagra* and transferred the *Houston* survivors, who were landed on St. Thomas on the evening of 18 May.

Water Everywhere, but Not a Drop to Drink

The Liberty ship *Richard Hovey,* sunk by a U-boat in the Arabian Sea on 29 March 1944, two days out of Bombay, won a certain posthumous fame for the ingenuity of her junior assistant engineer, Arthur Drechsler. When the lifeboat he was in was nearly out of drinking water, Drechsler rigged up a still out of odds and ends and successfully desalinated about sixty gallons of sea water, which materially helped the thirty-eight men in the boat to survive. After the survivors were landed and the story made known, he was awarded the U.S. Maritime Service's Distinguished Service Medal and his inventiveness and resourcefulness hailed in headlines back home.

The lifeboat had a capacity of thirty-one men and for a time carried thirty-nine, including the navy gunnery officer, Lt. (jg) Harry Chester Goudy. Two small life rafts were picked up and taken in tow. Although there were plenty of emergency rations, drinking water was in short supply, for two water casks had been shot up and their contents contaminated with sea water. The tiller had been destroyed. There were seven oars, which the healthy men manned in shifts, using one as a steering oar until the junior engineer devised a replacement tiller.

The off-duty oarsmen rested on the rafts between shifts. A sail was rigged for the lifeboat, and later for each raft, but a strong offshore current was canceling out the effect of their rowing northward toward land.

Having observed Arthur Drechsler's ingenuity at work on the tiller, Lieutenant Goudy asked him if it might be possible to distill sea water. Drechsler said it would be and set out to arrange it. Taking over one of the rafts for a workshop, he assembled such odds and ends as he could find. An unneeded steel container was flattened out for a firebox. An empty food container with a round opening in its top became a boiler.

Lifeboats carry oil to pour on threatening waves when needed, and the funnel-like device used to distribute it was used as a cone on top of the boiler to convey steam to a condenser. Then the young engineer took a pair of footrest brackets from the lifeboat to support the boiler over the firepan. An empty steel food container still in the bottom of the workshop raft was kept relatively cool by the sea. It was used for a storage tank.

Finally, a rubber hose from the lifeboat's bilge pump carried steam from the boiler to the storage tank. Steam would rise in the hose, condensing into pure water as it cooled, then flowing down into the tank.

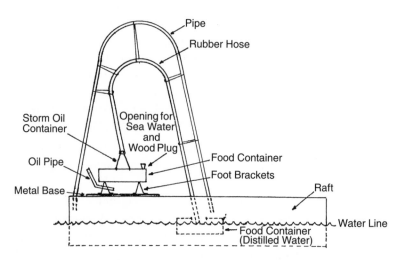

Ens. Goudy made this drawing of Arthur Drechsler's still, which was constructed from odds and ends from the lifeboat and two rafts. (National Archives, RG 38, Voyage Report of SS *Richard Hovey*)

(Air temperature—even of tropical air at the hottest time of day—is far cooler than the 212 degrees Fahrenheit at which steam condenses to water.)

Rags were used to caulk critical joints between hose and both boiler and tank. The other life raft was dismantled for fuel, a fire was kindled, the boiler charged with sea water, and in a few minutes distilled water began to drip into the storage tank. Over four days, the wood from the second raft was consumed, and between fifty and sixty gallons of potable water was produced. It had a slight rubbery flavor. There were no complaints.

A Tough, Gallant Carpenter

On 17 October 1942, the Bull Line freighter *Angelina* had fallen behind a convoy homebound from England when, just before midnight, she was torpedoed. The starboard boiler blew up, flooded the engine room, and darkened the ship. The *Angelina* was abandoned in 35-foot seas that ran three hundred feet from crest to crest. Forty-three of her crew crowded into a single lifeboat, which was quickly capsized. Several swimmers tried to return to the stricken *Angelina* and were sucked down with her as a second torpedo put her under fast.

✮

Back on the upturned lifeboat some of the cold, benumbed survivors despaired of rescue, but . . . Gustave Alm, the carpenter . . . urged them to hang on.

"Don't give up," he kept saying. "Don't give up. There's always a chance. Hang on. Hang on a while longer."

During the grueling hours of the night, a destroyer passed within a stone's throw, but no one on the warship saw them or heard their desperate cries. . . . One of the gunners gave up and drifted away, but Gus Alm struck out against the pounding seas and hauled the boy back.

The rescue ship *Bury* and a corvette had responded to the *Angelina*'s SOS and had [already] picked up the men on the raft . . . but it was not until dawn that they spotted the lifeboat, by now with only a handful of survivors clinging to the grab rails on the bottom.

While the corvette dumped oil to windward of the boat, Capt. L. E.

Brown of the *Bury* maneuvered his little vessel within a line's throw of the capsized craft.

Captain Brown counted five men on the wallowing lifeboat, but what amazed him was the superhuman exhibit of dogged stamina and courage by one of those sea-beaten five: Gustave Alm, the carpenter.

One man would be washed off, then another, but each time this man Alm, by feats of great courage and strength, managed to haul them back aboard the lifeboat's bottom.

[By deft seamanship the *Bury* got close enough to throw a line to Alm, who made it fast to a hold-rod on the boat.] As the big carpenter held one exhausted man on the grab rails, another one was swept off. [The *Bury* darted up close and one of its] crew reached over the side, grabbed his lifejacket, and dragged him aboard on the crest of a sea.

[Again and again Alm caught the *Bury*'s line and secured it to one of the exhausted men on the lifeboat so he could be hauled aboard the *Bury*.] When a line was finally thrown to Alm himself, he was almost too exhausted to secure it around his own waist.

☆   (Bunker, *Seafarers*, 17–18)

At last the men of the *Bury* fished the heroic carpenter onto their deck, bruised, bleeding, covered with oil, exhausted to the point of semi-consciousness, but alive. They gave him a shot of brandy, and he passed out like a light.

The British Captain Brown, of the *Bury*, wrote to the U.S. Maritime Commission, "I feel honored to have played a part in the rescue of a man with such spirit. He is a true American."

The commission agreed. It awarded Alm the merchant marine's Distinguished Service Medal.

Fighting off Sharks

Only fifteen of the seventy-two officers and men of the tanker *Esso Gettysburg* survived her sinking in the Atlantic off Savannah, Georgia, on 9 June 1943. She was bound for Philadelphia with a cargo of crude oil and was well armed. The navy gun crew was drilling on the forward gun. After a radio warning that a submarine had been reported nearby, she was on intense alert and intermittent escort by patrol aircraft. Still, no one saw the sub before the two torpedoes, four seconds apart, that set her afire and sank her.

Flames prevented launching any boats; those who survived jumped overboard, several without time to don life preservers. Ens. John S. Arnold II and six of his men, already at the 3-inch bow gun, spotted the sub and fired on it until the flames drove them overboard. Ensign Arnold was sprayed with burning oil, sustaining third-degree burns on his face, neck, and arms, but continued directing fire until the last moment, for which he was later awarded the Navy Cross.

Chief Mate Herman Kastberg and several others also went off the bow. While swimming away from the ship, he said,

☆

six of us got together. . . . suddenly a shark was among us. As I had previously got rid of my shoes, I felt him brush past my bare feet. Only three of us had life jackets, and we were supporting the other men. The shark circled off toward the ship but came back again and charged. . . . We all kicked and splashed and the shark again swerved away, but a few minutes later he charged again. We repeated the kicking and thrashing in the water and he went off.

[James Lane, an acting AB, and a navy gunner, S1c Sherman Doucette, had dived off the stern.] Neither of us had time to get life preservers, and we swam for about five hours. About five minutes after [we] dived into the water and got out of the oil, we saw about fifteen to twenty sharks constantly circling around us, at times disappearing then reappearing; they kept with us all the while. . . .

[Meanwhile, the chief mate's group of six men had gotten well clear of the burning oil around the ship, and they saw other swimmers to the north.] We hailed them and told them to join us so that we could all keep together. Soon afterward we saw Third Mate Crescenzo towing Ensign Arnold. Finally several other men joined us. We decided to swim closer to the burned out area, figuring that the oil would keep the sharks away.

This decision was fortunate, as it resulted in our finding two lifeboats that had drifted clear of the flames. Chapman and I swam toward the boat that seemed usable—lifeboat no. 3. On the way I picked up a navy issue first-aid kit; it belonged in the flare box and had apparently been blown overboard. The metal lifeboat was so hot that we had to splash water on it to cool it off. In reality it was just a burned-out hull, and it had shipped a considerable quantity of water. The water saved submerged material from the flames. We found the remains of three bodies in the boat. Largely untouched by the fire were three tanks of water and, in the gear box, a compass and a waterproof case containing a flare pistol and three flares. There was also a piece of tarpaulin.

We got in, put the bodies overboard, and started to bail the boat out so that she would ride higher in the water. Ten other survivors joined us and got into the boat. Soon afterward, we saw two men approaching; they were Able Seaman Lane and navy gunner Doucette. The navy man was blinded by oil, and we guided him by our voices. This was about four and a half hours after the torpedoing. There were then fourteen men in the boat.

Half an hour later we picked up another navy man, Gunner's Mate Third Class Edward S. Graves. He was hanging on to a fog buoy which had drifted away from the ship. His chest hurt him painfully; he had three fractured ribs. This was about 7 P.M., five hours after the disaster.

From available pieces of gratings we started to cut crude paddles. We organized ourselves and decided to stay near the scene of the attack until daylight. The bow of the *Esso Gettysburg* was still above the surface. Her tanks were exploding under water. Then the ammunition magazines exploded.

We decided that if help did not come by daybreak, we would start for shore. Believing we were one hundred miles off the coast, we figured it would take us fifteen days of paddling to reach land and that by rationing the drinking water we would have enough for thirty days.

We feared sharks and set watches for the night. Each man was given a drink of water and told he could not have another until daylight. We were drifting in the Gulf Stream faster than the wreck of the *Esso Gettysburg.* . . . We made a bed for Ensign Arnold to keep him as comfortable as possible. He was stoical and uncomplaining, waiting until daybreak for treatment of his burns. When there was light enough for me to see clearly, he asked me to cut some of the hanging flesh away from the burns. I did this carefully and applied a dressing from the first-aid kit. I also applied it to two other men.

We continued to make paddles, finally finished them, and set off in a westerly direction. Allowing for a known error of the compass, we laid out a course that would land us at Point Lookout.

About 8:30 A.M., we sighted a plane. It was flying as if to make a grid search, about fifteen miles away. We tried a flare, but it was not usable. We succeeded in firing the second flare, but the plane did not see it and disappeared.

Continuing to paddle, we sighted a ship on the horizon, about eight miles away. Then we saw another plane and fired our third and last flare. The plane saw us and approached. We waved everything we could, and I blinked my flashlight. The plane's lights blinked in recognition and flew on to report to the ship—the SS *George Washington*—which turned toward us.

When the *George Washington* came within hailing distance, we were asked what ship we were from and where she was attacked. The skipper did not want to risk stopping and told us to come over, but I called out that it would take us too long to paddle that far. The *George Washington* then stopped, lowered a boat, and picked us up.

The doctor on board treated the injured men and saved those who were burned from having severe scars. The skipper, Captain Park, asked us whether we wanted to be taken to the nearest port or to the ship's destination, New York. I told him we wanted to be landed as soon as possible on account of the injured men. The *George Washington* put us ashore in Charleston, South Carolina, that night. The navy took care of the seven survivors of the gun crew and the United Seamen's Service took charge of the eight survivors of the *Gettysburg:* they were fine, giving each of us a complete new outfit and a free telephone call to his home.

✭ (Standard Oil Company, *Ships of the Esso Fleet,* 458–59)

The Glorious End of the *Stephen Hopkins*

A lifeboat from the U.S. Liberty ship *Stephen Hopkins* made a month-long voyage from the African side of the South Atlantic to Brazil, after being sunk by a German raider, the *Stier,* and an accompanying blockade-runner, the *Tannenfels.* Five of the nineteen men aboard were gravely wounded, and four of them died in the passage, which began when the *Hopkins* went down a flaming wreck on 27 September 1942.

✭

Late that afternoon the lifeboat party sighted six more survivors on a small raft, some distance away, but couldn't recognize them, although they thought Jean Ziesel, the second cook, and one of the navy gunners were among them. The wind blew the raft out of sight in the mist before the boat could overtake it. Then they saw Third Mate Walter Nyberg in the wreck of another lifeboat, that also disappeared in the drifting mist before they could reach it.

The next day two rafts were sighted—the sign of another ship gone down—but no survivors were aboard. They took food and water from the rafts, but even so, by 1 October they had to cut their rations to six ounces per day so as to have more for the wounded men. All they could do for them was to soak their bandages in saltwater. . . .

Eugene McDaniel, a cook, died on 6 October, and Leonardo Romero, a utilityman, died two days later. Gunner Wallace Breck had a bad wound in his shoulder, and they operated on him without any anesthesia and removed a piece of shrapnel. He survived. But during the next two weeks Athenasios Demetriades and George Gelagotis, firemen, died.

Finally, on 27 October, the lifeboat pulled up on a Brazilian beach twenty-two miles north of Rio with fifteen survivors from the Liberty ship whose lone battle against two heavily armed raiders will long remain an epic of the sea.

☆   (Bunker, *Liberty Ships,* 108)

That epic, one of the great heroic legends of World War II, began on the morning of 27 September 1942, when the *Hopkins* was eight days out of Cape Town, running in ballast for Paramaribo, Dutch Guiana, on South America's north coast.

☆

Two strange ships broke out of a bank of haze off the starboard bow and Third Mate Walter Nyberg called Capt. Paul Buck to the bridge.

The captain took one look at the strangers and ordered the general alarm sounded. "I don't like the looks of this," he said. "Two ships wouldn't be stewing around here like that if they were freighters. They're up to something."

☆   (Bunker, *Liberty Ships,* 106)

Merchant seamen and armed guard sailors dashed to their stations. The *Hopkins* carried a 4-inch gun aft, two 37-millimeter guns on the bow, and six machine guns, four .50-caliber and two .30-caliber. The skipper ran up a new, large, U.S. flag.

The smaller ship was the German commerce-raider *Stier*, which had already sunk four merchantmen. She was armed like a destroyer, with six 150-millimeter (5.9-inch) guns and two torpedo tubes, plus machine guns. The raider was accompanied by the larger but more lightly armed blockade-runner *Tannenfels*.

At a range of more than a thousand yards, the *Stier* opened fire with a shot that splashed a hundred yards off the *Hopkins*'s bow. Three direct hits quickly followed, amidships and in the engine room, killing two men.

As the armed guard commander, Ens. Kenneth Willett, reached the *Hopkins*'s 4-inch gun aft, shrapnel ripped open his belly, but he took charge of the gun.

☆

It returned the German fire. The first shot from the *Hopkins* threw spray over the foredeck of the *Stier* and the next made a solid hit, with smoke and a plume of fire to prove it had done damage. Navy gunners and merchant seamen yelled and cheered.

"Aim low and make every shot count," Willett told the gun captain, who did exactly that. The gun crew urged Willett to go for medical aid, but he leaned against the ready ammo box and kept saying, "I'm all right. I'm all right." Between shots he yelled down the ammunition hoist, encouraging men who were passing up shells and powder from the magazine under the steering-engine room.

When the German ships closed the range to a thousand yards or so they opened up with small guns. Hot lead chattered and pinged against gun tubs and deckhouses. In the first excitement of battle, everyone around the stern gun was talking at once, but as machine-gun bullets sent a sailor reeling against the splinter shield with blood streaming from his chest they fell silent. A few moments later he died without saying a word.

In the engine room, boiler fires sputtered with the concussion of the stern gun, the electric lights shattered and went out, and the emergency lamps were switched on. Fireman Mike Fitzpatrick stood between the boilers watching the water in the gauge glasses jump with each shell burst. When a shot hit amidships the glasses broke, and hot water dripped onto the deck. Shock knocked insulation from the steam lines, and asbestos covered the floor plates like snow.

Hemmed in by a maze of pipe and steel Third Assistant Kenneth Vaughan and Oiler Andy Tsigonis could only wonder what was going on topside and wish they were on deck. The chatter of machine guns came down the ventilators like the racket of riveting hammers. They never knew what happened when a salvo of 5.9-inch shells from the *Stier* smashed through the thin hull plates, and the engine room filled with live steam, water, and choking cordite fumes. After that hit, the bridge rang the engine room, but there was no answer.

☆   (Bunker, *Liberty Ships,* 106–7)

The Germans rained fire on the freighter. As navy gunners were killed merchant crewmen stepped forward. The second mate and a messman manned the 37-millimeters at the bow and fired until the gun tub was filled with dead bluejackets and empty shell cases, and they too were killed. But before they went down they scored some telling hits on the *Stier's* gunners. The boatswain was killed trying to rig an emergency radio antenna on the flying bridge; a shell hit the radio shack and blew up the radio man as he frantically tried to get out an SOS on emergency power. The same shot felled the first mate.

Captain Buck, preparing to sink his ship's confidential papers, was blown off the bridge. The only gun on the *Hopkins* capable of major damage to the *Stier* was the 4-incher, and it was scoring consistently when its ammunition magazine blew up. Ensign Willett tried to pass the 50-pound 4-inch shells from the ready box to the gun but his gaping wound had sapped his strength.

The *Hopkins* was sinking with fires burning fore and aft. Edwin O'Hara, a nineteen-year-old engine room cadet from the Merchant Marine Academy, was bearing a hand everywhere aft, and after the magazine blew up he led the surviving gunners, all wounded, merchant and navy, to life rafts. Then he returned to the gun, where there were five shells left in the ready box. He lugged them to the gun and loaded and fired them all.

As he stepped down from the gun platform to help launch a raft, guns from both the *Stier* and the *Tannenfels* found the young cadet and blew him apart. Nearby, Ensign Willett, who now could hardly stand, was being helped to a boat by the ship's carpenter when both were cut down by machine gun fire. Second Engineer George Cronk helped lower a riddled lifeboat, then

✰

stuffed blankets into the shell holes. It was no boat for an ocean voyage of hundreds of miles with wounded men, but the survivors manned their oars and pulled away, just as the gallant *Stephen Hopkins*, ablaze from bow to stern, went down with her new U.S. flag still flying.

The *Stephen Hopkins* was gone, but her gunners had done well. [The *Stier*] was a flaming wreck . . . with smoke billowing out of her. [The *Hopkins*] was merely a freighter although she had fought like a cruiser. Outnumbered and outgunned, the *Hopkins* could, in all honor, have surrendered without firing a shot, but her crew chose to do battle against superior odds . . . and fought one of the great ship-against-ship battles of World War II. . . .

[Her] lifeboat finally held nineteen men, five of them painfully wounded, all that were left of fifty-six armed guard and merchant sailors (and a passenger). As they sailed away under a freshening wind, the Germans were soon obscured by mist and rain. Some time later a thunderous blast reached them as the *Stier* finally blew up and sank.

✰   (Bunker, *Liberty Ships,* 108–9)

The U.S. Navy's official historian, Samuel Eliot Morison, called the fight "an old-time sea battle . . . that recalls the war of 1812" (Morison, *Battle of the Atlantic,* 1:398).

Morison's British counterpart, Capt. Stephen W. Roskill, DSC, RN, saluted the freighter's crew in *The War at Sea:* "They fought an action of which all the Allied navies and merchant marines should be proud, and had rid the oceans of one of the heavily armed and dangerous German raiders" (Roskill, *War at Sea,* 2:266).

The U.S. War Shipping Administration named the *Stephen Hopkins* one of the Gallant Ships of World War II, and installed a bronze plaque at the Merchant Marine Academy bearing the following citation: "Two enemy raiders suddenly appeared out of the morning mist to attack the SS *Stephen Hopkins.* Heavy guns of one raider pounded her hull and machine-gun fire from the other sprayed her decks at close quarters. The lightly-armed merchantman exchange shot for shot with the enemy raiders, sinking one and setting the other afire before she, with boilers blown up, engines destroyed, and ablaze from stem to stern, went down carrying many of her gallant crew with her. The stark courage of her crew in their heroic stand against overpowering odds caused her name to be perpetuated as a Gallant Ship."

A Foe's Farewell Salute

And in his *Sea War,* Felix Riesenberg, second-generation sailor and chronicler of the merchant mariner, quotes (on page 169) the ultimate tribute to the *Hopkins* and her crew, which came from one of the Germans who had helped destroy her. Hans Grunert, a member of the *Tannenfels* crew, described the battle in a 1955 article for the German illustrated paper *Der Frontsoldat,* concluding "On the German side we had four dead and twenty injured. In spite of a search of two hours we did not find any survivors of the American ship. With our flag at half-mast we made a full circle around the spot where the Liberty ship had sunk thus rendering the last honors to our brave adversary."

Indeed.

Epilogue

Counting the Dead

About 7.8 million GIs came home from the war, leaving behind more than 400,000 dead companions, 71 percent of them killed in action. The marines lost 2.9 percent dead in battle, 3.6 percent overall. The navy's dead from all causes were 1.49 percent, 0.88 percent in action.

Of the 250,000 merchant mariners that sailed during the war, 6,845 were killed in various ways—shot, bombarded, drowned, incinerated, vaporized—2.73 percent. When the survivors got home, any big reception they received was from their individual families. No parades down Fifth Avenue and no GI Bill.

Forty years after the last military homecoming parade, the Pentagon, in a review ordered by a federal district court,* reversed its decades of denials and granted the status of veterans to oceangoing merchant mariners who served in World War II. This brought them no GI Bill of Rights or other substantial benefits, but it did honor their war service—and entitled them to an American flag for their caskets. It also enabled them to join existing veterans' organizations, and to organize several of their own, notably the American Merchant Marine Veterans' Association and the U.S. Merchant Marine Veterans of World War II. A number of states authorized modest bonuses for merchant marine veterans, generally for those who resided in the state before and returned as residents after their war service.

---

*The critical court decision came in a class action brought in 1986 by four merchant marine veterans, after six years of unavailing appeals to the Civilian/Military Service Review Board of the Department of Defense. One of the quartet was Lane Kirkland, a deck officer throughout the war, and then president of the AFL-CIO—whose maritime unions paid the costs of the eight-year legal battle. U.S. District Judge Louis F. Oberdorfer ordered the Pentagon review, and the resulting reversal was implemented at last on 19 January 1988.

Looking Ahead

The merchant marine itself effectively shriveled to its prewar status. Surplus ships were sold—1,113 of them to foreign operators. Its postwar fate had certain similarities to what happened after the Civil War and World War I; numbers of ships and jobs inevitably declined.

But more important factors than the end of the war were technological advances and economic considerations. Ships grew larger, faster, and fewer. Crews got smaller and pay better. Unions were smaller and richer. Vessels under the U.S. flag plummeted in number—from about 5,600 oceangoing ships at VJ-Day to near four hundred of them fifty years later.

Interactions between the military and the merchant marine have changed as dramatically as the technology. And there have been revolutionary changes in the wartime problem of safety of ships and mariners from enemy action.

TECHNOLOGICAL CHANGES

The size, speed, maneuverability, cargo-carrying facilities, and cargo-handling equipment of ships have undergone revolutionary change since 1945. Container ships started the revolution: their cargo is in what amounts to over-the-road trailer bodies; they are offloaded onto railroad flatcars, or flatbed trailers and driven to their destination. They are ubiquitous on American highways.

Roll-on, roll-off ships are a giant adaption of the LCT; cargo is driven off across a bow ramp. LASH (lighter aboard ship) vessels in effect carry cargo in large barges stowed athwartships on deck; in port the ship's own huge crane lifts them off and lowers them into the water.

But for all the increase in speed, passenger shipping has not been able to compete with airlines in business and point-to-point nonbusiness travel. The passenger liner has become the cruise ship, and sea travel and shore stops are the vacation.

Accompanying these developments have been colossal increases in size. The largest modern freighters are more than twice the length of a Liberty ship (1,000 feet versus 441, with a beam of 175 feet versus 59), and their deadweight tonnage—one million—is nearly a hundred times that of the Lib. Speeds range up to 30 knots and more. Crew size in the modern giants is half that of a World War II freighter or tanker in

American-flag ships; in Japan, e.g., that figure is one-quarter. Satellites have enabled global positioning systems that make navigation electronic, quick, and easy.

ECONOMIC CHANGES

These physical and mechanical and electronic changes have precipitated some great economic changes and accompanied others. As fewer seafarers—incidentally including a slowly increasing number of women, from captain to AB—run bigger and faster ships, salaries and overtime pay have skyrocketed on U.S. ships. This is a tribute to the maritime unions and their congressional allies, but the tremendous increases also reflect years of double-digit inflation in the mid-1970s.

The higher technology of modern ships has increased the educational requirements for ships' officers, and it still takes a captain, a chief engineer, and three mates or deck officers and three assistant engineers (and a steward and some cooks) to run a merchant vessel. The U.S. Merchant Marine Academy and a few other schools have risen to that challenge, and turn out superbly qualified marine officers—far more than there are ready berths in U.S. ships. These officers are in demand on foreign ships, where the jobs really are. But at lower salaries.

Radio officers face a declining prospect, as modern electronic communication has taken on more and more of a "plug-and-play," do-it-yourself character. Many captains now handle the radioman's responsibilities, almost in spare time. Telegraph keys have gone the way of the pterodactyl—to the museum.

The boatswain and the electrician survive. But the new ships require only a few ABs and oilers and only one or two wipers and ordinary seamen. Ships' carpenters are no more. Only the messboy has thrived in the bottom ranks, because even small and elite crews have to eat—but more and more, they do so from buffet tables.

U.S. shipping companies that remain in business enjoy more congenial relations with the unions than in the World War II era and before, and this is partly because of and partly the result of effective lobbying both interests have done on behalf of continuing maritime subsidies (now outright grants in exchange for companies' making ships available to the military in emergencies).

Meanwhile, the "flight from the flag" in the U.S. shipping industry continues, as more U.S.-owned ships are registered under foreign flags and sailed with foreign or mixed U.S.–foreign crews.

Military–Merchant Marine Relations

All military transportation operations have been consolidated under the U.S. Transportation Command, under which the Military Sealift Command (MSC) carries by far the greatest volume of cargo, and in ships manned by merchant crews. This has made it easier for congenial naval–civilian relations at the upper levels, and at least in peacetime there is no naval presence whatever at the individual ship level. The likelihood of an armed guard presence on merchant ships in a future war seems to be very much in limbo for the foreseeable future.

In a future war the kind of military–civilian and intramilitary disputes and disjunctions that sank so many ships and killed so many merchant seamen early in World War II virtually disappears, for the head of the Military Sealift Command is necessarily one of the most competent sea transport executives to be found, and the vital sea-transport decisions will fall to him or to her, and not to a future Admiral King or any other fleet, force, or theater commander.

In the Persian Gulf War the Military Sealift Command carried 85 percent of all dry-cargo military supplies to the theater, with dispatch and a generally high level of efficiency. This was accomplished by seven of its eight Fast Sealift Ships, which carried what it would have taken 120 World War II freighters to transport. These vessels are essentially container ships, modified to allow them to carry a mix of container and roll-on, roll-off cargo.

There are two other major elements of the MSC. The Afloat Prepositioning Force has thirteen Maritime Prepositioning Ships to carry combat equipment and supplies for the U.S. Marine Corps, and twelve other vessels to supply army and air force needs: seven freighters for ammunition and other supplies, four tankers, and one ship carrying a complete field hospital.

At the time of the Gulf War, the Ready Reserve Force (RRF) consisted of ninety-four vessels under the control of the U.S. Maritime Administration, MARAD in Federalese. Two-thirds of these ships are designated as ready for activation within five days and the others in ten to twenty days. "Flat racks" and "sea sheds" can be applied to these ships to accommodate "unit equipment," that is, tanks, self-propelled guns, and vehicles.

In actual service in the Gulf War, forty-nine of the lot were break-bulk freighters, eleven were tankers, and the remainder vessels of various specializations from roll-on, roll-off freighters to crane ships. The Military Sealift Command is authorized to charter ships from U.S. owners whether they operate under the U.S. flag or a foreign "flag of convenience," and it also can charter foreign-owned, foreign-flag ships.

One of the thorniest problems confronting the whole military sea transport enterprise is manpower. The Maritime Administration anticipates that the pool of merchant seafarers qualified to operate deep-draft ships will number some eleven thousand in the year 2000—down from forty-eight thousand in 1980 and twenty-five thousand in 1990.

SAFETY OF SHIPS AND CREWS

At the end of the twentieth century a sea war like either of the world wars does not seem a realistic prospect. If a superpower adversary does emerge, nuclear submarines and long-range or carrier-based bombers again would be offensive and defensive instruments, but to anticipate this is akin to the old generals' game—approaching a next war by studying how to win the last.

Nations must of course be prepared for such eventuality, but in the world of 2000-plus, the rogue microstate, the freelance terrorist country or religion, the renegade nuclear scientist or ex-Soviet general with plutonium to go is a constant threat. In a world of supertankers and superfreighters, the truck bomb or the suitcase nuclear bomb are as deadly as a torpedo and can be placed and detonated for pennies instead of billions.

Bright new futures confront new terrors as vicious as the warped human soul can devise.

The surrender of General Cornwallis to General Washington at Yorktown brought the American Revolution to an end. Who among the king's generals expected the upstart colonists to defeat the world's superpower? Small wonder that the British band arrayed at the surrender ceremonies, to Cornwallis's startlement, played a popular tune to which an English nursery-rhyme had been set: "The World Turned Upside-Down."

We live in such a world. Maybe we should dust off that tune.

Glossary

Abaft. Nautical preposition meaning aft of, or toward, the stern.

Abeam. Beside a ship. An object in the sea beside a ship is said to be abeam of it, or off the port or starboard beam.

Belaying pin. A metal pin up to a foot or so in length and about an inch in diameter. The movable pin fits holes in a ship's rail or elsewhere and is used to belay or secure rope rigging lines. Its shape and weight made it a handy impromptu weapon.

Bells (e.g., eight bells). Ship's bell signals the hour and half hour on each watch. Sea watches are four hours on duty, with eight hours off. The midnight watch begins at eight bells, or 2400. One bell is 0030 (12:30 A.M.), seven bells is 0330 or 3:30, and eight bells signals the change of watch at 0400. Eight bells therefore rings at midnight, four A.M., eight A.M., noon, four P.M., and eight P.M.

Bight (noun). A loop in a rope; (verb) to bind or fasten with such a loop.

Black gang. The engine-room crew of a steamship or motorship, so called (without reference to natural skin color) because of their variously sooty and oily environment, which, especially in the days of coal-fired boilers, blackened the clothing and exposed skin of wipers, oilers, firemen-water-tenders, and the engineer on watch.

Blockade. Closing of seaports to all commerce, enforced by warships of an enemy nation. In the American Revolution and, even more effectively, the War of 1812, British naval squadrons stood off all American ports and effectively shut down U.S. sea trade. Intermittently and to varying degrees, American privateers so treated Britain in those wars. The Union performed a similar role off Confederate ports during the Civil War.

Bomb (abbreviation of bombshell). See "Shell."

Bow. The foremost point of a ship; anything in the sea between dead ahead and abeam is said to be off its (port or starboard) bow.

Bow chaser. Swivel mounted, long-range cannon mounted at the bow of a ship, used to fire early shots at a pursued vessel.

Brig. Two-masted, square-rigged ship.

Bunting. A pennant (q.v.) flown from the masthead of a navy ship. The name came from a material (bunting) that proved unsatisfactory and was abandoned, though the name survived for some time.

Caliber. The diameter of a gun barrel; a gun's length is also often expressed in calibers; e.g., a 4-inch 33-caliber gun would be 4 × 33 inches (132 inches, or 11 feet) long.

Carcass or carcase (ammunition). A hollow iron ball with three holes; it was filled with inflammable material that ignites when the cannon is fired. Flame from the holes set fire to the target ship or structure.

Carronade. A light and short cannon, carriage-mounted and easily loaded, using a light charge of powder to throw a heavy projectile a relatively short distance. It was named for Scotland's Carron Company Ironworks, where it was developed for close-range battle.

Cartel. Document regulating an exchange of prisoners; also a vessel carrying prisoners to be released under such a document.

Case shot. Any kind of old iron, musket balls, or even stones, in a wooden or canvas case that would fit in the bore of a cannon and, on being fired, scatter on impact with the target.

Cat's-paw. A vagrant breeze rippling the sea's surface in a small area.

Chain shot. Cannot shot consisting of two balls connected by a chain or bar. On being fired, the assembly rotated in flight, and at the target slashes sails and tears rigging; sometimes only a considerable length of chain was used in this fashion.

Close-hauled. Sailing as close as possible into the wind, with sails hauled in so tightly they are nearly parallel with the keel.

Crossbar (as in cannon shot). A long bar, which whirled about in flight, and was used to cut or tear ropes and sails, or shear off masts.

Crosstrees. Horizontal spars projecting from a masthead to separate the upper shrouds or ropes that support the mast.

Crowbars (in gunnery). Ordinary crowbars used as cannon shot. A gun could be crammed to the muzzle with them, and, gyrating wildly in flight, they could sunder the sails and rigging of an enemy ship.

Cruise (in privateering). A privateer's total time at sea, a period of indeterminate length, seeking cargo ships to capture as prizes. Compare "Voyage."

Cruiser. A large, fast warship.

Cutwater. The foremost part of the bow or stem of a ship.

Deck engineer. On a freighter, the person responsible for operating winches and associated deck machinery used for handling cargo.

Double-shotted. Having a double load (i.e., loaded with two balls or charges of shot).

Draft (of a ship). The distance between a ship's keel or bottom and the waterline (e.g., her draft is eight feet, or she draws eight feet).

Fill (as in a ship filling away). To trim, or adjust, the sails to fill with wind.

Forecastle (universally pronounced and often spelled fo'c'sle). The part of a ship's deck forward of the foremast; also the space in the bow of a ship where seamen are quartered.

Frigate. A square-rigged, usually three-masted, warship mounting a main battery of twenty-four or more cannons on a single gun deck. It also would have guns on the forecastle and quarterdeck.

Grapeshot (or grape). Small iron balls, about the size of a walnut, used as a charge for cannons, usually directed against personnel; musket balls were often used as grape. The analogy to contemporary buckshot (which is some-what smaller) is clear. A charge of grape was piled on a wooden dowel that would fit in the bore, then wrapped with canvas and stored for action.

Grenade. A small bomb. A hollow iron sphere filled with gunpowder, differing in principle from modern grenades only in that its fuse had to be ignited by hand and then thrown at the enemy.

Guns and Gunnery:

Bore by projectile weight

Gun's common name	Bore diameter (approx.)
one-pounder	2 inches
two-pounder	2.4 inches
four-pounder	3 inches
six-pounder	3.5 inches
nine-pounder	4 inches
ten-pounder	5 inches
twelve-pounder	4.25 inches
twenty-eight-pounder	5.75 inches
thirty-two-pounder	6 inches
forty-two-pounder	6.55 inches
sixty-pounder	8 inches
100-pounder	9 inches

Projectile weight by bore diameter

Bore diameter	Projectile weight	
2-inches	1-lb.	ball or shell
2.4-inches	2-lb.	shell or shot
3-inches	4-lb.	"
4-inches	9-lb.	"
4.25-inches	12-lb.	"
5-inches	10-lb.	"
5.75-inches	28-lb.	"
6-inches	32-lb.	"
6.55-inches	42-lb.	"
8-inches	60-lb.	"
9-inches	100-lb.	"
11-inches	200-lb.	"

Gunwale (pronounced "gunn'l"). The upper edge of the side of a ship, used to support muskets and wallpieces, with openings cut into it for cannons.

Hanger. Sword resembling a shortened cavalry saber hung from the belt by seamen (among others) and used for combat in boarding or defense.

Hermaphrodite brig. Two-masted ship having a square-rigged mainmast and a schooner-rigged (fore-and-aft) mizzenmast.

Hulled. Said of a ship whose hull is penetrated by gunfire.

Knot. A nautical mile, or 1.15 statute miles. Also a measure of speed; a speed of 10 knots is 10 nautical miles per hour.

Langrage (also spelled langrace, or langrel). Type of cannon shot containing chunks and pieces of scrap iron that spread out in flight. Ostensibly designed to shred sails and rigging, it also was a vicious antipersonnel weapon that could sweep the deck of the ship fired on, inflicting grievous wounds on the men hit. It was often so used by privateers.

Larboard. Port, opposite of starboard.

Letter-of-marque trader (often abbreviated as "letter-of-marque"). An armed merchant vessel operating in time of war under a letter of marque. It lawfully could seize prize ships or ships carrying contraband to an enemy port. Its crew received regular seafarer's wages, plus a share of the proceeds of any prize vessels or cargoes.

Letters of marque and reprisal. A letter of reprisal (from the sovereign) was issued originally to a shipowner entitling him to recover by force of arms a vessel or its cargo unlawfully seized from him, or to satisfy an unpaid debt or damages inflicted on him by the owner of the seized ship, or prize (q.v.). Letters of reprisal were valid only in the territorial waters of the nation issuing them. The practice dates from the twelfth century and was common by the seventeenth. Raiding and seizing a prize outside territorial waters could be authorized by a letter of marque. These aims soon merged in a single letter of marque and reprisal, whose use was virtually universal among seafaring nations from the thirteenth century. The practice began to wane after the War of 1812. It was outlawed by the major European powers (excepting Spain) in the Paris Declaration (1876). The United States also held out until the growth of its navy made it a major sea power, and the practice was finally abolished by the second Hague International Peace Conference in 1907.

Libel. A document instituting a lawsuit or setting forth a legal claim.

Long Tom. A long-range cannon much favored on privateers. Typically they "were the first voice heard by an intended victim," in Jerome Garitee's phrase. A Long Tom might be a 9- or 12-pounder with a range of up to a mile. Such a gun mounted to permit it to traverse from side to side would be called a pivot or swivel gun and often was used as a bow or stern chaser (qq.v.).

Marque and reprisal. See "Letters of marque and reprisal."

Midshipman. In the British Navy, the rank between naval cadet and the lowest commissioned rank; a sublieutenant. In American usage a student officer ranking above a chief petty officer and below a warrant officer.

Mizzenmast. The rear, or aftermost, mast of a two- or three-masted ship; on four- and five-masters, the third mast.

Overfall. A line of short, breaking waves in a particular area and caused by a strong current over a shoal or by a convergence of conflicting currents.

Packet. Abbreviation for packet boat. A ship or boat plying a regular schedule between two ports, carrying mail, small freight, and passengers.

Parole. The release of a captured seamen on his pledge to observe the conditions stipulated in the document of parole.

Pennant (properly, pendant, though universally pronounced "pennant"). A long, narrow pendant or flag flown at the masthead of a warship commanded by a commissioned officer. It was flown day and night as long as a ship was in commission.

Plimsoll line or mark. Mark stenciled on the hull of a cargo ship, consisting of a set of horizontal lines showing maximum depth to which it could be safely loaded for various waters (e.g., fresh, tropical, winter, etc.). It is named for its originator, the nineteenth-century English merchant Samuel Plimsoll.

Poop. A partial deck, the aftermost and highest deck of a ship, often the roof of a stern cabin.

Privateer. From the mid-seventeenth century, a contraction of "private man of warre." The first edition of *Encyclopaedia Britannica* (1768–71) defined privateers as "a kind of private ships of war, fitted out by private persons at their own expence; who have leave granted them to keep what they can take from the enemy." The privateer operated under a letter of reprisal, or marque and reprisal, ordinarily issued by the government of the shipowner's country. The term came to be somewhat ambiguous and was sometimes used interchangeably—whether carelessly or pejoratively—with "pirate." A privateer was the vessel; it was captained and sailed by privateersmen—who were compensated only by a stated share of the proceeds of prizes taken.

Prize (as in prize of war). A vessel seized by a privateer operating under a letter of marque and/or reprisal. It had to be adjudicated a lawful prize, in the United States by a federal district court in a maritime district, after which it could be sold at auction with the proceeds divided according to agreement between the owner (as one party) and the officers and crew (as the second) of the vessel seizing the prize.

Prize master. An officer of a privateer capable of navigating, commanding a prize crew and prisoners, and sailing a prize or captured ship to a friendly port or a nonblockaded port in the privateer's nation, where disposition of the vessel would await a prize court's decision.

Quarter (on shipboard). The portion of the sea as seen from a ship lying between abeam and astern. An object in the sea in that relative position is said to be off a ship's starboard or port quarter.

Round or solid shot. A single projectile. A ball not containing an explosive charge, used for maximum range or distance.

Samson post, or Sampson post. A strong pillar or column projecting above the deck on which rigging is mounted for loading and unloading cargo.

Scantling. The heft and dimensions of timbers constituting the frame of a vessel.

Schooner. A two-masted ship, rigged fore and aft, of relatively shallow draft, though somewhat deeper aft, having a single deck and sharply raked masts. Schooners were designed for speed at the expense of cargo capacity, especially the famed Baltimore Clippers of the early nineteenth century. A schooner with topsails was designated a topsail schooner.

Sea anchor. A drag resembling a tapered, bottomless, canvas bucket attached by line to a lifeboat or raft to retard its drifting and keep its bow to the wind.

Shaft alley. A tunnel between engine room and the very stern of a propeller-driven ship; it houses the drive shaft by which the engine turns the propeller.

Shell. A projectile containing particles of iron, or in earlier times, stone, plus an explosive charge to burst the shell and scatter its fragments and contents as shrapnel; the charge is detonated by a fuse that ignites when the cannon is fired. Compare "Shot."

Ship (in pretwentieth-century parlance). A full-rigged (square-rigged) ship, with top and topgallant masts and sails.

Ship of the line, or line-of-battle ship. A large, three-masted, full-rigged warship, typically at the time of the Revolution carrying up to seventy-four guns, mostly 32- and 42-pounders, on two decks. Bigger ships of the line had an additional gun deck and as many as a hundred or more guns.

Shot. Any projectile not having an explosive charge to detonate en route to the target. Solid shot was used for maximum range and to hole or put a hole in the hull of an enemy ship. Smaller shot was used against personnel and jagged shot against sails and rigging. Variations include carcase, case shot, chain shot, crossbar, crowbars, grapeshot, langrage, round shot (qq.v.).

Sloop-of-war. Originally a brig or sloop used as an auxiliary to a ship of the line; by the time of the American Revolution, the ship sloop or sloop-of-war had evolved into a square-rigged three-master.

Sparks. Universal seafaring term for the radio operator.

Sponge (in gunnery). A wetted sponge affixed to a long stave, used to clean powder residue from a (muzzle-loading) gun barrel and quench any smoldering remnant before reloading.

Steering sail. See "Studding sail."

Stern chaser (cannon). A swivel mounted, long-range cannon mounted at the stern of a ship, used to fire at a pursuing enemy ship.

Studding sail (pronounced "studsl" or "stunsl"; also called steering sail). A light auxiliary sail on a square-rigged ship, extended by a boom beyond the foresail or mainsail (and top and topgallant sails) for additional speed in following winds, and, by adding a supplementary thrust to leeward, to assist steering.

Tender. A smaller vessel attending a warship, carrying provisions and serving as a sort of nautical errand boy, etc.

Top-gallant-sail (pronounced "t'gantsl"). On a square-rigged ship, the course of sail next above the topsails.

Top-hamper. Weight or encumbrance aloft (e.g., upper masts and rigging that are useless in a vessel's current role); later said also to be of extra weight or encumbrance on deck.

Truck. The wooden cap of a mast, with holes or sheaves for halyards and to mount a flagstaff; also a small wooden wheel of a gun carriage.

'Tween decks. The space between any two whole decks of a ship (thus excluding a partial deck, such as the poop deck at the stern). Hammocks could be slung in this open space for crew members or such passengers as prisoners.

Voyage (in privateering). A trip, with destinations and/or duration specified, of an armed, cargo-carrying merchant letter-of-marque trader that is licensed to capture prizes of opportunity, or to cruise if its master wished. Compare "Cruise."

Wallpiece. A heavy, large-bore musket, too long and heavy to fire accurately without resting it on a wall.

Wear (as in "he wore ship"). To turn about and run before the wind.

Wind sail. A long, wide tube made of sailcloth used for ventilation of a ship.

Yard (in ship's rigging). A spar to which the head (top) of a rectangular sail, or the foot of a fore-and-aft sail, is attached.

Bibliography

BOOKS

Albion, Robert Greenhalgh, and Jennie Barnes Pope. *Sea Lanes in Wartime: The American Experience, 1775–1945*. Hamden, Conn.: Archon Books, 1968.

Allen, Gardner W. *A Naval History of the American Revolution*. 2 vols. Boston and New York: Houghton Mifflin Company, 1913.

Boyne, Walter J. *Clash of Titans*. New York: Simon and Schuster, 1995.

Bunker, John. *Liberty Ships: The Ugly Ducklings of World War II*. Annapolis, Md.: Naval Institute Press, 1972.

Carse, Robert. *There Go the Ships*. New York: W. Morrow & Co., 1942.

Churchill, Winston. *The Second World War*, vol. 2, *Their Finest Hour*. Boston: Houghton Mifflin, 1949. Vol. 4, *The Hinge of Fate*, 1950. Vol. 5, *Closing the Ring*, 1951. Vol. 6, *Triumph and Tragedy*, 1953.

Clark, William H. *Ships and Sailors: The Story of Our Merchant Marine*. Boston: L. C. Page, 1938.

Cohn, Michael, and Michael K. H. Platzer. *Black Men of the Sea*. New York: Dodd, Mead, 1978.

Crowell, Benedict, and Robert Forrest Wilson. *How America Went to War: An Account from Official Sources of the Nation's War Activities, 1917–1920*. New Haven: Yale University Press, 1921. Vols. 2–3, *The Road to France*.

Dönitz, Karl. *Zehn Jahre und zwanzig Tage*. Bonn: Athenäum Verlag Junker und Dunnhaupt, 1958. Translated by R. H. Stevens under the title *Memoirs: Ten Years and Twenty Days* (London: Weidenfeld and Nicolson, 1959).

Dunn, Walter Scott, Jr. *Second Front Now*. University: University of Alabama Press, 1980.

Ellsberg, Edward. *The Far Shore*. New York: Dodd, Mead, 1960.

Gannon, Michael. *Operation Drumbeat: Germany's First U-Boat Attacks Along the American Coast in World War II*. New York: Harper & Row, 1990.

Garitee, Jerome R. *The Republic's Private Navy: The American Privateering Business as Practiced by Baltimore during the War of 1812*. Middletown, Conn.: Published for Mystic Seaport by Wesleyan University Press, 1977.

Gibson, Charles Dana. *Merchantman? Or Ship of War: A Synopsis of Laws,*

U.S. State Department Positions, and Practices Which Alter the Peaceful Character of U.S. Merchant Vessels in Time of War. Camden, Maine: Ensign Press, 1986.

Hartcup, Guy. *Code Name Mulberry: The Planning, Building, and Operation of the Mulberry Harbours.* New York: Hippocrene Books, 1977.

Hoehling, A. A. *The Fighting Liberty Ships: A Memoir.* Annapolis, Md.: Naval Institute Press, 1996.

Hoyt, Edwin P. *U-Boats Offshore: When Hitler Struck America.* New York: Stein and Day, 1978.

Kell, John McIntosh. *Recollections of a Naval Life, Including the Cruises of the Confederate States' Steamers "Sumter" and "Alabama."* Washington, D.C.: Neale, 1900.

King, Ernest J. *U.S. Navy at War, 1941–45.* Washington, D.C.: U.S. Department of the Navy, 1946.

———, and Walter Muir White. *Fleet Admiral King.* New York: W. W. Norton, 1952.

Little, George. "An 1812 Privateer Captures a British Letter of Marque," in Oliver G. Swan, ed., *Deep Water Days.* Philadelphia: Macrae Smith, 1929.

Maclay, Edgar Stanton. *A History of American Privateers.* New York: D. Appleton and Co., 1895.

———. "Privateers & Privateersmen," Chapter from *A History of American Privateers.* In Oliver G. Swan, ed., *Deep Water Days.* Philadelphia: Macrae Smith, 1929.

Marvin, Winthrop L. *The American Merchant Marine: Its History and Romance from 1620 to 1902.* New Haven: Yale University Press, 1919.

Meriwether, Colyer. *Raphael Semmes.* Philadelphia: G. W. Jacobs, 1913.

Morison, Samuel Eliot. *History of United States Naval Operations in World War II.* Boston: Little, Brown. Vol. 1, *The Battle of the Atlantic,* 1947; vol. 10, *The Atlantic Battle Won,* 1959.

Nevins, Allan. *Sail On: The Story of the American Merchant Marine.* New York: United States Lines Company, 1946.

Paine, Ralph D. *The Old Merchant Marine: A Chronicle of American Ships and Sailors.* New Haven: Yale University Press, 1921.

Pedraja, Rene De La. *The Rise and Decline of U.S. Merchant Shipping in the Twentieth Century.* New York: Twayne Publishers, 1992.

Porter, David D. *The Naval History of the Civil War.* New York: Sherman Publishing, 1886.

Riesenberg, Felix, Jr. *Sea War.* New York: Rinehart, 1956.

Roskill, Stephen W. *The War at Sea: vol. 2: The Period of Balance.* London: HM Stationery Office, 1956.

Schoenfeld, Max. "The Navies and Neptune." In *D-Day 1944,* Theodore A.

Wilson, ed. Lawrence: University Press of Kansas (published for the Eisenhower Foundation at Abilene), 1971, 1994.

Sherman, Rev. Andrew M. *Life of Captain Jeremiah O'Brien, Machias, Maine.* Morristown, N.J.: George W. Sherman, 1902.

Simmons, Thomas E. *Escape from Archangel: An American Merchant Seaman at War.* Jackson: University Press of Mississippi, 1990.

Spears, John R. *The History of Our Navy: From Its Origins to the End of the War with Spain 1775–1898,* vol. 1. New York: Charles Scribner's Sons, 1902.

————. *The Story of the American Merchant Marine.* New Haven: Yale University Press, 1919.

Standard Oil Company (New Jersey). *Ships of the Esso Fleet in World War II.* New York: Standard Oil Company, 1946.

Summersell, Charles Grayson. *CSS Alabama: Builder, Captain, and Plans.* University: University of Alabama Press, 1985.

Thomas, Lowell. *Raiders of the Deep.* Garden City, N.J.: Garden City Publishing, 1928.

————. *Count Luckner, the Sea Devil.* Garden City, N.J.: Garden City Publishing, 1932.

Waters, John M. *Bloody Winter.* Annapolis, Md.: Naval Institute Press, 1984.

West, Wallace. *Down to the Sea in Ships: The Story of the U.S. Merchant Marine.* New York: Noble and Noble, 1947.

NEWSPAPERS, MAGAZINES, AND SHORTER PUBLICATIONS

Bunker, John. *The Seafarers in World War II.* Detroit: SIUNA, 1951.

Cameron, John S. "The Sea Wolf's Prey." *Sunset,* August–November 1918.

Mapes, Harold T. "Wireless Man Tells of Silver Shell's Fight." *New York Times Magazine,* 8 July 1917, 7.

New York Times. "Gulflight Attack Arouses Washington," 3 May 1915, 1.

————. "Armed American Steamship Sunk; 11 Men Missing," 3 April 1917, 1.

————. "Beat Off U-Boat in 2½-Hour Fight," 3 March 1917, 1.

Pilot. National Maritime Union of America. New York.

————. "Former Member of PILOT Goes Down With Pan Mass," 27 February 1942.

————. "None Would Have Escaped Pan Mass But For 1st Ass't," George R. Lamb, 20 March 1942, 5.

————. *On a True Course: The Story of the National Maritime Union of America, AFL-CIO.* 1967.

Time. 21 December 1942.

West Coast Sailors. Sailors' Union of the Pacific.

Westcott, Alan. "Sinkings of American Merchantmen." *Current History,* October 1918: 104, 107.

GOVERNMENT DOCUMENTS

U.S. Congress. House. Committee on Merchant Marine and Fisheries. Subcommittee on Merchant Marine. *Hearings on Operation Desert Shield/Desert Storm: Sealift Performance and Future Sealift Requirements.* 102d Cong., 1st sess., 1991.

Marshall, George C. King memorandum of 19 June 1942 in Marshall Papers, Box 73, Folder 12, "King, Ernest J. 1942 May—1942 August," at George C. Marshall Research Library, Lexington, Va. Quoted in King and White, *Fleet Admiral King* (1952), 455–56.

National Archives, College Park, Md. Memorandum for File. Loss of SS *Mary Luckenbach* by Enemy Action 14 September 1942. Record Group 38. In Voyage Report of SS *Mary Luckenbach.*

———. Naval Armed Guard Reports. Record Group 38. Voyage Report of SS *Argon.* Ens. Harold Unterbert, USNR.

———. Naval Armed Guard Reports. Record Group 38. Voyage Report of SS *Daniel Morgan.* Lt. (jg) Morton E. Wolfson, USNR.

———. Naval Armed Guard Reports. Record Group 38. Voyage Report of SS *Deer Lodge.* 1. Ens. Thomas E. Delate, USNR; 2. Ens. J. Kenneth Malo, USNR.

———. Naval Armed Guard Reports. Record Group 38. Voyage Report of SS *Dunboyne.* Ens. Rufus T. Brinn, USNR.

———. Naval Armed Guard Reports. Record Group 38. Voyage Report of SS *Frederick Douglass.* Ens. John Roang, USNR.

———. Naval Armed Guard Reports. Record Group 38. Voyage Report of SS *Nathaniel Greene.* Lt. (jg) R. M. Billings, USNR.

———. Naval Armed Guard Reports. Record Group 38. Voyage Report of SS *Richard Hovey.* Lt. (jg) Harry Chester Goudy, USNR.

———. Naval Armed Guard Reports. Record Group 38. Voyage Report of SS *St. Olaf.* Lt. (jg) Wesley Norton Miller, USNR.

———. Summary of Statements by Survivors [of sunk American merchant vessels]. Record Group 38 . . .

———. Enemy Attacks on Merchant Ships. SS *Deer Lodge.* With Voyage Reports. 14 June 1943.

———. Memorandum for Commander in Chief, United States Fleet. 25 November 1944. Request for Consideration for Award of Operation and Engagement Star . . . Record Group 38. (In SS *Deer Lodge* file, inter al.)

Index

About the Author

Bruce Felknor entered World War II in 1944 as a radioman. After the war, he spent a decade in public relations, and in 1956 he was named executive director of the nonpartisan Fair Compaign Practices Committee, where he became a national authority on electioneering ethics. He published the classic *Dirty Politics* in 1966 and taught briefly at Hamilton College. He then joined Encyclopaedia Britannica, holding various executive and editorial positions, longest as executive editor, and retired in 1985. He lives with his wife in Lake Bluff, Illinois.

THE NAVAL INSTITUTE PRESS is the book-publishing arm of the U.S. Naval Institute, a private, nonprofit, membership society for sea service professionals and others who share an interest in naval and maritime affairs. Established in 1873 at the U.S. Naval Academy in Annapolis, Maryland, where its offices remain today, the Naval Institute has members worldwide.

Members of the Naval Institute support the education programs of the society and receive the influential monthly magazine *Proceedings* and discounts on fine nautical prints and on ship and aircraft photos. They also have access to the transcripts of the Institute's Oral History Program and get discounted admission to any of the Institute-sponsored seminars offered around the country.

The Naval Institute also publishes *Naval History* magazine. This colorful bi-monthly is filled with entertaining and thought-provoking articles, first-person reminiscences, and dramatic art and photography. Members receive a discount on *Naval History* subscriptions.

The Naval Institute's book-publishing program, begun in 1898 with base guides to naval practices, has broadened its scope in recent years to include books of more general interest. Now the Naval Institute Press publishes about 100 titles each year, ranging from how-to books on boating and navigation to battle histories, biographies, ship and aircraft guides, and novels. Institute members receive discounts of 20 to 50 percent on the Press's nearly 600 books in print.

Full-time students are eligible for special half-price membership rates. Life memberships are also available.

For a free catalog describing Naval Institute Press books currently available, and for further information about subscribing to *Naval History* magazine or about joining the U.S. Naval Institute, please write to:

Membership Department
U.S. NAVAL INSTITUTE
118 Maryland Avenue
Annapolis, MD 21402-5035
Telephone: (800) 233-8764
Fax: (410) 269-7940
Web address: www.usni.org

7/99^2 8/05^6